Deciding Where to Live

Deciding Where to Live

*Information Studies on
Where to Live in America*

Edited by
Melissa G. Ocepek and William Aspray

ROWMAN & LITTLEFIELD
Lanham • Boulder • New York • London

Published by Rowman & Littlefield
An imprint of The Rowman & Littlefield Publishing Group, Inc.
4501 Forbes Boulevard, Suite 200, Lanham, Maryland 20706
www.rowman.com

6 Tinworth Street, London, SE11 5AL, United Kingdom

Selection and editorial matter © 2021 The Rowman & Littlefield Publishing Group, Inc.
Copyright of individual chapters is held by the respective chapter authors.

All rights reserved. No part of this book may be reproduced in any form or by any electronic or mechanical means, including information storage and retrieval systems, without written permission from the publisher, except by a reviewer who may quote passages in a review.

British Library Cataloguing in Publication Information Available

Library of Congress Cataloging-in-Publication Data

Names: Ocepek, Melissa G., editor. | Aspray, William, editor.
Title: Deciding where to live : information studies on where to live in America / edited by William Aspray and Melissa Ocepek.
Description: Lanham : Rowman & Littlefield, [2021] | Includes bibliographical references and index. | Summary: "This book explores major themes related to where to live in America, not only about the acquisition of a home but also the ways in which where one lives relates to one's cultural identity. It shows how changes in media and information technology are shaping both our housing choices and our understanding of the meaning of personal place"— Provided by publisher.
Identifiers: LCCN 2020033344 (print) | LCCN 2020033345 (ebook) | ISBN 9781538183601 (paper) | ISBN 9781538139707 (ebook)
Subjects: LCSH: Housing—United States. | House buying—Social aspects—United States.
Classification: LCC HD7293 .D355 2021 (print) | LCC HD7293 (ebook) | DDC 333.33/80973—dc23
LC record available at https://lccn.loc.gov/2020033344
LC ebook record available at https://lccn.loc.gov/2020033345

Contents

Preface　　xi

1　**Where to Live as an Information Problem:
　Three Contemporary Examples**　　1
　William Aspray and Melissa G. Ocepek
　Case 1: The Information Tools of Today's House Buyers and
　　　Real Estate Agents　　2
　　Real Estate Search Goes Online　　3
　　Realtors' Work and Tools　　7
　　Traditional Information Sources for Home Buyers　　8
　　Chapters Related to This Case Study　　13
　Case 2: Keeping Austin Weird: Affordable, Sustainable, and
　　　Not Overrun with Californians　　14
　　Affordable　　15
　　Sustainable　　16
　　Californians　　17
　　The Weirdest, Best Place to Live　　18
　　Chapters Related to This Case Study　　19
　Case 3: Coronavirus and the Real Estate Market　　20
　　Commercial Real Estate　　21
　　Residential Real Estate—Buying and Renting　　22
　　Chapters Related to This Case Study　　25

2　**Turning in Place: Real Estate Agents and the Move
　from Information Custodians to Information Brokers**　　35
　Steve Sawyer
　Buying and Selling a Home　　37
　　The Rise of Intermediation　　39
　Real Estate Agents' Work　　40
　　The Structure of Real Estate Agents' Work　　41
　Information Sources and Flows　　42
　　The Multiple Listing Service　　42

v

	The Purchase and Sales Agreement	43
	The HUD1 Form	43
	Financial Data	43
	Home Data	44
	ICTs, Information Flows, and Intermediation	44
	From Information Custodian to Information Broker	46
	Adding Value	47
	The Informational and Social Value of Intermediation	48
3	**The Evolving Residential Real Estate Information Ecosystem: The Rise of Zillow**	57
	James W. Cortada	
	Structure of the Real Estate Industry before the Internet	58
	Effects of Computing on the Industry before the Arrival of the Internet	68
	Arrival of the Internet-Born Real Estate Industry	70
	Consumer Access to Information	71
	Changing Relations between Agents and Customers	73
	Emergence of an Internet-Based Real Estate Industry	75
	The Zillow.com Phenomenon	80
	Effect of the Coronavirus Pandemic on Real Estate	84
	Conclusions	85
4	**Privacy, Surveillance, and the "Smart Home"**	93
	Philip Doty	
	Surveillance in Contemporary America	94
	A Discursive and Terminological Aside	96
	Thinking of Home	97
	Home as a "Moral and Moralizing" Place	99
	The Dream of the Mechanized, Automated Home in America and Beyond	100
	So-Called Smart Homes and Surveillance	103
	Working Definitions of "Smart Homes"	103
	Why Do People Choose "Smart Homes"?	105
	A Counternarrative about Privacy, "Smart Homes," and the IoT	109
	Google's Nest Thermostats: An Abbreviated Case Study	111
	Considering How Information Studies Contributes to the Question about Where to Live	113
	Conclusion	114
	Considering How "Smart Homes" and Surveillance Influence Where We Live	116

5	***This Old House*, *Fixer Upper*, and *Better Homes and Gardens*: The Housing Crisis and Media Sources** *Melissa G. Ocepek*	**125**
	The Housing Crisis	126
	After the Crash: Opinions on Home Ownership Following the Housing Crisis	127
	Sources of Information	129
	History of Home and Garden Sources	130
	Magazine History	131
	Television History	132
	HGTV and the Housing Crisis	135
	Data Collection and Analysis	136
	Magazines	136
	HGTV	137
	Findings: Magazines	139
	Findings: HGTV	142
	Conclusions	144
6	**A Community Responds to Growth: An Information Story about What Makes for a Good Place to Live** *Hannah Weber, Vaughan M. Nagy, Janghee Cho, and William Aspray*	**151**
	Adjusting to Growth	154
	Traffic	156
	Construction of New and Affordable Housing	159
	Development of Open Land on the West Side of Arvada	159
	Affordable Housing	161
	Rocky Flats	163
	Educational Facilities	164
	Enriching Community and Environment	165
	Arvada Urban Renewal Authority	165
	Reimagining Olde Town	166
	Final Words	168
	Directions for Future Research	169
7	**The Valley between Us: The Meta-Hodology of Racial Segregation in Milwaukee, Wisconsin** *Judith Pintar*	**177**
	The HOLC Maps	179
	Meta-Hodology	182
	Real Estate Bias in Milwaukee	188
	Conclusions	203

8 Modeling Hope: Boundary Objects and Design Patterns in a Heartland Heterotopia — 211
David Hopping

- Epiphany — 212
- "So Old-Fashioned It's, Well, New" — 215
- Community as Intervention — 216
- The Scaffolding Framework — 219
  - Layer 1—Architecture and Site Design — 219
  - Layer 2—Routine and Special Events — 219
  - Layer 3—Volunteer Engagement — 220
  - Layer 4—Roles and Expectations — 220
  - Layer 5—Communication — 222
  - Layer 6–Professional Services and Material Supports — 222
  - The Generations of Hope Community Model — 222
- Heterotopia — 223
- Boundary Objects — 225
- The "Veil of Intervention" — 227
- The Pattern Language of Intentional Neighboring — 229
- Legacy — 232

9 Home Buying in Everyday Life: How Emotion and Time Pressure Shape High-Stakes Deciders' Information Behavior — 237
Carol F. Landry

- A Competitive Market — 238
- The Appearance of Emotion — 239
- The Presence of Time Pressure — 240
- Research Implementation — 241
  - The Mock Home-Buying Experience — 241
  - Semistructured Interviews — 242
  - Participant Observation — 243
- Experiencing Information — 243
  - The Dimensions of Emotion and Information Behavior — 243
    - How Information Use Affects High-Stakes Decision Makers — 243
    - Compelling Influence behind Emotion and Noninformation-Use Behaviors — 247
  - Time Pressure and Information Behavior — 247
    - Information Use Generates Time Urgency — 248
    - Time Pressure Propels Noninformation-Use Behavior — 248
  - The Interaction of Emotion and Time Pressure — 249
    - Information Use Induces the Co-Occurrence of Emotion and Time Pressure — 249
    - Noninformation Use Is Propelled by the Interaction of Emotion and Time Urgency — 250

	The Role of Information Use by Proxy	251
	Altering Information Behavior	252
	Conclusion	254
10	**In Search of Home: Examining Information Seeking and Sources That Help African Americans Determine Where to Live**	**259**
	Jamillah R. Gabriel	
	Theoretical Perspective	260
	Historical Overview	261
	The Information Behavior of House Searching	265
	Information Seeking and Search Strategies	266
	Information Sources and Ranking Lists	268
	Factors Affecting Decision Making	271
	Conclusion	274
11	**Where to Live in Retirement: A Complex Information Problem**	**281**
	William Aspray	
	Issues Facing Retirees about Where to Live	282
	Aging in Place—or Not	284
	Moving within the United States	287
	Moving outside the United States	290
	Exogenous Forces	293
	Final Words	296

Closing Statement	309
Index	313
About the Editors and Contributors	325

Preface

Where to live is one of the most important issues faced by every adult in the United States. From an economic point of view, the 80 million American families who own homes have a total of $27 trillion tied up in equity and mortgage—an amount greater than the entire U.S. economy in 2018. This does not count the 43 million apartments and homes serving as rental properties. Unsurprisingly, a large real estate industry—with more than 2 million active agents—is devoted to providing this housing. When one adds in commercial real estate and construction, real estate stands as the largest industry sector in the United States—at 14 percent of the economy—bigger than state and local government, banking, insurance, and durable manufacturing.[1]

Of course, economics does not tell the whole story. One's home is also an expression of one's self and the environment in which one's life plays out. One simple example of this is the pantry wall, where a series of pencil marks record the growth of one's kids over time. The home is chosen not only for what it is but also for where it is. People make choices about where their home is located so that they can live in a particular community that contains the type of people they want to live near to and that has the amenities (schools, churches, shopping, cultural institutions, parks, and so on) that they seek. They often choose to live where they can be near friends and family or to enable their work lives.

These economic and emotional aspects of where one lives are well understood. Less well recognized are the formidable information challenges concerning where to live. Consider the transaction of buying and moving in to a house. This transaction takes an entire village of specialists: real estate agents, mortgage brokers, various kinds of inspectors and repair people, movers, exterminators, lawn care and tree service people, and hardware and paint store clerks, among others. Information issues arise on both the macro and micro levels: what country, state, and neighborhood should I live in? Is it better to buy or rent in this market? What housing situation fits my life stage? What can I afford? Is the real estate agent experienced enough to get me successfully through the house-buying process? How will my dreams of home match the realities of my budget and the market? What amenities is this house near? Are the schools appropriate for my children? Will I and the people living with me be able to thrive in this setting? The list of questions goes on and on.

This book is about a variety of everyday information behaviors and attitudes concerning where to live: information seeking; information fear, avoidance, and other affective aspects of information; types of information used in making decisions, including the impact of media sources; issues of informational privacy and information bias related to one's home; the use of information and communication technologies in the acquisition of places to live; and the social, political, and cultural factors shaping and being shaped by informational decisions about where to live. In addressing these issues, this book draws on the literatures of sociology, political science, psychology, gender studies, cultural studies, and business—but most of all from information studies. This book explores, in a detailed way, a number of specific case studies related to how humans interact with information as they carry out their everyday lives.

The first section of the book addresses issues about how the work lives of realtors has been shaped by new information and communication technologies, such as the internet and social media, and how the industry itself has been changed by these same technological disruptors. The second section of the book draws on two well-established lines of scholarship in information studies—privacy and documentary studies—in understanding issues about home owners: privacy and surveillance issues related to the smart home and media and other sources consumed or incidentally experienced by home owners as they decide to fix up their homes, move, or be satisfied with the living environment as is. The third section of the book raises questions about community: how information techniques and technologies are employed to enable a town to remain a good place to live in the face of relentless growth; how people make cognitive and emotional decisions in superheated real estate markets, where there are multiple offers and one must react immediately; and how social and political issues affect information bias and racially inequitable housing in a community. The fourth section examines particular kinds of information-seeking behaviors: how African Americans decide where to live and how retirees decide whether to age in place, downsize, or move to a new community.

Both editors are professors in leading information schools. Indeed, every author in this book either is or has been a professor or student at one of five leading information schools: the University of Colorado, Boulder; the University of Illinois, Urbana-Champaign; Syracuse University; the University of Texas, Austin; and the University of Washington, Seattle.

(Author biographies are to be found at the back of the book.) These information schools are interdisciplinary places of research and study, drawing heavily on both the technology of computer science and the wide swath of social sciences—but even to some extent on the humanities disciplines and the creative disciplines of art, architecture, and design. While this book is academically rigorous, it discusses one of the most important issues of lived experience—where to live—and thus we have worked to make all of the chapters accessible to a general reader who might be interested in the topics covered rather than in what they contribute to the academic canon.

We appreciate the help that we have received from Charles Harmon, our editor at Rowman & Littlefield, and other staff members at the press: Natalie Mandziuk, Jessica McCleary, and Erinn Slanina. We appreciate the faculty start-up funds from the University of Colorado, Boulder, for William Aspray and support from the University of Illinois, Urbana-Champaign, for Melissa G. Ocepek.

NOTE

1. These statistics, plus many others—with citations—can be found at the beginning of chapter 3 in this book.

ONE

Where to Live as an Information Problem

Three Contemporary Examples

William Aspray and Melissa G. Ocepek

This is a book about the informational aspects of where to live. It is not too much of a stretch to say that the decision about where to live is one of the most important decisions that humans make. We discuss the complex process of buying a home (or, most typically, several homes) during one's lifetime. For most people, this is the largest purchase they ever make. Of course, home is not only about financial investment. It is about where and how we choose to live, about our identity as a person, and about how we interact with the larger society and culture to form our sense of home, of place, and of self. Thus, in this volume, we go well beyond the real estate transaction to talk about how one decides where to live and how society shapes or constrains these choices. We also discuss the cultural fascination with the question of where to live. For example, we consider why home and garden shows on television are so popular even when one does not own a home or is not planning to move. We do all of this from the perspective of an information scholar; indeed, each of the chapters is written by people who study information for a living.

There are many ways in which both information and information technologies play a role in decisions about where to live—more than we can cover with one book. The chapters in this volume cover four main topics: the impact of information and communication technologies on real estate work, the housing industries, and the privacy of the home; examining where to live from a community perspective by discussing stakeholders and exogenous factors that make a community a good or bad place to live; studying how specific populations, including retirees and African Americans, make decisions about where to live; and undertaking documentary studies that investigate the many kinds of sources that people actively or passively take into consideration as they make these decisions.

We use three brief case studies to introduce the chapters that follow. The first of these case studies concerns apps and websites as well as more traditional information sources used by both the house buyer and the real estate professional in searching for or buying a home. This study provides a way for us to introduce chapters on the changing nature of the work of the real estate agent (Steve Sawyer) and the changing nature of the real estate industry (James Cortada). It also gives us a way to introduce chapters on privacy issues in the home industry (Philip Doty) and the use of home and garden magazines and television shows as a source of information for home buyers and others (Melissa G. Ocepek).

The second brief case study concerns the housing market in Austin, Texas, and the resistance there to growth and change. This study enables us to introduce four chapters that discuss housing from a community perspective. These include chapters about the affective and cognitive elements of buying a house in a superheated local housing market (Carol Landry), the use of information to maintain the quality of life in a community in the face of rapid growth (Hannah Weber, Janghee Cho, Vaughan M. Nagy, and William Aspray), the institutionalization of racial inequity in a community through its housing policies and practices (Judith Pintar), and the creation of an experimental intergenerational housing community (David Hopping).

The third brief case study concerns the change in information questions that occurred almost overnight as the country was beset by the Covid-19 pandemic. This enables us to introduce two chapters about the information-seeking behaviors of other specific populations: African Americans (Jamillah Gabriel) and retirees (William Aspray).

CASE 1: THE INFORMATION TOOLS OF TODAY'S HOUSE BUYERS AND REAL ESTATE AGENTS

There are few—if any—industries that have not been helped greatly by a wealth of industry-specific apps. The real estate industry is no exception. Much like stock brokers, real estate agents have to stay on top of a wealth of information in an industry that is changing minute by minute. From changes in mortgage rates to rising and falling property values to local and world events that affect them, real estate agents need to have their finger on the constantly changing pulse of the local real estate market. Apps can help you do that.[1]

Agents . . . have traditionally been tied to their offices, digging through files and emails to find necessary information or faxing paperwork for signatures.[2]

Real Estate Search Goes Online

Prior to the National Association of Realtors' creation of the Realtor.com website in 1995, the practice of house hunting had not changed much for many years.[3] One would check the classified ads in the local newspaper; ask friends, family, and colleagues about houses they knew that were on the market or about to come on the market; tour neighborhoods in one's automobile searching out for-sale signs; or contact a realtor. If one were looking for a house in another geographic region, house hunting involved one or two costly trips of intensive house hunting over several days, with the houses selected by the real estate agent (who likely did not know the buyer and was only guessing at his or her needs), making the selection of homes to view with only minimal input from the buyer. The out-of-town buyer would have to choose a house typically from no more than about a dozen choices. Whether buying locally or at a distance, the process was almost always mediated by a realtor, who controlled access to information about available houses and their conditions.[4] Since 1995, the process has changed dramatically.

Table 1.1 provides some information taken from the 2017 annual survey conducted by the National Association of Realtors about the use of the internet and mobile devices for house hunting. We see from this table the growing importance of online information sources to the home buyer.

The National Association of Realtors kindly supplied us with information from some of its annual surveys, going back to 1995, which was the first year in which they asked a question about the information sources used by house buyers.[5] A few trends pop out of their survey results. We can see the rapid adoption of the internet as an information source in the late 1990s. In 1995, only 2 percent of respondents reported using the internet in their search, but that percentage had increased to 18 percent two years later and to 37 percent two years after that. By the time of the 2005 survey, 77 percent of buyers were consulting the internet, and in both the 2010 and the 2015 survey reports, 89 percent of buyers were consulting the internet.[6] Not surprisingly, the internet was used in their housing search by a greater percentage of young people than older people.[7] The internet has not displaced the realtor. In the 2000, 2005, 2010, and 2015 reports, realtors were an information source to 86 to 90 percent of house buyers, with no noticeable trend line. Open houses have remained a stable source of information to house buyers, serving between 41 and 51 percent of house buyers in 2000, 2005, 2010, and 2015, also with no noticeable trend. Newspaper advertisements have fallen off as an information source in home buying but remain significant: 51 percent in 2000, 50 percent in 2005, 36 percent in 2010, and 20 percent in 2015. The value of yard signs

Table 1.1. A 2017 Statistical Profile of Use of Online Information Sources for House Hunting[a]

Comparing Websites to Other Information Sources

- Websites and realtors were the most common sources of information for buyers, more important than open houses, yard signs, friends and neighbors, or builders; these were in turn more valuable than print newspaper advertisements, home magazines, billboards, relocation companies, or television.[b]
- Considering where a buyer found his or her house, looking at historical trends, the internet grew steadily from 8% in 2001 to 49% in 2017; real estate agent dropped steadily from 48% in 2001 to 31% in 2017; yard signs dropped off from 15% to 7% over this same time; no other source gained as much as 10% of the buyers throughout this entire period; home magazines have never been more than 2%, and they have been negligible since 2009.
- 88% of people found online sources useful; 79% found realtors useful sources of information.
- The first step for 42% of home buyers was to look online; for 17% of buyers, the first step was to contact a real estate agent.
- 95% of buyers used the internet in their search at some point in 2017 compared to 2% in 1995, 18% in 1997, and 90% in 2009.
- 49% of buyers found their house on the internet compared to only 8% in 2001.

Age Differences in Information Sources Used

- There were generally negligible differences by age in the information sources used; 18- to 24-year-olds used mobile devices more than other age-groups by approximately 5% to 10%. The biggest difference was in the use of home builders, used by 69% of those in the 45–64 category and not used by more than 22% by any other age category; this presumably reflects which age-group is buying new homes.
- Buyers who used the internet have an average age of 44 years and a median income of $90,800. Buyers who did not use the internet had an average age of 65 years and a median income of $69,900.

How the Internet Was Used

- When buyers used the internet, photos and detailed information about the property was the most useful; the next most important was information about floor plans, virtual tours, information about other houses for sale, and neighborhood information.
- Value of website features (in order, from most important): photos, detailed information about properties, floor plans, virtual tools, real estate agent contact information, detailed information about recently sold properties, neighborhood information, interactive maps, pending sales/contract status, videos, and information about upcoming open houses (all of these had at least 60% of buyers saying they were very or somewhat useful).
- First-time home buyers were more likely than repeat buyers (18% to 8%) to use the internet to learn about the home-buying process; repeat home buyers were more likely than first-time buyers to look online at properties as a first step.

How Mobile Devices Were Used

- Mobile devices were used in the search by 68% of buyers (up from 58% the previous year), with slightly more first-time buyers than repeat buyers using mobile apps (70% to 66%).

a. http://s3.amazonaws.com/sharebox.storage/documents/2666/2017_PROFILE_OF_HOME_BUYERS_AND_SELLERS_KCM.pdf?1516409811 (accessed June 5, 2019).

b. On the value of seminars for first-time home buyers, see the online discussion forum "Are First Time Home Buyers Seminars Worth Having," Trulia, initiated September 5, 2012, https://www.trulia.com/voices/Agent2Agent/are_first_time_home_buyer_seminars_worth_having_-429295 (accessed July 25, 2019).

has also fallen off some in the internet era: 77 percent in 2005, 45 percent in 2010, and 51 percent in 2015.

While realtors are still the most important element in the house-buying process—used by 88 percent of home buyers[8]—buyers today are much better informed because of the availability of numerous websites and apps that enable them to view house listings without having to gain access through a realtor. Not all of the searching is specifically goal directed to buying a house; it could instead be for entertainment purposes, to learn the value of their present home, or to identify neighborhoods in their price range, for example.[9]

While Realtor.com was the first real estate website, it is only the third most trafficked site today.[10] The two most heavily used real estate websites are Trulia (founded in 2004) and Zillow (founded in 2006). Trulia was originally an independent company but was purchased by Zillow in 2015. However, Trulia continues to operate its own independent website focused on housing acquisition, while Zillow has a whole-lifetime house-ownership focus. The acquisition was a boon to Zillow, whose traffic rose rapidly after the acquisition (an example of network-scale benefits).

While Zillow, Trulia, and Realtor.com are the three most trafficked real estate websites, there are many others.[11] As more and more Americans begin using smartphones, the number of real estate apps is growing rapidly; most of these apps have been developed since 2010. Websites and apps are used not only by buyers (and sellers) but also by real estate agents. Buyers and agents have different information needs, so we will consider them separately—looking at buyers first. Increasingly, real estate websites have a corresponding app, but there are some apps (especially those used by relators) that do not have a corresponding website.

In the crowded online real estate business, companies need to look for a feature that differentiates them from their competitors and gives them an edge. For example, Zillow includes a tool that estimates the value of a house, called Zestimate, which the company applies not only to houses currently on the market but to all houses.[12] Trulia provides interactive maps that inform the viewer about crime statistics, stores, restaurants, and schools in the vicinity of a house. Redfin provides more information than its competitors about foreclosures, short sales, and for-sale-by-owner listings. Xome provides good information about a home's walkability score as well as about local schools. HomeSnap enables the buyer to access information about a particular home by taking its photo. Many of these companies are introducing social networking elements into their apps and websites. For example, Redfin has integrated the ability to send housing descriptions to friends and family through text messaging, e-mail, or social networking platforms. And so it goes, with each company trying to find its own competitive advantage through the features it offers.[13]

Many of these real estate websites are like Swiss Army knives, providing numerous features on a single site. For example, Trulia offers filtering of listings, photo and video tours of homes, interactive maps, key word searches, an affordability calculator, an open house scheduler, a mortgage calculator, voice controls, a chat platform, and support for Android smart watches.[14] Table 1.2 lists a number of the leading real estate apps for home buyers and what each is good at.[15] This list suggests some of the issues that are on the minds of potential home buyers: not only the selection of a neighborhood and a home located there but also costs of a real estate transaction, mortgage rates, credit scores, and the opinions of people the buyer is close to or helping with the down payment on a house.[16]

Table 1.2. Features of Popular Real Estate Apps for Home Buyers (in Addition to Realtor.com, Zillow, and Trulia)

Redfin (discounted home-buying fees)
Bigger Pockets (learning about real estate)
LoopNet (commercial real estate)
HomeSnap (joint search with spouse or parents)
Xome (auctions)
Credit Karma (monitoring your credit score)
CO Everywhere (evaluating the neighborhood of a house of interest)

Why would someone want to build or use an app if there are powerful real estate websites available? While the buyer might look at real estate listings on their home computer, they may also want to look at listings while they are out and about—in the midst of a tour with a realtor, before or after viewing an open house, or simply when they come across a for-sale sign while they are out in the community—or, for curiosity's sake, even when they are traveling elsewhere in the country. Even though realtors conduct business from their offices or homes, they also conduct much of their business from their cars, such as while showing properties or running business errands. Apps are built for mobile use. They adapt features available on a real estate website for the smaller screens and touch capabilities of smartphones. They can focus on fewer features that are in most demand while in motion, leaving to real estate websites other features, such as home buyer guides, company biographies, and neighborhood descriptions. With fewer features, these apps not only are suited to the affordances of a smartphone (e.g., small screens) but also may be simpler for a potential buyer to understand and use. Millennials in particular are used to doing much of their online business on a smartphone, so this can be a preferred medium for their house-searching experience.[17]

Realtors' Work and Tools

The process of showing and closing house sales is a complex business. It is often carried out by a team and involves many different players: buyers, sellers, parents of buyers, mortgage companies, closing companies, real estate company management, various kinds of inspectors, companies that prepare photographic or virtual reality tours of homes, and so on. Thus, real estate agents need not only specialized tools that provide information about available real estate but also tools that are used by other small businesses for communication, printing, and so on (see figure 1.1).[18] Table 1.3 lists the work responsibilities of a realtor (buyer agent).

One business writer identified three criteria for an effective real estate app for agents—all of them information centered:[19]

- "Makes it easy to share important information with agents, buyers, or sellers (or all three)
- "Centralizes information for a specific stage (or stages) of the lifecycle, so you can act and react faster
- "Empowers you to create and manage new programs and activities, with little ramp-up time or without relying on anyone else"

Figure 1.1. Real Estate Office, Poteet, Texas, March 1939. *Library of Congress Prints & Photographs Division, Washington, D.C. 20540 USA.*

Table 1.3. Work Responsibilities of a Realtor (Buyer's Agent)[a]

- Prospect for both seller and buyer leads, convert leads to appointments, and close for buyer agency agreements
- Conduct a thorough needs analysis to ensure fiduciary service to all buyer clients
- Ensure that buyer clients are prequalified with mortgage lender
- Show homes to prospective home buyer clients
- Identify homes to show that meet buyers' criteria
- Schedule showings of homes with buyer clients, listing agents and/or home sellers
- Refine buyers' criteria and select additional homes to show as necessary
- Write and submit all offers to purchase homes for buyer clients
- Negotiate offers to purchase and oversee entire negotiation process
- Schedule and attend on-site property inspections with clients and vendors
- Negotiate all inspection repairs
- Provide buyer clients access to homes under contract as needed for measuring, inspecting, etc.
- Promptly return all buyer client telephone calls, texts, and e-mails
- Gather and answer buyer questions about potential homes and local community information
- Provide buyer clients pricing information and market research
- Educate buyer clients about home buying process
- Regularly ensure buyer clients that lead agent is involved and informed—promote the team concept
- Keep lead agent informed on all client communications and developments (copied on all e-mails and update notes in customer relationship management software)
- Close buyer clients to written offers to purchase
- Train, mentor, and assist in the hiring of additional buyer's agents and showing assistants
- Communicate diligently with administrative staff to ensure the highest level of service to buyer clients from initial contact through contract to close
- Regularly attend team meetings
- Attend all office training for working with buyer clients

a. Icenhower Coaching & Consulting, "A Real Estate Buyer's Agent Job Description," The Real Estate Trainer, December 12, 2015, https://therealestatetrainer.com/2015/12/12/real-estate-buyers-agent-job-description (slightly edited).

Table 1.4 provides another business writer's view of the forty (!) essential apps necessary for the real estate agent.[20]

Every week, new articles appear online, written by specific vendors or the general business press, encouraging real estate agents to modernize and use apps for their business information needs as a means to become more efficient and effective in their operations. Table 1.5 provides some additional apps that have appeared recently in the business press that were not listed above.[21] As one can see, the number of apps is practically endless.

Traditional Information Sources for Home Buyers

There are, of course, other sources of information about house buying besides websites and apps. One major source is self-help books on the

Table 1.4. Useful Real Estate Apps for Agents

1. Zillow Premier Agent (lead generation)
2. RealScout (nurturing)
3. Showing Suite (showing real estate)
4. Cloud CMA (comparative market analysis)
5. Real Geeks (customer relationship management)
6. Structurely (artificial intelligence–based lead qualification)
7. RPR Mobile (property reports)
8. Showcase IDX (plug-in to integrate listings with your website)
9. Zumper (rental listing)
10. Placester (building an IDX website)
11. Area Pulse (market data)
12. Everlance (mileage tracking)
13. KeyMe (key copying using cell phone)
14. Spacio (open house management)
15. BombBomb (video e-mail management)
16. Smarter Agent Mobile (customizing app for a brokerage)
17. VRX Staging (virtual staging)
18. RealtyMX (rental listings management)
19. Revaluate (move predictor)
20. Grasshopper (vanity phone numbers)
21. CSS (showing coordination)
22. Home Value Leads (home valuation)
23. Prempoint (lockbox replacement)
24. Homesnap (buyer–agent collaboration)
25. Zurple (lead generation and nurturing)
26. Qualia (real estate settlements)
27. Rently (facilitate showing of rentals)
28. HouseCanary (real estate valuation)
29. REIPro (real estate investment)
30. CityBlast (social media lead nurturing)
31. Cloud MLX (Multiple Listing Service customization)
32. Brokermint (back-office real estate tools)
33. BrokerKit (agent recruiting and retention)
34. Dotloop (electronic signature and transaction)
35. REDX Storm Dialer (automatic dialing)
36. Zapier (work flow automation)
37. Waze (crowdsourced communication tool while in traffic)
38. Videolicious (video editing)
39. Slack (team communication)
40. Planoly (Instagram management and scheduling)

general or specific aspects of buying a house.[22] Some of the books, such as *Home Buying for Dummies*,[23] are general works that are intended for a wide audience with various goals in their house buying and that guide the home buyer through each step of the process. For example, this Dummies book covers whether to buy, getting a mortgage and other financial issues, selecting a realtor, valuing a property, negotiating, the many-step

Table 1.5. Additional Apps Recommended for Real Estate Agents

10BII Financial Calculator (for real estate investors)
Ad Manager (Facebook)
Airbnb (for real estate investors—private homes for rent site)
Amitree Folio (e-mail assistant to gather files, contacts, and e-mails in one place)
BackAgent (real estate transaction management and work flow)
Buffer (schedule posts to social networks and analyze results)
CamScanner (scan documents on your mobile device)
Canva (design and print business cards and presentations)
Charlie (professional and personal background of people you meet with)
Citrix Podio (organize team communication and shared data)
Close.io (customer relationship management)
Cloud Attract (build real estate landing pages)
Cloze (integrate e-mail, contacts, calendar, and to-do list)
Contactually (customer relationship management)
Disclosures.io (organizing and sharing disclosures)
DocuSign (electronic document signing)
Drift (conversational marketing platform)
DropBox (store documents in the cloud)
EverNote (take notes and clip images from Web)
Feedback Pro (feedback solicitation tool)
Folio (organize in-box)
Follow Up Boss (centralize communications)
FlipComp (finds best deals for investors)
FreshChat (messaging software for teams)
Google Maps (maps)
Hotjar (heatmaps of what users want; capture info about use of your website)
HotPads (apartment rentals listing)
Houzz (home design, decorating, and remodeling)
Hubspot (social media marketing and Web analytics)
Hutch (virtual interior design)
Insightly (customer relationship management)
Lead Simple (report real estate leads and sales)
Lion Desk (record and embed video in e-mail and texts)
Live (Facebook—digital media strategy)
Live Chat (online customer service software)
LoopNet (online listings for commercial properties)
MagicPlan (measure and create floor plans using phone)
Marketo (marketing automation software)
Mashvisor (property search for real estate investors)
Matterport (virtual reality tool)
Mojo Dialer (dialing real estate leads)
Mortgage Calculator by Quicken Loans
Neighborhoods & Apartments (walkability scores)
OneNote (Microsoft—take notes and clip images from Web)
OnSpot Social (collect contact information at events)
Palm Agent ONE (estimate closing costs)

PDF Escape (add signature to PDF documents)
PlanOmatic (real estate photography and interactive floor plans)
Premier Clip (Adobe—video creation)
Property Fixer (for real estate investors)
Realtor.com (house listings)
Realeflow (general tool for real estate investors)
Redfin (real estate listings)
SentriSmart (integrate data about home with Sentri lockbox)
Sign Easy (sign from a mobile device)
Sitegeist (data about your surrounding area)
Skyslope (real estate transaction management)
StreetEasy (New York City real estate listings)
Swype (text faster with more accuracy)
Trello (Web-based list-making software)
Trulia (real estate listings)
Updater (organize moving-related tasks)
Vert (conversion tool for size, weight, and volume)
Wise Agent (real estate marketing automation)
Xome (real estate listings)
Zip Realty (augmented reality for real estate)

process of buying, how to read contracts and inspection reports, and a little on real estate investing. The number of house-buying books has multiplied so that now there are easy-to-use platforms for self-publishing and marketing, such as those provided by Amazon for both print books and e-books. There are a number of books that are targeted specifically at first-time buyers, who presumably know less about the process and may feel more intimidated by it.[24] Some books are targeted at specific groups of buyers, such as millennials or military veterans.[25] Other books are marketed by touting the expertise of the author, such as the lawyer,[26] the house inspector,[27] the real estate agent,[28] the mortgage broker,[29] the person just like you who has recently gone through the house-buying experience,[30] or the celebrity from a television house-buying show.[31] There are a number of books targeted at people who want to make money from real estate, including the flipping of houses.[32] Some books address fears that potential home buyers have, such as buying a house with dangerous mold.[33] There are also books providing guidance about buying houses in specific geographic locations.[34]

Of course, real estate agents also provide information to buyers.[35] There is material, known as a *buyer's packet*, commonly provided when a buyer first meets with an agent and contractually agrees to use that agent exclusively for the purchase of real estate for some specified period of time. Table 1.6 lists the information typically found in a buyer's

Table 1.6. A Typical Buyer Package[a]

- A color graphical cover page
- A list of what they should expect from their REALTOR®
- A list of reasons why you are the best REALTOR® for their needs
- A list of commitments from you to your buyers of what they can expect from your services
- An explanation of agency (sellers agency, buyer agency, and transaction brokerage)
- The advantage of working with a buyer's agent
- Information on the pre-approval process
- An overview of what they should expect through the process (the home search, writing an offer, earnest money, negotiations, inspections and appraisals, title work, the closing process)
- Common buyer mistakes
- A map of the area (if they are moving from out of town)
- A blank copy of a real estate contract
- Testimonials from happy clients
- A glossary of real estate terms

a. Real Estate Business Resources, "How to Create an Impressive Buyer's Packet!," https://rebr.com/whats-in-an-impressive-buyers-packet (accessed June 4, 2019). The content of this table is taken verbatim from this source. There is much more discussion in the real estate literature about seller's packets, often known as pre-listing packets, provided when one is attempting to convince a seller to provide their listing to the agent. See, for example, Matt Bonelli, "The Perfect Pre-Listing Packet for Real Estate Agents—Are You Using It?," Inman, February 8, 2017, https://www.inman.com/2017/02/08/perfect-pre-listing-packet-using (accessed June 4, 2019); Emile L'Eplattenier, "Pre Listing Package: Guide the Conversation before You Pitch," Fit Small Business, May 9, 2017, https://fitsmallbusiness.com/pre-listing-package (accessed June 4, 2019); and Icenhower Coaching and Consulting, "Pre-Listing Package Content & Strategies for REALTORS," The Real Estate Trainer, January 22, 2016, https://therealestatetrainer.com/2016/01/22/pre-listing-package-content (accessed June 4, 2019).

packet. When the agent shows a house to the buyer they are working with, they commonly make a copy of the Multiple Listing Service (MLS) listing for the buyer. When a buyer becomes serious about making an offer on a house, the realtor will prepare and share with the buyer *comps*, which compare the house in question with other, similar houses that have sold recently in the area or that are currently on the market. The real estate agent will also typically help the buyer with referrals to third parties who are involved in the real estate transaction, such as mortgage brokers, inspectors of various sorts, and closing companies. The agent will also use his or her experience to counsel the buyer about what is reasonable behavior, such as how much the buyer should offer above or below asking price, based on the agent's recent experience with the local housing market.

Thus, we have seen that the buying and selling of a house is an information-intense process. Both buyer and agent need access to the various kinds of information available about a house and related topics, such as neighborhood and mortgage rates. This information is presented in various forms: person to person, in print, and online. Agents in addition need information tools to carry out their business activities.

Chapters Related to This Case Study

We have seen above that the real estate agent works in an information-intense environment and that in recent years agents have had numerous online tools at their disposal to supplement the traditional information sources available to them. They also have access to an extraordinary increase in the amount of information about real estate to make available to all the stakeholders. As Steve Sawyer argues in chapter 2, the role of the real estate agent is changing rapidly today. In the past, agents were primarily information custodians; their principal job was to maintain and provide access to information to buyers, sellers, and others involved in the process. They were market intermediaries. Today, their role as market intermediaries still exists but is being challenged by means that can eliminate the need to go through the agent for relevant information. Instead, today's agent is increasingly an information broker, a person whose principal job is to explain the complex information ecosystem of real estate, not simply to provide access to information.

Just as all this new information and information technology is changing the work role of the real estate agent, it is also changing the nature of the real estate industry. James Cortada explains these changes to the real estate industry in chapter 3. Cortada describes the strategy of firms and the structure of the traditional real estate industry and presents a brief history of this industry in the United States. He then contrasts this traditional industry with the evolving industry by providing a case study of Zillow, one of the leading online real estate companies. He then explains that there are four types of business models for internet-based real estate: the Web advertising, brokerage, virtual value chain, and diversified models.

With this abundance of information, there are important questions about equitable access to information, bias and quality of information, and privacy of information. In chapter 4, Philip Doty examines an important aspect of the privacy issue as it relates to real estate: the so-called smart homes that have become increasingly available in the past decade. Drawing deeply from the literatures of privacy, surveillance states, and feminist-informed research in science and technology studies, he explains how these smart homes enable companies and governments to learn about us, target advertising to us (including what is advertised and its timing), sell data about us, and influence people's behavior.

This introductory case study has surveyed a number of websites, apps, and more traditional publications and other types of information (e.g., buyer packages) that are used by buyers and agents in the buying and selling of houses. In chapter 5, Melissa Ocepek discusses two additional information sources related to where to live: magazines and television shows about home and garden themes. She examines in particular the way that these sources relate to the Great Recession that began in 2007.

CASE 2: KEEPING AUSTIN WEIRD: AFFORDABLE, SUSTAINABLE, AND NOT OVERRUN WITH CALIFORNIANS

> Welcome to Austin—Please don't move here—I hear Dallas is great!
>
> —A design on a popular T-shirt made for SXSW in 2012[36]

Austin, Texas, is known for many things: music, festivals, and queso. It has also come to be known as one of the top U.S. cities to live in. Austin is also a place where both the editors of this volume and the authors of this chapter lived and worked. Austin's popularity has led to tremendous population and economic growth throughout the past few decades. The Great Recession affected Austin like the rest of the United States, but since then, Austin has had one of the hottest housing markets in the country. The housing market in the Austin metro area grew by 126 percent in the past ten years, or by $141 billion.[37] From 2012 to 2015, houses sold in Austin were regularly receiving "10 to 20 offers at $20,000 to $50,000 over list in the first 48 hours."[38] Also during this time, about 117,000 new homes were built, as were around 68,000 new apartment units.[39] The median home price in Austin reached $406,000 in September 2019.[40] All of this growth has affected Austin in many ways, and a vocal contingent of residents are not pleased with the change. Since at least 1997, the popular music, film, and tech festival SXSW has been known for popular T-shirts encouraging visitors to enjoy the city but "Don't move here."[41] Sending an unusual message for most growing cities, you are welcome to visit, but please do not stay.

Austin is thriving today in part because of the creative and cultural hub it has been throughout its history, but most musicians and artists who have always been a major part of the Austin's scene cannot afford a $400,000 home.[42] This has created a strong and vibrant creative resistance movement in Austin that can trace its roots back before the Great Recession and Austin's current real estate explosion. This section describes Austin's creative resistance to the dramatic population and economic growth that has been epitomized by the popularity of the city's unofficial slogan: "Keep Austin Weird."

The slogan was coined by Red Wassenich in 2000 when he called a local radio station to donate and support the radio show and the city he loved.[43] Wassenich and his wife Karen Pavelka soon created and began distributing bumper stickers printed with the slogan throughout Austin.[44] The slogan took off and soon could be seen on cars, buildings, and people.[45] "Keep Austin Weird" has become the rallying cry of many different groups and local businesses fighting to maintain what makes Austin special. It has been used consistently to highlight opposition to the homogenization and gentrification that can occur when a city experiences unchecked growth, especially in terms of affordability, sustainability, and to avoid becoming too much like California.

Affordable

The Austin housing market has dramatically changed in terms of pricing in the past few years. The fastest-growing home values are in a popular East Austin ZIP code, where, from 2009 to 2019, the median home price jumped from $137,400 to $315,400, or a 130 percent increase. This growth affects all residents, whether they are home owners or renters, in different ways.

Home owners can be priced out of their homes when their property taxes increase without home owners doing anything to increase their home's value. It is one thing when home owners decide to renovate their homes to increase the value; it is another when the neighborhood changes around them so quickly that they can no longer pay their property taxes. In some areas, property tax rates began eclipsing mortgage payments, forcing residents to relocate.[46] For many renters, rising real estate costs make home ownership farther out of reach or create the conditions that individuals can afford a home only on the outskirts of town or in the surrounding suburbs. In fact, the price of rent in a neighborhood can double or triple in as little as ten years due to the lack of rent control policies in Austin.[47]

The Austin real estate market has made it so that many home owners and renters have had to leave their neighborhoods or even become homeless.[48] Relocating out of formerly affordable neighborhoods can be especially difficult to working-class residents. Moving takes time and money that individuals may not have and can break apart communities. It also may increase commute times or make use of public transportation no longer feasible. In 2019, Austin ranked as the fourteenth-most traffic-congested city in America, and it is estimated that Austin commuters lost $1,270 annually in fuel and lost productivity costs due to traffic.[49]

Rising real estate and rent prices also affects businesses, which can lead to an overall increase in the cost of living that affects all members of a city regardless of their living situation. As Austin grows economically, many of the artists, musicians, and other creative and cultural creators who made the city such a desirable place to live may find that it is no longer a feasible place to live.[50] This leads many Austinites to reject and fight against the city's growth.

A 2003 survey found that the majority of Austinites (56 percent) surveyed responded that growth brings more costs than benefits to the community.[51] Most respondents also wanted the local government to slow (42 percent), stop (15 percent), or even discourage (11 percent) growth. Even at the start of the housing crisis in 2007, Long, a human geographer, found through interviewing Austinites that the concerns over growth in Austin continued, with most of his interviewees describing challenges for the city including "higher cost of living, loss of cultural character, rising rents, and changes to the downtown area."[52] To counteract these concerns, Austin city leaders adopted a plan called the "Austin Smart Growth Initiative," which included plans for downtown redevelopment, neighborhood planning, affordable housing projects, open space preservation, and green builder programs.[53] The last two items were especially important to many members of the Austin community who value environmental protection and sustainability as a cornerstone of the Austin of the past and future.

Sustainable

The city of Austin has a large, active group of individuals intensely concerned with the environmental impacts of the city's growth. This concern has been present for several decades. Throughout the 1970s, Austin city council meetings became spaces where environmentalists regularly shared their concerns with city leaders and pushed against development projects.[54] In 1979, Austin passed the "Austin Tomorrow Plan," which articulated planning and development goals with an emphasis on environmental impact. Neighborhood and community organizations formed throughout the 1980s, noting environmental changes taking place throughout the city, including a group that took it on themselves to measure the city's water quality and share their results with the local press. In the 1990s, environmental activists worked with the city to share their concerns over a proposed development project within the Barton Springs watershed. The city eventually placed a water ordinance referendum on the ballot, and when it passed by a two-to-one margin, it marked a notable shift in Austin city politics away from a growth agenda and toward a green sustainability agenda.[55]

Following the water ordinance referendum, many environmental and leftist activists became city leaders, and Austin became a city known for its environmental policies. These policies included some of the leading programs and policies related to recycling, composting, and green building as well as its tens of thousands of acres of protected land spread among several nature and wildlife preservations.[56] Although Austin's environmental focus predates the "Keep Austin Weird" slogan, it is an integral part of the weird, antigrowth spirit at the heart of Austin's creative resistance.

The fight for environmental policies throughout the 1970s, 1980s, and 1990s continues today in Austin. Recently, the city has set a goal of becoming carbon neutral by 2050, requiring new homes to be capable of producing as much electricity as they consume.[57] This is part of an effort to minimize the environmental impact of population growth throughout the city. Austin has also been working to develop green housing solutions in parts of the city that were previously large industrial sites, including the former municipal airport and a decommissioned steam power plant. Both sites have become some of the most sought-after real estate in the city. In and near downtown Austin, both developments are highly walkable with many shops, restaurants, and green spaces to enjoy. These sites highlight what has made Austin stand out as a sustainable city, a growth plan with a clear focus on green design that emphasizes the drives that bring people into the city in the first place.

This environmental legacy influenced Austin city politics and culture. The environmentalists of the 1970s created a political norm around protesting, attending, and shaping city council meetings. These tactics have been used for decades by other groups and businesses to ensure that Austin is not changing too fast or losing what makes Austin the city it is.[58] There has long been an understanding that Austin is a liberal bastion in deeply conservative Texas and that its environmental policies helped it to stand out as a weird city in a conservative, oil-loving state.

Californians

The belief that many of the problems in Austin were caused by Californians is well known and has existed for decades.[59] Throughout that time, Austin changed in many ways, and in addition to the issues with growth mentioned above, many residents also saw the city experience a loss of weirdness in the form of new McMansions, luxury retailers, valet parking, dress codes, noise ordinances, and fish tacos.[60] Austin and California have many similarities that have enticed many Californians to relocate—the climate, cultural industries, exciting food scene, and tech start-ups—with one huge difference: the cost of living. According to the CNN Money cost-of-living calculator, using 2018 data, living in Austin instead of Los Angeles, an individual can expect to save 54 percent on housing, 27 percent on transportation, and 20 percent on groceries. While living in Austin instead of San Francisco, an individual can expect to save 71 percent on housing, 34 percent on transportation, and 27 percent on groceries.

The fear of the invading Californians can be nicely summarized by the following excerpt from an article in the *Austin Chronicle* from 1995, and although this article is from twenty-five years ago, it represents many of the same concerns in Austin today:

> While the high-pitched battle over growth and development rages on here in Austin, this isn't a notion that sits easy with some locals. After all, the idea

behind intelligent, managed growth is to avoid overdeveloping our naturally abundant Central Texas region in the same way that parts of California (like Los Angeles, the San Francisco Bay area, Orange County and the San Jose/Silicon Valley region) went from slices of paradise on Earth to crime-ridden, overcrowded, overpriced urban and suburban landscapes. With the increase of local problems like traffic and gang activity, and such issues of land and water rights coming to the fore, our verdant hills of Central Texas are now echoing with the same crises much of California faced in the last three decades—battles that the state appears to have lost. So it's no wonder that Austinites—including those, like this writer, who moved here from elsewhere—are worried that Austin is not just going to become another Dallas or Houston, but in fact become Californicated.[61]

The scapegoating of Californians as the cause of many of Austin's problems is largely not supported by demographic data. The majority of population growth in Austin from 2010 to 2019 was in fact from Texans moving to Austin from other parts of the state.[62] The largest number of out-of-state residents moving to Austin are indeed coming from California, but that is likely due to Texas and California being the two most populous states and the prominence of similar industries, including the tech sector.[63] In fact, between 2010 and 2014, Austin received 7,317 new residents from California's twenty-six metro areas and lost 4,353 residents to those same areas. While that is an overall increase in population, it pales in comparison to the migration from other Texans.

Californians are certainly moving to Austin and changing the city, but so are Floridians, New Yorkers, and Wisconsinites (who can be seen taking over Star Bar on West 6th Street during every Green Bay Packers and Wisconsin Badger football game, along with one of the authors' sister). The derision that is hoisted on Californians really just provides a tidy package for Austin's creative resistance to economic and population growth. Turning a city of 250,000 people in 1970, 465,000 in 1990, and 790,000 in 2010 to a city of approaching more than a million residents in 2019 will cause a lot of changes that may upset long-tenured residents. Indeed, Austin is now larger than San Francisco. Turning that anger into action has been a major reason that Austin is largely considered a success story today. The creative resistance of its residents, local officials, and business owners to keep Austin weird has also kept Austin growing and thriving.[64]

The Weirdest, Best Place to Live

In 2019, Austin was named the best place to live in the United States by *U.S. News and World Report*.[65] It was the third consecutive year that Austin had received this honor.[66] The rankings are based on a formula that considers a number of factors, including a city's job market index, housing affordability index, quality-of-life index, desirability index, and net migration. Austin ranked especially high in desirability and net migration. Desirability is important to note because it speaks to how people feel about Austin. It is measured through a survey of 2,500 people throughout the United States asking them where they would most like to live, and Austin was one of the top cities among respondents.[67] One of the reasons Austin is so desirable is because it is a city that has a unique cultural identity and a strong countercultural streak, or, stated more simply, it is cool in large part because it is weird. The "Keep Austin Weird" slogan has not only become ubiquitous with the capital of Texas but also spawned a movement of weird cities with "Keep ___ Weird" stickers popping up in Portland, Oregon; Santa Cruz, California; Boulder, Colorado; Cincinnati, Ohio; Mobile, Alabama; Asheville, North Carolina; Albuquerque, New Mexico; and Louisville, Kentucky.[68] Weirdness has become a symbol for authenticity, creativity, and uniqueness because Austin has been able to succeed as a growing city with a weird soul.

Chapters Related to This Case Study

Austin is a city that has defined itself in opposition to population and economic growth that may have taken the small (by Texas standards), oddball capital and turned it into another Dallas. This story highlights how the Austin community broadcasts its identity to potential and current residents. While most cities try to encourage potential buyers to move there and through messages suggest that the community is safe, welcoming, filled with gainful employment, and near an economic center, Austin was more confrontational. More typical community messages are explored in chapter 6 through the information that Arvada, Colorado, shares with its current and potential residents. Information and its use, creation, and dissemination are at the heart of this chapter, but its perspective—that of a community instead of a resident—presents a unique entry point to explore the informational issues around where to live. Chapter 7 explores Milwaukee, Wisconsin, and the policies and processes throughout its history that led to its remaining one of the most racially segregated cities in the United States. This chapter takes a data storytelling perspective to explore the maps that were used to define and manipulate the real estate market to advance the interest of white families above all other racial and ethnic groups. Chapter 8 considers how a novel type of planned community was created around multigenerational relationships and support structures for families adopting children out of the foster care system and retirees. This story is examined through three theoretical lenses from sociology and information science to explore the social realities of this community and how it can become a replicable model. Chapter 9 brings together several of the themes explored throughout this volume by exploring the information behaviors of home buyers in an especially competitive and stressful housing market. While the home-buying process is rife with complicated decision making at almost every level of the process, this chapter focuses on how the time pressures of a competitive market impact the emotional experience of home buying. All together, these four chapters explore a variety of different communities to emphasize the complexity of selecting, planning, and designing areas that people chose to live in and the information that shapes those places and decisions.

CASE 3: CORONAVIRUS AND THE REAL ESTATE MARKET

> The U.S. housing industry is on lockdown. New construction sales centers are empty. In most states real estate agents can't show houses. Inspectors won't inspect. Appraisers can't appraise. Even cash buyers willing to waive contingencies can't get an appointment. Closings for homes that went under contract before America put its economy on ice—if they happen at all—are now done virtually via Zoom, Docusign, and drive-through title companies in order to comply with stay-at-home orders and social distancing guidelines.
>
> Real estate's clobbering runs wide and deep. Hospitality, including hotels, restaurants, and bars, took the first body blow. . . . Malls, shopping centers, and sporting and entertainment venues locked down next. . . . Short-term vacation and AirBnB rentals, which briefly saw a reservation surge in popular tourist destinations and remote rural communities as people fled dense urban hotspots like New York City, were promptly banned by many local city councils.[69]

This case study considers the first effects in early 2020 of the new coronavirus (Covid-19) on the commercial and residential real estate industries. This is written during the height of the pandemic, and no doubt some of the details will seem outdated as time passes and we gain a longer-term perspective on what happened. However, we intend this to be a snapshot of a particular point in time and do not need to update as the situation evolves. Even at this early time in the run of the pandemic, the coronavirus provides an apt case study of how exogenous forces can create new and urgent information needs and do so almost overnight.

Buyers and sellers, tenants and landlords, agents, and people from the various secondary services that support real estate transactions (appraisers, mortgage companies, closing companies, insurance companies, and so on) all are clamoring for information about how long the pandemic will last, what ways of ordinary business are no longer possible, what work-around processes can be implemented, what kind of financial aid the government is offering and what kinds of regulations it is imposing, and how the real estate industry will change over the longer term. Since this is an ongoing event, we have not written of it in the past tense, even though when our readers get to this case study, it will hopefully be something that we have successfully put behind us.

Commercial Real Estate

In March and April 2020, in response to the new coronavirus, numerous articles began to appear online about the impact on the commercial real estate market, targeted at both large commercial real estate firms and small investors. These articles were written by real estate consultants, lawyers serving the real estate industry, real estate trade groups, and the trade press, among others. For example, the Building Owners and Managers Association International instituted a Coronavirus Resource Center.[70] The National Association of Realtors (NAR) is providing information to its members related to its advocacy efforts concerning the CARES Act,[71] the Small Business Administration Injury Disaster Loans program and Paycheck Protection Program, mortgage forbearance programs of Fannie Mae and Freddie Mac, and various tax provisions, such as business tax offsets and 1031 Like-Kind Exchange programs. NAR provides a Q&A section on its website that addresses commonly asked questions about coronavirus and real estate. The website points readers to information pages of the CCIM Institute (Certified Commercial Investment Member—a leader in real estate training) and IREM (the Institute of Real Estate Management).[72]

The precipitous drop in the stock market, together with the high market volatility that has accompanied the coronavirus, has harmed the confidence of investors in commercial real estate.[73] This has hit both public and private investment in commercial real estate. This is unusual because public real estate investment trusts (REITs) typically do well in down markets, but nevertheless they dropped in share value by 35 percent in late February and early March 2020.[74] The REITs are instead sitting on cash, reducing the amount they are using for investments.[75] The market value of commercial real estate overall fell 24 percent in the period from February 21 to March 17, 2020. Senior housing (−49 percent), skilled nursing facilities (−38 percent), and lodging (−36 percent) fell the most, while data centers (−11 percent), cell towers (−13 percent), and self-storage facilities (−16 percent) were the least hard hit.[76] Similarly, some secondary real estate markets are also struggling; for example, flex-space providers

(Knotel and Convene), short-term rental companies (Sonder and Zeus Living), brokerages (Redfin and Compass), and property insurance brokers (Jetty) are laying off or furloughing large numbers of employees. Firms that provide instant offers on homes (so-called iBuyers) are under duress, and Zillow and Opendoor have suspended this capital-intense portion of their business for now.[77]

Concerns over the pandemic have resulted in a rapidly growing literature that provides commercial property owners with guidance on the general situation[78] as well as unusual issues that might arise in connection with the coronavirus. Topics include personal safety (for employees, contractors, and vendors), public safety (in common areas such as bathrooms, lobbies, and parking lots), management of tenant relationships (e.g., following agreements spelled out in leases and forms of communication), force majeure lease provisions (controlling who is excused from which provisions of a lease when terrorist acts, natural disasters, or other acts of God occur),[79] methods for supporting self-quarantined tenants, issues about operating covenants (e.g., requirement to operate businesses in the rented property during certain specified hours), co-tenancy provisions (e.g., reduced rent for small business leaser if a department store moves out of the same shopping mall), special insurance issues (whose insurance covers coronavirus events, landlord or tenant?),[80] default (what triggers a default on a commercial lease, and what period of time is given to rectify the problem?), business tax offsets, privacy and security issues (legal interrogation of people who entered premises about presence of coronavirus and responsibility to screen people entering the building), rent relief for tenants, and compliance with local, state, and federal regulations (including emergency regulations).[81]

Residential Real Estate—Buying and Renting

The coronavirus has also had a swift impact on the residential real estate market.[82] Redfin has reported that the median price for newly listed homes in the United States was $309,000 the week of March 29, which represented a drop of 6 percent from the week before ($21,000 drop). Moreover, the number of listings decreased by 33 percent and the number of sales by 42 percent compared to the same week one year earlier.[83] (Because there has been a shortage of houses on the market for the past decade, the prices have not dropped as much from the pandemic as they might otherwise have; sellers are at least somewhat resistant at listing for lower prices or caving in to lower offers.)

Given that millions of people are losing their jobs because of the coronavirus, residential sales are unlikely to rebound quickly. The timing could not have been worse for the residential real estate industry inasmuch as spring is traditionally the hottest time of year for this market, for it is connected with families who want to move during the summer and be in their new home in time for the new school year. Some sellers have an urgent need to move, for example, because of a new job in a different location, while others without this urgency are holding off on active searching, at least temporarily.[84] With buyers being more cautious, this leaves some sellers in the precarious transitional position of having to carry two mortgages (on their home being marketed and a newly purchased home). The house-flipping market has also taken a hit, as investors are unwilling to buy fixer properties if they do not know whether their workers will be allowed on the property to do the renovations. Even when someone has purchased a new condo and is ready to move in, there have been cases where the condo association is not permitting move-ins because they do not want the virus tracked into the building.[85]

The implementation of social distancing and the closure by the majority of governors who allowed only essential businesses to remain open have placed a major damper on house buying[86] as well as on those companies and agents focused on residential real estate. In most states, this industry was not deemed essential, and the showing of houses almost immediately ended. Any business being transacted had to be conducted online, both for viewing houses and moving through the transactional process of buying a house. The real estate industry cried foul when it was not deemed an essential business:[87]

> It's hard not to whiff some political favoritism here. Pennsylvania Governor Tom Wolf put bike repair shops on his "life-sustaining" business list—as well as his own kitchen cabinet supply company—but placed realtors on lockdown. In Massachusetts, wood chippers still grind away since someone effectively lobbied Governor Charlie Baker's office to make landscapers essential, while real estate agents sit idly at home.[88]

But the real estate industry is fighting back. The Pennsylvania Association of Realtors has filed a lawsuit against Governor Wolf to make real estate an essential business.

The real estate agency has tried to make the best of the situation and turned to online means to transact their business.[89] Some agencies are also investing in expensive services from Matterport to create high-end virtual tours since physical visiting of properties is contrary to social distancing rules.[90] Virtual open houses are being broadcast on Facebook, Instagram, and websites. Video chats with the listing agent at the house provide a chance for prospective buyers to ask specific questions and receive a visual answer in response to these questions. Digital mortgage platforms are available to verify employment and assets. Mortgages were already being applied for either by phone or online, but now the entire mortgage process can be handled without any in-person meetings. About half of the states allow virtual notarization, which makes the closing process much easier to accomplish. Banks are allowing desktop appraisals (e.g., using tools such as Clear Capital's OwnerInsight), and co-op boards are interviewing prospective residents on Zoom. Some MLSs are discontinuing the days-on-market counter so as to not discourage buyers in these unusual times.[91]

There has been an explosion in requests from home owners for *forbearance*: temporary relief from having to pay one's mortgage payments. By April 13, 2020, approximately 2 million people had applied.[92] Under the CARES Act, if a home owner holds a federally backed mortgage (e.g., those backed by Fannie Mae, Freddie Mac, the Federal Housing Administration, or the Veterans Administration), they are entitled to a 180-day period in which they can pay no or reduced mortgage payments, and they can petition for an additional 180 days at the end of the initial period. Both periods of forbearance will be granted routinely if the home owner can demonstrate need. Moreover, these delays in mortgage payment cannot be reported to credit agencies and used to reduce credit ratings.[93]

While we have focused here on house buying, a similar phenomenon is occurring with renters. Approximately two-thirds of property managers and half of individual landlords reported at least some tenants having difficulty paying their rent. Forty-six percent of property managers and 27 percent of individual landlords offered these tenants accommodation, while 7 percent of property managers and 5 percent of individual landlords terminated leases instead.[94] The challenges of showing an apartment or house for rent are similar to those of showing a house for sale. There are similar issues with getting lease agreements signed, although generally the paperwork is much less substantial than in the case of a sale. Some aspects of the process, such as appraisals and inspections, either do not exist or are greatly streamlined in the case of rentals. Financial qualification of renters is more important than ever today, but it is less complicated than qualifying a buyer.

Many of the online articles cited in writing this section have been focused on a general audience, of interest to buyers, sellers, and agents alike. However, some of the more data-driven material is of interest primarily to the agents. Some of the real estate industry associations also have resource pages online for their members. For example, the NAR has a coronavirus site online that is regularly updated. It offers general guidance, information about shelter-in-place and nonessential business edicts, and information about real estate transactions (listed properties, properties in escrow, and leased properties).[95]

Chapters Related to This Case Study

In the case of both commercial and residential real estate, what we are facing are issues that information studies scholars call information-seeking behavior. Buyers, sellers, leasers, agents, and people from the many secondary parts of the real estate industry (e.g., appraisers, mortgage brokers, inspectors, insurance agents, and so on) are facing an unprecedented situation, and they need specific information not only to act in an effective manner but also to ease their minds and make them more confident in their actions. Thus, the information these people seek has both a cognitive and an affective dimension. The coronavirus situation is exceptional—an event that people will remember and discuss for many years into the future. However, in people's lives, every day they confront various kinds of issues for which they need specific information and in which they craft specific kinds of information-seeking strategies and sources. Two of our chapters are about differentiated populations and their information-seeking behaviors. In chapter 10, Jamillah Gabriel discusses the information-seeking behaviors of African Americans when they are trying to decide where to live. William Aspray's chapter 11 addresses a different information-seeking behavior, when people decide where and how to live in retirement. The coronavirus introduces a new set of questions for all parties in commercial and residential real estate, different from those in a normal real estate market. Similarly, the information-seeking behaviors of African Americans and retirees pose a special set of issues and information-seeking strategies compared to the decision processes that the majority of American adults confront during most of their lives when they decide where to live.

NOTES

1. Will in Real Estate Marketing, "Top 6 iPad Apps for Real Estate Agents and Realtors," On Spot Social, June 4, 2018, https://onspotsocial.com/apps-real-estate-agents (accessed May 16, 2019).

2. Emily Esposito, "The Best Real Estate Software in 2019: 13 Apps for Real Estate Agents," Zapier, May 20, 2019, https://zapier.com/blog/best-real-estate-software (accessed May 17, 2019).

3. To keep the story simpler, we are going to discuss only websites and apps to purchase houses in this section. There is, however, a parallel development for renting a place to live. See, for example. Apartments.com, Zumper, and many others, such as Rentals.com, Rentdigs.com, Rent.com, Rent Jungle, Realrentals.com, Sublet.com, Hotpads, and Trovit.

4. Digital Trends Staff, "Looking for a House? The Best Real Estate Apps Will Make It Easier," January 23, 2018, https://www.digitaltrends.com/mobile/best-real-estate-apps (accessed May 16, 2019).

5. In particular, we have examined table 4.2 from the 1995 report, II-3 (2000), 3-3 (2005), 3-3 and 3-4 (2010), and 3-3 and 3-4 (2015). There are methodological differences in the way in which the results are reported in these reports. For example, the 1995 report identifies a single most important source of information for home buyers, while the later ones allow people to identify more than one source as important. For example, it looks as though the average number of information sources consulted by a home buyer who took the NAR survey was 4.8. Thanks to Brandi Snowden of NAR for supplying us with these data.

6. The 2015 survey was the first survey that separated out tablet and mobile technologies from online technologies. In 2015, online website use was 89 percent, while mobile or tablet website or application was 57 percent.

7. Comparing the 18- to 24-year-old population with those 65 or older, the percentages were 95 to 62 in 2010 and 92 to 77 in 2015—so use of the internet by older people for house searching has been increasing in the 2010s.

8. Daria Bulatovych and Kate Abrosimova, "How to Develop a Real Estate App Like Zillow," Yalantis, blog, n.d., https://yalantis.com/blog/mobile-real-estate-app-development-usa-zillow-trulia-apps-technology (accessed May 21, 2019).

9. For example, in May 2015, Zillow's website received approximately 36 million visits, while Trulia's received 23 million visits. While much of this activity is goal directed to buying a home, there is also what one might call "real estate lifestyle surfing" in which one is curious about homes and communities but not in the midst of a search to buy a home (Bulatovych and Abrosimova, n.d.).

10. For example, in the third quarter of 2018, combined traffic to the Zillow website and app was approximately 186 million monthly visitors, while Realtor.com received approximately 60 million visitors during this same period (Bulatovych and Abrosimova, n.d.).

11. Fourth and a distant fifth are Yahoo! Homes and Redfin, respectively. (Kate Abrosimova, "What Technology Stack Do Zillow, Redfin and Realtor.com Use for Property Listings," Yalantis, blog, n.d., https://yalantis.com/blog/what-technology-stack-do-zillow-redfin-and-realtorcom-use-for-property-listings (accessed May 21, 2019).)

12. In fact, Zillow allows its users to see listings for all homes, not just for those currently listed.

13. Digital Trends Staff, "Looking for a House?"

14. Digital Trends Staff, "Looking for a House?"

15. The information in table 1.2 is taken from the following articles: Joe Hindy, "5 Best House Hunting Apps and Real Estate Apps for Android," Android Authority, September 22, 2018, https://www.androidauthority.com/best-house-hunting-apps-real-estate-apps-android-783885 (accessed May 24, 2019); Eric Rosenberg, "The 8 Best Real Estate Apps of 2019," The Balance, February 28, 2019, https://www.thebalance.com/best-real-estate-apps-4163003 (accessed May 24, 2019); Devon Thorsby, "The Best Apps for Househunting," U.S. News and World Report, December 12, 2018, https://realestate.usnews.com/real-estate/slideshows/the-best-apps-for-house-hunting (accessed May 24, 2019); Adam Verwymeren, "Best Apps for Finding a Home," Fox News, May 28, 2015, https://www.foxnews.com/real-estate/best-apps-for-finding-a-home (accessed May 16, 2019).

16. While most of the literature talks about the use of apps by buyers, not sellers, these apps are also used by sellers to identify the state of the market, find houses that are competitive with theirs, and check that they are pricing and marketing their house in effective ways. And, of course, many people who are selling a home will turn around and buy another home.

17. Real Estate Webmasters, "Why Every Agent or Broker Needs a Real Estate App," Real Estate Webmasters, blog, October 2018, https://www.realestatewebmasters.com/blog/why-every-agent-or-broker-should-have-a-real-estate-app (accessed May 22, 2019).

18. There is rapid innovation going on to develop new real estate apps. One current area of research is to use augmented reality in real estate apps. "Augmented reality means that the reality of the display by camera images is enhanced with the GPS and compass information on the smartphone and combined with supplementary data from external knowledge bases, social media networks or real estate search engines" (Veronika Lang and Peter Sittler, "Augmented Reality for Real Estate," 18th Annual Pacific-Rim Real Estate Society Conference, Adelaide, Australia, January 15–18, 2012, http://www.prres.net/papers/Lang_Augmented_Reality_for_Real_Estate_final.pdf (accessed May 28, 2019).

19. Esposito, "The Best Real Estate Software in 2019."

20. Kiah Treece, "40 Best Real Estate Software and Tools for Top Agents in 2019," Fit Small Business, May 22, 2019, https://fitsmallbusiness.com/best-real-estate-software (accessed May 22, 2019).

21. The apps listed in table 1.2 are taken from the following online articles: Abdallah Allabadi, "The Best Real Estate Apps of 2018," Mashvisor, October 10, 2018, https://www.mashvisor.com/blog/best-real-estate-apps-2018 (accessed May 22, 2019); Emile L'Eplattenier, "20 Best FREE Real Estate Apps for 2019," The Close, January 9, 2019, https://theclose.com/real-estate-apps (accessed May 21, 2019); Paul Esajian, "14 Best Real Estate Apps for Buyers, Sellers, and Investors," Fortune Builders, https://www.fortunebuilders.com/real-estate-apps (accessed May 24, 2019); Esposito, "The Best Real Estate Software in 2019"; Melanie Haselmayr, "10 Best Apps for Real Estate Agents and Brokers," Forbes, June 24, 2014, https://www.forbes.com/sites/allbusiness/2014/06/24/10-best-apps-for-real-estate-agents-and-brokers/#609b9fae7453 (accessed May 16, 2019); Realtors Property Resource, "14 Best Apps for Real Estate Agents in 2017," http://blog.narrpr.com/tips/best-apps-real-estate-agents-2017 (accessed May 16, 2019); TDG, "Best Real Estate Apps for Home Buyers, Sellers, Apartment Rentals, and Investors," The Droid Guy, October 27, 2018, https://thedroidguy.com/2018/10/best-real-estate-apps-home-buyers-sellers-apartment-rentals-investors-1061872 (accessed May 22, 2019); Ben Weger, "25 Best Apps and Software for Real Estate Agents and Brokers," Updater, May 22, 2018, https://www.updater.com/blog/best-apps-for-real-estate-agents-and-brokers (accessed May 21, 2019); Will in Real Estate Marketing, "Top 6 iPad Apps for Real Estate Agents and Realtors."

22. When we conducted a search on the term "buying a house" on Amazon Books (June 4, 2019), we got 75 pages of hits, with slightly more than 20 hits per page. There were a number of irrelevant items among those "hits" and some duplication, but it is clear that there are hundreds of practical books written to guide the reader in buying a house.

23. Eric Tyson and Ray Brown, *Home Buying for Dummies*, 2nd ed. (For Dummies, 2001) (updated, same authors and publisher, 2016, as *Home Buying Kit for Dummies*). Other examples of general house-buying books include Mark Ferguson and Gregory Helmerick, *How to Buy a House* (independently published, 2017), and Alysse Musgrave, *Buying a Home: Don't Let Them Make a Monkey Out of You!*, 6th ed. (CreateSpace Independent Publishing, 2017).

24. See, for example, Anthony Park, *How to Buy Your Perfect First Home: What Every First-Time Homebuyer Needs to Know* (independently published, 2018), and Jeff Leighton, *How to Buy a House: First Time Home Buyers Quick and Easy Guide to Buying a Home* (independently published, 2018).

25. Lauren Bowling, *The Millennial Homeowner: A Guide to Successfully Navigating Your First Home Purchase* (Coventry House, 2017); David E. Nelson Jr., *Making the Most of Your Veterans Affairs (VA) Home Loan Benefits: An Active Duty Service Member and Veteran's Guide to Home Ownership* (Atlantic Publishing Group, 2018).

26. Ilona Bray, Alayna Schroeder, and Stewart Stewart, *Nolo's Essential Guide to Buying Your First Home*, 6th ed. (Nolo, 2016).

27. Dylan Chalk, *The Confident House Hunter: A Home Inspector's Tips for Finding Your Perfect Home* (Cedar Fort, 2016).

28. Ilyce R. Glink, *100 Questions Every First-Time Home Buyer Should Ask: With Answers from Top Brokers from around the Country*, 4th ed. (Three Rivers Press, 2018).

29. Elysia Stobbe, *How to Get Approved for the Best Mortgage without Sticking a Fork in Your Eye: A Comprehensive Guide for First Time Home Buyers and Home Buyers . . . Since the Mortgage Crisis of 2008* (Ponto Alto Publishing, 2015).

30. Rick Schultz, *101 Things I Wish I Knew before I Bought My First Home: How to Reduce the Stress of Your First Purchase* (independently published, 2016).

31. Jonathan Scott and Drew Scott, *Dream Home: The Property Brothers' Ultimate Guide to Finding and Fixing Your Perfect House* (Houghton Mifflin Harcourt, 2016).

32. Jordan Riches, *Real Estate Investing for Beginners* (independently published, 2019); J. Scott, *The Book on Flipping Houses*, 2nd ed. (Bigger Pockets, 2019); Ralph R. Roberts, *Flipping Houses for Dummies*, 3rd ed. (For Dummies, 2017). On becoming a landlord, see Mike Butler, *Landlording on AutoPilot: A Simple, No-Brainer System for Higher Profits, Less Work, and More Fun (Do It All from Your Smartphone or Tablet)*, 2nd ed. (Wiley, 2018). On buying at auctions, see Danni Ackerman, *Buying at Auction Houses for Fun & Profit* (CreateSpace, 2013).

33. Steve Worsley, *Black Mold and Home Inspections: What Your Realtor Won't Tell You When Buying a Home* (independently published, 2019); Andrew Trim, *Real Estate Dangers and How to Avoid Them* (Wiley, 2019).

34. Ira Serkes, George Devine, and Ilona Bray, *How to Buy a House in California*, 16th ed. (Nolo, 2017); Nicholas Wallword, *Investing in International Real Estate for Dummies* (For Dummies, 2019); Tom Kelly and Mitch Creekmore, *Cashing in on a Second Home in Mexico* (Crabman Publishing, 2007).

35. Most agents who are representing buyers are also representing sellers, and where there is a conflict of interest, the agent represents the seller. However, it is possible to contractually sign up for a buyer's agent who is exclusively beholden to the buyer. For a description of the duties and responsibilities of a buyer's agent, see Icenhower Coaching and Consulting, "A Real Estate Buyer's

Agent Job Description," *The Real Estate Trainer*, December 12, 2015, https://therealestatetrainer.com/2015/12/12/real-estate-buyers-agent-job-description (accessed June 4, 2019).

36. "The Story of The Sassy Shirt," *Austin Monthly Magazine*, May 31, 2012.

37. Erin Edgemon, "Austin's Total Home Value Grew at Staggering Rate in Past Decade," *Austin Business Journal*, January, 20 2020, https://www.bizjournals.com/austin/news/2020/01/20/austins-total-home-value-grew-at-staggering-rate.html.

38. Mary Ann Azevedo, "Austin Housing Market Braces as Newcomers Continue to Move In," *Forbes*, May 28, 2019, "Looking at the Numbers" section, para. 6, https://www.forbes.com/sites/maryannazevedo/2019/05/28/austin-housing-market-braces-as-transplants-continue-to-move-in.

39. Edgemon, "Austin's Total Home Value Grew at Staggering Rate in Past Decade."

40. Paul Thompson, "20 Austin Neighborhoods Where Home Values Skyrocket," *Austin Business Journal*, October 22, 2019, https://www.bizjournals.com/austin/news/2019/10/22/housing-boom-the-austin-neighborhoods-that-deliver.html.

41. Wells Dunbar, "In Time for SXSW, a Brief History of Austin's 'Don't Move Here' T-Shirts," KUT 90.5, Austin's NPR Station, March 7, 2014, https://www.kut.org/post/time-sxsw-brief-history-austins-dont-move-here-t-shirts.

42. Joshua Long, *Weird City—Sense of Place and Creative Resistance in Austin, Texas* (Austin: University of Texas Press, 2010), 54.

43. Red Wassenich has recently passed away, but his words and impact are still felt throughout Austin. For a more detailed account of the creation of "Keep Austin Weird" slogan, see Long, *Weird City*.

44. Both Wassenich and Pavelka are members of the field of library and information science. Wassenich worked as a librarian at Austin Community College and taught courses there and at the School of Information at the University of Texas, Austin, along with Pavelka, who is a senior lecturer.

45. For much more about creative resistance in Austin, see Long, *Weird City*.

46. Long, *Weird City*, 56.

47. Long, *Weird City*, 56.

48. Long, *Weird City*, 56.

49. Katie Hall, "Austin Traffic Worsens, Now Ranking 14th Most Congested City in Nation," *Austin American-Statesman*, https://www.statesman.com/news/20190822/austin-traffic-worsens-now-ranking-14th-most-congested-city-in-nation.

50. Long, *Weird City*, 54.

51. Opinion Analysts, "Community Priorities For a Healthy Economy—A Survey of Austin Residents by Liveable City," 2003.

52. Long, *Weird City*, 60.

53. Long, *Weird City*, 58–59.

54. Long, *Weird City*, 32–33.

55. Long, *Weird City*, 35.

56. Long, *Weird City*, 36.

57. Laura Parker, "How One City Turned Industrial Zones into Green Enclaves," *National Geographic,* December 9, 2016. https://www.nationalgeographic.com/environment/urban-expeditions/austin/austin-green-buildings-fight-urban-sprawl.

58. For a list of campaigns to preserve Austin businesses and traditions through the use of the "Keep Austin Weird" slogan, see Long, *Weird City,* chap. 5.

59. Long, *Weird City,* 85–91; Rob Patterson, "Austin, California?," *Austin Chronicle,* June 30, 1995, https://www.austinchronicle.com/news/1995-06-30/533708/; KVUE Staff, "VERIFY: Are Californians Really 'Invading' Austin?," *kvue.com,* May 16, 2019, https://www.kvue.com/article/news/verify/verify-are-californians-really-invading-austin/269-a972ffc8-353d-49f7-865c-c95b32bc5ec6.

60. Long, *Weird City,* 85.

61. Patterson, "Austin, California?," para. 3.

62. KVUE Staff, "VERIFY."

63. John Egan, "How Many Californians Are Moving to Austin? The Numbers Will Surprise You," *CultureMap Austin,* December 12, 2016, https://austin.culturemap.com/news/city-life/12-2-16-californians-moving-to-austin-census-data.

64. City of Austin, "City of Austin Population History–1840 to 2019," 2019. https://www.austintexas.gov/sites/default/files/files/Planning/Demographics/population_history_pub_2019.pdf; Daniel Salazar, "Census: Austin Nears 1M Residents, Suburbs Keep Booming," *Austin Business Journal,* May 23, 2019, https://www.bizjournals.com/austin/news/2019/05/23/austin-nears-1-million-residents-suburbs-keeps.html.

65. Eva Ruth Moravec, "Austin Is One of the Best Places to Live in America," *U.S. News and World Report,* 2019, https://realestate.usnews.com/places/texas/austin?src=usn_fb&utm_source=austin-tx.

66. Jimmy Im, "These Are the 10 Best Places to Live in the US in 2019," *CNBC,* April 15, 2019, https://www.cnbc.com/2019/04/15/us-news-world-report-best-places-to-live-in-the-us-in-2019.html.

67. *U.S. News and World Report,* "How We Rank the Best Places to Live & Retire," 2019, https://realestate.usnews.com/places/methodology?src=usn_fb&utm_source=how-we-rank-the-best-places-to-live-retire.

68. Long, *Weird City,* 94–95.

69. Peter Lane Taylor, "What Will America's Housing Market Look Like after the Coronavirus Pandemic Ends: Here's What 5 Top Producing Real Estate Agents Had to Say," *Forbes,* April 12, 2020, accessed through Apple News, April 13, 2020.

70. See the BOMA website, https://www.boma.org (accessed April 13, 2020). Other trade associations addressing this issue are the Alternative and Direct Securities Association, the American Hotel and Lodging Association, the American Seniors Housing Association, Building Owners and Managers Association, International Council of Shopping Centers, the National Apartment Association, the National Association of Realtors, the National Association of Real Estate Investment Management, the National Association of Real Estate Investment Trusts, the National Multifamily Housing Council, the Real Estate Roundtable, and the Society of Industrial and Office Realtors (Commercial Real Estate Industry Coronavirus Research Center, https://realestatedaily-news.com/commercial-real-estate-industry-coronavirus-resource-center, accessed April 13, 2020).

71. Coronavirus Aid, Relief, and Economic Security Act, passed by the U.S. Congress on March 27, 2020.

72. National Association of Realtors, "Coronavirus Guidance: Commercial Real Estate," April 10, 2020, https://www.nar.realtor/coronavirus-guidance-commercial-real-estate (accessed April 13, 2020).

73. For specific examples of commercial real estate transactions that are being bollixed by the coronavirus, see "Commercial Property Freezes: 'There's Widespread Panic,'" Crain's Chicago Business, March 20, 2020, https://www.chicagobusiness.com/commercial-real-estate/commercial-property-freezes-theres-widespread-panic (accessed April 13, 2020). To see how recently people were still touting commercial real estate investment even in the face of the coronavirus, see Mark Heschmeyer, "State of the Market Video: Coronavirus Hits Commercial Real Estate: Industry's Attributes Can Still Appeal to Investors, Even in Uncertain Times," CoStar News, March 16, 2020, https://www.costar.com/article/1854056636/state-of-the-market-video-coronavirus-hits-commercial-real-estate (accessed April 13, 2020). For a more upbeat account of how tenants and landlords can work together to get through the problems, see Kirk Pinho, "Don't Fret Just Yet about Commercial Real Estate Debt Threat," Crain's Detroit Business, March 17, 2020, https://www.crainsdetroit.com/real-estate/dont-fret-just-yet-about-commercial-real-estate-debt-threat (accessed April 13, 2020).

74. Jonathan Lansner, "Bubble Watch: Coronavirus Slashes Commercial Property Values 24%," *Orange County Register*, March 17, 2020, https://www.ocregister.com/2020/03/17/bubble-watch-coronavirus-slashes-commercial-property-values-24 (accessed April 13, 2020). For more industry news about REITs, see Calvin Schnure and Nareit Staff, "The Coronavirus, Commercial Real Estate and REITs," Nareit Real Estate, March 5, 2020, https://www.reit.com/news/blog/market-commentary/coronavirus-commercial-real-estate-and-reits (accessed April 13, 2020), and Paul Fiorilla, "Commercial Real Estate Finding It's Not Immune to the Coronavirus," Commercial Property Executive, n.d., https://www.cpexecutive.com/post/commercial-real-estate-finding-its-not-immune-to-the-coronavirus (accessed April 13, 2020).

75. Mary Diduch, "How Will Coronavirus Affect Global CRE Deal Volume?," *The Real Deal*, March 23, 2020, https://therealdeal.com/2020/03/23/how-will-coronavirus-affect-global-cre-deal-volume (accessed April 13, 2020). On the real estate market in China and around the world, see Kevin Thorpe and Rebecca Rockey, "Coronavirus: Impact on the Global Property Markets," Cushman and Wakefield, February 28, 2020, https://www.cushmanwakefield.com/en/united-states/insights/2020-coronavirus-and-impact-on-the-property-markets (accessed April 13, 2020), and their accompanying page of insights, n.d., https://www.cushmanwakefield.com/en/united-states/insights/2020-coronavirus-and-impact-on-the-property-markets (accessed April 13, 2020).

76. Lansner "Bubble Watch." For additional statistical information, see Alex Nicoli, "7 Charts Show How the Coronavirus Could Clobber Real Estate, from Retail Vacancies of Nearly 15% to Plunging Office Rents in Texas Cities," Business Insider, https://www.businessinsider.com/seven-charts-show-how-coronavirus-could-clobber-commercial-real-estate-2020-3 (accessed April 13, 2020).

77. Alex O. Nicoll, "Coronavirus Is Clobbering the Real Estate Industry. From a Frenzy of Flex-Office Layoffs to Big Deals Falling Apart, Here's Everything You Need to Know," Business Insider, April 13, 2020, https://www.businessinsider.com/the-latest-coronavirus-and-commercial-real-estate-news-2020-3 (accessed April 14, 2020).

78. See, for example, Tim Wang, "Covid-19, Volatility and U.S. Commercial Real Estate," Clarion Partners, Legg Mason Global Asset Management, March 30, 2020, https://www.leggmason.com/en-us/insights/market-outlook/cp-coronavirus-volatility-commercial-real-estate.html (accessed April 13, 2020), or Paul Moore, "Commercial Real Estate: How Coronavirus Could Change the Landscape in 2020 and Beyond," Bigger Pockets, April 8, 2020, https://www.biggerpockets.com/blog/coronavirus-change-commercial-real-estate-landscape (accessed April 13, 2020). On the political situation at the national level and its impact on commercial real estate over the next twenty years, see Michael Barnard and Adam Crozier, "Politics of Coronavirus, Climate, & Commercial Real Estate, Part 1 (of 2)," Clean Technica, April 3, 2020, https://cleantechnica.com/2020/04/03/politics-of-coronavirus-climate-commercial-real-estate-part-1-2, and "Coronavirus, Climate, & Commercial Real Estate, Part 2 (of 2)," April 3, 2020, https://cleantechnica.com/2020/04/03/coronavirus-climate-commercial-real-estate-part-2-2 (both accessed April 13, 2020).

79. For more information about leases and, in particular, force majeure provisions, see Matthew T. Harris, Christian Scheutz, and Jeffrey M. Pomeroy, "Coronavirus: Impact on Office, Retail, and Industrial Leases, Baker Donelson, March 19, 2020, https://www.bakerdonelson.com/coronavirus-impact-on-office-retail-and-industrial-leases (accessed April 13, 2020); Christian S. Bruno, Matthew S. Robbins, and Jon M. Schoenwetter, "Coronavirus and Commercial Real Estate Leases," Cozen O'Connor, March 18, 2020, https://www.cozen.com/news-resources/publications/2020/coronavirus-and-commercial-real-estate-leases (accessed April 13, 2020); Jennifer Perkins, "The Impact of Coronavirus on Existing Commercial Leases," Arnold & Porter, March 24, 2020, https://www.arnoldporter.com/en/perspectives/publications/2020/03/the-impact-of-coronavirus-on-existing (accessed April 13, 2020); and Joshua Stein, "A First Look at Legal Issues in Leases, Thanks to Coronavirus," Commercial Observer, March 21, 2020, https://commercialobserver.com/2020/03/a-first-look-at-legal-issues-in-leases-thanks-to-coronavirus (accessed April 13, 2020).

80. Specifically on insurance, including business interruption and liability insurance, see Tyrone R. Childress, Matthew L. Jacobs, and Jason B. Lissy, "Time for a Policy Checkup: Maximizing Insurance Coverage for Coronavirus Losses," Jones Day, February 2020, https://www.jonesday.com/en/insights/2020/02/time-for-a-policy-checkup (accessed April 13, 2020).

81. See Patrick Abell, "INSIGHT: Coronavirus Challenges Facing Commercial Property Owners," Bureau of National Affairs, Bloomberg Law, March 18, 2020, https://news.bloomberglaw.com/corporate-governance/insight-coronavirus-challenges-facing-commercial-property-owners (accessed April 13, 2020); National Association of Realtors, "Coronavirus Guidance: Commercial Real Estate," April 10, 2020, https://www.nar.realtor/coronavirus-guidance-commercial-real-estate (accessed April 13, 2020); James E. Anderson et al., "Coronavirus and

the US Commercial Real Estate Sector," DLA Piper, March 13, 2020, https://www.dlapiper.com/en/us/insights/publications/2020/03/coronavirus-and-the-commercial-real-estate-sector (accessed April 13, 2020); Ethan C. Geis and Michael Van Someron, "Coronavirus Challenges for Commercial Landlords," *National Law Review*, April 13, 2020, https://www.natlawreview.com/article/coronavirus-challenges-commercial-landlords (accessed April 13, 2020); and Eric L. Altman et al., "Commercial Real Estate Tips of the Week: Practical Answers from Sheppard Mullin's Coronavirus Task Force," *National Law Review*, April 10, 2020, https://www.natlawreview.com/article/commercial-real-estate-tips-week-practical-answers-sheppard-mullin-s-coronavirus (accessed April 13, 2020). For general, practical advice for commercial landlords for handling tenants, see the Cauble Group, "How to Handle Coronavirus for Commercial Landlords," April 9, 2020, https://www.tylercauble.com/blog/coronavirus-for-commercial-landlords (accessed April 13, 2020).

82. One data study indicates that the impact of the coronavirus on the residential real estate market is not distributed evenly across the country. Clusters of counties in New Jersey and Florida, together with a few counties in New York and Connecticut, are most at risk, while the Midwest, Southwest, and West have lower risk. This risk is based on foreclosures, homes underwater (i.e., worth less than the remaining mortgage amount), and cost of property ownership compared to local wages (AZ Big Media, "Here Are the U.S. Housing Markets Vulnerable to Coronavirus Impact," April 13, 2020, https://azbigmedia.com/real-estate/residential-real-estate/here-are-the-u-s-housing-markets-vulnerable-to-coronavirus-impact [accessed April 14, 2020]). We have heard anecdotally that the top 5 percent of the market has been less impacted by the coronavirus because there was already a severe shortage of high-end housing stock available, and what becomes available moves quickly.

83. Harsh Chauhan, "Coronavirus May Have Already Triggered a U.S. Housing Market Crash," CCN, April 11, 2020, https://www.ccn.com/coronavirus-may-have-already-triggered-a-u-s-housing-market-crash (accessed April 14, 2020).

84. Clare Trapasso, "This Is How the Coronavirus Crisis Is Ravaging the U.S. Housing Market," Realtor.com, April 9, 2020, https://www.realtor.com/news/real-estate-news/this-is-how-the-coronavirus-crisis-is-ravaging-the-u-s-housing-market (accessed April 14, 2020). This is based on a survey of approximately 6,000 realtors taken on April 5–6, 2020.

85. Real examples of all the problems listed in this paragraph, drawn from the Philadelphia area, can be found in Michelle Bond and Jeremy Roebuck, "Coronavirus Leaves Home Buyers and Sellers in Limbo—and at Financial Risk," *Philadelphia Inquirer*, April 8, 2020, https://www.ccn.com/coronavirus-may-have-already-triggered-a-u-s-housing-market-crash (accessed April 14, 2020).

86. For example, as the details of the coronavirus became public knowledge but before Virginia Governor Ralph Northam had signed an executive order, average showings of a listed property in Arlington, Virginia, had dropped from fifteen to two (Eli Tucker, "Ask Eli: Impact of Coronavirus on the Real Estate Market, Part 4)," ARL Now, March 31, 2020, https://www.arlnow.com/2020/03/31/ask-eli-impact-of-coronavirus-on-the-real-estate-market-part-4 [accessed April 14, 2020]).

87. There are some exceptions. Real estate is deemed an essential service in Wisconsin and Connecticut, and California changed its mind and made it an

essential service after first deeming it nonessential (Dana George, "What Does Coronavirus Mean for the Housing Market?," The Ascent, April 3, 2020, https://www.fool.com/the-ascent/mortgages/articles/coronavirus-housing-market [accessed April 14, 2020]). In taking an industry-friendly stance on Virginia's Executive Order 55 in response to the coronavirus, the Northern Virginia Association of Realtors and the Virginia Association of Realtors decided that they were allowed to continue operations as long as they practiced social distancing, followed measures from the Centers for Disease Control, and avoided gatherings of more than ten people. (Tucker, "Ask Eli"). While open houses are not allowed in Washington State, showings that uphold social distancing are permitted.

88. Taylor, "What Will America's Housing Market Look Like after the Coronavirus Pandemic Ends."

89. One sign that the online solution is only a partial success is that traffic to Zillow and Redfin have dropped approximately 40 percent compared to pre-virus traffic (Jeff Andrews, "How Coronavirus Is Impacting the Housing Market," Curbed.com, April 9, 2020, https://www.curbed.com/2020/3/6/21163523/coronavirus-economic-impact-housing-market [accessed April 14, 2020]).

90. There are a few places that are still permitting in-person property visits. Here are the caveats for showing a house given to agents in the San Francisco Bay Area now that the governor has changed the rules and made real estate essential: "no flyers, appointments only, no more than two family members in a house. Once inside, social distancing mandates apply. House must be unoccupied by sellers." It was also noted that some agents were showing homes in California, ignoring the initial edict that real estate was nonessential (Louis Hansen, "Coronavirus Slows, but Doesn't Stop Bay Area Real Estate Agents," Mercury News, April 6, 2020, https://www.mercurynews.com/2020/04/06/coronavirus-slows-but-doesnt-stop-bay-area-real-estate-agents [accessed April 14, 2020]).

91. Taylor, "What Will America's Housing Market Look Like after the Coronavirus Pandemic Ends"; Michele Lerner, "Real Estate Goes Virtual: 3D Home Tours Now the Norm for Those Trying to Buy," *Washington Post*, April 9, 2020, accessed through Apple News, April 13, 2020.

92. Diana Olick, "Around Two Million Borrowers Have Applied for Forbearance Programs, CNBC Business News, April 13, 2020, https://www.cnbc.com/video/2020/04/13/around-two-million-borrowers-have-applied-for-forbearance-programs.html (accessed April 14, 2020).

93. Jacob Passy, "Are You a Homeowner Seeking Forbearance on Your Mortgage? Watch Out for the Red Flags," *MarketWatch*, April 11, 2020, accessed through Apple News, April 13, 2020.

94. Statistics from the April 5–6, 2020, realtor survey (Trapasso, "This How the Coronavirus Crisis Is Ravaging the U.S. Housing Market").

95. National Association of Realtors, "Coronavirus: A Guide for Realtors," April 7, 2020, https://www.nar.realtor/coronavirus-a-guide-for-realtors (accessed April 14, 2020).

Two

Turning in Place

Real Estate Agents and the Move from Information Custodians to Information Brokers

Steve Sawyer

I focus on the roles of real estate agents in the selling and buying of homes,[1] guided by two questions. First, what roles do real estate agents play in the selling and buying of people's homes? Second, how are these roles evolving? Responding to these questions, I advance two contributions. First, real estate agents continue to provide value as market intermediaries, even as their position is being challenged by other potential intermediaries. Second, real estate agents have been able to maintain, if not further secure, their role as market intermediaries because they have shifted their attention from being information custodians to being information brokers: from providing access to explaining.

The motivation for this chapter comes from the confluence of two things. First, residential real estate is important in the United States, where buying and selling a house remains the largest financial transaction that most people experience in their lives. Second, and in the face of this and as detailed below, the work I and my colleagues have done challenge the too-common thinking that the rise of internet-accessible house-for-sale listings from the 1990s would lead to widespread disintermediation in the real estate workforce.[2] To this point, there are more real estate agents working now than there were in 1997 despite the rise in online access to information on housing, the real estate crash of 2008, and other factors.

Most pundits, economists, and both home sellers and home buyers see real estate as a two-sided market transaction: a buyer and seller find each other and transact a house. Such a view may help people understand buying a candy bar or toilet paper. However, the size of the financial transaction, the factors being considered, and the likelihood that a purchase of one house is tied to the sale of another make real estate a more complex financial exchange than buying toilet paper. More broadly, one of the secondary points made in this chapter is that simplified views of buying and selling homes[3] are empirically unsupportable relative to what is happening in real estate.[4]

In contrast, and building on scholars and professionals with analytic perspectives rooted in economic sociology and sociotechnical perspectives, I look to the socially embedded nature of real estate transaction, the relationality of information, the complexity of multiparty negotiations, and the evolving uses and functionality of digital platforms.[5] These perspectives build on concepts of economic sociology and see market intermediaries as adding value. This is particularly so in the case of complex and consequential transactions that rely on informational exchanges and extensive interpretation.[6] Building from this, my premise is that real estate agents are market intermediaries who add value through *information brokerage*.[7] Information brokers use their knowledge to guide others to pursue a transaction. Information brokerage is at the core of online dating, financial services, and social media influencers' efforts.

Without information brokers' market-making efforts, buyers and sellers would have a more difficult time finding each other and consummating a purchase and sale. Others have noted that this intermediary role arose out of an awareness that it was hard for sellers and buyers to find each other[8] and that it was hard for sellers and buyers to effectively transact without additional help. A core insight from this chapter is that real estate agents are information brokers, and they now serve more to explain than provide information. The rest of this chapter provides me the means to make the case for how the real estate agent is an important intermediary, now emphasizing the informational and social nature of home buying.

The argument developed in this chapter builds on secondary data collection, interviews with real estate professionals, and ongoing synthesis of relevant contemporary literature. This work, done to advance the argument made here, extends from and builds on a long-running study of real estate agents' uses of information and communications technologies (ICT).[9]

The chapter continues in four sections, beginning with an overview of buying and selling a home and more discussion on intermediation. This is followed by a discussion of the roles played by real estate agents. The third section provides a short overview of the information flows involved in transacting real estate and some discussion on the rise of ICTs (the digital materiality) that enables and frames the flow and storage of all the data and information. The final section highlights the shift toward agents being information brokers and the social nature of housing market information.

BUYING AND SELLING A HOME

For most people, buying or selling a house is one of the most substantive economic transactions they commit. In 2019, slightly more than 64 percent of American families owned a home (down about 4 percent from 2007—before the housing-market-bubble-bursting recession of 2008).[10] According to data from 2013 from the National Association of Homebuilders, most of these 70 million families who own a home buy or sell three times in their lifetime on average. The typical home price is several times a family's household income, requiring substantial borrowing (via a mortgage or loan secured against the value of that home).[11] Home selling and buying is both consequential and done infrequently. Americans pursue this risky, infrequent, and expensive effort because home ownership reflects both the hopes and the dreams of the American dream and the economic reality that this is likely the core financial asset to propel wealth accumulation.

As noted in the first chapter and summarized again here, real estate is an important part of the U.S. economy. In 2018, about 5.5 million houses were sold and purchased. These account for about $1.76 trillion in total sales,[12] roughly 8.7 percent of the total U.S. economy. These are gross figures, and there are many ways to explore this level of summary data. A rough estimate is that 4 to 5 percent of this total is taken in real estate agent commissions (more on this below): perhaps $8 billion. These commissions are paid to the agents and brokers, home inspectors, building surveyors, title agents, mortgage brokers and bank officers, lawyers, and others. There are taxes and other fees, and a more extensive economic analysis would highlight that most houses are purchased by borrowing money. These loans and their interest contribute more to the economy above the purchase and sale price.

As another measure of real estate's role in the U.S. economy, in 2019, there were about 1.4 million real estate agents,[13] 41,000 home inspectors,[14] 49,000 building surveyors,[15] 4,500 title agents (who are not lawyers),[16] 53,000 mortgage brokers,[17] thousands of lawyers trafficking in real estate, and many others working in support of the selling and buying of homes, such as home decorators, house stagers, contractors, landscapers, and so on. There are also employees at the National Association of Realtors, the Mortgage Bankers Association, and the National Land Title Association—all of whom represent and politic the issues for various real estate activities—and the several thousand employees who work for state and federal agencies who oversee real estate activities in their jurisdictions. Employees at Zillow, Redfin, Trulia; the many other technology vendors who provide products and services to real estate agents; the many regional and local multiple listing services; and the administrative staffs of the regional and national real estate companies are involved in real estate. All this helps to make clear that up to 2 million people working in the United States make a living from real estate.[18] Residential real estate is a big part of the U.S. economy.

For most of us, however, buying and selling a house—a home—is as emotional as it is economic. For most sellers and buyers, buying a house is also connected to selling another or to making significant changes to funds and assets. That is, to afford buying the new house requires us to sell the other, making this a relational effort. Selling and buying are also locational:[19] moving to a new school district, buying a larger house but staying in the current neighborhood, and making decisions about commuting, lifestyle, or access to work are framed by the cost of the house and the costs of living, commuting, marital and familial needs, and many more things.

In the face of this reality, much of the theorizing by economists—for example, that any one house transaction is independent of another or that decision making is a dispassionate financial decision based on full information—oversimplifies the socially embedded nature of selling and buying a home. Simplified views of real estate markets would have you thinking that as more information is available to the buyer and seller, there will be less of a need for market intermediaries. That is, this is seen as the singular, market-distorting role played by real estate agents in this simplified economic rationality.[20]

The evidence that this simplified rationality is not helpful comes in three forms. First, as noted, there are more real estate agents now (about 1.4 million) than there were when internet-accessible house-for-sale listings began to appear on the internet in 1997 (roughly 0.9 million). Second, instead of disintermediation, or the rise in the number of sales directly between sellers and buyers (known as "for sale by owner" [FSBO]), the number of FSBO sales has dropped from 15 to 11 percent of total sales over the past twenty years.[21,22] Third, there are now a number of powerful online players, such as Redfin, Zillow, and others, that seek to intermediate the buyer–seller relationships. Their presence serves as a platform to connect sellers and buyers via the internet—a digital-enabled intermediary that often competes with and sometimes works with real estate agents. Likewise, the local, regional, and national multiple listing services (MLS) and most real estate agencies/brokerages provide digital platforms that can bolster intermediation.

Along with this increased intermediary competition, there are a stunning number of other online sources of complementary information (e.g., sites to provide analytic comparisons of neighborhoods, school comparison and ranking sites, sites that detail crime and consumption patterns at the neighborhood level, and so on).[23] In sum, the housing market intermediation space is more crowded, not less, with the advent of the internet and digital access to a range of information sources and types.

The Rise of Intermediation

There are at least four reasons for this increased intermediary effort. These four reasons also reinforce each other and, together, make a case for the continued reliance on real estate agents. First, as noted, there is a lot of money involved in real estate, and markets with money draw in participants.[24] Second, the online sites that claim to be serving to disintermediate real estate are, themselves, intermediaries—just of a different (more digital) form.[25] This sets them up as competitors to one another and with real estate agents. Third, the buyers, sellers, and the many intermediaries are bound up in a slowly evolving and interconnected web of online platforms, rules, and regulations governing the flows of information and money.

This interconnected web of digital arrangements, rules, and regulations about uses and the uses themselves is a "sociotechnical" arrangement. That is, this arrangement combines both technological and social in ways that make it impossible to see one as distinct from the other. As such, these arrangements have to be treated as a system.[26] One way to see this playing out is the ability of the real estate agents, mortgage brokers, technology platform purveyors, and other participants to find ways to become or stay involved by leveraging their social (organizational or political) position in the current arrangements or by creating new technological arrangements to maximize their role and value.

A fourth reason for all this intermediation comes from the increased access to information about housing and housing-related issues, such as neighborhood health and safety, school quality, and lifestyle options (e.g., walkability or access to stores). Financing options, home redesign, decoration and contracting, tax and property values, repair rates, and other means to compare, estimate, or assess options combine to provide the potential seller and buyer substantially more information about housing, challenging them to make sense of what they can learn. I focus on this fourth reason—massively expanded information access—even as I acknowledge that it is both bound up in the first three reasons and situated in the trajectory of real estate work.

The core of the argument I advance in response to the research questions posed above is that access to such a range of informational resources requires market intermediation. That is, when so much information becomes available, market players find it increasingly difficult to sort out the important information and to use it to make decisions. In the face of all this information, Simon's[27] concept of satisficing guides action: actors seek a reasonable path in a complex space. In these "over-informed" market spaces, actors that can help sellers and buyers make sense of what they learn add significant value and in many cases may be market-making mechanisms.[28]

My argument is that real estate agents have, over the past twenty years, shifted their roles from market brokers, controlling access to information, to be market makers, focusing on helping sellers and buyers make sales. As part of this, I argue that real estate agents are using their market-making position to leverage other market intermediaries, such as the digital real estate platforms, mortgage agents, and others who have some informational control in the transacting of real estate.

REAL ESTATE AGENTS' WORK

Again, real estate agents' role is to bring together the seller and buyer of a property: they act as an intermediary in a two-sided market (of buyers and sellers). Most agents are paid a commission on the consummation of a sale. This serves to incentivize them to bring the seller and buyer to completion (the "closing"). A typical house purchase and sale has the buyer and seller negotiating via the intermediation of a buyer's agent and a seller's agent. These agents share the two "sides" of the commission paid by the seller when a house is sold and purchased. These commissions range from 4 to 7 percent of the total price of the home.

From the interesting beginnings of the profession in the 1850s into the late 1990s, agents represented the seller and had a duty to do their best to sell the house, even if they were working with buyers.[29] This makes some sense, as agents are more likely to make money since the rules of realty give them exclusive rights to list and market the seller's property (for whatever period of time is legally designated by the location or negotiated by the agents, sellers, and perhaps the buyer).

As house prices increase and in the face of relentless pressure by many buyers and sellers to find ways to save money and by others involved in securing some of the money being exchanged, there has been downward pressure on the percentage of the sale price that agents charge, particularly for high-priced houses and in particular markets. In the face of this market pressure, some agents have moved from a full-service model to a task- or item-based pricing (charging a flat rate to list the house in an MLS, a set fee for showing the house, and so on). In many ways, this is similar to what has happened to travel agents, car dealers, and other market intermediaries. Perhaps the biggest difference across these comparisons is that a house does not move; rather, the owners do. Houses are unique assets for this reason, whereas airplane tickets can be consumed and cars get replaced.

In residential real estate, cost and savings pressures, along with pressure from buyers, have also given rise to "buyer agency,"[30] which changes the relationships among the seller, the buyer, and this agent. "Buyer's agency" means that buyers sign an exclusive agreement with an agent whose job is to help them find suitable properties among those offered for sale. This, in turn, provides the buyer with more equal representation in the transaction. Without buyer's agency, agents are beholden to represent the seller's interests, leaving the buyer more exposed to risk than is the seller. The fundamental structure of the transaction continues between buyers and sellers. However, buyer's agency increases attention to serving the buyer's needs (not just the seller's). This provides agents with more ways to provide value-adding services and gain market power.

Some closings are consummated through the skill and persistence of the home seller's effort. These are FSBO transactions. As noted, FSBO transactions represent a small and decreasing percentage of the housing market (falling to 11 percent of all sales in 2018 from about 15 percent in 1981, with many of these reflecting sales within a family).[31] This suggests that even with all the pressure for saving money and cutting transaction costs, the financial implications of a potential mistake lead most sellers and buyers to seek intermediation.

The Structure of Real Estate Agents' Work

Real estate agents are independent contractors required by law to work in the service of one (licensed) broker who oversees the closing.[32] These brokers are paid a share of the commission earned by the listing agent or both agents, depending on the laws of the location where the house is closed. Real estate agents typically work for an agency: these range in size from a single broker-agent to those with several brokers, dozens (hundreds, or thousands) of agents, and additional clerical and managerial staff. Some real estate agencies are franchises of national corporations; others are local or regional institutions.

Agents receive a variety of services from the broker's firm (the agency) and, in return, give the broker and the firm a share of the commission they receive for successfully completing the purchase or sale of a client's property. Productive agents have the bargaining power to negotiate for additional services or a more favorable commission split. Independent broker-agents provide their own resources and develop their own professional networks.

INFORMATION SOURCES AND FLOWS

This overview of buying and selling homes and the roles of real estate agents in these efforts provides the background to better understand the informational aspects of their work. Here I outline the five sources and flows of information that matter to selling or buying a home. Each of these flows and sources are to be found in a data store controlled by one of the participants in the selling and purchasing of a house. Most of these information flows are contained in one of the documents (or structured data forms) that make up the legal documents that come together to represent the change in ownership of the home. And most of these documents and the data they carry are stewarded by the real estate agents involved in the sale and purchase.

The Multiple Listing Service

Central to a transaction are data about the home, much of which are stored in the federated set of databases known as the multiple listing service (MLS) in partnership with the National Association of Realtors (NAR).[33] The MLS is a database about houses for sale, with access provided to those who agree to share information and abide by rules of use. An MLS is formed by and serves its members: dues-paying real estate agents. In this way, the MLS is a cooperative venture. An MLS's database provides digital access to listings of properties for sale, now also available online for buyers and sellers to see (some of what is available).

An MLS is a local effort taking place nationwide. As such, it is actually a set of federated databases, each slightly different than the other. So, even as there is a single national portal to the MLS,[34] there are also regional and local portals. Given the costs of operating an MLS, there have been multiple waves of local-to-regional consolidation. By 2019, the number of MLSs in the United States had dropped to less than 600:[35] 300 fewer than a decade before and half of what existed in 1997. And more than 500 of the remaining MLSs are operated by companies chartered by the local Realtors' board; the others are run by privately held companies independent of the local Realtor organization.[36]

Data are shared among MLSs, and this sharing is governed by the specific agreements stipulating what data are to be shared and used.[37] There are several efforts to provide an alternative to MLS data via public sites available on the internet, such as Zillow and others, that focus on serving regions or specific sellers/buyers. None of the current competitors have usurped the MLS's centrality, but these expand the options for consumers and agents to share and find house information.

The Purchase and Sales Agreement

Second, one of the primary legal vehicles is the purchase and sale (P&S) agreement.[38] The P&S contains all the details about the transaction of the house. This is a legal document, carefully tracked and reviewed by the lawyers, agents, and both the sellers and the buyers. While the P&S differs from location to location based on variations in state and local laws, legal precedent and procedures, and norms of behavior, it remains a recognizable and core element of the transaction. The agent representing the seller creates the P&S, negotiating through the seller's agent with the sellers, to create a P&S that both buyer and seller will sign once all contingencies (home inspection, title, appraisal, cleaning and repair, and so on) are removed. Beyond the agents, buyers, and sellers, the many lawyers, lenders, insurance and title agents, and perhaps others all pay attention to the P&S.

The HUD1 Form

A third information source is the federal Department of Housing and Urban Development (HUD)[39] forms (known as the HUD1) that are required parts of a house transaction. Some of this is done by the listing agent, but most of this form is completed by the sellers following guidance from their agent. The P&S and HUD1 forms contain much of the information about the houses, the purchasers, the sellers, and the conditions for the transaction.

Financial Data

A fourth flow of information comes together across multiple forms to support the financing or payments of the seller and buyer. These include mortgage and tax data and the buyer's savings, tax, and income data related to securing a mortgage. Additional data on assets and liabilities to assess the buyer's ability to purchase are often required (e.g., credit scores, additional support and funds, and so on). All buyers and sellers are required to show they have the funds for the work needed to bring the purchase to closing. These funds include legal fees, taxes, and loan origination and other fees, often held in escrow by one or both of the real estate agents involved. There is no singular source of all data bound up in a home transaction. Instead, these data are found on the P&S, the HUD1, the tax records (held by the cognizant local government), and the mortgage records (held by the bank) of the buyers and sellers and perhaps kept by the lawyers involved.

Home Data

Finally, there are additional data from home inspections, appraisals, property tax estimations, insurance assessments, and perhaps construction and repair work that are held by the vendors or civil servants hired or required to do these things. Some of these data are recorded in or mentioned in the MLS, P&S, HUD1, and multiple financial records.

Each of the information sources and flows are touched by one or both real estate agents and either the buyer or the seller. Often, these data are made available to both sellers and buyers, their agents, relevant lawyers supporting the seller or buyer, the broker overseeing the transaction, and perhaps others. Seen from the perspective of information sources and flows, the real estate agent's roles are to guide and explain to sellers and buyers what all the data and information mean, how these data and information are shared, the roles of the forms, the implications of sharing, and the ways in which all of these sources and flows come together to become the transaction that is the sale and purchase of a home. It seems worth noting that the house itself never moves, nor is much changed by all this work to collect, organize, share, and agree on the informational things that represent the physical asset.

ICTS, INFORMATION FLOWS, AND INTERMEDIATION

Nearly thirty years after home data began to be accessible online, almost all prospective buyers search for properties online via various national and regional MLS websites, agents' websites, and other online sources, such as Zillow.[40] And nearly 50 percent of buyers first contact an agent having already done much of the house search online. Even as recently as the late 1990s, house searching required working with a real estate agent to look at the MLS. Less than a generation later (or less than the length of a thirty-year mortgage), agents rarely identify houses for buyers.

Now, potential buyers look online, comparing and sorting their interests. Most home buyers are not sophisticated at searching for houses, relying primarily on their own knowledge, guidance from friends and family, and perhaps previous experience. This typically means that the agent is presented with a list of potential houses and lots of questions when a potential buyer contacts them. Here is also the core of the change in agents' roles: agents are now explaining, not delivering, information to these buyers.[41]

Moving house data online and the widespread digitalization of data means that information-centric work is also ICT work. Real estate agents, like most workers, use ICTs to support their work. So they have had to computerize in order to keep current in their work. As such, and as most buyers and sellers would now expect, real estate agents have become facile consumers of the many real estate–related sites and platforms to be found on the internet. A viable agent makes extensive use of their smartphones for contact management, texting, e-mail, and Web capabilities. Most agents cannot conceive of carrying out their work without their phone. As one of our longtime confederates texted, "If you don't have a smart phone, you're not a serious agent."

As detailed in the first chapter of the book, the impressive and steadily expanding range of digital services and specialty software applications leveraging the MLS has grown into a multi-million-dollar industry.[42] These third-party vendors provide agents with the means to automate routine queries, support customized analysis of sales and transactions, and allow special reporting functions. The traditional lockbox[43] has been replaced with digital lockboxes that record all access to that house's key, providing the selling agent with a digital record of who has viewed the property. Digital pictures and video are standard components of a house listing. Agents either invest in high-quality digital video cameras or subcontract the photo and video shootings to third parties. Most agents take advantage of digital forms software for the P&S, HUD1, and other contractual documents. These digital forms range from simple PDFs to more sophisticated dynamic data entry and tracking applications that work on smartphones and PCs. And, while fax machines can still be found in every office, their use is now (distantly) secondary to the nearly ubiquitous e-mail sharing of digital documents.

Agents are keen to have their listed homes be visible online. They work to get these listings posted to multiple websites, such as their own professional site, their agency site, the local MLS site, http://www.realtor.com, and others. And they are happy to be listed as a contact agent on Zillow and to a preferred agent for other sites. Beyond these devices and applications, many websites now provide additional data on mortgage and financing, neighborhoods and schools, comparisons of economic indices, community data, commuting times, and other possibly relevant data. Some of these websites leverage data from the MLS to provide value-adding services.[44] In the course of their work, agents build up a collection of preferred sites, often linking to them from their own professional websites. This set of individualized professional resources serves, in part, as a representation of their ability to provide process support and value-adding services: the suite of ICT that agents can bring to bear is embedded into their approach to supporting their clients.

Over the past ten years, agents have taken up social media and are now committed, high-profile, and often expert participants.[45] The specific platforms favored by agents vary. Pinterest, Instagram, and Facebook groups (and ads) are now a core part of an agent's job. In some real ways, social media serve agents very well. Social media provide a visible and shareable means to create attention. Real estate agents can use social media to allow for light social touches, sharing information about services, houses, and experiences. Social media provide a means of staying visible to people's digital social networks. The desire to have large contact lists and be visible to these contacts in many ways means that social media play to agents' roles as intermediaries.

More broadly, ICT uses are embedded in and enable most all elements of the agent's practice: personal software for querying the MLS, contact management software, professional websites for sharing house data and links to useful sites, digital cameras, smartphones, digital lockboxes, and so on. Beyond this growth of individualized use, note the growth in work and contact management systems put in place by brokers and agents. The implication of these work and customer management systems is to increase the options available to agents while also trying to retain some of the agent's intellectual capital as an organizational asset. And, finally, while there exists a stunning variety of devices, software packages, Web-based applications, and ways of using these, any one agent's collection of ICT seems to be functionally similar to others.

FROM INFORMATION CUSTODIAN TO INFORMATION BROKER

The combination of the growth in digital data, multiple access points to and sources of these data, and the number of competing sources of information demands that agents keep close track of this computerization of their work. From the perspective of a seller, these sources of data provide both an impressive and a challenging range of options to learn about and consider readying a house for sale, putting it on the market in both physical and digital ways, and assessing interests and pricing. Buyers enter their local real estate market faced with a second set of data sources, each offering some benefits but providing incomplete data that are often hard to source or compare.

For both the seller and the buyer, real estate agents become a "go-to" source to make sense of the flows and sources of digital (and nondigital) data. Agents are involved with helping sellers sort out the pricing of their property and the costs of closing. Agents are also involved with buyers to both assess what they can afford (often helping them to prequalify or prepare for securing a mortgage) and outline the costs of purchase. Most sellers and buyers can see homes for sale via multiple online sources. This change of search time for buyers and sellers shifts the role of agents to learning from the buyer and seller. Then agents use this knowledge of interests and preferences to shape and guide additional search and discovery. Agents are involved in drafting and negotiating the purchase and sale and then working with both buyer and seller to work through the contingencies and ensure that the house's ownership changes hands. Real estate agents are part of every information flow in a real estate transaction.

As my colleagues and others have noted, real estate agents have always served three roles: information sharing, process consultation, and providing value-adding services.[46] In this more "informated" market space and in the face of a rise of data-providing sites and competition for intermediation, agents have leveraged their market position and value-adding services to retain their place. They have done this in three ways, each reinforcing the other.

Buyer agency is the first mechanism, as it allows agents to serve both the seller and the buyer in equitable ways. Along with greater access to information, buyer's agency provides an educational and buffering role relative to the information sources and flows and for the negotiations and subtleties of the sale and purchase of a house, balancing the seller's agent privilege. In market terms, buyer's agency is a means to reduce the "information asymmetry" that exists between sellers and buyers.[47] That is, buyer's agents help buyers know more about the purchase and sale than would the agents acting only to the benefit of the seller.

The second role that agents serve, as process consultant, deserves more attention than that given in this chapter. I noted at the outset that the process is not done often, has substantial financial implications, and is often part of a chain of decisions. Here note that the purchase or sale of a house is almost always a familial decision: spouses negotiating, children being involved, family members being engaged, friends offering ideas, and school quality, commuting, safety, and egos all being bound together. These forces make for an emotional experience, something that real estate agents work through for every transaction: moving nervous families through a potentially confusing legal process. Process consultation is also a form of relationship therapy, contrasting with the dehumanized economic rationality that scholars who rely on simplified economic models of markets seem to expect.[48]

Adding Value

The third role, adding value, is where the agents have turned in place. The rest of this section focuses on two aspects of adding value: the shift from controlling access to information to the current role of helping buyers and sellers make sense of information. The second role of adding value is the real estate agent's participation in all the information flows that create a purchase and sale of a house. As discussed above, the shift in agents' attention from access to explanation reflects the greater consumer access to data about homes and housing, buyer and seller choices and experiences, and a means to respond to the competitive pressure of online intermediaries, such as Zillow, Redfin, Trulia, and other regional efforts.

Real estate agents find themselves straddling the information flows that combine into a transaction. Other potential intermediaries are connected to one or two of the flows and sources, while real estate agents touch all of them as part of their services to the seller or buyer. Since real estate agents are helping to manage and track these flows, they are provided with knowledge about both the transaction's elements and the other actors. Agents use this knowledge to help their client (be it the buyers or the sellers) to also work through the uncertainties and emotion, negotiations with the other party, and the relationship therapy that goes along with helping multiple people in the same family. These additional and admittedly social activities reinforce the role of agents as intermediaries.

THE INFORMATIONAL AND SOCIAL VALUE OF INTERMEDIATION

I began this chapter making a case that real estate agents add value through their role as market intermediaries. This required situating the rapid growth in digital forms of data that are now available via multiple online platforms and sources as having helped shift real estate agent from a market role focused on controlling consumers' access to housing data to a market role designed to provide guidance for how to make these data into information they can use.

More broadly, information asymmetries remain a concern of two-sided markets and intermediation.[49] So even as this economic perspective assumes that both parties pursue a single transaction in the face of full (or "perfect") information, the issue of one side knowing more than the other is troubling. My contention is that the social nature of information, the relational nature of the transaction, the emotional and personal investments that are part of home ownership, the process of satisficing, and the lack of full knowledge regarding all the steps required to ensure the purchases and sales of houses require assistance to reduce the information asymmetry.[50]

People's hopes and beliefs are less clear-eyed than economists' models. Intermediaries make sense in consequential efforts: it is useful to have a third party's voice. Perhaps the issue is less about intermediation and more about valuing an information service. Real estate agents provide a service, and services are hard to price. As service providers often rue, if everything goes smoothly, most people feel like they paid too much. But if a service experience falls short of what you need or expect, it seems as if you did not get the right expertise or paid too much for what you received. One of the issues with informational services is that, once explained, it often seems relatively simple to understand: the value is in the framing and explaining. This may be one reason that the real estate agent's intermediating role is constantly challenged.

My framing of the real estate agent's role builds from the social construction of markets and their socially embedded rationale.[51] With my colleagues, we have made this case before.[52] My contribution here is to focus attention on the ways in which the flows and sources of information reinforce agents' sociality, providing them with a stronger position in the competition for intermediation. Turning in place, from custodians to brokers, has solidified the real estate agent's role, for now, as an intermediary who adds value in the sale and purchase of residential real estate in the United States.

NOTES

This work was supported in part by the U.S. National Science Foundation grants IIS 97-32799 and 00-00178, the National Center for Real Estate Research (with particular thanks to Dr. Paul Bishop), the Office of the Dean of the School of Information Studies at Syracuse University, the Maulden-Entergy endowment at the University of Arkansas at Little Rock, and the Greater Syracuse Association of Realtors. The views presented here are mine. These views do not represent those of the funders, and I do not speak for my colleagues.

1. My focus is on residential sales in the United States, deferring for other places and times analytic discussions of rental markets, the broader topic of commercial property, and other countries.

2. See J. Baen and R. Guttery, "The Coming Downsizing of Real Estate: Implications of Technology," *Journal of Real Estate Portfolio Management* 3, no. 1 (1997): 1–18, and R. Guttery, J. Baen, and J. Benjamin, "Alamo Realty: The Effect of Technology Changes of Real Estate Brokerage," *Journal of Real Estate Practice and Education* 3, no. 1 (2000): 71–84.

3. See M. Nadel, "A Critical Assessment of the Traditional Residential Real Estate Broker Commission Rate Structure," *Cornell Real Estate Review* 12 (2007): paper 5, https://scholarship.sha.cornell.edu/cgi/viewcontent.cgi?article=1160&context=crer.

4. A recent example of this appeared in the February 8, 2020, issue of *The Economist*: "Tearing Down the House," 61–63. Two things about this article are worth noting: first, the efforts to compare housing to other kinds of markets (in the current case, bond markets) in order to make a case that neoliberal economic principles make sense and, second, that some form of artificial intelligence—this one leveraging housing price data—will become the thing that finally replaces

real estate agents. The narrow thinking regarding the first point dooms the second. More broadly, there has been a sustained and steadily growing discourse on the roles of automation and work, now including extensive attention to an expansively defined concept of artificially intelligent digital systems replacing and augmenting knowledge work. Relative to the roles of real estate agents, such efforts are noted in both chapter 1 and chapter 3 of this volume.

5. See H. White, "Where Do Markets Come From?," *American Journal of Sociology* 87, no. 3 (1981): 517–47; R. Swedberg and M. Granovetter, *The Sociology of Economic Life* (Boulder, CO: Westview Press, 2001); P. Yost, "Internet Challenges for Non-Media Industries, Firms, and Workers: Travel Agencies, Realtors, Mortgage Brokers, Personal Computer Manufacturers, and IT Services Professionals," in *The Internet and American Business*, ed. W. Aspray and P. Ceruzzi (Cambridge, MA: MIT Press, 2008), 315–50; J. Seely Brown and P. Duguid, *The Social Life of Information* (Cambridge, MA: Harvard Business School Press, 2000); and S. Sawyer, R. Wigand, and K. Crowston, "Digital Assemblages: Evidence and Theorizing from a Study of Residential Real Estate," *New Technology, Work, and Employment* 29, no. 1 (2014): 40–54.

6. See K. Crowston, S. Sawyer, and R. Wigand, "Social Networks and the Success of Market Intermediaries: Evidence from the US Residential Real Estate Industry," *The Information Society* 31, no. 5 (2015): 361–78, http://10.1080/019722 43.2015.1041665, and P. DiMaggio and H. Louch, "Socially Embedded Consumer Transactions: For What Kinds of Purchases Do People Use Networks Most?," *American Sociological Review* 63 (1998): 619–37.

7. See White, "Where Do Markets Come From?"; Swedberg and Granovetter, *The Sociology of Economic Life*; and J. Lie, "The Sociology of Markets," *Annual Review of Sociology* 23 (1997): 341–60.

8. This is detailed in M. Weiss, *The Rise of Community Builders: The American Real Estate Industry and Urban Land Planning* (New York: Columbia University Press, 1989).

9. See Crowston et al., "Social Networks and the Success of Market Intermediaries"; K. Crowston, S. Sawyer, and R. Wigand, "The Interplay between Structure and Technology: Investigating the Roles of Information Technologies in the Residential Real Estate Industry," *Information Technology and People* 14, no. 2 (2001): 163–83; K. Crowston, S. Sawyer, R. Wigand, and M. Allbritton, "How Do Information and Communication Technologies Reshape Work? Evidence from the Residential Real Estate Industry," in *The 2000 International Conference on Information Systems*, ed. W. Orlikowski, S. Ang, P. Weill, H. Krcmar, and J. DeGross (New York: ACM Press, 2000); S. Sawyer and F. Yi, "The Computerization of Service: Evidence of the Effects of Information and Communication Technologies in Real Estate," in *IT and Change in the Service Economy: Challenges and Possibilities for the 21st Century*, ed. E. Davidson, M. Barrett, and J. DeGross (London: Kluwer, 2008), 199–212.; S. Sawyer, R. Wigand, and K. Crowston, "Redefining Access: Uses and Roles of Information and Communications Technologies in the Residential Real Estate Industry from 1995–2005," *Journal of Information Technology* 20, no 4. (2005): 3–14; and S. Sawyer, K. Crowston, R. Wigand, and M. Allbritton, "The Social Embeddedness of Transactions: Evidence from the Residential Real Estate Industry," *The Information Society* 19, no. 2 (2003): 135–54.

10. See https://getpocket.com/explore/item/who-owns-a-home-in-america-in-12-charts?utm_source=pocket-newtab.

11. Home prices are rising more quickly than are household incomes and particularly so in the many urban and suburban locations seeing the greatest population growth; see https://www.census.gov/housing/hvs/index.html.

12. Data drawn from https://tradingeconomics.com/united-states/existing-home-sales and using $320k for average house price (accessed January 30, 2020).

13. See https://www.nar.realtor/research-and-statistics/quick-real-estate-statistics (accessed April 21, 2020).

14. See https://www.ibisworld.com/united-states/market-research-reports/building-inspectors-industry (accessed February 12, 2020).

15. See https://www.bls.gov/ooh/architecture-and-engineering/surveyors.htm (accessed February 12, 2020).

16. See https://nailta.org (accessed February 12, 2020).

17. See https://www.statista.com/topics/1685/mortgage-industry-of-the-united-states (accessed February 12, 2020).

18. It seems important to note that this chapter was written during the 2020 Covid-19 pandemic. In early March 2020, there were about 175 million people in the United States either seeking work or working, with unemployment at a relatively low 3.5 percent (6.125 million). By May 2020, nearly 40 million of these 175 million people were officially unemployed. And even more people (doing informal work, sex work, drug trades, and so on) were no longer working—even as their labor was not officially counted. Everyone lives someplace, even if they do not get to live in a building that we consider real estate.

19. Points made in specific detail in later chapters.

20. For more detail on the simplified economic view discussed of markets, see Nadel, "A Critical Assessment of the Traditional Residential Real Estate Broker Commission Rate Structure." Fundamental to the argument carried forward, I contrast this simplified economic view of markets and of market intermediaries with the more empirically supportable and socially embedded view of economic life as advanced by Lie, "The Sociology of Markets," and White, "Where Do Markets Come From?" The first part of this chapter contains a brilliant summary of these contrasts: D. Mackenzie, "Economic and Sociological Explanation of Technical Change," in *Technological Change and Company Strategy*, ed. R. Coombs, P. Saviotti, and V. Walsh (London: Academic Press, 1992), 26–48.

21. The market structure of residential housing in the United States resembles the structure of yacht sales, private planes, or rare cars, with two differences: houses do not move, and yachts, planes, and rare cars are all luxury goods. In all four cases, the cost and uniqueness of the asset lends itself to brokerage, not private sale. Relative to other high-capital transactions like small businesses, the market and tax rules are different, encouraging open brokerage.

22. See also I. Hendel, A. Nevo, and F. Ortalo-Magné, "The Relative Performance of Real Estate Marketing Platforms: MLS versus FSBOMadison.com," *American Economic Review* 99, no. 5 (2009): 1878–98. They highlight that FSBO sales are more likely in highly desirable locations that have limited availability: location matters in real estate.

23. Much of the discussion in the first chapter of this volume helps to illustrate this point.

24. See White, "Where Do Markets Come From?," and R. Latham and S. Sassen, *Digital Formations: IT and New Architectures in the Global Realm* (Princeton, NJ: Princeton University Press, 2005).

25. See F. Bar, "The Construction of Marketplace Architecture," in *Tracking a Transformation: E-Commerce and the Terms of Competition in Industries*, ed. BRIE-IGCC Economy Project Task Force on the Internet (Washington, DC: Brookings Institution Press, 2001), 27–49, and R. Schmiede, "Knowledge, Work and Subject in Informational Capitalism," in *Social Informatics: An Information Society for All?*, ed. J. Berleur, M. Nurminen, and J. Impagliazzo (New York: Springer, 2006), 333–54.

26. See Bar, "The Construction of Marketplace Architecture," and Latham and Sassen, *Digital Formations*.

27. See H. Simon, "Rational Choice and the Structure of the Environment," *Psychological Review* 63, no. 2 (1956): 129–38. The empirical prevalence supporting buyers and sellers pursuing satisficing challenges simplified economic models of markets that are premised on transactions occurring in the face of fully informed buyers and sellers.

28. For more, see White, "Where Do Markets Come From?"; Bar, "The Construction of Marketplace Architecture"; Swedberg and Granovetter, *The Sociology of Economic Life*; and S. Zuboff, *In the Age of the Smart Machine: The Future of Work and Power* (New York: Basic Books, 1988). By market making, I mean the roles of actors in a market to bring together buyers and sellers or to create a means of exchange. A friend who introduces you to your future spouse is acting as a market maker. LinkedIn's efforts to make people's work relations visible is also a market-making effort. A third example is when a local government decides to set up a regional farmer's market, designing rules and fees for sellers, locating a space, and supporting shoppers to participate. A market maker works to create both the opportunity and the operating rules to encourage exchange.

29. See J. Hornstein, *A Nation of Realtors: A Cultural History of the Twentieth Century American Middle Class* (Durham, NC: Duke University Press, 2005). Hornstein makes a compelling case that real estate agents are embedded in the neighborhoods and economic activity of (mostly white) suburban growth and the middle-class imaginary of the post–World War II economic boom and, as such, are more than intermediaries or economic agents; they were positioned as the vehicle to achieving such a dream.

30. See https://www.forbes.com/sites/zillow/2013/10/29/what-does-a-real-estate-buyers-agent-do/#2cead9e466bf.

31. See National Association of Realtors, *2019 Profile of Buyers and Sellers* (Washington, DC: National Association of Realtors, 2019), https://store.realtor.org/product/report/2019-nar-profile-home-buyers-and-sellers-download.

32. See B. Waller and A. Jubran, "The Impact of Agent Experience on the Real Estate Transaction," *Journal of Housing Research* 33, no. 1 (2012): 67–82.

33. See http://nar.realtor.

34. See http://realtor.com.

35. The exact number of local/regional MLSs continues to change. The trend is toward fewer and more regional MLSs. Real estate agents and others must pay

annual fees to participate in an MLS. Typically, membership in the local realtor association is required to join an MLS. This membership also covers dues for the NAR (see http://www.realtor.org). As an aside, real estate agents who are members of the NAR are called "Realtors," a trademarked term.

36. See https://www.inman.com/2019/02/26/what-the-mls-landscape-will-look-like-in-2019 (accessed February 3, 2020).

37. The technical and governance agreement to share MLS data are detailed in the NAR's "IDX" agreement. For more details, see https://www.nar.realtor/about-nar/policies/internet-data-exchange-idx/2018-revisions-to-idx-policy (accessed December 28, 2019).

38. To learn more about the elements and purpose of a purchase and sales agreement, a useful summary can be found at https://themortgagereports.com/37569/understanding-a-real-estate-contract-or-purchase-agreement.

39. For more on the HUD1 form, see https://www.hud.gov/sites/documents/1.PDF and https://www.hud.gov/sites/documents/10-39MLATCH.PDF. In the United States, the Department of Housing and Urban Development oversees the transacting of real estate in the same way that the U.S. Securities and Exchange Commission provides oversight to financial transactions. The HUD1 form contains detailed information (in a line-by-line format in two columns, for the buyer and for the seller) of the expenses incurred for selling and buying a property.

40. See http://www.zillow.com. See also chapter 3 in this volume.

41. See Waller and Jubran, "The Impact of Agent Experience on the Real Estate Transaction"; J. Xie, "Who Is 'Misleading' Whom in Real Estate Transactions?," *Real Estate Economics* 46, no. 3 (2018): 527–58; and H. Perkins, D. Thorns, and B. Newton, "Real Estate Advertising and Intraurban Place Meaning: Real Estate Sales Consultants at Work," *Environment and Planning* 40 (2008): 2061–79. This shift to explaining raises three critical questions about real estate agents' roles. First, what is the core body of knowledge they need to succeed? Second, how quickly can this be acquired? Third, who should pay the extra costs when an agent makes a mistake? In the current market arrangement, there is a clear value for experienced agents over new agents given that experience (via apprenticeships or practice) seems to be the primary vehicle for learning.

42. One of the fastest-growing parts of this ecology of ICT-based services for real estate are drones. Although it is hard to get a full accounting, it appears that houses that have drone footage included as part of the listing sell faster and closer to asking than do homes without drone footage, and about 40 percent of all drone video footage is in support of home sales.

43. A lockbox is a secure container attached to the door of a home for sale. It contains the key to open that house. Traditional lockboxes were opened by a key provided to agents who belonged to the local realtor association.

44. For example, Zillow.com combines some data on houses for sale with details of other houses' selling prices and property tax data and presents this information together on maps.

45. The extensive uses of social media by agents reflects the convergence of the value-adding services leveraging MLS data and the increased digital reach of agents who use their contact network to communicate with buyers, sellers, and

others. At this point, data on uses are almost moot given the visibility of this activity in our social media feeds. One proxy for such evidence is to do a Web search on social media and real estate to see how many courses are offered. A second proxy is to scan the schedule of any real estate professionals conference or seminar to see that social media use sessions often are more than 50 percent of all content.

46. For more, see DiMaggio and Louch, "Socially Embedded Consumer Transactions"; Crowston et al., "The Interplay between Structure and Technology"; and Sawyer et al., "The Social Embeddedness of Transactions."

47. See J. Cremer and F. Khalil, "Gathering Information before Signing a Contract," *American Economic Review* 82, no 3 (1992): 566–78, and D. Genesove and L. Han, "Search and Matching in the Housing Market," *Journal of Urban Economics* 72 (2012): 31–45. In classic economic thinking, an asymmetry is a market failure because the transaction is conducted with one party facing incomplete information or misinformation. From the relational perspective of economic sociology, an asymmetry is about gaining access to flows of information that they can draw on as needed.

48. Simplified views of real estate markets tend to undervalue emotion and other elements that play into the concept of satisficing put forth by Simon in "Rational Choice and the Structure of the Environment." For example, and in addition to Nadel, "A Critical Assessment of the Traditional Residential Real Estate Broker Commission Rate Structure," see J. Albrecht, P. Gautier, and S. Vroman, "Directed Search in the Housing Market," *Review of Economic Dynamics* 19 (2016); 218–31, and Xie, "Who Is 'Misleading' Whom in Real Estate Transactions?"

49. See J. Rochet and J. Tirole, "Platform Competition in Two-Sided Markets," *Journal of the European Economic Association* 1, no. 4 (2003): 990–1029.

50. See also DiMaggio and Louch, "Socially Embedded Consumer Transactions," and J. Seely Brown and P. Duguid, *The Social Life of Information* (Cambridge, MA: Harvard Business School Press, 2000).

51. See, again, White, "Where Do Markets Come From?"; Swedberg and Granovetter, *The Sociology of Economic Life*; and DiMaggio and Louch, "Socially Embedded Consumer Transactions."

52. See Crowston et al., "The Interplay between Structure and Technology," and "Social Networks and the Success of Market Intermediaries."

BIBLIOGRAPHY

Albrecht, J., P. Gautier, and S. Vroman. 2016. "Directed Search in the Housing Market." *Review of Economic Dynamics* 19: 218–31.

Baen, J., and R. Guttery. 1997. "The Coming Downsizing of Real Estate: Implications of Technology." *Journal of Real Estate Portfolio Management* 3, no. 1: 1–18.

Bar, F. 2001. "The Construction of Marketplace Architecture." In *Tracking a Transformation: E-Commerce and the Terms of Competition in Industries*, edited by BRIE-IGCC Economy Project Task Force on the Internet, 27–49. Washington, DC: Brookings Institution Press.

Cremer, J., and F. Khalil. 1992. "Gathering Information before Signing a Contract." *American Economic Review* 82, no. 3: 566–78.

Crowston, K., S. Sawyer, and R. Wigand. 2001. "The Interplay between Structure and Technology: Investigating the Roles of Information Technologies in the Residential Real Estate Industry." *Information Technology and People* 14, no. 2: 163–83.

———. 2015. "Social Networks and the Success of Market Intermediaries: Evidence from the US Residential Real Estate Industry." *The Information Society* 31, no. 5: 361–78. http://10.1080/01972243.2015.1041665.

Crowston, K., S. Sawyer, R. Wigand, and M. Allbritton. 2000. "How Do Information and Communication Technologies Reshape Work? Evidence from the Residential Real Estate Industry." In *The Proceedings of the 2000 International Conference on Information Systems*, edited by W. Orlikowski, S. Ang, P. Weill, H. Krcmar, and J. DeGross. New York: ACM Press. Paper 65. Available online at https://aisel.aisnet.org/icis2000/65.

DiMaggio, P., and H. Louch. 1998. "Socially Embedded Consumer Transactions: For What Kinds of Purchases Do People Use Networks Most?" *American Sociological Review* 63: 619–37.

Genesove, D., and L. Han. 2012. "Search and Matching in the Housing Market." *Journal of Urban Economics* 72: 31–45.

Guttery, R., J. Baen, and J. Benjamin. 2000. "Alamo Realty: The Effect of Technology Changes of Real Estate Brokerage." *Journal of Real Estate Practice and Education* 3, no. 1: 71–84.

Hendel, I., A. Nevo, and F. Ortalo-Magné. 2009. "The Relative Performance of Real Estate Marketing Platforms: MLS versus FSBOMadison.com." *American Economic Review* 99, no. 5: 1878–98.

Hornstein, J. 2005. *A Nation of Realtors: A Cultural History of the Twentieth Century American Middle Class*. Durham, NC: Duke University Press.

Latham, R., and S. Sassen. 2005. *Digital Formations: IT and New Architectures in the Global Realm*. Princeton, NJ: Princeton University Press.

Lie, J. 1997. "The Sociology of Markets." *Annual Review of Sociology* 23: 341–60.

Mackenzie, D. 1992. "Economic and Sociological Explanation of Technical Change." In *Technological Change and Company Strategy*, edited by R. Coombs, P. Saviotti, and V. Walsh, 26–48. London: Academic Press.

Nadel, M. 2007. "A Critical Assessment of the Traditional Residential Real Estate Broker Commission Rate Structure." *Cornell Real Estate Review* 12: paper 5. https://scholarship.sha.cornell.edu/cgi/viewcontent.cgi?article=1160&context=crer.

National Association of Realtors. 2019. *2019 Profile of Buyers and Sellers*. Washington, DC: National Association of Realtors. https://store.realtor.org/product/report/2019-nar-profile-home-buyers-and-sellers-download.

Perkins, H., D. Thorns, and B. Newton. 2008. "Real Estate Advertising and Intraurban Place Meaning: Real Estate Sales Consultants at Work." *Environment and Planning* 40: 2061–79.

Rochet, J., and J. Tirole. 2003. "Platform Competition in Two-Sided Markets." *Journal of the European Economic Association* 1, no. 4: 990–1029. https://doi.org/10.1162/154247603322493212.

Sawyer, S., K. Crowston, R. Wigand, and M. Allbritton. 2003. "The Social Embeddedness of Transactions: Evidence from the Residential Real Estate Industry." *The Information Society* 19, no. 2: 135–54.

Sawyer, S., R. Wigand, and K. Crowston. 2005. "Redefining Access: Uses and Roles of Information and Communications Technologies in the Residential Real Estate Industry from 1995–2005." *Journal of Information Technology* 20, no. 4: 3–14.

———. 2014. "Digital Assemblages: Evidence and Theorizing from a Study of Residential Real Estate." *New Technology, Work, and Employment* 29, no. 1: 40–54. http://10.1111/ntwe.12020.

Sawyer, S., and F. Yi. 2008. "The Computerization of Service: Evidence of the Effects of Information and Communication Technologies in Real Estate." In *IT and Change in the Service Economy: Challenges and Possibilities for the 21st Century*, edited by E. Davidson, M. Barrett, and J. DeGross, 199–212. London: Kluwer.

Schmiede, R. 2006. "Knowledge, Work and Subject in Informational Capitalism." In *Social Informatics: An Information Society for All?*, edited by J. Berleur, M. Nurminen, and J. Impagliazzo, 333–54. New York: Springer.

Seely Brown, J., and P. Duguid. 2000. *The Social Life of Information*. Cambridge, MA: Harvard Business School Press.

Simon, H. 1956. "Rational Choice and the Structure of the Environment." *Psychological Review* 63, no. 2: 129–38.

Swedberg R., and M. Granovetter. 2001. *The Sociology of Economic Life*. Boulder, CO: Westview Press.

Waller, B., and A. Jubran. 2012. "The Impact of Agent Experience on the Real Estate Transaction." *Journal of Housing Research* 33, no. 1: 67–82.

Weiss, M. 1989. *The Rise of Community Builders: The American Real Estate Industry and Urban Land Planning*. New York: Columbia University Press.

White, H. 1981."Where Do Markets Come From?" *American Journal of Sociology* 87, no. 3: 517–47.

Xie, J. 2018. "Who Is 'Misleading' Whom in Real Estate Transactions?" *Real Estate Economics* 46, no. 3: 527–58.

Yost, P. 2008."Internet Challenges for Non-Media Industries, Firms, and Workers: Travel Agencies, Realtors, Mortgage Brokers, Personal Computer Manufacturers, and IT Services Professionals." In *The Internet and American Business*, edited by W. Aspray and P. Ceruzzi, 315–50. Cambridge, MA: MIT Press.

Zuboff, S. 1988. *In the Age of the Smart Machine: The Future of Work and Power*. New York: Basic Books.

Three

The Evolving Residential Real Estate Information Ecosystem

The Rise of Zillow

James W. Cortada

> For the real estate industry, the old model has been killed by the presence of real estate and financing information on the Internet.
>
> —John Tuccillo[1]

Every adult in the United States has encountered some facet of the real estate industry since the mid-twentieth century. Residents engage with the industry through its more than 2 million active real estate agents, of which 1.3 million are formally credentialed through state and industry licensing or by using the internet. In 2018, residents purchased 5.34 million homes, of which nearly 670,000 were newly constructed. There are more than 86,000 real estate brokerage firms focused on consumers and their families. Home ownership by individuals in the United States is one of the highest in the world (nearly 64 percent of all families). As of 2018, nearly 90 percent of all home purchases were conducted with the services of a real estate agent or broker, up from nearly 70 percent in 2001.[2]

For most residents, their homes are their largest economic asset. Household equity in 2019 amounted to $16.4 trillion. These investments were coupled to mortgages amounting to nearly $11 trillion (in combination with other household debts), their largest economic exposure.[3] Combined equity and debt totaled $27.2 trillion or, put another way, $5 trillion more than the total economic output of the U.S. economy in the previous year, the largest economy in the world.[4] None of these statistics include the home and apartment rental market, which consists of another 43 million housing units in addition to the nearly 80 million owner-occupied homes. Such high levels of ownership existed for a long time. In 1975, for example, Americans owned nearly 47 million houses and condos, more than 56 million in 1985, and more than 75 million each year since the dawn of the new century.[5]

When combined, all facets of the industry—home sales, rentals, commercial real estate, construction, and so forth—make up the single largest industry in the U.S. economy, accounting for nearly 14 percent, making it bigger than all of state and local government in the economy or such other industries as banking, insurance, and durable manufacturing. Of the economic sectors that most immediately touch individuals, only the health industry was larger, making up 18 percent of U.S. gross domestic product (GDP) as of 2019.[6] So it should be no surprise that a large, well-organized real estate industry should exist to serve more than 300 million residents. Because of the large volume of money flowing through this industry, one can anticipate more agents and firms to participate in this sector of the economy and thus influence how individuals acquire homes. The case study of Zillow is an example of that process already at work.

The industry's size and influence on American life explains why this chapter is included in a study of how people make decisions about how and where they wish to live. Its purpose is to introduce the structure of the real estate industry but with a focus on that piece with which most residents engage in the United States: noncommercial property real estate agents and their firms. We do this through a historical lens in combination with the way an economist or business manager would view its development. Because computing (and later the internet) played such a profound role in the uses of information by agents and customers, I discuss the effects of these technologies on both, arguing that the internet, in particular, is fundamentally changing how agents and home owners interact and affect each other's decisions. Because Zillow.com is one of the industry's best-known real estate firms and one receiving much attention as an internet-based innovation operating in the housing market, I concluded that it needed to be included in this volume.

STRUCTURE OF THE REAL ESTATE INDUSTRY BEFORE THE INTERNET

While the industry has grown and changed continuously during the past 150 years, its fundamental components remained essentially intact and can conveniently be described as four related businesses. Each has its own business model, that is, how it works, how it is organized, and where its revenues and profits come from. Each interacts with the other three episodically or sometimes continuously. Information is shared, as needed, across these four business functions. These businesses are brokerage, agent, local and national associations, and the Multiple Listing Service

(MLS). Much is left out in this paradigm, such as banks loaning mortgage money to potential home buyers, property insurance firms offering protection for buildings and their contents and to secure the viability of a loan should the home buyer default on payments, construction firms that build houses or provide repairs and remodeling, property assessors who establish home values for home owners, and real estate agents, insurance companies, and local property taxing officials. But it is the four discussed here that often (but not always) most influence decisions by residents about where to live and how to pay for their decisions.

These organizations operate in a patchwork of local real estate markets, not in some national integrated one. The fragmented nature of the market is reflected in the existence of local and regional agencies and associations. We will see in this chapter that attempts to make regional markets larger and more integrated, even attempts to consolidate these markets into a national one, have been under way for decades and have picked up momentum thanks to the likes of Zillow and others, but buyers and renters remain localized. They do not, for example, as a course of events compare housing in the Midwest with those in the South or in Denver to determine where they can get the most house for their dollar. They have already decided to live in a particular area and so are focused on finding the optimal in housing only within that chosen local market.

Brokers recruit real estate agents—salespeople—to bring home sellers and buyers together. Brokers and agents shared (and still share) sales commissions, while brokers often bear the burden of expenses running sales offices. Brokers generated revenue by taking a percentage of the commission, and so the more sales agents they had, the more money and profit they could earn. Franchises that were local or national were variants of the broker model in that they ran offices around the country and had standard processes for conducting the buying and selling of homes. Beginning in the 1970s, agents could begin keeping all the commissions but reimbursed brokers for such expenses as office space, advertising, and other operating fees, although it is unclear how many did (just that many began moving to the new arrangement). Brokers always worked through sales agents until the early 2000s, when they began to reach out to consumers, offering them the technical services required to prepare sales contracts, access to databases of information about available houses for sale, and so forth. A small but slowly growing discernible trend surfaced, better known in many other industries as unbundling of services. But ultimately, it was always the real estate agent who retained the closest contact with buyers and sellers and who, in the parlance of the industry, "owned the customer." For their part, customers were less enamored with cafeteria-like services that they did not understand well despite the efforts of some agencies to promote the idea.

The real estate agent is as iconic and visible in American society as a police officer, mail carrier, or teacher. Hollywood, for example, has been making real estate movies for decades. Recent popular films include *American Beauty* (1999), and who can forget the recent *Big Short* (2015)? But it began in 1909 with *Blissville the Beautiful*, followed up with *Her Own Money* (1922) and *Worldly Goods* (1924).[7] For more than a century, they could be seen in every neighborhood in America, bringing sellers and buyers together, officiating at "closings," recommending to home buyers what banks to use and where to find repair people, and even shaping who lived in a neighborhood by what homes they showed.[8] Since the 1940s, they chauffeured potential buyers from one house to another, chatting up the strengths and weaknesses of various homes, communities, school districts, crime levels, and local amenities. They shaped the reputation of neighborhoods and were often a community's most consistent and long-serving boosters. By the 1970s, they were largely women who could work flexible hours in the evening and weekends, when potential buyers had time to "house hunt."[9] For decades, they did not (and still do not) need to have a college education or advanced degree, although credentialing has long been required by state licensing boards that required agents to understand local real estate laws and contracting, while national credentialing industry associations had their own bodies of knowledge to transmit and enforce regarding, for example, business models and selling but also their values, practices, and codes of conduct.

Central to the iconic role of real estate agents is that they controlled access and relations with customers. Agents developed networks of friends, prior customers, and family to obtain referrals for new business. They were paid not salaries but rather commissions based on a percent of the sales value of the home that was "closed" (i.e., sold), so having an active network of contacts for new customers helped to create the demand for their services. For more than a half a century before widely available information about homes and neighborhoods existed on the internet, agents were the primary source of information for consumers. Thus, a second source of their economic power after controlling information was the reverse: the lack of general knowledge and experience in the housing market by home owners and purchasers. For example, agents vigorously guarded access to information about what houses were available for sale. Their power lay in their access to information and buyers.

Agents shared commissions with other agents who became involved in a sale, such as one representing the "seller" with the agent who brought a buyer to the deal. They shared commissions, too, with a broker because states required agents to be associated with brokers. Commissions varied over the decades, but from a customer's or a buyer's perspective, the gross amount was usually 5 to 6 percent of the sales price of a property.

Figure 3.1. The ideal real estate agent in serving the seller from 1952. *National Association of Real Estate Boards.*

Sometimes that amount could be negotiated or, if a seller sold their home without the assistance of an agent or with only partial assistance, could eliminate or substantially reduce that amount, often passing on part of the savings to a purchaser by lowering the price of the home.[10]

Key to understanding the role of agents is their doling out of information to all parties. Less acknowledged is that they also gathered information. One observer of their work in the 1960s described what agents did to determine what houses to show buyers:

> They "qualify" the prospect by means of an interview and then determine which houses to show on this basis. This interview is conducted even though the prospect may come to the agent in response to an advertisement of a particular house.
>
> Through the qualifying interview the agent attempts to determine: the prospect's needs and desire regarding the size and type of house, including any special requirements (e.g., a fenced-in yard, a two-car garage, etc.); the general area in which he would like to live; and, most importantly, the financial resources of the prospect. The agents also take other factors into consideration when selecting the properties to be shown a customer, including the general appearance of the prospects . . . they tried to match the prospect to a particular house.[11]

Thus, the agent served as a gatekeeper for all involved. In a survey done in the 1960s of real estate agents, some two-thirds reported that they felt responsible to "protect a neighborhood from undesirable persons"; to protect their own reputations and business as an obligation to current, former, and future clients; and to ensure maintenance of property values.[12]

A third group of participants in the real estate business relevant to residents are associations. They exist at the local, state, and national levels; real estate agents were expected to join them by both custom and local licensing regulators. In exchange, agents participated in industry and local real estate networks, accessed professional education, identified with statewide codes of ethics, resolved disputes over such matters as commission sharing, lobbied state regulators and legislatures, and served as a source of industry trends and information. But, as one industry expert observed, "at its heart, an association is an information business, and like all information businesses, trade associations" have been challenged in their near monopoly of housing data by the availability of similar facts accessible over the internet to potential home buyers.[13] Associations compete against each other in providing information over the internet as well. As the same observer noted, "All of this has given rise to the concept of transactional membership. If the association delivers more value than it asks in dues, the members see a reason for belonging. Otherwise they will walk."[14] This reality existed by the end of the 1900s, competing with local monopolies on information about housing—known as MLS—the heart of a real estate agent's monopoly power over consumers for decades. The variety of memberships offered by local boards and regional and national associations varied but were modeled only at the national level. The National Association of Realtors (NAR) describes itself as a professional society; rivals call it a trade association. MLS agreements favor NAR members. For the NAR, upstart firms like Zillow serve as a foil to demonstrate that the former is not a monopoly.[15] To understand the real estate industry and how it has affected and served consumers, it is essential to appreciate the role of the MLS business, the fourth major component of the consumer-facing part of the industry.

MLS is a collection of services used by real estate agents to carry out their work. Private MLS companies, real estate associations, and real estate companies offer these regionally and nationally.[16] In 2020, there existed some 800 MLSs, with some of the larger ones with tens of thousands of members, in such places as New York and California.[17] An MLS accumulates and makes available to agents all manner of information regarding values of homes for appraisals and to inform pricing strategies, detailed descriptions of individual homes (e.g., number of bedrooms, type of flooring, amount of property tax, and so forth), and other texts needed to consummate sales.

Brokers and agents who are members of the association that get preferred access to the MLS have used and shared for decades this information among themselves to match buyers with sellers. Not until the availability of internet databases could consumers directly access such information without going through an agent. This restricted database originated in the late 1800s as agents informally shared information about local opportunities. In the next century, MLS lists became formalized with publications that agents updated routinely but that they made available only to each other and to their brokerage firms. That limitation of access has long been a bone of contention, even litigation, with the public at large, but it remained the bedrock information fortress fiercely defended by the industry over the past century.

The information asymmetry considered so precious by the industry is exactly what it needed for decades to facilitate bringing buyer and seller together. The concept of information asymmetry is crucial in understanding a great deal of what made the real estate industry function. The phrase comes from economics, where it is also known as information failure. It is the notion that in a transaction, one party has more information than the other that is material to the deal on the table. In this instance, the real estate agent knows more, for example, about the true value of a property, its features, and possibly what the owner selling it might be willing to sell it for. That imbalance can be useful to a real estate agent who is assisting a potential buyer find a property but also can be negative if that agent is hiding a fact about a potential problem with a property, such as a title dispute or that it has a leaky basement that is not evident during the dry season. MLS facts were always valued as asymmetric information in the industry, which explains why, as those kinds of data became available to buyers and sellers after the arrival of the internet, the industry so resisted its release to the general public.

Table 3.1 lists routine types of information that such MLS systems collected: facts needed to announce the availability of a home and that a buyer would want to see. MLS data structures vary widely across regional and local levels, so what one sees in an MLS search from, say, Realtor.com is a superset of the possible presentation of information and would, of course, have an interface to block or limit data scraping by rivals and others.[18] Over the decades, the amount of information added to such profiles has expanded, such as video late in the twentieth century, state educational rankings for academic achievement by schools, and, finally, data on crime levels in a neighborhood or entire city compared to others in the 2010s. The use of computers in the last quarter of the twentieth century made sorting easy by price, ZIP codes, style of home, and so forth as well. One could also check information about housing anywhere in the United States, no longer constrained to only local information.

For the entire twentieth century, these four components of the real estate industry—broker, agent, association, and MLS—complemented one another in a collaborative manner, making it possible to monopolize infor-

Table 3.1. Type of Information in an MLS Listing, 1950s–2020

Property details	Condition, number of bedrooms, number of full bathrooms, total number of rooms, types of appliances, air conditioning and heating, garage, square footage, lot size, if a neighborhood association exists, address, building style, and if, for example, a single family home, condo, or apartment
Property history	Prior sales of the home, prices of those transactions, history of property taxes
Nearby schools	Names of schools, data on the performance of students, size, location
Neighborhood	Number of homes, location, reputation, profiles of residents
Monthly payments	A recent addition, suggesting monthly rental or mortgage payments
Agent information	Listing agent and his or her contact information; planned marketing events, such as open house events; how to gain access for viewing
Images	Photographs of exterior and interior; in recent years also video of both types of images
Listing price	What the seller is asking as a sales price for the property; also any conditions (e.g., owner willing to finance a mortgage)

mation about the availability of homes for sale, to control who became an agent, to establish how commissions were set and distributed, and to set rules of behavior and practices. Consumers long understood this reality and, until the internet became the disruptive technology that fractured this arrangement, were subject to the industry's will despite their complaints, periodic lawsuits, and federal and state antitrust initiatives.[19]

State and federal courts and agencies long found problematic the real estate industry's attempt to constrain and control competition by how it managed access to the MLS and licensing. For decades, firms wishing to acquire more access to the market, especially by those that were internet born, filed antitrust suits.[20] This desire predated the arrival of the internet, yet its availability encouraged such aspirations. Increasingly in the late 1990s, they gained that access through the courts and other federal and state regulatory actions.[21] In 2007, the U.S. Department of Justice and the Federal Trade Commission (FTC) published a joint report detailing the rising levels of consumer access through the internet but also the stubbornness of the industry to monopolize information. The FTC noted that the industry routinely did not clarify for whom an agent worked, the seller or buyer, thereby hiding conflicts of interests. Price fixing and sharing of commissions increasingly again became a matter of concern to the FTC, the courts, and consumers. The report cited dozens of cases where state laws supported such behavior, others that attempted to open up the market, and still other cases filed by individuals and upstart realtors over the course of the prior pre-internet and early years of the internet. Access to the internet was helping buyers, however. Simultaneously, "the FTC sued to prevent MLSs from discriminating as to the listings that are made available on the Internet, and DOJ sued to prevent NAR from establishing rules against VOWs [virtual offer website] that limit the ability of a broker's client to see via the Internet all the listing information formerly screened by the broker."[22]

In 2008, the Department of Justice and the NAR concluded an agreement to limit anticompetitive practices that, for example, had limited the entry of new internet-based firms, now giving them access to MLS data.[23] Agents could begin, too, to offer à la carte fee-based menus of services, thereby breaking the 5 to 6 percent commission fee practice of old. As one lawyer involved noted in 2018, any future attempts to restrict access to the MLS or the market would probably no longer work.[24] The 2008 consent decree expired in 2018, when the Trump administration chose not to pursue its extension. However, the NAR publicly announced that it would continue to honor its terms.[25]

With the arrival of new business models (discussed below), the collaborative nature of this arrangement fractured, creating competition among themselves while increasing the ability of consumers to pick and choose what services they wanted, in the process driving down commissions. One could observe that reality by the early twentieth century, when the real estate industry had settled into an effective business model that worked for its members, as suggested by table 3.2.

So how did pre-internet real estate work? By the 1920s, the American public had been conditioned to go to a local real estate agency when they wanted to buy or sell a home because the agents had all the information required to price, market, find, negotiate sales prices, and conclude sales transactions. This monopoly over information extending over the entire spectrum of the buying and selling process made this behavior essential. All services were designed to facilitate the completion of a sale. Thus,

Table 3.2. Major Events in the Development of the U.S. Real Estate Industry

Year	Event
1855	Oldest existing brokerage firm established, Baird Warner
1908	National Association of Real Estate Agents founded (future National Association of Realtors, 1972)
1922	Establishment of Appraisal Institute
1933	Establishment of Institute of Real Estate Management
1938	Fannie Mae created to provide mortgages to poor and middle-income buyers
1960s	MLSs established state by state
1968	Establishment of Council of Real Estate Brokerage Managers
1970	Freddie Mac (Federal Home Loan Mortgage Composition) created
1975	National Association of Realtors, largest U.S. trade association with 400,000 members
1976	Council of Residential Specialists
1994	Real estate listing begin to appear over the internet
1995	HouseHunt, an early internet-born real estate agency, founded
1996	Real Estate Buyer's Agent Council
2000	908,000 new homes sold
2002	Broker reciprocity, known as IDX, established to make consumer searches easier for house listings
2004	Zillow established
2006	1 million new homes sold, down from 1.2 million in 2005
2007–2009	Housing bubble crises, most severe since 1930s
2011	Lowest number of new house sales in decades (323,000)
2011	More than 1.9 million properties received foreclosure notices
2015	Foreclosures declined for the fourth year in a row
2016	Existing home sales increases year over year from 5.25 million to 5.45 million
2017	Sales of new houses increased to 613,000 from 561,000 in 2016
2018	Housing values increased at fastest pace since 2006, but sales of existing homes declined to 5.34 million, down from 5.51 million in 2017
2019	National Association of Realtors claims 1.3 million members, 54 state associations (including U.S. possessions), and more than 1,130 local associations

agents could direct potential buyers to specific homes for their consideration, specific banks for mortgages, title insurers, appraisers, inspectors, repair people, companies selling home owners' insurance, and lawyers able to prepare closing (sales) contracts. They were also the primary source of information about communities and features of neighborhoods: important knowledge for those customers coming into a city or town from, say, another state.[26]

Agents often directed buyers to specific neighborhoods and housing options based on what they thought would be most compatible between buyers and residents, such as sending young families to one neighborhood or older upper-middle-class professionals to another. They also encouraged segregation: Blacks to one area and whites to another, known as *redlining*, which became the subject of many complaints, litigation, and regulatory activity beginning during the era of the civil rights movement of the 1960s and 1970s.[27] Regulators began monitoring and shaping the industry's monopolistic behavior as early as the 1920s but were not able to restructure the industry; that happened with the availability of the internet.[28]

The old system worked, however, in facilitating home purchases. Prior to the late 1800s, only wealthy and upper-middle-class families owned homes in towns and cities and farmers in rural areas. After its arrival, home ownership expanded rapidly to larger swaths of the American public: to 47.8 percent of the adult population in 1890, to 55 percent by 1950, to nearly 65 percent in the 1980s, and to 66.5 percent in 2010, after which ownership dipped slightly to just over 64 percent in 2018.[29] Beginning in the 1860s but expanding massively after 1890, banks began offering mortgages, enabling people to acquire homes. In the early 1900s, one might have paid 50 percent of the purchase price of a home (down payment) and carry the rest as a mortgage over five years. Those terms changed over the decades as the percent one could put down declined and the length of the mortgage expanded by decades. To promote home ownership, the Federal Housing Administration in 1934 introduced a mortgage insurance offering, an amortization plan, and terms ranging from fifteen to twenty years. Today's offerings are still compliant with mortgage insurance offerings made by both the public and the private sector. By the late 1900s, it was typical that one might put 20 percent cash down on a house and then carry a fifteen- or thirty-year mortgage on the balance. Banks and real estate agents were careful to "qualify" a potential purchaser, that is, determine if they could afford to make such payments and had the necessary character to be trusted. Hence, potential purchasers had to defend their ability to make such a purchase. During periods of economic turmoil, the process would falter, with up to 10 percent of such arrangements leading to bankruptcies and bank foreclosures, such as during the Great Depression of the 1930s and again after

2007. Periodically, they were also assisted by government programs, such as the Veterans Administration home loan initiatives funded by post–World War II GI Bills that assisted millions of home buyers in the 1940s and 1950s. But the key fact is that more than half of Americans owned or were buying the homes they lived in by the 1950s at the dawn of the greatest period of prosperity in U.S. history.

From the 1880s to the present, home prices increased steadily, making one's home often a family's single most important investment and hence not only a shelter.[30] In addition, the size of homes increased. The median size of a home constructed in 1973 averaged 1,525 square feet but by 2016 had expanded to 2,422 square feet, while some rooms expanded substantially, notably kitchens, which doubled in size, and bedrooms, which grew nearly as much. Ironically, the number of people living in homes shrank in the same period from an average of 2.9 occupants in 1973 to 2.5 in 2016. In other words, the amount of living space per person had increased from 526 to 969 square feet.[31]

EFFECTS OF COMPUTING ON THE INDUSTRY BEFORE THE ARRIVAL OF THE INTERNET

Not all facets of the real estate industry were immune to the effects of computing on their work, particularly since its key asset was data that could be automated and manipulated cost effectively from the earliest days of computing. While the real estate industry was accused of not embracing computing as fast as it could have—largely because of its nearly monopolistic control over its markets, which did not motivate its members to transform as quickly as other industries[32]—it did nonetheless appropriate computers long before the arrival of the internet, stimulating changes in the industry. Industry observers leave out two other contemporaneous features of the U.S. economy that should be kept in mind. First, computing affected other industries at the same time as it did real estate, leading industries to learn from each other; thus, real estate did not operate in isolation. Second, users of the industry's services—sellers and buyers—were exposed to computers in their own industries and jobs, most notably to the benefits of using personal computers (PCs) in the 1980s and accessing online databases beginning in the 1970s. These buyers and sellers (home owners) often acquired greater skills earlier than brokers and real estate agents and thus pushed the latter for greater access to such bodies of information as MLS listings online, not only to quarterly paper-based editions. To be clear, the real estate industry was a late adopter of computers, while its customers proved savvier about their potential. Computer users were sufficiently proficient that when the internet became widely accessible; they pushed the industry for access and, in the process, forced fundamental changes in the information balance of power to the extent discussed in all the other chapters of this volume. This is exactly the profile of the founders of Zillow.com (discussed later).

Use of computing prior to the availability of PCs in the 1980s remained extremely limited because so many brokers and agents operated tiny enterprises that could not cost justify expensive computing. That began to change in the mid- to late 1980s, when online access to data and the ability to use PCs to prepare documents and calculate with spreadsheets using devices that cost less than $3,000 became available. But the move was slow. The earliest adopters were the MLSs that embraced computers before brokers, agents, and agencies did. They did this at the local level with little guidance ("best practices") available from the industry at large.

However, by the time the internet had become available in the mid-1990s, some of the extensive paperwork associated with closings (sales) was beginning to be automated, sometimes thanks to the efforts of banks and in other cases to law firms and large real estate brokerage houses that could justify the expense of acquiring such systems. Home insurance agencies, which by their nature were associated with large enterprises, began using computing in the 1960s to create policies, so small bits and pieces of the agent–customer interaction began to feel the presence of computing. MLS publications became largely digital files in the 1990s, although regional listings were technologically incompatible with others around the country, limiting access to multiple listings across the nation until the 2000s.

Not until the availability of e-mail over the internet did real estate agencies and their information ecosystems (clients too) apply this technology. As recently as the late 1990s, industry observers spoke less about extant computing than about computing as a development they anticipated, demonstrating the paper-bound nature of industry practices even at the advent of the internet.[33] As described in chapter 1 of this volume, real estate agents stepped through essential applications to access relevant information: both paper and, later, digital. By the end of 1998, however, there were more than 3,600 websites in the industry.[34] With minimal competition and fixed fees applied universally, little incentive existed within the industry to automate to either reduce operating costs or provide additional services to clients. Computing in the real estate industry essentially did not become important until it was forced to embrace the use of the internet by the combination of emerging new internet-born rivals, digitalized legal and banking "paperwork" requirements, and the growing demand of consumers.

Whenever economists or historians discuss the effects of computing on a business or industry, they encounter the thorny problem of technological determinism, a topic too lengthy to discuss fully here. But it is an issue to keep in mind as we shift discussion to the role of the internet. Essentially, the idea is that the adoption and subsequent reliance on a particular technology compel its users to work in ways in which they have no choice to deviate from. For example, if the reader is a user of Microsoft's operating system, then things must be done the Microsoft way. Because the real estate industry was slow to embrace computing between the 1950s and the end of the 1970s, its agents, brokers, and associations did not face issues related to technological determinism. But after they began embracing the internet, did they? Did consumers of their services compel altered behavior shaped by the technology, and, if so, to what extent? Most scholars would argue that humans had free will and could choose to some extent not to be dictated by a technology. As you read the rest of this chapter, consider what role technology played in the behavior of the industry. The evidence so far suggests that the disintermediation (i.e., the breakup of services into cafeteria-style services) of real estate services has not yet happened. Zillow, discussed in further detail, sought to pull various disparate offerings together, that is, to become an intermediary by appropriating technology to do so. A quarter of a century of experience using the internet has yet to fundamentally cause a restructuring of the industry, although much has changed due to its availability. The degree to which technology influenced the work and business models in real estate thus remains an open question. To approach a better understanding of the issues involved, we turn to that portion of its work affected by the internet.

ARRIVAL OF THE INTERNET-BORN REAL ESTATE INDUSTRY

The presence of the internet's technologies appeared on both sides of the real estate market—the industry and the client—beginning almost immediately when the availability of the World Wide Web and such nonexpert search engines as AltaVista, Yahoo!, Bing, and Ask Jeeves, among others, made the internet easy, inexpensive, and practical to use by the mid-1990s. It would be difficult to exaggerate the effect of this technology's availability to all participants working in and with the real estate industry. Given the size of this industry, the disintermediation (a widely used term in the 1990s to define the elimination of the "middleman" in many transactions) of the real estate industry had the potential to be the largest example of the restructuring of a cluster of businesses caused by the effects of internet-based computing. That a quarter of a century after the wide availability of the Web the industry appears to have retained some of the structural elements of the past is remarkable, a circumstance that will someday need to attract the attention of historians.[35] But that is not to say that profound changes did not take place; indeed, they did. By no later than 2005, the information balance of power had shifted from the nearly total monopoly of the industry to, at a minimum, parity with what customers had: access to the same MLS-type information and power of the purse to demand lower fees from real estate agents, bankers, and appraisers, among others, and to break apart the total bundled "package" of services traditionally offered by a real estate agent, resulting in a cafeteria smorgasbord of services that a home buyer could pick from. This happened so quickly that even a quarter of a century later, industry observers have yet to credibly articulate how Americans have been affected by this technology. It is one of the reasons that so many authors came together to put this volume together, namely, to start assessing the massive changes still under way. What strikes one as remarkable is how long the industry could ward off the kinds of fundamental changes in both the use of technology and the business models given what was occurring in so many other industries.

The first discernible substantive shift of the industry to the use of new computing technologies became evident between 1995 and 2005. In these years, real estate agents and brokerage firms embraced more than online databases over the internet, although these were important, indeed crucial, to how they operated since the late 1990s. They tapped into municipal geographic information systems then widely being deployed, cellular phones and pagers, and, by the early 2000s, e-mail among themselves and with buyers and sellers. In such behaviors, they mimicked what was occurring across the U.S. economy in other professions. Listing activities went digital, such as MLS databases, although these continued to be controlled by the agents.

CONSUMER ACCESS TO INFORMATION

Search functions, however, slowly became increasingly accessible to potential buyers and sellers, such as online property tax information, land sales, online newspapers for sale data, and so forth. These files augmented what real estate agents tried to control, enriching a consumer's font of information. These additional collections of relevant information were controlled not by the real estate industry but instead by local governments, community newspapers, and other organizations. Digitized MLS systems began offering other capabilities, such as online documents necessary for closings. By 2005, computing was making it possible to shift house searches to buyers before they reached out to agents. Potential buyers gained access to MLS listings and did not hesitate to visit such databases. Computing made it easy for agents to communicate more through portable phones and e-mail with potential buyers and sellers, thereby speeding up the sales cycle. They began to use semiautomated process steps, such as preparation of the myriad documents required for closings. Others began to specialize in narrower types of sales, such as for very expensive homes, recreational properties, or specific neighborhoods. Implementation of computer-based documents led to changes in both content and format, such as those developed and mandated by the U.S. government. Each of these digitized functions was widely in use within the first decade of the internet's availability.[36]

It was the public's access to the MLS listings that most fundamentally changed the information balance of power in these years.[37] These online data were augmented by other, often municipal and state databases that further informed consumers. These included information about neighborhoods, entire cities and regions, schools, houses for sales, deed and title data, more about local taxes, and open litigation. These additional data sets increasingly linked together in the decade following 2005, thereby expanding the menu of information available to buyers and sellers.[38]

The effects built up quickly. As early as 2000–2002, consumers already had years of experience challenging the fees charged by agents since they (buyers and sellers) could now do some of the work conducted by the former in earlier times by using the internet. Studies conducted on consumer behavior in the 1990s had already begun to track this growing consumer activism.[39] The near monopoly on local knowledge held by agents was now being challenged even more insistently by buyers, for example, living in other states who could check multiple online sources for specific information about a potential community or house. Agencies began to consolidate to improve their efficiencies and to scale up to differentiate themselves through the use of expensive technologies.[40]

A study conducted by the California Association of Realtors in 2000 showed how quickly buyers were changing their behavior. It observed that some 25 percent of buyers who used the internet found the house they ultimately purchased, that 78 percent recruited their agents over the internet whose name was attached to the description of a house of interest to them, and that home buyers reported that their internet experience was useful. That same study noted that the time from considering a purchase to closing was shrinking and that for those who used the internet, the time shrank from five months to three months.[41] As in so many other industries, the cycle of business was speeding up, creating some fear in the real estate industry that others might enter their business online, such as banks and internet-born enterprises, a concern that became a reality in subsequent years.[42]

Fast-forward to the early years of the second decade of the new century, and the landscape has changed dramatically. It seemed that everyone was accessing the internet for information to buy and sell homes. More houses were bought and sold in cities where consumers extensively used the internet to inform their decisions, with nearly 90 percent who had used the internet actually making a purchase. Internet-based real estate firms now existed and were challenging traditional agents for business. The new competitors were prepared to provide some or all services individually or packaged together (as in traditional business practice) and increasingly discounted, threatening both the old profit streams and the business monopolies of the industry.[43] The internet made it easier for agents to offer ever-growing amounts of information quicker to potential buyers, for example. Home buyers were thrilled at the vast amounts of new information they could quickly collect and conveniently peruse.

CHANGING RELATIONS BETWEEN AGENTS AND CUSTOMERS

Agents quickly embraced use of the internet's databases because they too could learn more about how to assist their customers. For example, a listing agent could post more information, including photographs and videos, that more people could look at without having to consume the time of an agent to show a home that turned out to be of little interest to a potential buyer. Thus, better-qualified customers came knocking. In real estate terms, "better qualified" meant two things. First, it meant that a potential buyer's financial resources and credit rating showed that they could afford to buy what was being presented to them. Second, it also meant that the tastes and desires of the buyer were sufficiently understood by the agent so that he or she was required to show only homes that fit these criteria, such as the need for a fenced-in backyard or a desire to live in a neighborhood filled with professionals or academics.

Agents who used technology effectively increased incrementally the number of sales in these years because they could, for example, speed up communications back and forth among buyers and sellers and more quickly transmit information and documents that needed signing—all activities that involved the exchange of the same kinds of information as before the arrival of online communications but that now could be done faster. One student of the process noted that much of the legwork for a sale began shifting to buyers and sellers prior to engaging agents:

> Market intermediaries and individuals who connect buyers and sellers rather than buying or selling themselves can use information technology (IT) to connect buyers and sellers with agents to keep the traditional real estate professional in business and increase profits over time. The steps to the e-commerce real estate process include (a) entering the house in a listing database, (b) making the property searchable and suitable for prospective buyers, (c) evalu-

ation in-person through a walk-through or showing, and (d) negotiation of price. All four steps, made easier with IT, allow sellers to do the majority of the work on their own, essentially bypassing a real estate professional.[44]

Consumers increasingly now identified to agents the homes they wanted to look at rather than waiting for the agent to select them. These various activities essentially took an opaque market and made it transparent in a period of less than fifteen years. Lifting the veil occurred across the vast landscape of real estate transactions, involving every step of the buyer–seller–agent engagement. Transparency existed in what was for sale locally and anywhere across the nation; what each property had in the way of amenities, features, neighborhood stores, and schools; data about local taxes and cost of living; rankings of schools near these properties; and available financing and local banks, among other sources of information. The ability to link together various sets of data—such as tax records and comparative costs of multiple housing options—made it possible to create a clearer composite view of an option in excess of what a potential buyer could piece together prior to their extensive access to online information. Asymmetry in real estate information was beginning to melt away.

Consumers now had many options, too, of where to get their information that agents also could use, such as Yahoo!, Redfin.com, Realtor.com, Trulia.com, Zillow.com, and Craigslist, the half dozen most widely consulted sources by 2014, a point expanded on in chapter 1.[45] To be sure, the services and data varied from one internet based-source/business to another. For example, Redfin made available live chat services, Zillow online property appraisals, and Realtor.com digital signatures for legal documents to save everyone time at closings.

Before discussing these internet-born businesses, consumer behavior warrants additional commentary. What exactly could they find? Incrementally, since the late 1990s and full throated by 2010–2012, they could obtain, independently of a broker or agent if they wished (and most did), possible homes to buy, the best mortgage rates nationwide offering the most favorable interest rates and terms, access to online loan applications that were less expensive to process for them and the lenders, home inspectors, appraisers, attorneys, and title insurance. With respect to schools, whose quality profoundly influences purchase decisions by young families, they found statistics on student demographics, test scores, rankings, graduation rates, levels of criminal and misbehavior, seniority of teachers, and parent testimonials about the quality and culture of the school. I already mentioned details about housing markets and descriptions of specific houses, now also including virtual tours. Most websites do not charge for accessing their information, nor do most city and state government agencies that provide additional information about crime,

Table 3.3. Widely Consulted Real Estate Websites, circa 2012

Foreclosure.com	Properties in pre-foreclosure, foreclosure, or bankruptcy
Homes.com	Listings of home selling and buying, mortgage loans
Homescape.com	Regional MLS listings
Homeseekers.com	Information in multiple languages, demographics, crime
Realsites.com	Listing service for properties, home evaluations with involving an agent
Rebuz.com	Lists real estate associations, appraisers, etc.
Trulia.com	All manner of listing nationwide, historical data on sales prices
Zillow.com	Listings for new and resale homes, foreclosures, nationwide data

Source: Heather Richardson and Leonard V. Zumpano, "Further Assessment of the Efficiency Effects of Internet Use in Home Search," *Journal of Real Estate Research* 34, no. 4 (2012): 519.

local economic conditions, and city services. Table 3.3 is a brief list of the kinds of websites widely consulted by 2012. In the years following, many websites and internet-born real estate firms consolidated these widely disparate sets of data into one-stop-shopping sites, as the Zillow.com case demonstrates. Consumer behavior with regard to real estate information began to mimic information searches in other industries. These included iterative searches for hard facts, articles in the general and trade press, and comparisons of options, among others.[46]

EMERGENCE OF AN INTERNET-BASED REAL ESTATE INDUSTRY

Zillow.com represents an example of a new broad-based business model now evident in the real estate industry originating out of the twin influences of the capabilities of the Internet and other forms of IT and in response to the rapidly expanding appetite of buyers and sellers to leverage these technologies for their convenience, pleasure, and effectiveness. Zillow exemplifies how the industry is responding to the changes that occurred in the transformation of the information balance of power that occurred in the real estate market over the past quarter century. It is not unique, as many other firms are similarly structured to respond to the realities of today's real estate market, but it is one of the most visible, successful, and increasingly large examples familiar to tens of millions of buyers and sellers. It is the most used real estate website in the United States, now routinely visited by three times as many people as Trulia.com or Realtor.com, the second and third most accessed websites, respectively.[47]

The challenge to real estate agents is that disruptive innovation is forcing them to create new forms of enterprises and implement new business models. For observers, this is a process currently under way and not yet settled. Part of what is happening is that consumers of real estate information and services are becoming increasingly self-serving, having now reached a point where every kind of traditional real estate research, transaction, and service can be done with or without involving real estate agents or brokers. Agents, however, continue to be in demand for highly specialized market segments, such for the sale and purchase of multi-million-dollar apartments in Manhattan, homes in Beverly Hills, and large recreational properties in Colorado's ski country, for example.[48]

Put another way, a sufficient number of individuals studied in this volume have adopted cafeteria-style services from the industry that it appears that old business formats that had sufficed for more than a century are in decline. To be more precise, agents have not gone the way of the woolly mammoth because transactions are still complicated, so they remain active participants, and new business models take into account their activities as transactions are automated.[49]

Consumers have long suspected that agents were more interested in selling quickly than in holding out for higher prices for homes, so unbundling services became a strategy for mitigating some of that possible behavior. Increasingly, consumers see online agencies as a way to replace agents, and among these new providers, some of the most widely embraced are Zillow, Realtor.com, and Trulia.com. By early 2018, 50 percent of buyers were finding the homes they purchased over the internet, 28 percent through real estate agents, and the rest through friends, relatives, and other miscellaneous sources.[50] Brokers are unbundling their services to meet the specific needs of these buyers and sellers. The fact that regulators and the Department of Justice have long questioned existing laws and practices that supported the old nearly monopolistic behavior of agencies is consistent with an emerging, more competitive model of behavior by the industry.[51]

It was becoming apparent to the industry, too, that the number of individuals acquiring homes without the aid of an agent was rising and that the top four reasons for doing so in descending order were that they were purchasing from someone they knew, they could save on the cost of commissions, they were confident that they could conduct the selling and closing themselves, or they bought directly from a builder.[52] The successful business models offered by eBay, PayPal, and Amazon were compelling models to appropriate.

New entrants into the industry, such as Zillow, began by being information aggregators, bringing together into one website increasing amounts of the various types of information that tech-savvy consumers wanted to examine. Then these information providers expanded their offerings, adding incrementally automated portions of traditional agent-provided services, offering these either free of charge or for a fee that was competitive or less costly than before. Competition among these new firms emerged on an offering-by-offering basis, which proved attractive to increasing numbers of consumers. For example, sellers could post onto MLS databases the availability of their homes, selecting from such vendors as Owners.com or ForSaleByOwner.com, a common practice by 2014.[53] The most widely consulted real estate websites rapidly became Zillow, followed by local MLS sites, then Realtor.com, Trulia.com, and Redfin.com, as discussed in chapter 1. Survey work done in 2015–2016 suggested that by then, some 60 percent of consumers were willing to work with such real estate enterprises. Yet it was also reported that due to the complexity of real estate transactions, as many as 77 percent of them might still need the services of a human agent, suggesting both an opportunity and a challenge to the newly emerging internet businesses, such as Zillow. Half said that they would be willing to sell their homes on their own if the right digital applications were available.[54]

So what do these new businesses look like? Two observers of the industry, Emma Cherif and Delvin Grant, began exploring that question in the early 2010s. Using classical business model analysis (such as one might learn in a business administration master's program and also used by venture capitalists and entrepreneurs), they discovered both obvious and not-so-obvious patterns. Clearly, the internet made it easier to collect, present, and use information; expanded the number of people using such data; improved "seamless collaboration between agents, buyers, sellers, and financiers"; and made it easier to do business, especially for participants with limited knowledge of the real estate business and its complexities.[55]

Cherif and Grant identified four variants of internet-based businesses that responded to these technological realities (see table 3.4). Each relies

Table 3.4. Internet-Based Real Estate Business Models

Type	Description
Web-advertising model	Broadcasts information, advertises; offers free information; sells advertising, such as Realestate.yahoo.com, Realtor.com, Trulia.com, Zillow.com
Brokerage model	Brings brokers, sellers, and buyers together to conduct business, with broker charging fees to at least one participant in a transaction, enabling search for properties; provides brokerage services, such as Redfin.com and Realtor.com
Virtual value-chain model	Supports traditional real estate model with technology; information is a value-creating opportunity when information and transactions can be done digitally
Diversified model	Assists companies to expand their core business to related services, relying on networks, to create national brands and more diversified offerings

Source: Emma Cherif and Delvin Grant, "Analysis of e-Business Models in Real Estate," *Electronic Consumer Research* 14 (2014): 31–32.

on the internet for handling dialogues with potential buyers and sellers, provides diverse methods for monetizing its use, and reflects practices becoming evident simultaneously in other industries. Differences also include the extent to which they rely on partnerships across firms. The first method, which relies on Web advertising, is one of the earliest business models used in many industries, beginning in the 1990s: broadcasting information to potential buyers and selling advertising to real estate agencies, including to early internet-born real estate firms. A second method, the brokerage model, takes the first approach and adds the ability to conduct transactions online, an early twenty-first-century innovation. In this case, a site charges a fee for transactions conducted through its facility. The third method, which the researchers labeled a virtual value-chain model, essentially automates the back-office operations of a traditional real estate firm and facilitates connections between agents and buyers and sellers. The fourth method, which they labeled diversified, builds on the third by creating networks among participants to establish national brands, more diversified offerings, and collaboration across agencies nationwide.[56]

Some of these businesses have become quite substantial. For example, Trulia.com, a new start-up in 2010, quickly brought in an estimated $700 million in revenue, while Redfin.com brought in some $230 million. Zillow had data on 100 million homes and generated $30 million of revenue in 2010. Their market shares were all under 10 percent at the time, a circumstance that changed. Zillow, the largest real estate website, reported in 2019 that it tracked more than 110 million properties, had a market cap of $9.7 billion in midyear, and had experienced 7 billion visits in 2018, with its revenue increasing year over year by one-third. By any measure, these are very large numbers.[57]

Their value propositions (i.e., what they offer of value) varied. Zillow appraises the value of a property, Redfin.com provides online access to agents, DocuSign lets agents conduct legal signatures online for sales documents, Trulia.com offers estimates of property value, and Realestate.yahoo.com displays data on an agent's home page once a client has landed on it. These were all identified in chapter 1 as instructive major participants in the issues addressed throughout this volume. All claim high customer service and routinely improve use of their websites as technologies evolve. All aim to serve the same market segments: buyers, sellers, house owners, brokers, agents, and banks.

Table 3.5 lists the services provided by six internet-based providers. These are all offered over the internet, thus representing the core of Web-based businesses, with fees and/or advertisements being their source of revenues, although that is changing as they add services in addition to their core information offerings. Note a pattern: many of the services are similar in type, although each formats and displays data differently, but

Table 3.5. Core Offerings of Internet-Based Real Estate Firms, circa 2014

Firm	Offerings
Zillow.com	Establishes accounts, MLS listings, finds agents, location searches, saved searches, advice forum, mobile device access, value analysis, alerts, maps, analytics, demographic data
Redfin.com	Establishes accounts, MLS listings, finds agents, location searches, saved searches, advice forum, new listings, mobile device access, alerts, value analytics, maps, demographic data
Realtor.com	Establishes accounts, MLS listings, finds agents, location searches, saved searches, advice forum, new listings, mobile device access, alerts, value analytics, maps
Trulia.com	Establishes accounts, MLS listings, finds agents, location searches, saved searches, advice forum, new listings, mobile device access, alerts, value analytics, maps, Trulia Stats widget and Slide Show widget
Realestate.yahoo	Establishes accounts, MLS listings, finds agents, location searches, saved searches, advice forum, new listings, mobile device access, alerts, value analytics, maps, demographic data, no mobile device access
Craigslist.com	MLS listings, prices, advice forum, advanced searches, new listings

Source: Modified from table 1 in Emma Cherif and Delvin Grant, "Analysis of e-Business Models in Real Estate," *Electronic Consumer Research* 14 (2014): 37.

all tap into other existing databases while offering such common features as account log-in and access through newer technologies, such as mobile devices. Instead of brick-and-mortar offices, they all have an IT platform located on the internet. Table 3.6 summarizes their sources of revenue as of 2014. In this table, we see more variations (but even here not so much).

In other words, the data in these various tables demonstrate that a relatively similar business model had emerged by the early 2010s. Customers were similar, they could customize what services they acquired, and the information made available to all or most was typical, often

Table 3.6. Sources of Revenue of Internet-Based Real Estate Firms, circa 2014

Firm	Sources of Revenues
Zillow.com	Broker, agent, bank advertisements
Realtor.com	Realtors pay monthly fees to show up on lists of top 10 percent of time in rotation
Trulia.com	Sells ad space, sells agents more features
Realestate .yahoo.com	Sells ads to new home builders, real estate agents, brokers; partners with Zillow on advertising and sharing of listings
Craigslist.com	Places job advertisements in San Francisco, Los Angeles, and New York

Source: Modified from table 1 in Emma Cherif and Delvin Grant, "Analysis of e-Business Models in Real Estate," *Electronic Consumer Research* 14 (2014): 39.

drawing from the exact data sets. Zillow did more than the others to add new types and qualities of information (discussed next). All these firms had formed various partnerships with other websites to acquire and share information as well. All used the same channels of distribution and had invested continuously in enhancing their websites and its offerings and tools.[58] But rather than form a de facto monopoly, their corporate cultures called on them to compete with one another by adding to, changing, and improving their services on a continuous but fast-paced manner. That behavior represented a sharp departure from the old, pre-internet business model, where competition always existed but seemed less intense than in the internet market.

THE ZILLOW.COM PHENOMENON

To put a finer point on the new way of doing business, this section explores how Zillow.com became the largest online real estate company in the United States. As a type of business, it is first and foremost a media company, offering information to the greater market, even though it is focused on all manner of real estate data. Equally important, it is an e-business, following much of the same model and strategies as other iconic firms, such as eBay and Amazon. Its history reads like a West Coast/Silicon Valley start-up; in fact, its founders came from Expedia and Microsoft. Like other highly successful digital start-ups, it grew rapidly at speeds not normally seen in pre-internet brick-and-mortar companies but often evident in the Silicon Valley world. The company was cofounded in 2005 by a former chief executive officer of Expedia, Rich Barton, and by Lloyd Frink, also from Expedia, the latter having worked at Microsoft as well, locating the new business in Seattle, Washington. In February 2006, they launched their website as Zillow.com. Like so many other start-ups, they experienced a need and identified a solution. Before founding Zillow, they needed to find housing. They could not conveniently obtain the information required to make sound decisions. Zillow's chief executive officer, Spencer Rascoff, explained that "shopping for a home was like being in a dark room where only the agent was holding a flashlight. She'd shine it on two or three homes—listings or 'comps' she had chosen for you—but all you wanted to do was grab the flashlight and wield it yourself." Further, "that is why we created Zillow: to turn on the lights and bring transparency to one of our country's largest and most opaque industries."[59]

Its initial offering was Zestimate, the ability to calculate the value of a home; in time, its algorithms did that for most homes in America. The founders reported that within several days of their website becoming available, hundreds of thousands of people visited it, crashing their little servers. Visits increased so much that by 2014–2015, it had more than 140 million unique visitors every month with access to more than 140 million homes, offering far more information than in 2006.[60] It became evident that the value of homes proved to be central to people's interest in Zillow's data; they were able to report that how people searched for home listings online sorted results by home prices. Very quickly, they expanded their various data sets such that one could quickly describe the firm as a provider of assistance to buyers, home builders, sellers, real estate agents, landlords, renters, mortgage professionals, and property managers to access information relevant to their work and modified their algorithms as well. All of that became possible within a decade of its founding.

As a media company, Zillow generated revenues by selling advertising to professionals across the real estate industry while connecting potential buyers—mortgage shoppers—with those who could assist them within the industry. Much of its history is about incrementally adding channels of distribution for its information, such as through more than 180 newspapers and other online websites. In 2011, Zillow launched a partnership with Yahoo! to establish what quickly became the largest real estate advertising network resident on the Web. That was a special year, too, for Zillow because it held its initial public offering and began appearing on the NASDAQ in July at $20 per share. Two years later, the stock was selling for $66 per share, giving the firm a value of $2.3 billion. By the end of 2017, Zillow was generating $1.1 billion, spinning off $94.4 million in net income. It valued its assets at $3.1 billion on its tenth anniversary in 2016.[61] In late 2019, the stock was selling for nearly $40 per share, resulting in a market cap of $8.3 billion.[62] So, within half a decade, Zillow.com had access to sufficient amounts of capital to expand its offerings and business.

But, like other successful digitally born firms, it did not grow only by adding information and people visiting its website; it also acquired other firms that sped up its expansion and growing dominance in its chosen market. Acquisitions included Postlets, an online real estate creation and distribution platform, and Diverse Solutions, both in 2011; RentJuice, a software-as-a-service company servicing landlords and property managers leasing units in 2012; and Buyfolio, which was also acquired in 2012, to increase its access to a real estate shopping and collaboration platform while in that same year picking up two other firms. It made the largest of its early acquisitions in 2013, StreetEasy, for $50 million and the following year its first in Canada. But the most strategic acquisition came in 2014, when it acquired its largest competitor, Trulia, for $3.5 billion. Zillow management left Trulia operating as a separate brand to encourage the latter's users to continue visiting that platform.

Zillow reorganized into the Zillow Group to manage its growing portfolio of companies. All of that occurred during its first decade of operation; other acquisitions followed, all of which involved real estate. As of 2016, it employed more than 2,000 people. By then, it was the largest information provider in the industry.

Its business model of relying on analytics proved crucial. It is how one learned, for example, that homes within a mile of a Starbucks were worth more than similar homes in another part of town or that people began their searches by sorting by price. Their central offering, Zestimate, proved attractive and controversial. The controversy concerned the degree of its accuracy. Critics argued largely that it took merely square footage and applied a dollar value per square foot to calculate a value, an accusation that Zillow denied.[63] It is software that determines the value of a home based on all manner of available information about the property. Its accuracy varied, stimulating the controversy, but Zillow made it possible for estimates to be compared against actual selling prices in the same regional markets. Periodically, Zillow releases statistical data on Zestimate's accuracy. The firm begins by saying that Zestimate is never 100 percent accurate, as too many variables are involved, but it does claim to be accurate within 10 percent of the final selling price. Zillow maintains that its data provide "a range of prices" and that these do not replace a normal property appraisal that takes other factors into consideration, such as the quality of the home or its amenities.[64] As early as 2007, the *Wall Street Journal* concluded that it was reasonably accurate, while charges that its algorithms emphasized, for example, too much square footage of a home did not affect the attraction of the firm's estimates.[65] As it added more information and acquired more "eyeballs," the databases and algorithms that provided the superstructure of the tool became more central to its attraction.[66]

Zillow's use of data for its Zestimate and other services proved that the company could effectively use such information. It was able to develop a collective insight of what consumers wanted. The business value of Zestimate was enormous, and the firm did not hesitate to patent protect this asset as one of its central intellectual properties.[67] Its availability was less about empowering buyers and sellers with free information (although that happened) and more about leveraging such information to help Zillow and agents and sellers generate sales.

What kind of data were available, say, by 2019–2020? Several were offered from the beginning that were enhanced with volume and variety in what the firm refers to as its Zillow Home Value Index (ZHVI), and that has become the source of much economic analysis prepared by the firm. These data types include home listings and sales by type, location, price, and so forth; rental values, similarly sliced by category of location and so forth; rental listings similarly segmented; forecasts of future values and trends; and various other metrics, such as on rising sea levels, affordability of mortgages and rents, price-to-income ratios, and mortgage rates, among others. It routinely publishes a wide variety of metrics, more than two dozen on a regular basis, all related to real estate pricing and transactions.[68] Many of its methods for data analysis mirror traditional practices of an economist and of industry participants, such as appraisers and mortgage lenders.[69] Zillow's data today encompass the bulk of the U.S. housing market. To put a fine point on the matter, in 2019, residential investments accounted for between 3 and 5 percent of GDP, which includes new home construction and residential remodeling and brokers' fees, and between 12 and 13 percent of GDP devoted to consumption spending on housing services, which includes such components as rent and cost of utilities.[70]

To conclude our discussion of Zillow, one might ask, what happened as a result of the housing bubble of 2007–2012? While housing prices declined, foreclosures increased, and the nation entered a recession, Zillow continued to flourish, as its services became of greater interest. It expanded its business model to enter the home loan business, providing preapprovals and financing in 2019, while the year before, it had launched iBuying, entering the market for instant home buying (the house-flipping business) based on Zillow's understanding of a particular home's value and offering cash payments in nearly instant time but for a fee of roughly 7.5 percent. However, home owners would not need to prepare or repair their homes for a showing, to clean them, and so forth. Zillow's executives anticipated being able to purchase 5,000 homes per month, a subject of controversy among its stockholders, who wondered what would happen if the company owned a great number of properties during a future downturn in the market.[71]

An interesting question going forward with Zillow—and one that cannot be fully answered at this time as the business transforms from a pure media company into a business that buys and sells homes—is to what extent its attempts to provide objective information will be colored by its new business initiatives. Will one aspect of its business undermine or transform another aspect? This is undoubtedly becoming an urgent question within the firm, not only to the public, as Zillow increases its acquisitions of homes. As of 2020, this new initiative was not yet profitable, and the company had to defend its activities. For Zillow and all other i-buyers, the issue remained small, as they collectively bought only 60,000 homes in 2019 valued at $8.9 billion, which represented only 0.5 percent of all transactions. In the meantime (so far), prices that Zillow paid for homes were 98.6 percent of the price that normal real estate models demonstrate should be paid, suggesting that home owners selling to

Zillow, Opendoor, or other i-buyers were giving up only 1.4 percent as a discount for the convenience of the quick sale as opposed to what they normally would sell their properties for in a traditional manner.[72] Thus, one could speculate that its core Zestimates will continue to be driven more by the pursuit of accuracy than by a need to tip the scales in support of its new initiatives because the older model represents the lion's share of its revenue, at least for the time being.

EFFECT OF THE CORONAVIRUS PANDEMIC ON REAL ESTATE

As this chapter was being written in 2020, the coronavirus pandemic was washing over the United States, with its devastating effects on the economy, families, and communities. Recall that some state governors and mayors mandated that businesses shutter and that people not leave their homes and apartments for weeks and months except to buy groceries and medicines, to visit doctors, and to continue working if their jobs were considered essential. Various public officials also mandated that landlords could not evict tenants for most of the usual reasons, nor could banks similarly foreclose on homes. Officials wanted people to remain physically sheltered in their dwellings.

It is too soon to assess the long-term consequences on the industry and its customers; however, some insights are evident. The pandemic spread dramatically in the late winter to the start of the spring of 2020 at the exact moment when buyers and sellers normally begin their annual season of greatest economic activity and as tenants begin moving from one apartment or home to another. These activities continued during this period; however, their volume declined. With unemployment so high, there was early evidence by March that consumers and their agents were rethinking housing priorities. The industry looked to its experiences in 2008 during the Great Recession for insights on what to expect and found a few lessons. In 2008, for example, home owners had already in the prior three years cashed out $824 billion in equity that left them exposed to foreclosures as unemployment rose. Between 2017 and 2020, they had pulled out only $232 billion in equity, meaning that home owners had more equity in 2020 than in the earlier period. That difference alone suggested that fewer people would feel the pressure to have to sell their homes. In fact, 37 percent had no mortgage in 2020; they owned their homes. Of the remaining two-thirds, one-quarter of those owners had 50 percent or more equity.[73] Meanwhile, the pent-up demand for homes that had existed right through 2019, particularly for first-time buyers, had not changed fundamentally but was simply unsatisfied more quickly than might otherwise have been the case. Where activity occurred, agents and the public relied more on computing than before, showing houses through videoconferencing or doing more virtual closings and digital transfers of documents and signatures. Even online notarization could be done, as was occurring in Florida. The buying and selling processes of the past had been sufficiently digitized for most agents to conduct entire transactions over the internet.[74]

CONCLUSIONS

We finally need to ask about business cycles in the real estate industry and call attention to the growing role of big data and artificial intelligence, as both affect how people make decisions concerning their housing.

The U.S. real estate industry has increasingly experienced roughly ten- to eighteen-year business cycles involving expanding business, plateaus, crises (shrinkages), and transformations in recent decades, while throughout the nineteenth and early twentieth centuries, cycles averaged eighteen years. Its features have been well understood since the 1930s and involved booms, slumps, and recoveries.[75] Rising prices, overly optimistic underwriting, declining values, and a return to fundamental values characterize these cycles. Recent intervals in peaks have involved seven years in 1980, ten in 1990, and seventeen to eighteen years in 2006–2007, and questions are being asked in 2020 if another peak is about to occur.[76] Each evolution in the real estate market encouraged or constrained the enthusiasm of consumers to commit to renting or purchasing homes, condos, and apartments. Primary drivers influencing behavior include government policies that encourage home ownership, access to affordable mortgages, the quality of the job market and salaries, demographic shifts such as age, the availability of roads and other infrastructure, and the supply of housing. Secondary drivers always include state and local regulations and zoning stipulations, the economic performance of small businesses, advancements in both household and computing technologies, and household formations and incomes. During the 1980s, abundant capital (mortgage credit) and tax incentives encouraged expanded real estate activities; in the 1990s so too from industry consolidations, securitization of debt to lower risk for lenders, and expansion of both the digital and the general U.S. economy. In the first decade of the twenty-first century, inexpensive debt—indeed too much of it—fueled growth in industry transactions along with unprecedented consumer debt and an expanding stock market. From 2008 through a severe reversal in expansion that crashed through the industry, new homes were not built, many mortgages morphed into foreclosures, and consumers became wary about acquiring homes in the post-2012 years, in part driven by a younger workforce reluctant to commit to long-term residency in one community or home. Meanwhile, housing booms returned to both coasts, as had been the case throughout the second half of the twentieth century.[77]

Industry observers in 2019 almost universally believed that purchasing homes over the internet—fashionably called i-buying—would increase, some forecasting from a fraction of 1 percent of all purchases in 2018 to more than 3 percent by 2030, representing a steadily increasing percentage.[78] Real estate agents were not going away—acquisition of homes remained too complicated—and they had appropriated IT in sufficient forms to continue being of value to the market.[79]

As this chapter and this volume were being written, all industries and the world of IT consulting and computer science were abuzz about big data and artificial intelligence. One article's headline on the real estate industry read, "Why Buying and Selling a House Could Soon Be as Simple as Trading Stocks."[80] The expectation built on what Zillow.com and other digitally born firms understood: that with the vast amount of data available online, coupled with growing software capabilities with which to analyze literally trillions of pieces of information about individuals' behaviors and what they looked at online, linked to vast quantities of data about their jobs, preferences, specific facts about homes and apartments, and so forth, both consumers and participants in real estate transactions might be led by, influenced by, or subject to the effects of computer systems. This software could be guided if not influenced by what these inanimate objects learn about people and their preferences and capabilities, combined with business practices and policies participating in the broad information ecosystem of the real estate industry.

While here is not the place to discuss big data, its features should at least be called out. Big data maximizes computational power and algorithmic accuracy to gather and analyze vast quantities of data quickly, cheaply, and effectively. That is happening already. Zillow does that in the United States, RealEstate.com.au in Australia, and Zoopla in the United Kingdom; it is now a worldwide feature of the industry. Internet-based real estate transactions are becoming worldwide, expanding across Canada, Japan, southeastern China, the United Kingdom, and western Europe, among other localities. Sparse data would suggest that it is most widespread in the United States and remains a fragmented market despite the long-standing practice of, for example, wealthy Russians buying properties in New York and London or Asians in Vancouver.[81]

Regarding analysis, software can now identify patterns of acquisition and expenditures, for example, to advise individuals and participants in the industry on how best to make a decision, including providing recommendations. Finally, with respect to methodologies, there exists the wide belief that tapping into massive sets of data provides a higher form of intelligence and understanding (knowledge) on the verge of exceeding that of humans making housing decisions. Such an acceptance currently contributes to giving such decisions the patina of truth, objectivity, accuracy, and, consequently, security in the belief that they have optimized their decision making.[82] Time will tell how all this unfolds.

NOTES

1. John Tuccillo, *New Business Models for a New Economy: Remaking the Four Businesses of Real Estate* (Chicago: Dearborn Real Estate Education, 2002), 45.

2. National Association of Realtors, "Quick Real Estate Statistics," May 11, 2018, https://www.nar.realtor/research-and-statistics/quick-real-estate-statistics (accessed November 14, 2019).

3. Various statistics, U.S. Federal Reserve Flow of Funds and Urban Institute, March 2019.

4. Urban Institute, *Housing Finance at a Glance: A Monthly Chartbook, April 2019* (Washington, DC: Urban Institute, 2019).

5. Statista, November 11, 2019, https://www.statista.com/statistics/187576/housing-units-occupied-by-owner-in-the-us-since-1975 (accessed November 14, 2019).

6. Statista, https://www.statista.com/statistics/84968/us-health-expenditures-as-percent-of-gdp-sico19601 (accessed April 2, 2020).

7. For a list of such movies, see *AFI Catalog*, https://catalog.afi.com/Search?searchField=Subjects&searchText=real+estate&sortType=sortByRelevance (accessed February 27, 2020).

8. The dark side, discussed later in this chapter, is redlining, by which agents kept certain people out of a neighborhood, such as African Americans out of white communities. For details, see Keeanga-Yamahtta Taylor, *Race for Profit: How Banks and the Real Estate Industry Undermined Homeownership* (Chapel Hill: University of North Carolina Press, 2019).

9. More than half women by the end of the 1970s. See Jeffrey M. Hornstein, *A Nation of Realtors: A Cultural History of The Twentieth-Century American Middle Class* (Durham, NC: Duke University Press, 2005), 156–201, and Grace Stetson, "The Untold History behind Why Most Real Estate Agents Are Women," *Apartment Therapy*, March 30, 2019, https://www.apartmenttherapy.com/women-in-real-estate-history-268098 (accessed February 27, 2020).

10. Tuccillo, *New Business Models for a New Economy*, 28.

11. Charles M. Barresi, "The Role of the Real Estate Agent in Residential Location," *Sociological Focus* 1, no. 4 (Summer 1968): 62.

12. Barresi, "The Role of the Real Estate Agent in Residential Location," 65.

13. Tuccillo, *New Business Models for a New Economy*, 29.

14. Tuccillo, *New Business Models for a New Economy*, 29.

15. There has also been the tangential line of discussion (indeed debate) within the industry for decades about whether agents are professionals with a shared

standardized body of knowledge and licensing, code of conduct, and so forth or are tradespeople who apprentice with minimal certification and licensing requirements. If they are the former, then their institutions are professional associations; if they are the latter, then their institutions are trade associations. The industry has elements of both types of job descriptions, all made even more confusing by discussions concerning the role of women versus men in this industry as well. It remains an unresolved discussion.

16. Real estate agents began sharing information about sales opportunities in the United States in the late 1800s. MLS is a generic term referring to local lists and thus why there is not one but many lists that today are linked digitally into national versions; National Association of Realtors, "Multiple Listing Service (MLS): What Is It?," https://www.nar.realtor/nar-doj-settlement/multiple-listing-service-mls-what-is-it (accessed February 27, 2020).

17. For an example, see one for Massachusetts at https://mlspin.com/about_mls_pin.aspx (accessed November 15, 2019).

18. There is no substantive research on how that warfare occurs. However, competition appears, too, to be handled in more traditional ways, such as acquiring a rival firm or forming collaborative partnerships. An example of the latter is the partnership formed by Redfin and Opendoor. For an explanation of data scraping in real estate, see Vytautas Kirjazovas, "How Data Scraping Is Revolutionizing Real Estate Industry," *Oxylabs*, November 6, 2019, https://oxylabs.io/blog/data-scraping-for-real-estate (accessed April 2, 2020).

19. These actions continue as this chapter was being written in 2020. See, for example, U.S. Department of Justice, "Enforcing Antitrust Laws in the Real Estate Industry," https://www.justice.gov/atr/enforcing-antitrust-laws-real-estate-industry (accessed February 27, 2020).

20. Bruce M. Owen, "Kickbacks, Specialization, Price Fixing, and Efficiency in Residential Real Estate Markets," *Stanford Law Review* 29, no. 5 (1977): 931–67.

21. Beth Nagalski, "Ending the Uniformity of Residential Real Estate Brokerage Services: Analyzing the National Association of Realtors' Multiple Listing Service under the Sherman Act," *Brooklyn Law Review* 73, no. 2 (2008), https://broooklynworks.brooklaw.edu/blr/vol73/iss2/7 (accessed February 27, 2020).

22. U.S. Department of Justice and Federal Trade Commission, *Competition in the Real Estate Brokerage Industry* (Washington, DC: U.S. Government Printing Office, April 2007): 69. VOW means "virtual office website," where information is made available to consumers and agents beyond traditional MLSs.

23. U.S. Department of Justice, "Final Judgment: U.S. v. National Association of Realtors," November 18, 2008, Civil Action No. 05 C 5140, https://www.justice.gov/atr/case-document/final-judgment-142 (accessed February 27, 2020).

24. Andrea Riquier, "Realtors Will Soon Be Free of 10-Year-Old Justice Department Decree—So What Happens to Housing Now?," *MarketWatch*, March 21, 2018, https://www.marketwatch.com/story/realtors-will-soon-be-free-of-10-year-old-justice-department-decree-so-what-happens-to-housing-now-2018-02-06 (accessed February 27, 2020).

25. National Association of Realtors, "The Future of VOW Policy after the DOJ-NAR Agreement Expiration," November 27, 2018, https://www.nar.realtor/the

-future-of-vow-policy-after-the-doj-nar-agreement-expiration (accessed February 27, 2020).

26. For an introduction to the historiographical literature, see Marc A. Weiss, "Real Estate History: An Overview and Research Agenda," *Business History Review* 63, no. 2 (Summer 1989): 241–82. On the economics of information monopoly, see Steven D. Levitt and Chad Syverson, "Market Distortions When Agents Are Better Informed: The Value of Information in Real Estate Transactions," *Review of Economics and Statistics* 90, no. 4 (2008): 599–611.

27. William H. Brown Jr., "Access to Housing: The Role of the Real Estate Industry," *Economic Geography* 48, no. 1 (1972): 66–78; Stephen L. Ross and Margery Austin Turner, "Housing Discrimination in Metropolitan America: Explaining Changes between 1989 and 2000," *Social Problems* 52, no. 2 (2005): 152–80; Mary Szto, "Real Estate Agents as Agents of Social Change: Redlining, Reverse Redlining, and Greenlining," *Seattle Journal for Social Justice* 12, no. 1, Article 2 http://digitalcommons.law.seattleu.edu/sjsj/vol12/iss1/2 (accessed November 15, 2019).

28. A. D. Theobald, "Real Estate License Laws in Theory and Practice," *Journal of Land & Public Utility Economics* 7, no. 2 (1931): 138–54; Anupam Nanda and Katherine A. Pancak, "Real Estate Brokers' Duties to the Clients: Why Some States Mandate Minimum Service Requirements," *Cityscape* 12, no. 2 (2010): 105–25.

29. Various tables, U.S. Census Bureau and Federal Reserve Bank of St. Louis.

30. "Online Data Robert Shiller," http://www.econ.yale.edu/~shiller/data.htm for housing values since 1890 (accessed November 16, 2019).

31. "Online Data Robert Shiller," as reported by J. D. Roth, "A Brief History of U.S. Homeownership," May 1, 2018, https://www.getrichslowly.org/homeownership (accessed November 16, 2019).

32. Isaac Megboluge, "Residential Real Estate in the Age of Information Technology," *Housing Finance International* 1997: 22; Tuccillo, *New Business Models for a New Economy*, 11.

33. Steve Sawyer, Kevin Crowston, Rolf T. Wigand, and Marcel Allbritton, "The Social Embeddedness of Transactions: Evidence from the Residential Real Estate Industry," *The Information Society* 19, no. 2 (2003): 135–46, esp. 13.

34. Sawyer et al., "The Social Embeddedness of Transactions," 13.

35. One could speculate, based on behaviors evident in other industries, that a variety of factors were in play: poor computing skills of individuals working in the industry, inadequate training (a complaint raised at the same time by teachers, for example), and insufficient need to improve productivity due to the "baked-in" economics of a virtually guaranteed 6 percent commission that fit the preexisting business model of the industry honed over the previous half a century.

36. Steve Sawyer, Rolf T. Wigand, and Kevin Crowston, "Redefining Access: Uses and Roles of Information and Communication Technologies in the US Residential Real Estate Industry from 1995 to 2005," *Journal of Information Technology* 20 (2005): 216–18.

37. Sawyer et al, "Redefining Access," 218.

38. These linkages occurred outside the MLS world, driven by the expansion in the use of websites by cities, towns, counties, and state and federal agencies.

Many states, large counties, and cities had used computing since the 1960s (even local governments by the late 1980s) and thus brought considerable experience to digitizing additional files after the availability of the internet. Tax and property values were some of the earliest records to be digitized, followed by geographic information system engineering information. For a history of local computing, see James W. Cortada, *The Digital Hand: How Computers Changed the Work of American Public Sector Industries* (New York: Oxford University Press, 2008), 211–50, and Kenneth L. Kraemer and John Leslie King, *Computers and Local Government: Vol. 1. A Manager's Guide* (New York: Praeger, 1977). For the recent smart city movement, see Anthony M. Townsend, *Smart Cities: Big Data, Civic Hackers, and the Quest for the New Utopias* (New York: Norton, 2014).

39. See, for example, the highly documented studies by Karen M. Gibler and Susan Nelson, "Consumer Behavior Applications to Real Estate Education," *Journal of Real Estate Practice and Education* 6, no. 1 (2003): 63–83.

40. Tuccillo, *New Business Models for a New Economy*, 23–24.

41. Study summarized in Tuccillo, *New Business Models for a New Economy*, 46.

42. Glenn S. Dorfman, *Real Estate Industry Scan: Trends, Industry Practice, Innovation and Change* (Minneapolis: Minnesota Realtors, 2004), 6.

43. E. Beracha and M. B. Wintoki, "Forecasting Residential Real Estate Price Changes from Online Search Activity," *Journal of Real Estate Research* 35 (2013): 283–312; R. Rutherford and A. Yavas, "Discount Brokerage in Residential Real Estate Markets," *Real Estate Economics* 40 (2012): 508–35.

44. Jennifer J. Dorwart, "Strategies for Real Estate Professionals to Compete with Internet Organizations," PhD diss., Walden University, 2016, 30–31.

45. For details on the nature of the searches, see Y. Jung and S. D. Pawlowski, "Virtual Goods, Real Goals: Exploring Means-End Goal Structures of Consumers in Social Virtual Worlds," *Information & Management* 51 (2014): 520–31.

46. For the theory, behavior, and discussion of relevant literature, see Prashant Das, "Online Information Search, Market Fundamentals and Apartment Real Estate," PhD diss., Georgia State University, 2013, summary available at https://scholarworks.gsu.edu/real_estate_dis/14 (accessed November 18, 2019).

47. Tyler Zey, "The Top Ten Real Estate Websites," https://www.easyagentpro.com/blog/top-10-real-estate-websites (accessed February 27, 2020).

48. They are also used to manage properties, help construction firms sell properties in newly developed subdivisions and apartment buildings, conduct appraisals, and participate in apartment brokerage transactions.

49. L. Han and S. H. Hong, "Understanding in-House Transactions in the Real Estate Brokerage Industry," *RAND Journal of Economics* 47, no. 4 (2016): 1057–86.

50. National Association of Realtors, "Quick Real Estate Statistics," May 11, 2018, https://www.nar.realtor/research-and-statistics/quick-real-estate-statistics (accessed February 27, 2020).

51. B. D. Bernheim and J. Meer, "Do Real Estate Brokers Add Value When Listing Services Are Unbundled?," *Economic Inquiry* 51, no. 2 (2013): 1166–82; L. Blas, "Cashing In on Commissions? Estimating a Realtor's Value Added," *Yale Economic Review* 5, no. 1 (2009): 10.

52. For an example of such a survey from around 2015, see L. Cusumano, "Real Estate Agents Will Lose Value as Digital Peer-to-Peer Exchange Platforms

Couple Exponentially with Technological Advancements," M.A. thesis, Realtor University, 2017, 19.

53. L. Kamping-Carder, "Some Homeowners Go Solo to Sell Their Real Estate," *Wall Street Journal*, quoted in Cusumano, "Real Estate Agents Will Lose Value as Digital Peer-to-Peer Exchange Platforms Couple Exponentially with Technological Advancements," 21.

54. Cusumano, "Real Estate Agents Will Lose Value as Digital Peer-to-Peer Exchange Platforms Couple Exponentially with Technological Advancements," 32, 33, 36.

55. Emma Cherif and Delvin Grant, "Analysis of e-Business Models in Real Estate," *Electronic Consumer Research* 14 (2014): 26.

56. Cherif and Grant, "Analysis of e-Business Models in Real Estate," 25–50.

57. iPropertyManagement, "Zillow Statistics," https://ipropertymanagement.com/zillow-statistics (accessed November 20, 2019).

58. The discussion of the previous several paragraphs are drawn largely from Cherif and Grant, "Analysis of e-Business Models in Real Estate," 25–49.

59. Spencer Rascoff and Stan Humphries (Zillow's chief economist), *Zillow Talk: Rewriting the Rules of Real Estate* (New York: Grand Central Publishing, 2016), 8.

60. Rascoff and Humphries, *Zillow Talk*, 9.

61. Yahoo! Finance, "Zillow Group," https://finance.yahoo.com/quote/Z/financials?p=Z (accessed November 20, 2019).

62. The 2019 share value had declined from the company's all-time high of $62.74 in July 2018. Regardless, the stock had tripled in value in less than a decade.

63. For a sample criticism, see Kenneth R. Harney, "Inaccurate Zillow 'Zestimates' a Source of Conflict over Home Prices," *Los Angeles Times*, February 8, 2015, https://www.latimes.com/business/realestate/la-fi-harney-20150208-story.html (accessed February 27, 2020).

64. For an analysis of its accuracy with examples, see Elizabeth Weintraub, "Learn How Accurate Zillow Estimates Are," *The Balance*, June 25, 2019, https://www.thebalance.com/how-accurate-are-zillow-home-estimates-1798268 (accessed February 27, 2019).

65. James R. Hagerty, "How Good Are Zillow's Estimates?," *Wall Street Journal*, February 14, 2007; Harney, "Inaccurate Zillow 'Zestimates' a Source of Conflict over Home Prices."

66. John Cook, "Zillow at 10: Rich Barton, Spencer Rascoff and Lloyd Frink on the Rise of the Real Estate Media Titan," *Geekwire*, February 4, 2016, https://www.geekwire.com/2016/zillow-10-years (accessed November 20, 2019).

67. In 2012, for example, Zillow sued Trulia, alleging that Trulia had infringed on part of its patent for Zestimate, although there was some question as to what Zillow could patent in the first place. See John Cook, "Patent Office: Most Zillow Claims around Zestimate Valuation Tool Are 'Unpatentable,'" *GeekWire*, March 28, 2014, https://www.geekwire.com/2014/patent-office-rules-zillow-claims-around-zestimate-valuation-tool-unpatentable (accessed April 2, 2020).

68. For a technical discussion of its data sets, see https://www.zillow.com/research/about-us (accessed November 20, 2019).

69. See the technical discussion of methods by Eduard Hromada, "Real Estate Valuation Using Data Mining Software," *Procedia Engineering* 164 (2016): 284–91.

70. These kinds of data are published routinely by such industry groups as the National Association of Home Builders, the U.S. Department of Commerce, and the industry press.

71. Rebecca Shore, "Could Zillow's Fears Be the Key to Zillow's Growth?," *The Motley Fool*, November 5, 2019, https://www.fool.com/investing/2019/11/05/could-zillows-fears-be-the-key-to-zillows-growth.aspx (accessed November 20, 2019).

72. "Tearing Down the House," *The Economist*, February 15, 2020, 61–63.

73. Christina Vazquez, "Real Estate Market Feeling Impact of Coronavirus Pandemic," *Local10.com*, March 26, 2020, https://www.local10.com/news/local/2020/03/25/real-estate-market-feeling-impact-of-coronavirus-pandemic (accessed April 2, 2020).

74. Larry Altman, "What Effect Will COVID-19 and the Stay-at-Home Order Have on the Real Estate Market? Agents Work to Makes Sales without Open Houses," *KCET*, March 26, 2020, https://www.kcet.org/shows/socal-connected/what-effect-will-covid-19-and-the-stay-at-home-order-have-on-the-real-estate (accessed April 2, 2020).

75. Homer Hoyt, *One Hundred Years of Land Values in Chicago* (New York: Arno Press, 1970; original ed. 1933). It is the seminal work that originally defined real estate cycles; Liz Brumer-Smith, "Understanding Real Estate Cycles to Find Profitable Investments in Any Market," *Millionacres*, October 7, 2019, https://www.fool.com/millionacres/real-estate-market/articles/understanding-real-estate-cycles-find-profitable-investments-any-market (accessed February 27, 2020); Kieran Trass, *The Housing Bubble* (New York: Penguin, 2008).

76. "How Long Does a Seller's Market Last? Analyzing Real Estate Cycles," *Berkshire Hathaway*, December 16, 2019, https://berkshirehathawayhs.tomieraines.com/Blog/ID/368/How-Long-Does-a-Sellers-Market-Last-Analyzing-Real-Estate-Cycles (accessed February 27, 2020).

77. Christopher Lee, "Real Estate Cycles: They Exist . . . and Are Predictable," *Center for Real Estate Quarterly Journal* 5, no. 2 (Spring 2011): 5–11.

78. Various Morgan Stanley Research reports.

79. Rascoff and Humphries, *Zillow Talk*, 148–51; Jennifer Dorwart, "Strategies for Real Estate Professionals to Compete with Internet Organizations," *Walden University ScholarWorks*, 2016, https://scholarworks.waldenu.edu/dissertations/2810 (accessed November 20, 2019).

80. Andrea Riquier, "Why Buying and Selling a House Could Soon Be as Simple as Trading Stocks," *MarketWatch*, September 12, 2019, https://www.marketwatch.com/story/how-buying-and-selling-a-home-could-soon-be-as-simple-as-trading-stocks-2019-09-11 (accessed November 20, 2019).

81. For an example that mimics the U.S. experience, see https://www.listglobally.com (accessed February 27, 2020).

82. Kimberly Winson-Geideman and Andy Krause, "Transformation in Real Estate Research: The Big Data Revolution," 22nd Annual Pacific-Rim Real Estate Society Conference, January 17–20, 2016, http://www.prres.net/papers/Geideman_Transformations_in_RE_Research.pdf (accessed November 20, 2019).

Four

Privacy, Surveillance, and the "Smart Home"

Philip Doty

> "Smart" is a euphemism for rendition: intelligence that is designed to render some tiny corner of lived experience as behavioral data. . . . Products, services, and applications march to the drumbeat of inevitabilism toward the promise of surveillance resources hacked from the still-wild spaces of what we call "my reality," "my home," "my life," and "my body."[1]
>
> As homes shift from defendable places to watched spaces . . . the human body is abstracted from territory.[2]

The first epigraph from Zuboff's book on contemporary surveillance capitalism indicates how the many elements of our worlds, including our homes, undergo "rendition." Rendition is taking our phenomenologically vital selves, habits, and locations and reducing them to behavioral data by powerful business and state interests, what the second epigraph by Rapoport illustrates as we are rendered incorporeal. This process is enabled by surveillance of all kinds. Public and private enterprises, often in partnership, detect patterns of our past behavior using techniques such as data mining and then manipulate these data using computationally complex and powerful, if flawed, predictive algorithms. They do so in the context of our consumer culture to learn about us, target advertising to us, sell data about us, observe and control our movements across borders and into buildings, and more to achieve two dreams:

1. The dream of advertisers for centuries—to predict when a consumer is ready to buy a particular product in order to have that product in the forefront of their attention at that time, a key to what Crang and Graham and others identify as the "fantasy of friction-free consumption."[3]

2. The dream of the modern state also for centuries—to be able to govern people within and without its borders by knowing about and influencing their behavior.[4]

They are after the accumulation of so much data that they can ascertain the merely possible rather than the probable in order to control the uncertainty and govern the variability of the contemporary economy and nation-state.[5] While the tools of probability (descriptive and inferential statistics) grew up to serve the modern nation-state, the primary tools to control uncertainty under current regimes of commercial and governmental surveillance are those of risk management, especially data mining and predictive algorithms. As Amoore notes, "risk technologies . . . hold out the promise of managing uncertainty and making an unknowable future knowable and calculable" in an "information-driven utopia of governance."[6] As with all surveillance, the goal of such knowledge is classification and other forms of action.

It is not only our buying habits, travel and border-crossing history, physiological characteristics, exercise and leisure patterns, and reading and communication that are so rendered but also our homes and what happens in them. This chapter examines the surveillance that occurs in the modern American "smart home." The chapter begins with some observations about the surveillance that surrounds us more generally and the symbolic value of home in the United States, then moves to the chapter's main focus of "smart home" surveillance both for good and for ill.

As the chapters in this volume show, choosing a place to live in America is a complex decision invoking many criteria and judgments as well as factors beyond our general knowledge and influence. Among the characteristics to consider about a place to live, particularly when buying or building homes, is living places' digital connectivity. Similar concerns also color the decisions about placements for aging relatives, children, or others. Such decisions can be informed by home buyers' or home builders' concerns about the internet of things (IoT), big data, and surveillance.

SURVEILLANCE IN CONTEMPORARY AMERICA

Despite their deep historical roots, both liberal democracy and the nation-state, including the study of characteristics of the state *state-istics*, are the products of early modernity. So is the relentless documentation and surveillance that it has also imposed across the breadth of personal, civic, and economic life[7] and, increasingly, at home. As Lyon, Gandy, and other scholars of surveillance remind us, the goal of surveillance is not observation in itself. It is rather to classify, to discriminate, to make judgments about groups and individuals. Surveillance is "focused, systematic and routine attention to personal details for purposes of influence, management, protection or direction,"[8] enabling social sorting.[9] While surveillance certainly is "about" a fundamental asymmetry of power and its exercise, surveillance exists and is intentional in its attempts to control and to govern in its broadest sense, particularly those populations considered "other" by virtue of race, religion, and economic circumstance.

The discriminatory character of surveillance is complex and multifaceted. It involves racial, ethnic, linguistic, economic, geographic, and other forms of bias.[10] It also involves other forms of categorization across a multitude of activities, such as shopping and the prediction of likely consumers and their purchases, predictive policing, crime detection, border crossings, health, traffic control, and more. The border between the home and the outside world is one place where surveillance is dynamically determined, particularly as new social practices, digital technologies and systems, and political values emerge.[11] The recent development and increasingly strong symbolic value of "smart homes" and other "smart" devices make contemporary surveillance more common than it would otherwise be. Thus, the classification that surveillance allows and facilitates, including the monetization of information about us and our behavior, is more intrusive and more internalized as well. We are increasingly complicit in our own surveillance, and, as many scholars assert, we are increasingly reduced to data, although we have long been inclined to participate in our own surveillance for any number of reasons.[12] While there are advantages to this increase in surveillance as outlined below (e.g., potentially more independent and safer living for older persons), we face a new kind of question: Do we want to live this way? Answering that question influences both how and where we live.

There are many theories of surveillance, and they come from a variety of perspectives.[13] Particularly influential theories include the following:

- The panopticon of Jeremy Bentham, especially as used by Michel Foucault as the dominant if increasingly questioned metaphor for ubiquitous surveillance[14]
- The surveillance assemblage, particularly to "demolish" the panopticon[15]
- The discriminatory, participatory panopticon[16]
- Contextual integrity as the key to autonomy, privacy, and interpersonal relations[17]
- The culture of surveillance[18]
- Surveillance capitalism[19]

- Emerging important topics such as self-surveillance, including the quantification of self; big data analytics, machine learning, and artificial intelligence; and algorithmic bias[20]

While this list does not claim to be comprehensive, it gives an indication of the increasingly interwoven forms of surveillance that modern life entails and demands for full social, political, and economic participation.

A Discursive and Terminological Aside

The many and growing literatures about "smart homes" generally include them as participants in the IoT, a concept with similar cultural and professional currency. A technology assessment of the IoT for the Congress by the U.S. Government Accountability Office's Center for Science, Technology, and Engineering noted that interconnected objects of various kinds have long existed. They identify four recent changes in the social and technological landscape that have facilitated a much wider, faster, and more heterogeneous uptake of devices connected to the internet and to each other: miniaturized and inexpensive electronics, increasingly ubiquitous connectivity, cloud computing, and data analytics.[21] Shuhaiber and Mashal quote sources to the effect that the global IoT market will reach between $3.9 trillion and $11.1 trillion by 2025, the number of connected "smart objects" will reach $212 billion in 2020, and a "typical family home" might have more than 500 smart devices.[22] Others estimate that 40 million American homes (of about 140 million nationwide) have hundreds of millions of "smart" devices already connected to the internet. Expectations are that the number of connected "smart homes" in America will increase to 80 million.[23] Zuboff notes a Reuters report from February 2018 that "the global 'smart home' market was valued at $36 billion and expected to reach $151 billion by 2023"[24]—all an indication of the scale and social interest in "smart" home systems.

Here is a good time to note why I include quotation marks around "smart homes," "smart cities," and similar terms. The usage is common in many thoughtful examinations of "smart" devices, homes, and the like, and it is naive to dismiss this orthographical choice as "scare quotes." Rather, the quotation marks indicate reasonable skepticism about the ideological work done by three interrelated claims about "smart" devices, sometimes explicit, sometimes not. Briefly, they are that (1) objects or processes can display intelligence and thus be "smart," (2) machines can "learn," and (3) predictive algorithms are free from bias because of the apparent "objectivity" of quantitative data and methods. None of these claims is true. Intelligence is a characteristic of sentient beings, and use of the terms "smart" or "intelligent" is a loose figurative claim that has come to dominate professional and scholarly argot. Reifying the figurative use, giving it misplaced concreteness, is a conceptual and political error. Similarly, claiming that machines can learn is figurative. Machines and processes driven by machines, using powerful observational and analytic methods, offer almost unimaginable computational power. But the complexity of these methods and our inability to describe them precisely does not mean that the machines have intentionality or purpose. Instead, they are doing what we tell them to do in the ways we tell them to do it. Finally, the putative unassailability of predictive algorithms is, in fact, a major discursive and political and ideological step subject to the same sort of examination that all political and ideological claims merit.

Such claims are usually hiding in plain sight but are not, as their supporters claim, prepolitical and thus immune to critique. There are many scholars' works of the past century demonstrating the reasonableness and power of this sort of political, ideological analysis. Sadowski and Bendor's 2019 paper about the "smart city," major corporations' narratives, and the use of the trope of the sociotechnical imaginary is useful here. It is a recent, summative example of how such analysis bears valuable fruit, especially about how the partnership of state and commercial interests achieves discursive hegemony, how they "successfully propagate their smart city [and "smart home"] imaginary and dominate the smart city discourse."[25] Now it is useful to bring some of the skeptical scholarly analysis noted above to the concepts of home, surveillance, and the "smart home."

THINKING OF HOME

It is important to remember that the political and social ethos of the United States has been one where the concept of the home is one that has "been fundamental to the construction of conceptualizations of privacy." That is, as privacy helps to define "home," home helps to define "privacy" and how we think of it, operationalize it, articulate it, and look to achieve it. As expected, many scholars discuss the home as a "bastion of seclusion and isolation," and Shapiro continues, quoting Lasch's 1979 well-known adage of home as a "haven in a heartless world."[26] Echoing Shapiro, Rapoport reminds us that surveillance in the home "challenges readings on boundary and privacy," foundational to the classical liberal home in policy, legal, and cultural contexts, by undermining the home's ability to guarantee personal space, autonomy, retreat, and privacy.[27] Home surveillance especially erodes our ability, as individuals, families, and groups, to dream and to produce reverie, citing Bachelard on the poetics of space. It is this dreaming that makes a physical space a place to dwell rather than simply a place to be. Home also deliberately limits access to the body and mind, clearly linking the concepts of home and privacy, and provides respite and "a familiar and localizable way of being that renders inactivity and a setting of the 'outside' world aside possible."[28] At the same time, however, the home is also a site for social interaction and "never completely severed from the public gaze"[29] and is thereby a site for development and expression of a freer self than is normal publicly. At the same time, however, the home is a site for normalization and the imposition of discipline on behavior and identity by the self and others as we are socialized in the many ways that we are. Friedewald et al. continue in a similar key, saying that home is "an emotionally charged and personally furnished cradle of living, physical space as much as a socio-cultural context and state of mind."[30]

There are, of course, other important readings of home, especially in the past several decades identifying the home as a place of labor of all kinds and oppression of and violence against women, children, and others unable to defend themselves. Useful here are some early and continuing feminist readings as against privacy and "the private," such as the work of Anita Allen, Patricia Boling, and Catherine MacKinnon.[31] For a review of much of this early and continuing theme of feminist critique of privacy, especially in the home, see Doty on "gendered perspectives on privacy."[32]

Further, as feminist-informed research in science and technology studies has also shown, the concepts of a freestanding, privately owned home; concepts of family life; and personal and shared autonomy are deeply intertwined. For example, in her groundbreaking book-length study *More Work for Mother: The Ironies of Household Technology from the Open Hearth to the Microwave*, famed historian of technology and science and technology studies scholar Ruth Schwartz Cowan notes that[33] "the majority of people [in the United States]—whether rich or poor, owners or workers, male or female—chose to preserve in both the realm of symbol and the realm of fact, those activities that they deemed crucial to the creation and the maintenance of family life. . . . Most people prefer to live in their own homes, with their own relatives, rearing their own children, regularly sitting down to meals together, decorating their quarters according to their own lights, dressing themselves according to their own tastes, and controlling the tools with which they have to do their work."

This powerful impulse has been key to the development of the United States as a polity and as an organic society. Cowan continues, "Most people will opt to increase the possibility of exercising their right to privacy and autonomy." Clearly, hundreds of millions of us have acted on this set of internalized norms and expectations for centuries in buying or building our own homes. The proliferation of "smart" devices and functions, however, including those we wear, those that we introduce or that are built into our homes, and those that increasingly define the neighborhoods and cities where we live, pose new challenges to this ideology of home, autonomy, and privacy. For example, Shapiro particularly notes the barrier that the home provides between safety and danger in moral terms,[34] and it is to this theme we turn to next to give us further insight into how IoT-connected "smart home" devices and the ubiquitous, always-on surveillance that they enable undermine what home means.

Home as a "Moral and Moralizing" Place

An important theme in the literature about home in America is what Rapoport and others term a "moralized and moralizing space as residents voluntarily monitor themselves and their families."[35] This is true generally about home in America especially given the nineteenth-century cult of domesticity and the intertwined historical movement identified as the feminization of American culture.[36] These two historical movements have been the subject of serious critique, especially for their questionable affirmation of "separate spheres" for women (home, domestic relations, and "labors of love") and men (work, politics, and economic relations). This chapter cannot address the large and growing literature about these movements and critiques,[37] but there is rich material for further work, including that about "smart homes." Of specific interest here is that the moral oversight at work in the contemporary home is increased—and some would say exacerbated—as more Americans willingly open their family lives to "continuous inspection" by increasing surveillance and interconnectivity with the IoT in the home. Obliquely echoing the work of Foucault on the disciplinary effects of school, work, prison, hospital, and the modern state, Rapoport continues, "Similarly to the school . . . the home becomes a site in which social discourses are internalized and in which individuals learn to govern themselves."[38]

Reprising and anticipating common themes in the appreciation of the symbolic value of home in America, Tognoli cites a large literature in multiple disciplines that home is "comfortable . . . familiar and warm . . . a place . . . for restoration, energy, and regeneration."[39] He discusses the nineteenth-century American ideology of separate spheres and the cult of domesticity, especially the work of Harriet Beecher Stowe and her sister Katherine Beecher.[40] Tognoli makes plain how home, privacy, and the moral influence of women have long been ideologically and symbolically connected, noting that women were expected to help protect men and children from the world's temptations and moral dangers by making the home "spiritually and physically clean." Privacy was a means to ensure that cleanliness.

Liisa Mäkinen is a Finnish scholar of surveillance and geography. In her empirical study of Finnish adopters of "smart home" technology, she cites scholarship that notes that many persons feel that their homes are sites of moral rectitude and protection: "In this context, the outside is seen as 'dangerous' and the inside as 'pure.'"[41] Giving us even further insight into this value dynamic, Mäkinen refers to some respondents' use of the Finnish term *koskemattomuus*, which includes not only physical integrity but also "a feeling of being untouchable, autonomous and 'intact.'"[42] This concept, difficult to appreciate in English, is reinforced by one respondent's saying that the "untouchability" of their "smart home" was a prime rationale for the purchase and use of an integrated security system.[43] This concern and corresponding claims about the moral, physical, and "intact" character of their home gives us important insight into the ideology of home in America as well and to the symbolic dynamic linking home, privacy, and surveillance in the "smart home" as an instantiation of the IoT.

The Dream of the Mechanized, Automated Home in America and Beyond

For quite some time, women have largely done the domestic labor or labor in the home.[44] While this division of labor has never been absolute, an oxymoronic outcome of the increased number and kinds of household appliances has been no significant decrease in the effort, time, and kinds of tasks that women spend doing what is commonly called housework. Time spent, for example, doing laundry is reallocated to child care and adherence to a heightened standard of cleanliness.[45] But the dream of a mechanized or automated home, the precursors of the "smart home," has a long history, especially in the United States. Walt Disney's animation of the automated broom toting water out of control under Mickey Mouse as the Sorcerer's Apprentice in *Fantasia* (1940), an animation of Paul Dukas's 1897 musical setting of Goethe's 1797 poem of the same name, is an amusing if harrowing vision of the animated household task gone wrong. Bonnie Fox provides a content analysis of seventy years of advertisements in *Ladies Home Journal* (published monthly from its founding in 1883 until 2014, now published quarterly), perhaps the premier bourgeois women's magazine in the twentieth century.[46] The *Journal* had more than 1 million paid subscribers early in that century, ranking first in circulation of women's magazines between 1932 and 1961, then either second or third behind *McCall's* or *Better Homes and Gardens* for the remainder of the century.[47] Of particular value is her observation that advertisers had to engage women's ideological consciousness about what being a good housekeeper, spouse, and mother is *supposed* to be as well as to help shape that consciousness[48] because "advertising is ideological by nature."[49] This point is of special import as a reminder about several elements related to "smart homes" and surveillance: the discursive power of ads for "smart home" and IoT devices and services,[50] the central role and unquestioned iconographic status of the digital and the internet in modern American life,[51] and our shared social scripts. The ads documented in Fox and Koskela highlight how effective appeals to the combination of fear and guilt can be, whether about the mechanized or the IoT-connected "smart home."

A recurring theme in Koskela's 2014 review of Finnish ads for surveillance and security technologies intended to "automate" home and work is "techno-fetishism," of interest to American life. Her goal is to determine the manifold meanings of these advertisements in the context of the way we currently imagine and operationalize the governance of security across society, with special focus on appeals to the politics of fear and the politics of care. As noted by Sadowski and Bendor, "Surveillance marketing . . . promote[s] a particular kind of agenda: setting security in the consumer society and claiming that technical equipment is a powerful solution,"[52] often by highlighting threats, whether reasonable or not, and then offering a technological "solution." Citing the work of Chris Hackley, Koskela says that advertising works generally by disarming potential consumers, looking to "resonate with their fantasies and aspirations and normalize consumption practices."[53] In addition to the usual bag of marketing tricks used to market surveillance, Koskela identifies additional elements, noted by many other observers:[54]

1. Appeal to technical expertise embodied in the devices and available as services
2. Trust especially strong, customized client services
3. Explicit and evocative use of the politics of fear, the "semiotics of danger" especially since 9/11, featuring a supposed "need for increased security" as "the ideology of contemporary society—something assumed as self-evidently true," referring to Jonathan Bignell's work on media semiotics

Koskela enhances her argument by noting that the quotidian character of surveillance in contemporary society, not just in Finland but around the world, hides the threats that surveillance holds—oppression, intrusiveness, and relentless observation—as instantiated by the partnership of private and public enterprises that persuades us to accept surveillance not only as inevitable but also as desirable.

As noted above, Koskela's observations about advertising and techno-fetishism apply equally well to American homes that have been full of mechanical, automated, and timed devices long before the arrival of the internet and the "smart home." For example, the alarm clock, invented as early as the thirteenth century, has been widely available for home use in a variety of sizes, designs, and prices since early in the nineteenth century.[55] Even a cursory glance at many twentieth-century American homes would have included these kinds of mechanical, automated, and timed devices:

- Automatic garage door openers
- Thermostats to control heating and/or air conditioning
- Automatic light timers
- Smoke and carbon monoxide detectors
- Intercom systems and audio baby monitors
- Motion detector lights
- Power tools
- Automated lawn sprinklers and irrigation systems
- Electric heating elements in driveways and walkways to melt ice and snow
- Appliances such as
    - Coffee makers
    - Stoves and ovens
    - Clothes washers and dryers
    - Refrigerators with automatic ice makers and defrosting capabilities
    - Dish washers
    - Radios
    - In-wall vacuum cleaners
    - Space heaters and (e.g., quartz-based) heaters that warm objects rather than the air
    - Ceiling, box, and tabletop fans; exhaust fans in kitchens, bathrooms, and workshops
    - Humidifiers, dehumidifiers, and air filters
    - Televisions and recording devices, such as videocassette recorders

What makes these devices and appliances different from "smart" devices and homes are four major characteristics.

First, these devices and appliances *stand alone*; they are not connected to the internet, making them quite distinct from the interconnected devices in the IoT in the "smart home." Second, they are *"dumb,"* that is, not enabled by so-called artificial intelligence and/or machine learning, contrasting them to those devices and appliances in the "smart home." Third, they are initiated and stopped by *direct human intervention*, while "smart home" devices and appliances may rely on some combination of human initiation and machine-controlled learning or, instead, even passive observation of people's behavior and use of devices and appliances and internet connectivity to begin, continue, and cease operation. Fourth, these devices and appliances are deliberately controlled to be *on or off*, while "smart home" devices and appliances are always on, always gathering, analyzing, and sharing data—often without home owners' knowledge or consent. "Smart homes" differ on all four of these characteristics, and it is these differences that make "smart homes" indefatigable means of surveillance.

SO-CALLED SMART HOMES AND SURVEILLANCE

While the term "smart homes" has a great deal of currency, it has seen significant social circulation since about 1988.[56] There is no canonical definition of what a "smart home" is.[57] Naturally, we should not expect agreement on what such a widely used term might mean, especially given its origins in advertising, computer science, and elsewhere as well as the potentially confusing colloquial uses of "smart" in common parlance. Looking at several working definitions in the research literature of what a "smart home" is purported to be, however, will help focus this discussion and clarify what I intend when I use the term.

Working Definitions of "Smart Homes"

Illustrative examples describing the surveillance capabilities and components of the "smart home" include the following. Steven Alter, exercising a sociotechnical analytic, quotes a 2015 editorial in *Service Science* that a "smart system" is a

> system capable of learning, dynamic adaptation, and decision making based upon data received, transmitted, and/or processed to improve its response to a future situation. The system does so through self-detection, self-diagnosing, self-correcting, self-monitoring, self-organizing, self-replicating, or self-controlled functions. These capabilities are the result of the incorporation of technologies for sensing, actuation, coordination, communication, control, etc.[58]

While such a broad definition may seem less than useful, it helps us understand what an IoT-connected "smart home" is and how it works.

For example, Marikyan and colleagues' 2019 systematic review of literature of 143 papers and reports from 2002 to 2017 about the "smart home," with a supposed emphasis on the user perspective (more on that below), says that smart technologies possess "some degree of artificial intelligence," interconnection, and interoperability that allow them to "acquire information from the surrounding environment and react accordingly" to enhance the well-being of the home's residents. Further, a "smart home" is a "residence equipped with smart technologies aimed at providing tailored services for users. Smart technologies make it possible to monitor, control and support residents, which can enhance the quality [of] life and promote independent living."[59] They lament in passing the lack of engagement in their sample of ethnographic methods, policy questions such as privacy, financial concerns, users' emotions and psychological states, or ethical questions. Instead, the literature they review refers overwhelmingly to only the technological characteristics of "smart home" systems and does so in a manner we might term technologically determinist as well as a direct result of an unquestioned and unreflective technological enthusiasm. Why did they observe such a result? They relied on Scopus to generate their sample.

Scopus's overwhelming emphasis is on STEM disciplines, and the most represented genres are papers published in scientific journals and scientific reports. There are few if any humanistic investigations represented in the database and few books and chapters in books, much more common in the humanities and some social scientific disciplines. Thus, STEM disciplines and their defining genres are disproportionately represented in the database and, therefore, in their sample. Thus, description of technological characteristics dominated their sample and why they found little engagement with wider topics related to "smart home" users and little skepticism about technological and commercial claims about "smart homes."

Rapoport identifies five characteristics of home surveillance technologies, or systems, that do the following:

1. "continuously observe particular zones (rooms, outdoor spaces, thresholds) and architectural elements (doors, windows, gates) in order to prevent unwanted and unaccepted access/penetration into dwelling areas"
2. "monitor undesired and disorderly behavior within the home, such as those of service providers (nannies, hired caregivers, etc.) and family members (teenagers)"
3. "simulate/replace humans in their capacity as caregivers (who monitor and supervise the elderly, infirm, handicapped, and young)"
4. are "used as deterrents (mostly against in intrusion by unwanted strangers) and in order to record and store data"
5. "monitor the presence of residents in order to adjust ambient conditions accordingly" (e.g., heating, cooling, lighting, power usage, and food preparation)[60]

This typology, as well as the descriptions above, give us an indication of some of the reasons that "smart homes" are attractive to various people in the United States (and beyond). It is worthwhile to review some of the empirical data that show why "smart homes" are built and/or retrofitted. There is a growing literature to help us understand this phenomenon, especially a growing number of small-scale empirical studies and surveys, mostly by personal interview. There are no substantial large-scale surveys (wide but usually shallow investigations) about attitudes toward "smart homes," although such studies are likely to be done in the near future, often in concert with a growing number of empirical studies (deeper but more narrow research). The data from the smaller studies discussed below, however, show considerable consistency and what many researchers call data saturation, indicating a growing likelihood that many (but not all) of the most important of the attitudes about "smart homes" are beginning to be identified.

Why Do People Choose "Smart Homes"?

Friedewald and colleagues emphasize that an important goal of home automation, including automation itself and security, is achievement of the long-held hope of "a future home equipped with technical devices that reduce burdens and make life easier."[61] But they ask, "Will it fulfil the promises or is it just an illusion—offering apparently easy living while actually increasing the complexity of life?"[62] More specific goals include support of the independent living of older persons and others with mobility and other significant physical limitations by (1) monitoring their health, safety, physical location, and other characteristics but also (2) having the ability to "compensate [for] possible functional impairments" (e.g., through remote control of doors and appliances), (3) increasing security (by having caregivers notified about fire and burglary alarms as well as the use of automatic protection mechanisms for appliances such as ovens and irons), and (4) most importantly to some researchers and smart home occupants, providing the ability to communicate from remote locations with people at home.

Not only are these benefits of integrated security and surveillance systems according to Friedewald and colleagues important in themselves, but independent living and enhanced communication afforded by such systems can increase the ability of homebound persons to participate in civil society and their ability to influence public decisions, findings echoed by many of the technology enthusiasts who dominate the literature review by Marikyan and colleagues.[63] Other goals of such systems that Friedewald and colleagues mention are the enhancement of rest/sleep, increased personal hygiene, entertainment and participation in hobbies, and physical fitness and participation in sports (think of streaming fitness apps related to home workouts, yoga, cycling, and so on).

Zheng and colleagues' 2018 interview study with "smart home" owners revealed a number of reasons that these homes attract buyers and remodelers. Two reasons are particularly prominent and supported by many other studies. The first is their informants' interest in "seamlessly integrating the physical and digital worlds inside the home," reminding us that "smart" devices of all kinds look to make digital or encode the world around us, including our homes. The second theme to underscore strongly in Zheng and colleagues' study is related to the first—the fact that "convenience and connectedness are [high] priorities for smart home owners, and these values dictate privacy opinions and behaviors directed at external entities that create, manage, track, or regulate IoT devices and their data." The primacy of convenience runs clearly through this study and other empirical investigations of what "smart home" inhabitants want. Convenience is "a primary justification for sacrificing privacy for IoT device owners" more broadly,[64] as is concern about the benefits from external entities for surrendering information about the home and its occupants' behaviors (more on this below).

Zheng and colleagues' study provides a number of statements from their participants that provide us with important insight into those informants' reasoning as well as attitudes and affect about "smart homes":[65]

- Respondent 5—"It's cool and also convenient. I can control my lights with my voice, which is pretty nice."
- Respondent 4—"controlling the thermostat from one's phone rather than at the thermostat panel was important [because] . . . it's more convenient to be under your warm covers and not have to run downstairs and check the temperature."
- Respondent 7—feels "a huge sense of closeness to my family just checking in on them . . . [e.g.,] the lamp's on by my husband's chair, he must be sitting there reading, or . . . if it's extra warm in there [the kitchen] they might be cooking dinner. It's like being with my family when I'm not."
- Respondent 8—"In terms of big data there's continuously going to be a trade-off, right? I would be willing to give up a bit of privacy to create *a seamless experience* because it makes life easier. . . . It feels as a consumer, if there is a better, *more seamless experience* to advertise to me, like I should benefit in some way" [emphasis added].

Importantly to considering surveillance, Zheng and colleagues conclude that since smart home users interacted with their IoT devices primarily by cell phone apps, a fundamental challenge is to design creative means of protecting privacy without completely compromising users' ability to use "smart home" and IoT devices relatively conveniently.[66]

In her 2016 paper, Liisa Mäkinen notes that ads for integrated "smart home" security systems emphasize protecting not just property but the family as well, a particularly important characteristic since many of her informants used such systems in their vacation or other second homes. She offers a four-part typology of surveillance in the homes of her informants and expands on the meaning of this typology:

1. Protection or controlling surveillance of the home—noting a reaction in part to the contemporary atmosphere of fear of crime where it is "better to be safe than sorry" (as articulated in this context by sociologist of fear Frank Furedi in 2002), accompanied by a faith that records of such surveillance will not be abused by system operators and monitors. Mäkinen discusses related research showing that "people frequently place blind trust in these systems" to deter, observe, and contribute to the prosecution of criminals "recognized" by home surveillance systems. Her respondents shared this faith.
2. Caring surveillance of family members or pets—which Mäkinen further clarifies as "sincere" surveillance; for example, the motive of their surveillance of their home is not spying or eavesdropping but care for children, disabled family members, pets, and others who cannot care fully for themselves. Her informants maintained that "a child is watched in order to ensure his safety, but that watching is not to be done without him being aware of it. The situation where adult family members were monitored happened mainly in the context of bi-directional communication," noted in item 4 below.
3. Recreational surveillance—such as using home surveillance cameras for "playful or social purposes or merely to pass the time" or to observe wildlife, natural settings, and the weather, particularly at vacation homes; she mentions related research that discuss uses such as voluntary self-display and participation in surveillance games on the internet.
4. Communicational surveillance—to communicate directly and conveniently with family members in the home where the "'camera becomes a proxy for human presence.'"[67]

As Mäkinen shows, the categories in this typology are not mutually exclusive, but they do give us further insight into why "smart homes" are attractive. Recalling the analysis of surveillance advertisements' appeal to emotions in Koskela,[68] Mäkinen says that such ads (1) exaggerate the success of such systems in deterring crime, (2) reach out to potential customers as "informed consumers," and (3) emphasize how the purchase and use of such integrated surveillance systems show that the customers are acting as responsible parents, partners, and pet owners. This last point brings to mind the similar ideological work done in the nineteenth century by the concept of so-called separate spheres and the cult of domesticity discussed above.

In their review of 143 papers about "smart homes" from 2002 to 2017, Marikyan and colleagues reiterate many of these rationales for the building, remodeling, or choosing of "smart homes" by their inhabitants.[69] For example, they found that studies of "smart homes" and their IoT offerings of interest to buyers included controlling and monitoring IoT devices and services, energy management and sustainability, cost efficiency, comfort (e.g., automation of daily routine tasks and remote management of home access), emotional support (e.g., robotic companions and rehabilitation devices, audible beacons, and remote control tied to voice recognition), a general sense of security, support of health care for oneself and family members (e.g., wearable sensors, temperature sensors, video displays for those with hearing challenges, and telemedicine), and general quality of life.[70] Their table 3 summarizes potential and perceived benefits for users of "smart home" adoption, identifying short-term and long-term benefits.[71] The long-term benefits include promotion of the well-being of older persons (mentioned in forty-one papers they reviewed), reduction of the carbon footprint and an increase in environmental sustainability (in twenty-eight papers), increasing the affordability of health care (twenty-four papers), and overcoming social isolation (eight papers).

The respondents in Zeng and colleagues' study mentioned the importance of these devices to their integrated and interconnected use of a "smart home": lights, "intelligent" digital personal assistants, thermostats, power outlets and switches, motion sensors, integrating electronic hubs for the system, door locks, smoke detectors, and leak detectors.[72] Their respondents, like those in other studies mentioned here,[73] expressed wide lack of concern about any privacy and security problems of which they were aware related to ownership of "smart homes." They articulated four reasons for their lack of worry: trust in managers of their systems and in the large companies handling their data (e.g., Amazon and Facebook), their belief that they were not "worthwhile targets" of security adversaries (not considering widespread denial-of-service attacks that have affected similarly "unworthwhile" targets), an assertion that they had "nothing to hide," and their faith that they had sufficiently secured all parts of their "smart homes" and their integration with the IoT in part because of some respondents' technological expertise.

These rationales and opinions of "smart home" owners and others, especially as supported by lists of characteristics of home surveillance systems, seem overwhelmingly if not entirely positive. Further, one of the touchstones of the field of information studies and other disciplines that study people's uses of all kinds of information and communication technologies (ICTs) is that users are the experts about their own attitudes, beliefs, and reasons for action. But, given that fundamental commitment to the user perspective, the study of ICTs involves many kinds of investigations, many kinds of methods, and many sources and kinds of evidence. It is useful, then, to recall the discursive and ideological work that the apparently innocent listing of technical capabilities of ICT systems and users' enthusiasms for technologies do. Particularly valuable is remembering that the costs of surveillance, particularly at home, are usually hidden and often emergent.

A Counternarrative about Privacy, "Smart Homes," and the IoT

As noted above, the many conveniences and functions that "smart homes" offer are considerable, as are the many costs affiliated with them. Fifteen years ago, Friedewald and colleagues articulated a series of warnings about ambient computing, an earlier analogue to ubiquitous computing, the IoT, and "smart" devices we now speak about. These problems included the following:

- Cognitive and emotional overload managing devices and the informated household
- Intentional or unintentional misuse of data gathered by such devices
- Malfunctions of devices, services, and systems
- Obsolescence of those devices, services, and systems
- Undermining appreciation of the embodied, material experience of being human, "promoting an extreme dematerialization of the body," especially for older people[74]

They continue with a special warning against losing sight of the fact that "there is no typical, uniform user and use but rather a diversity of users and uses . . . [because device and service providers] generally have difficulties in understanding the user market in a qualitative way." Certainly, that last concern about the limited understanding of users continues to be true but in ways they could not have anticipated. The growth of connectivity, the IoT, and, most important, information capitalism and surveillance capitalism provide no incentive whatsoever for device and service providers to understand and protect users' interest beyond their roles as consumers and sources of increasingly valuable data profiles. Friedewald and colleagues' warnings were cogent then and continue to be even more so today as demonstrated by the growing research about "smart" devices, whether in the home or elsewhere. What they left out, of course, was an explicit consideration of surveillance per se even though it was an underlying theme of their list of problems of ubiquitous computing.

Among the expected boons of ubiquitous computing that Friedewald and colleagues mentioned are clearly ambivalent and problematic. One is what they identify as the need to meet increased expectations of home hygiene and cleanliness, recalling Cowan in *More Work for Mother* and others. On a related note, such systems can increase the amount of unpaid work in the home, including the time, cognitive burden, and frustration of configuring and maintaining such complex systems. Further, the enhanced ability to work at home is, at best, a mixed blessing, as work encroaches on our time, familial relations, and consciousness on an increasingly 24/7 schedule.

While space limitations prohibit a deep dive here into the many and broad literatures cataloging privacy concerns about all things "smart," a brief mention of more themes not yet discussed is worthwhile. Among the specific themes of the literature about "smart homes" and their extensions of "smart neighborhoods" and "smart cities" are the intrusive use of "lifestyle" and health monitoring, especially of older adults and persons with intellectual disabilities, often without their knowledge or explicit permission. That concern intensifies because of intellectual impairments, whether congenital, the result of injury or disease (e.g., dementia), or the result of age-related cognitive decline. Also particularly problematic is the increased surveillance of the poor, people of color, and those in neighborhoods with ethnic, linguistic, and religious minority groups. Such surveillance involves but is not limited to the increased use of predictive policing and related governmental modes to effect surveillance using data mining and the predictive algorithms of sophisticated data analytics. A last general theme to note here of concern to millions of users is how voice-controlled digital assistants (especially as integrating controls for "smart homes," such as Google Home and Amazon Echo/Alexa, as long as they have power, are always on, are always listening, and are able to activate even without the use of their start words.

Just as Sadowski and Bendor remind us about "smart cities," we can see "smart homes" as an example of the production of "crises and technological salvation" from the partnership of commercial and state organizations.[75] The commercial and governmental narrative emphasizes a politics of danger and insecurity, energy waste, financial exigencies, and even care and more as threats and the necessity of ubiquitous surveillance for "our own protection" and to protect and care for our families. We must do better than sheepishly accept this sort of ideological and political claim wrapped in information-technological inevitabilism as noted in Zuboff's epigraph above. As citizens, scholars, and home dwellers, we must muster appropriate skepticism, not dismissive cynicism, about these sorts of claims. To do so is imperative. Not to do so leaves us as targets, individually, as families, and as home dwellers, of predatory data collection, data mining, pattern analysis, and predictive analytics. In that vision, we are not human beings but rather data objects to be manipulated and taken advantage of, even at home.

Google's Nest Thermostats: An Abbreviated Case Study

While in-home thermostats have long been standard in many if not most homes in the United States, so-called smart thermostats are key parts of the "smart home" and the IoT. The Nest thermostat from Google is a useful case study for specifying the functionalities of such devices, their surveillance capabilities, how they are advertised and discursively constructed, and their critiques. Alphabet (Google's parent holding company) purchased Nest's home company and then merged it with Google in 2018. Currently, Nest resides at the Google Store and has a full panoply of "smart home" and security devices: thermostats, cameras, doorbells, a fully integrated alarm system, door and window locks, and carbon monoxide and smoke alarms. One of the Nest thermostats is advertised as a "learning" thermostat as compared to programmable thermostats, which Nest advertising identifies as incapable of saving much energy.[76] Instead, this particular Nest model learns, and "Learning changed everything," illustrative of the usual hyperbole that characterizes much of marketing, especially of digital and other "high-tech" devices and services.

Another recent Nest thermostat ad asks,

> Why should you have to figure out your thermostat? The Nest Thermostat learns from you. Just turn it up and down for the first few days. The Nest Thermostat will get to know the temperatures you like and when you like them. Then it programs itself and creates a schedule for you. The Nest Thermostat even learns from your home and figures out how it heats or cools, because no two homes are exactly the same.

The emphasis here is on the device's ability to save energy (estimates range from 10 to 12 percent on heating and 15 percent on cooling) when compared to other thermostats, whether programmable or not, to make the household more efficient, both by the device's own "intelligence" and by its ability to interface with other systems. These systems include cell phones, the electrical power grid, locks, cars, appliances such as stoves and ovens, Wi-Fi systems, digital beds, personal fitness devices, key fobs, garage door openers, and lighting and audio/video systems. Using algorithms based on what is commonly referred to as "artificial intelligence," the ad describes Nest's other functions such as these:

- "It learns what you like," including preferred times to go to sleep and when to rise and preferred temperatures in the house at those times.

- "It knows when you're away," adjusting the heating or cooling temperature to preferred levels for when the house is empty. It uses its own sensors and geo-location of cell phones synchronized with the system as well as the ability to integrate with varying levels of success with home security systems.
- "It learns about your home."
- "Control it from anywhere" by cell phone with the Nest app.

Nest thermostats use motion sensors as well as indoor and outdoor cameras, some with facial recognition and communication functions, to enhance their connectivity and power.

But all is not well here. Zuboff warns that the terms of service and oppressive privacy policies from Nest/Google enable information about homes and their inhabitants to be shared "with other smart devices, unnamed personnel, and third parties for the purposes of predictive analyses and sales to other unspecified parties."[77] Not only are we the products rather than just the customers of such devices and services, but, as known widely, we provide the training set for advancing the power, adaptability, and applicability of predictive analytic systems. We enable their so-called machine learning, thereby exposing ourselves, homes, and families to further predations of parties over whom we and the U.S. government have little power.

Zuboff notes that, should a Nest purchaser refuse to accept the conditions about data collection, sharing, and analysis imposed by Google,

> the terms of service indicate that the functionality and security of the thermostat will be deeply compromised, no longer supported by the necessary updates meant to ensure its reliability and safety. The consequences can range from frozen pipes to failed smoke alarms to an easily hacked internal home system.[78]

This example illustrates how systems meant to inspire confidence about their ability to protect one's home and increase its efficiency can, in fact, be the precise means to make one's home *unsafe*, more vulnerable to failures of many kinds, and more exposed to bad actors as well as accidents.

While there is a large literature about these kinds of "unintended" (sometimes termed "iatrogenic") consequences in science and technology studies, Mäkinen's 2016 empirical study of "smart home" owners in Finland illustrates a similar concern. More specifically, respondents in her study discuss their unease that, while a security system is installed to protect the family from unwanted intrusion, Wi-Fi cameras' observations in particular can be intercepted in real time or broken into afterward.[79] I term this situation the *paradox of exposure*, part of many "smart home" owners' reactions to the IoT-connected security systems they use.

Apthorpe and colleagues show clearly the ease with which the packet streams that make up network traffic can be separated into those specific to each of the four widely available "smart" devices used in their study: a Sense sleep monitor, a Nest Cam indoor security camera, a Belkin WeMo switch, and an Amazon Echo. Internet Wi-Fi traffic patterns and the associated metadata can reveal sensitive information *"even when traffic ... is encrypted."*[80] A passive observer, such as an internet service provider (cited as a particular concern of many of the technically savvy respondents in Zheng and colleagues' study),[81] can use only the send/receive rates of each device to determine users' behavior, including when they were sleeping or simply in bed, the presence of motion in the house and its frequency, a state change from off to on or vice versa of the switch, and usage spikes when using the Echo.[82] Encryption alone could not prevent the determination of such private behavior in the home, even with no need to examine the packets themselves, posing nettling concerns about privacy, physical security, security of electrical power, vulnerability to advertisers, and more.

This brief look at Nest, other devices, and the problems that their always-on surveillance poses is a useful way to focus concerns about privacy, surveillance, and "smart homes." Apthorpe and colleagues remind us why "smart home" devices and the IoT are of increasing concern: they "encode the physical world in network traffic."[83] That does *not* mean that we blithely accept the reduction of people and their behavior to data for the surveillance machine of government and private enterprise. Instead, it means that we need to understand this simple fact of representation in order to conceptualize, communicate, and address the concerns that these technologies and business practices give rise to in the context of home. As this volume demonstrates, information studies has much to add to that discussion.

CONSIDERING HOW INFORMATION STUDIES CONTRIBUTES TO THE QUESTION ABOUT WHERE TO LIVE

One can respond to the question in two registers, the first in general terms, the second in more domain-specific terms. To begin, one of our field's primary strengths is its theoretical and methodological sophistication and catholicity as well as our centuries-long understanding of the phenomenological complexity of social life (including at home) and information's role in it. Information studies scholars have a long history of contributions to both theoretical and empirical understandings of topics related to how we decide where to live (e.g., of people's information behavior), ranging across user studies, use of critical incident techniques, policy research, user experience and human–computer interaction scholarship, historical research, surveys, and more in an integrated methodological toolkit. The field's emphasis on rigorous empirical investigations of individuals and groups, based on sound and deep theoretical footings, provides unique perspectives on how people in America go about deciding where to live.

Further, information studies has expertise in and dedication to the public interest, operationalized by, for example, the following:

- A skeptical attitude toward technophoria, or the breathless enthusiasm for digital technologies in particular, especially their newest evolutions
- A pragmatic and realistic approach to the evaluation of information technology systems and applications hand in hand with the reasonably skeptical attitude about blind enthusiasms mentioned above
- A wide interpretation of what the manifold public interests are both when they intersect with commercial interests and when they do not
- A deep understanding of the nature, weaknesses, and strengths of the use of particular databases for doing research

In addition, however, information studies has special expertise in considering privacy, surveillance, and home.

Such expertise includes the ability to problematize any utopian or dystopian fantasies about the IoT as well as about "smart" cities, "smart neighborhoods," and "smart" homes. Further, even though information studies privileges the category "information," it also exercises some skepticism about the ideology of information that dominates contemporary culture.[84] It is an especially acute need for all concerned citizens and academics to contribute their critical faculties to embrace and question our informated moment. Information studies contributes to undermining the belief that increasingly ubiquitous surveillance, information capitalism generally, and surveillance capitalism are desirable, unquestionable, and inevitable. They are not.

CONCLUSION

In his well-known presidential address to the Society for the History of Technology in 1985, subsequently published in the society's major organ, *Technology and Culture*, Melvin Kranzberg emphasized the importance of what we term the sociotechnical view of technology. He argued that we need to examine "the significance in human affairs of the history of technology and the value of the contextual approach in understanding technical developments."[85] This perspective favors neither the social nor the technical in understanding how technologies develop, are adopted, are adapted, are deployed, are used, and evolve—fully embracing both the social and the technical elements of this constantly unfolding story.

In the address, Kranzberg postulated his now famous, gnomic first law of technology: technology is neither good nor bad nor neutral. He explains that it is the duty of scholars, especially historians, to

> compare short-term versus long-term results, the utopian hopes versus the spotted actuality, the what-might-have-been against what actually happened, and the trade-offs among various "goods" and possible "bads." All this can be done only by seeing how technology interacts in different ways with different values and institutions, indeed with the entire sociocultural milieu.[86]

This chapter operationalizes Kranzberg's scholarly call to arms by examining utopian claims, hopes, and beliefs about "smart homes," especially in the technical and other literatures that feature hyperbolic claims of unbridled technical boosterism in public and private sectors. The chapter has compared such technophoria to more tempered, realistic, and contextualizing perspectives on "smart homes." In particular, we have seen that the surveillance properties of "smart homes," greatly desired and appreciated by some, are part of the expanding web of surveillance by private actors and governments, especially in the operation of information capitalism, surveillance capitalism, and post-9/11 securitization. Let us consider in closing what that complex situation means, especially for people deciding how and where to live.

In the absence of local, state, and federal regulation and legislation, the proliferation of surveillance in the United States not only will continue but also is likely to accelerate under the presumed imperatives of surveillance capitalism, digital triumphalism, and the cachet of "smart" devices. We are subjected to unrelenting surveillance in the workplace, in financial and commercial transactions, during our use of communication devices, on public transportation, in public spaces of all kinds, in travel, and even in political activity. Surveillance will continue its incursion into our homes as always-on "smart" devices and systems record, analyze, and share data about us in the IoT. There is and will be increasing pressure to participate in this rendition of our lives and the abstraction from our bodies that Zuboff and Rapoport describe in the epigraphs to this chapter.

Sadowski and Bendor remind us that any conversation about "smart" devices, home, neighborhoods, and cities, "like other sociotechnical imaginings . . . is a field of struggle over the political imagination." Similarly, as with the use of phrases such as "seamless experience" and emphasis on the primacy of "connectedness" noted below, locutions about technological "solutions" and the "smartness" of devices is "more than just an idle label." Citing the work of Ian Bogost, contributing writer at *The Atlantic*, they show that such locutions indicate surrender to technological thinking so that it dominates *all* modes of thinking.[87] For "smart home" and IoT enthusiasts, this is how things should be.

Considering How "Smart Homes" and Surveillance Influence Where We Live

As noted at the beginning of this chapter, digital connectivity and the ability to integrate "smart" devices throughout a home's functions are criteria for potential buyers, renters, and remodelers to consider about where to live. Zheng and colleagues' respondents had little demonstrable concern with privacy beyond some general reservations. Most of these reservations were made moot by their participants' faith in brand-name devices and service providers so that their decisions were *not* "intentional purchasing and device interaction decisions made based on privacy considerations . . . situated in the everyday contexts of home routines,"[88] themes that appear in the general privacy and surveillance literatures. Despite its reductionism, it may be analytically useful to posit three kinds of decision makers in the context of "smart home" living: those who actively choose such homes, members of demographic and socioeconomic groups who have increased "smartness" thrust on them, and those who choose to minimize their participation in the IoT, especially at home.

The first group, as discussed throughout this chapter, comprises the many millions of our fellow citizens in the United States as well as elsewhere who actively seek out and embrace the "smart home." Convenience, protection of family members and property, increased interactive communication, modernity, and even recreation and the "cool factor" are the watchwords here. Of paramount importance from this perspective is the integration of "smart home" systems with cell phones and apps that millions of Americans use to define and organize their lives. Also important are the techno-fetishism noted above[89] and technophiliac imaginings[90] as well as "the technological way of life per se of many young urban people"[91] that has only intensified and accelerated. Many of the quotations in the work of Zheng and colleagues[92] are strong examples of this combination of techno-fetishism, industry capture of the users' self-image as consumers and as technically adept, and the importance of having "smart home" apps integrated with so-called smartphones, especially among the young and affluent. Marketing terms such as "seamless experience" and "connectedness" in their respondents' interviews show the triumph and effectiveness of techno-advertising and the related "smart" imaginary, especially among those financially able to invest in "smart homes" and other major IoT devices and services.

For IoT and "smart home" enthusiasts, however, there are additional important reasons for embracing these technologies, including ways to secure and to care for children, disabled family members, pets, and others. Looking at the surveillance of care more closely for a moment is enlightening. Research shows that home can provide children privacy to develop self-esteem and self-reliance, engage in "positive" social behavior, and individuate/separate from others.[93] However, as the empirical data discussed in the section on why people choose "smart homes" show, inhabitants of such homes develop practices to walk the fine line between the potentially oppressive surveillance of care on the one hand and respect for children's dignity and privacy on the other. These are strong reasons to purchase a "smart home."

In the increasingly fraught atmosphere of fear that characterizes many Americans' lives (whether of pandemics, political terrorism, financial ruin, and more), "smart homes" offer a sense of security. Rapoport says that "smart home" surveillance systems offer "confidence and freedom that is a result of their being watched, protected, and secured," leading to "a sense of physical and mental well-being."[94] The empirical findings discussed in this chapter and elsewhere certainly support this sense of protection of self, others, and property as the major attraction for "smart home" users in concert with the ever-present convenience.

In the context of "smart cities" and the ubiquitous sensing, data analysis, and comparisons in relational databases that characterize such informated places, we have reason to be skeptical. David Lyon reminds us, "If everyone is observed, automatically and constantly, questions about surveillance deserve to be raised."[95] What such unrelenting scrutiny means is multifaceted. Some of us have *little choice* but to more fully participate in surveillance even at home as our homes (especially rentals), neighborhoods, and cities are purportedly made "smarter." Particularly vulnerable groups include the poor and residents in majority-minority neighborhoods who are already disadvantaged by the discriminatory deployment of surveillance in many cities and the many hidden biases of data-analytic algorithms.[96] They are in a seriously disadvantaged position with little or no ability to choose being the target of "smart" devices or not. Our fellow citizens in these categories increasingly cannot escape, for example, the use of facial recognition technologies as suggested in New York City high-rise public housing projects, the deployment of additional police presence using predictive policing algorithms in cities large and small throughout the United States, the proliferation of tracking algorithms and data-analytic techniques in the criminal justice system, and other technologies.

While closed-circuit television (CCTV) cameras are deployed worldwide, a look at a September 2019 list of the most surveilled cities in the world measured by number of CCTV cameras per 1,000 inhabitants holds some value.[97] Chinese cities occupy the first five positions (and three other positions in the "top ten") with values ranging from 168 to 73.8

CCTV cameras per 1,000 inhabitants, while London, often presumed to be a leader in the use of such cameras, is in the sixth position with 68.4. What is of particular interest in this context, however, is that Atlanta ranks tenth with 15.6 CCTV cameras per 1,000 inhabitants, or 7,800 cameras for just over 500,000 inhabitants, the smallest city in the list by an order of magnitude and more. What makes this ranking noteworthy, of course, is Atlanta's position as the center for much of African American culture, education, and more. This situation is not entirely dispositive, certainly, but it indicates an oxymoron in thinking about "smart" locations and surveillance. More financially privileged actors in the first group discussed above embrace "smart homes," "smart neighborhoods," and "smart cities" and deliberately choose to move into them. At the same time, however, less advantaged, less mobile Americans often cannot move *out* of them. This situation, deeply involved with decisions about where to live, is a public policy matter of the first order, with implications well beyond concerns about surveillance in the "smart home."

The third group in this analysis includes people who choose to limit their participation in the IoT, especially by limiting or avoiding their use of "smart home" technologies. Among other criteria, such people may find ontological security, a concept from Anthony Giddens's book *The Consequences of Modernity*,[98] important in decisions about home. Dupuis and Thorns note that "Giddens . . . describes ontological security as the confidence that most human beings have in the continuity of their self-identity and in the constancy of their social and material environment."[99] Home serves those purposes in four ways:[100]

1. The constancy of social and material environments
2. Daily routines
3. Freedom from surveillance, providing a place where people "feel most in control of their lives"
4. A "secure base" for the construction of identities

Home, as the primary safeguard of privacy, for the family if not for the individual,[101] is for some a sort of "second body" ensuring our integrity, identity, and inviolability.[102] These are important elements in deciding where to live, not only for choosing one's home but also choosing the contexts of neighborhood and city.

Some of us will choose to live in "smart homes," "smart neighborhoods," and "smart cities" for the many opportunities, protections, and, often, conveniences they afford us. Some will not be able to choose in any meaningful way. Many of us, however, will choose *not* to live in "smart" environments in order, instead, to experience the remove, protections, and succor of home in ways that we could not otherwise.

In a variation on a well-known aphorism, variously attributed to Winston Churchill (about buildings) and media scholar John Culkin (about tools), we make our homes, and then our homes make us. They make us particularly by doing important boundary work distinguishing home from other places, and, to those of us concerned about surveillance and privacy at home and elsewhere, home provides a refuge from the unrelenting surveillance that characterizes our world. Clearly, choices about surveillance, "smart homes," and related technologies will increasingly determine where we live, how we live, and what home is.

NOTES

1. Shoshana Zuboff, *The Age of Surveillance Capitalism: The Fight for a Human Future at the New Frontier of Power* (New York: Public Affairs, 2019), 238.

2. Michele Rapoport, "The Home under Surveillance: A Tripartite Assemblage," *Surveillance & Society* 10, no. 3/4 (2012): 326.

3. Mike Crang and Stephen Graham, "Sentient Cities: Ambient Intelligence and the Politics of Urban Space," *Information, Communication & Society* 10, no. 6 (2007): 794ff.

4. Graham Burchell, Colin Gordon, and Peter Miller, eds., *The Foucault Effect: Studies in Governmentality* (Chicago: University of Chicago Press, 1991).

5. Louise Amoore, *The Politics of Possibility: Risk and Security beyond Probability* (Durham, NC: Duke University Press, 2013).

6. Amoore, *The Politics of Possibility*, 7, 8.

7. Michel Foucault, *Discipline and Punish: The Birth of the Prison*, trans. Alan Sheridan (New York: Pantheon, 1977); Sarah E. Igo, *Known Citizen: A History of Privacy in Modern America* (Cambridge, MA: Harvard University Press, 2018).

8. David Lyon, *The Electronic Eye: The Rise of Surveillance Society* (Cambridge: Polity Press, 1994), 14.

9. David Lyon, ed., *Surveillance as Social Sorting: Privacy, Risk and Digital Discrimination* (London: Routledge, 2003).

10. Oscar H. Gandy, "It's Discrimination, Stupid!," in *Resisting the Virtual Life: The Culture and Politics of Information*, ed. James Brook and Iain A. Boal, 35–47 (San Francisco: City Lights, 1995); Oscar H. Gandy, *Coming to Terms with Chance: Engaging Rational Discrimination and Cumulative Disadvantage* (London: Ashgate, 2010); Mary Madden, Michele Gilman, Karen Levy, and Alice Marwick, "Privacy, Poverty, and Big Data: A Matrix of Vulnerabilities for Poor Americans," *Washington University Law Review* 95, no. 1 (2017): 53–126; Safiya Umoja Noble, *Algorithms of Oppression: How Search Engines Reinforce Racism* (New York: New York University Press, 2018); Cathy O'Neil, *Weapons of Math Destruction: How Big Data Increases Inequality and Threatens Democracy* (New York: Crown/Random House, 2016).

11. Stuart Shapiro, "Places and Spaces: The Historical Interaction of Technology, Home, and Privacy," *The Information Society* 14, no. 4 (1998): 275–84.

12. Oscar H. Gandy, *The Panoptic Sort: A Political Economy of Personal Information* (Boulder, CO: Westview Press, 1993); Reg Whitaker, *The End of Privacy: How Total Surveillance Is Becoming a Reality* (New York: New Press, 1999).

13. David Lyon, ed., *Theorizing Surveillance: The Panopticon and Beyond* (Portland, OR: Willan, 2006); David Lyon, *The Culture of Surveillance: Watching as a Way of Life* (Cambridge: Polity Press, 2018); Masa Galic, Tjerk Timan, and Bert-Jaap Koops, "Bentham, Deleuze and Beyond: An Overview of Surveillance Theories from the Panopticon to Participation," *Philosophy & Technology* 30 (2017): 9–37; Zuboff, *The Age of Surveillance Capitalism*.

14. Foucault, *Discipline and Punish*.

15. Kevin D. Haggerty, "Tear Down the Walls: On Demolishing the Panopticon," in Lyon, *Theorizing Surveillance*, 23–45; Kevin D. Haggerty and Richard V. Ericson, "The Surveillant Assemblage," *British Journal of Sociology* 51, no. 4 (2000): 605–22.

16. Gandy, *The Panoptic Sort*; Gandy, "It's Discrimination, Stupid!"; Oscar H. Gandy, "Data Mining, Surveillance, and Discrimination in the Post-9/11 Environment," in *The New Politics of Surveillance and Visibility*, ed. Kevin D. Haggerty and Richard V. Ericson, 363–84 (Toronto: University of Toronto Press, 2003); Lyon, *Surveillance as Social Sorting*; Whitaker, *The End of Privacy*.

17. Helen N. Nissenbaum, "Privacy as Contextual Integrity," *Washington Law Review* 79, no. 1 (2004): 119–57; Helen N. Nissenbaum, *Privacy in Context: Technology, Policy, and the Integrity of Social Life* (Stanford, CA: Stanford Law Books, 2010).

18. Lyon, *The Culture of Surveillance*.

19. Shoshana Zuboff, "Big Other: Surveillance Capitalism and the Prospects of an Information Civilization," *Journal of Information Technology* 30 (2015): 75–89; Zuboff, *The Age of Surveillance Capitalism*.

20. Gandy, "Data Mining, Surveillance, and Discrimination in the Post-9/11 Environment"; Gandy, *Coming to Terms with Chance*; Noble, *Algorithms of Oppression*; O'Neil, *Weapons of Math Destruction*; Frank Pasquale, *The Black Box Society: The Secret Algorithms That Control Money and Information* (Cambridge, MA: Harvard University Press, 2015); Bruce Schneier, *Data and Goliath: The Hidden Battles to Collect Your Data and Control Your World* (New York: Norton, 2015).

21. U.S. Government Accountability Office, *Internet of Things: Status and Implications of an Increasingly Connected World*, GAO-17-75, 2017, https://www.gao.gov/assets/690/684590.pdf.

22. Ahmed Shuhaiber and Ibrahim Mashal, "Understanding Users' Acceptance of Smart Homes," *Technology in Society* 58 (2019): 101–2.

23. Eric Zeng, Shrirang Mare, and Franziska Roesner, "End User Security and Privacy Concerns with Smart Homes," *Proceedings of the Thirteenth Symposium on Usable Privacy and Security (SOUPS 2017)*, 2017, https://www.usenix.org/system/files/conference/soups2017/soups2017-zeng.pdf.

24. Zuboff, *The Age of Surveillance Capitalism*, 6.

25. Jathan Sadowski and Roy Bendor, "Selling Smartness: Corporate Narratives and the Smart City as a Sociotechnical Imaginary," *Science, Technology, & Human Values* 44, no. 3 (2019): 556.

26. Shapiro, "Places and Spaces," 275.

27. Rapoport, "The Home under Surveillance," 320, 322.

28. Rapoport, "The Home under Surveillance," 321–23, 327.

29. Rapoport, "The Home under Surveillance," 323.

30. Michael Friedewald, Olivier Da Costa, Yves Punie, Petteri Alahuhta, and Sirkka Heinonen, "Perspectives of Ambient Intelligence in the Home Environment," *Telematics and Informatics* 22 (2005): 224.

31. Anita L. Allen, *Uneasy Access: Privacy for Women in a Free Society* (Totowa, NJ: Rowman & Littlefield, 1988); Anita L. Allen, "Privacy Torts: Unreliable Remedies for LGBT Plaintiffs," in *Privacy in America: Interdisciplinary Perspectives*, ed. William Aspray and Philip Doty, 27–84 (Lanham, MD: Scarecrow Press, 2011); Anita L. Allen, *Unpopular Privacy: What Must We Hide?* (Oxford: Oxford University Press, 2011); Patricia Boling, *Privacy and the Politics of Intimate Life* (Ithaca, NY: Cornell University Press, 1996); Catherine A. MacKinnon, "Privacy and Equality: Beyond Roe v. Wade," in *Feminism Unmodified: Discourses on Life and Law*, 93–102 (Cambridge, MA: Harvard University Press, 1987).

32. Philip Doty, "Digital Privacy: Toward a New Politics and Discursive Practice," in *Annual Review of Information Science & Technology*, vol. 35, ed. Martha Williams, 192–98 (Medford, NJ: Information Today, 2001).

33. Ruth Schwartz Cowan, *More Work for Mother: The Ironies of Household Technology from the Open Hearth to the Microwave* (New York: Basic Books, 1983), 149.

34. Shapiro, "Places and Spaces," 281.

35. Rapoport, "The Home under Surveillance," 323.

36. Cowan, *More Work for Mother*; Ann Douglas, *The Feminization of American Culture* (New York: Farrar, Straus and Giroux, 1977); Linda K. Kerber, "Separate Spheres, Female Worlds, Woman's Place: The Rhetoric of Women's History," *Journal of American History* 75, no. 1 (1988): 9–39; Barbara Welter, "The Cult of True Womanhood, 1820–1860," *American Quarterly* 18, no. 2, pt. 1 (Summer 1966): 151–74.

37. Ruth Gavison, "Feminism and the Public/Private Distinction," *Stanford Law Review* 45, no. 1 (1992): 1–45; Judith A. McGaw, "No Passive Victims, No Separate Spheres: A Feminist Perspective on Technology's History," in *In Context: History and the History of Technology: Essays in Honor of Melvin Kranzberg*, ed. Stephen H. Cutcliffe and Robert C. Post, 172–91 (Bethlehem, PA: Lehigh University Press, 1989).

38. Rapoport, "The Home under Surveillance," 323.

39. Jerome Tognoli, "Residential Environments," in *Handbook of Environmental Psychology*, ed. Daniel Stokols and Irwin Altman, 655–90 (New York: John Wiley & Sons, 1987), 660.

40. On the influence of the work of these women, both individually and together, see also Cowan, *More Work for Mother*, 43ff.

41. Liisa A. Mäkinen, "Surveillance On/Off: Examining Home Surveillance Systems from the User's Perspective," *Surveillance & Society* 14, no. 1 (2016): 64.

42. Mäkinen, "Surveillance On/Off," 65 n. 3.

43. Mäkinen, "Surveillance On/Off," 72.

44. Cowan, *More Work for Mother*.

45. Cowan, *More Work for Mother*; Bonnie J. Fox, "Selling the Mechanized Household: 70 Years of Ads in *Ladies Home Journal*," *Gender & Society* 4, no. 1 (1990): 25–40.

46. Fox, "Selling the Mechanized Household."

47. Fox, "Selling the Mechanized Household," 28.

48. Fox, "Selling the Mechanized Household," 26.

49. Fox, "Selling the Mechanized Household," 28.

50. Hille Koskela, "'Capture Every Moment'—The Profane Semiotics of Surveillance Advertisements," *Social Semiotics* 24, no. 3 (2014): 324–44; Sadowski and Bendor, "Selling Smartness."

51. David E. Nye, *Technology Matters: Questions to Live With* (Cambridge, MA: MIT Press, 1987).
52. Sadowski and Bendor, "Selling Smartness," 325.
53. Koskela, "'Capture Every Moment,'" 326.
54. Koskela, "'Capture Every Moment,'" 326–27.
55. https://clockhistory.com/alarmClockHistory.
56. Google Ngram viewer, https://books.google.com/ngrams#.
57. For an engaging and theoretically rich discussion of the need for definitional clarity in discussing "smart" things, especially given their remarkable diversity, see Steven Alter, "Making Sense of Smart Living, Working, and Organizing Enhanced by Supposedly Smart Objects and Systems," in *Smart Working, Living and Organising*, ed. Elbanna Amany, Yogesh K. Dwivedi, Deborah Bunker, and David Wastell, 247–60 (Cham: Springer, 2018).
58. Alter, "Making Sense of Smart Living, Working, and Organizing Enhanced by Supposedly Smart Objects and Systems," 5.
59. Davit Marikyan, Savvas Papagiannidis, and Eleftherios Alamanos, "A Systematic Review of the Smart Home Literature: A User Perspective," *Technological Forecasting & Social Change* 138 (2019): 139.
60. Rapoport, "The Home under Surveillance," 324 n. 10.
61. Friedewald et al., "Perspectives of Ambient Intelligence in the Home Environment," 235.
62. Friedewald et al., "Perspectives of Ambient Intelligence in the Home Environment," 221.
63. Marikyan et al., "A Systematic Review of the Smart Home Literature."
64. Serena Zheng, Noah Apthorpe, Marshini Chetty, and Nick Feamster, "User Perceptions of Smart Home IoT Privacy," *Proceedings ACM Human-Computer Interaction* 2, no. CSCW, Article 200 (2018): 2.
65. Zheng et al., "User Perceptions of Smart Home IoT Privacy," 9ff.
66. Zheng et al., "User Perceptions of Smart Home IoT Privacy," 15; see also Rene Cardona Jr., "Is My Smart Home a Private Home? Improving the User Experience of Consent and Privacy Awareness of Internet-Connected Home Devices," master's thesis, University of Texas, Austin, 2017.
67. Mäkinen, "Surveillance On/Off," citing John MacGregor Wise, 425.
68. Koskela, "'Capture Every Moment.'"
69. Marikyan et al., "A Systematic Review of the Smart Home Literature."
70. Marikyan et al., "A Systematic Review of the Smart Home Literature," tables 1 and 2, 144, 146.
71. Marikyan et al., "A Systematic Review of the Smart Home Literature," 147.
72. Zeng et al., "End User Security and Privacy Concerns with Smart Homes," table 2, 69.
73. Mäkinen, "Surveillance On/Off"; Zheng et al., "User Perceptions of Smart Home IoT Privacy."
74. Friedewald et al., "Perspectives of Ambient Intelligence in the Home Environment," 236.
75. Sadowski and Bendor, "Selling Smartness," 540.
76. Nest.com (accessed March 13, 2020).
77. Zuboff, *The Age of Surveillance Capitalism*, 6–7.

78. Zuboff, *The Age of Surveillance Capitalism*, 7.
79. Mäkinen, "Surveillance On/Off," 72.
80. Noah Apthorpe, Dillon Reisman, and Nick Feamster, "A Smart Home Is No Castle: Privacy Vulnerabilities of Encrypted IoT Traffic," 2017, https://arxiv.org/abs/1705.06805, 1, emphasis added.
81. Zheng et al., "User Perceptions of Smart Home IoT Privacy."
82. Apthorpe et al., "A Smart Home Is No Castle," 2–3.
83. Apthorpe et al., "A Smart Home Is No Castle," 4.
84. Jean-François Blanchette, "A Material History of Bits," *Journal of the American Society for Information Science and Technology* 62, no. 6 (2011): 1042–57; Ronald E. Day, "Poststructuralism and Information Studies," in *Annual Review of Information Science and Technology*, vol. 39, ed. Martha Williams, 575–609 (Medford, NJ: Information Today, 2005); Philip Doty and Ramona Broussard, "Fiction as Informative and Its Implications for Information Science Theory," *Proceedings of the Association for Information Science and Technology* 54, no. 1 (2017): 61–70, https://doi.org/10.1002/pra2.2017.14505401008; Bernd Frohmann, *Deflating Information: From Science Studies to Documentation* (Toronto: University of Toronto Press, 2004); Geoffrey Nunberg, "Farewell to the Information Age," in *The Future of the Book*, 103–33 (Berkeley: University of California Press, 1996).
85. Melvin Kranzberg, "Technology and History: 'Kranzberg's Laws,'" *Technology and Culture* 27, no. 3 (1986): 544.
86. Kranzberg, "Technology and History," 547–48.
87. Sadowski and Bendor, "Selling Smartness," 552–53.
88. Zheng et al., "User Perceptions of Smart Home IoT Privacy," 2.
89. Koskela, "'Capture Every Moment.'"
90. Crang and Graham, "Sentient Cities," 804–5.
91. Friedewald et al., "Perspectives of Ambient Intelligence in the Home Environment," 224.
92. Zheng et al., "User Perceptions of Smart Home IoT Privacy," esp. 9–11.
93. Tognoli, "Residential Environments," 661.
94. Rapoport, "The Home under Surveillance," 328.
95. Lyon, *The Culture of Surveillance*, 100.
96. Gandy, "It's Discrimination, Stupid!"; Gandy, "Data Mining, Surveillance, and Discrimination in the Post-9/11 Environment"; Gandy, *Coming to Terms with Chance*; Lyon, *Surveillance as Social Sorting*; Madden et al., "Privacy, Poverty, and Big Data"; Noble, *Algorithms of Oppression*; O'Neil, *Weapons of Math Destruction*.
97. https://www.statista.com/chart/19256/the-most-surveilled-cities-in-the-world.
98. Anthony Giddens, *The Consequences of Modernity* (Stanford, CA: Stanford University Press, 1990).
99. Ann Dupuis and David C. Thorns, "Home, Home Ownership and the Search for Ontological Security," *Sociological Review* 46, no. 1 (1998): 27.
100. Dupuis and Thorns, "Home, Home Ownership and the Search for Ontological Security," 29.
101. Shapiro, "Places and Spaces," 278.
102. Kirsten Jacobson, "A Developed Nature: A Phenomenological Account of the Experience of Home," *Continental Philosophical Review* 42 (2009): 355–73.

Five

This Old House, *Fixer Upper*, and *Better Homes and Gardens*

The Housing Crisis and Media Sources

Melissa G. Ocepek

"Home is where the heart is," "Home away from home," and "Go big or go home" are just some of the dozens of clichés we have in America that emphasize the centrality of home to our language and our lives. The concept of home is multifaceted, complex, and shifting. How one feels about one's home can be just as dynamic. The 2007 housing crisis led to a long and difficult economic recession in the United States and around the world that affected global markets, industries, and the way millions of people felt about their home. During times of uncertainty and chaos, many people take emotional as well as physical shelter in their safe spaces: spaces where they can turn on the TV, curl up with some light reading, and forget about their problems. For millions of Americans, home and garden programming, twenty-four hours of which can be found every day on HGTV, and home and garden magazines offer a beautiful, calming escape.

HGTV came into my life when I was the most unsettled, nearing the end of graduate school with an unknown future ahead. I found *House Hunters*, *Flip or Flop*, and *Love It or List It* the perfect antidotes to the anxiety and existential dread that comes from large-scale life change. I was following a trend that the creator and former head of HGTV, Kenneth Lowe, identified in 1995 when he told the Associated Press,

> Some people live in an apartment, some in a half-million dollar home. Yet their common interest is that sanctuary where they live.... The passion is the same, and the sensibility is the same—improving your home. *There is nothing new here. It is the cocooning trend.*[1]

"Cocooning" is a term used throughout the coverage of the rise of HGTV as one of the most watched cable networks.[2] The concept comes from futurist Faith Popcorn and is described in her book *The Popcorn Report* as "the impulse to go *inside* when it just gets too tough and scary *outside* . . . a sort of hyper-nesting."[3] Popcorn has used her concept, first developed in the late 1970s, to help explain the success of HGTV and home and garden magazines in the mid-1990s.

Whether or not it is true, cocooning has become a major way that many journalists and popular media critics describe the success of home and garden sources in the mid-1990s, including the launch of HGTV in 1994.[4] The term came back into usage with a new focus after 9/11. Steve Thomas, host of *Ask This Old House* (a *This Old House* spin-off), reflected on the popularity of his show and other home and garden sources since 9/11, saying, "The trend that used to be called 'cocooning' was in place before 9/11, but that [event] helped sharpen people's focus [on their home]."[5] As the world seemed to become more chaotic, more people spent more time with the comfort of home and garden sources.

The one force that could maybe break people out of their cocoons and time spent watching HGTV or flipping through *Better Homes and Gardens* might have been the housing crisis. The chaos and uncertainty of the world around us was suddenly put on display with for-sale signs, abandoned building projects, and eviction notices. The housing crisis serves as an important backdrop to explore how mass media home and garden sources influence narratives around home ownership and the ideal of home in the United States. To begin this exploration, I briefly summarize the housing crisis and its effect on opinions on home ownership, followed by a brief description of information sources derived from the scholarly tradition of library and information science. I then present a brief history of two of the most prevalent forms of home and garden information sources—magazines and television—including a brief discussion of HGTV's theorized role in the crisis. Before describing the trends present in home and garden sources, I briefly describe my data collection methods and analysis before articulating my findings and concluding thoughts.

THE HOUSING CRISIS

The U.S. housing crisis, also known as the subprime mortgage crisis, lasted roughly from 2007 through 2011. Before the crisis, in 2006, until its end, in 2011, housing prices declined more than 30 percent nationally, and $8 trillion in home equity was lost.[6] Between 2008 and 2011, approximately 4 million home owners had their homes foreclosed on in addition to the one-quarter of home owners whose home values sunk below the amount they owed on their mortgages.[7]

In Phoenix, home prices declined by 56 percent during the crisis, making it only the third-worst-affected area.[8] In Florida, a report using Zillow home pricing statistics found that statewide home prices fell 52.7 percent from the peak in April 2006 to the trough in October 2011.[9] Recent reports have found that mainly Black and Hispanic communities experienced many of the worst rates of foreclosure. Communities that are mainly Black and Hispanic experienced foreclosures at 2 and 2.5 times higher rates, respectively, than white communities between January 2007 and December 2015. Foreclosed homes in these communities also experienced a greater decrease in value than homes in white communities and compared to all homes nationally.[10] In certain metropolitan areas, the foreclosure rates were far worse. For example, Minneapolis, Boston, Cleveland, and San Francisco all had more than three times the foreclosure rates in Black than in white communities, while Hispanic communities experienced 3 and 3.3 times the foreclosure rates in New York and San Francisco, respectively, and 4.1 and 4.5 times in Boston and San Jose, respectively.

The housing crisis was the epicenter of the Great Recession: the longest recession in the United States since World War II. The Great Recession began in December 2007 and lasted until June 2009.[11] In addition to being long, the Great Recession was quite severe. The U.S. real gross domestic product fell 4.3 percent, the largest decline since World War II, and the unemployment rate doubled from 5 percent in December 2007 to 10 percent in October 2009.[12] The net worth of U.S. households and nonprofit organizations fell from approximately $69 trillion in 2007 to $55 trillion in 2009.

All the economic indicators also speak to a larger psychological toll of uncertainty, loss, and fear experienced by many Americans. The combination of the housing crisis and the Great Recession increased stress-related health problems throughout the United States, including decreased fertility rates, decreased self-rated health, and increased morbidity, psychological distress, and suicide.[13] For the millions directly affected by the housing crisis and the Great Recession, their safe cocoons were becoming the cause of much chaos and uncertainty.

AFTER THE CRASH: OPINIONS ON HOME OWNERSHIP FOLLOWING THE HOUSING CRISIS

The housing crisis and the Great Recession affected Americans in myriad ways. Millions lost their homes, jobs, and savings that were tied up in the stock market. Americans also were faced with a new and unsettling reality: their homes were no longer the safe economic investment they had come to count on. Many people looked at their homes and their economic futures differently during the height of the crisis. A report by the Joint Center for Housing Studies at Harvard University found that the housing crisis did negatively impact Americans' views on the benefits of home ownership but that those declines were short lived.[14] The report found that

> the available evidence suggests that people's perceptions of homeownership as a good investment were impacted by the Housing Crisis. The percentage of people holding those views certainly dropped during the early stages of the Housing Crisis, but they seem to have rebounded relatively quickly.[15]

Another early report by the Joint Center for Housing Studies found that "the desire to own a home has changed little and remains strong."[16] Both of these reports found that even for people directly impacted by the housing crisis, the ideal of home ownership was not completely lost and that many looked forward to buying again.

While public opinion on housing rebounded quickly after the crisis, many families are still dealing with financial fallout of the loss in value of their single largest investment. The Landi family is one of the millions of American families that lost their home in 2010 when it was foreclosed on.[17] John Landi was forced into early retirement by the Great Recession and was no longer able to keep up with his mortgage payments. His home, initially purchased in 1970 for $41,000, was later valued at $750,000 after renovations and additions. During the foreclosure process, it was valued at $450,000, far less than the mortgage on it. After failing to gain relief through loan modification or bankruptcy, the Landis lost their home of forty years. With their poor credit score, John and his wife Maria struggled to find a rental. They eventually were able to buy another home, but their new mortgage had a much higher interest rate due to their poor credit score. The Landis are one of many families involved in the housing recovery, but even with a new home, they are worse off financially than they were before.

Individuals who lost their homes in the housing crisis due to foreclosures or short sales (when home owners sell their homes for less than they owe but avoid foreclosure) typically have to wait three to seven years to purchase a home again.[18] One study found that 11.5 percent of 2.8 million former home owners who experienced a foreclosure, short sale, or bankruptcy had obtained a new mortgage. That means that millions of former home owners have not become home owners again. A 2019 survey has found that of Americans who lost a home in the past ten years due to a financial event, 61 percent have not purchased again, and of that 61 percent, 20 percent say they never plan to buy again, while 58 percent want to buy in the next five years.[19]

After the housing crisis, the rate of home ownership is starting to improve.[20] In the second quarter of 2018, 64.3 percent of households owned their homes, up from a low of 63 percent[21] and down from a high of 69.2 percent in the fourth quarter of 2004.[22] While the housing recovery brought new and former home owners into the real estate market, those home ownership rates are not consistent across different racial and ethnic groups. In 2017, 41.3 percent of Black households and 47 percent of Hispanic households owned their homes, while the white home ownership rate was 71.9 percent.[23] One reason for this large difference is that after the housing crisis, banks and mortgage providers were forced to intensify their lending standards. This has hit Black and Hispanic home buyers especially hard. In 2015, 27.4 percent of Black mortgage applicants and 19.2 percent of Hispanic applicants were denied mortgages, while the denial rate for white and Asian applicants was only about 11 percent. Throughout the precrisis boom, throughout the crisis, and during the recovery, Blacks have consistently been denied mortgages the most or second most—after Native Americans in the most recent years—among racial groups. Many factors go into a mortgage denial, including several factors that are strongly impacted by institutional racism and the long tail of housing discrimination discussed in chapters 7 and 10 in this volume.

The decision to purchase a home after losing one is more than a financial decision for many; it can also be deeply emotional. For example, Mark and Teresa Taunton of Celebration, Florida, were in a financial position to purchase a home back in 2014 after the three-year waiting period imposed on them by their short sale had passed, but they were still emotionally grieving the loss of their home. Mark told *USA Today*, "The memory was still sore."[24] Eventually, after renting and saving money, the Tauntons found a home that was considerably less expensive than the home they lost. Although they had qualified for a much larger mortgage, the fear that another financial event could jeopardize their new home clearly affected their purchase decision, exemplifying how economics is but one factor in the home-buying process.

The Tauntons and the Landis are examples of what the reports by the Joint Center for Housing Studies found: "Americans yearn for homeownership."[25] That desire is powerful, and it is fueled in large part by our culture and our insistence in what the American dream looks like. The white picket fence is a symbol of stability and responsibility and the pride of personal accomplishment that comes with home ownership.

SOURCES OF INFORMATION

Our understanding of home and the way we think and feel about our homes is influenced by a wide variety of sources of information. These sources may be magazines, television programs, or news stories, and they may be directly about homes or housing or indirectly about the housing market and home design trends. Before examining the home and garden sources reviewed for this chapter, I briefly discuss information sources as they are understood by library and information science scholars.

Information sources can be an individual or institution that originates some piece of information.[26] Information sources are typically categorized by type and run the gamut from formal sources, such as academic journal articles, to informal conversations with friends. In Krikelas's model of information-seeking behavior, sources are categorized by whether they are internal or external to an individual.[27] For example, an experience with a home improvement project is an internal source of information, while a YouTube how-to video that provides guidance for the project would be considered external. Recent research has begun to address the sensory experience of information, including sensory-based information sources.[28]

It can be difficult to understand the impact of a source because a lot of information is shared without attribution to the original source. For example, Facebook has been making news over the past several years because of its power as an unregulated source of information sharing misinformation alongside reputable news content. A few of you reading this chapter may have never seen an episode of *House Hunters* on HGTV, but because of the cultural importance of the show and the influence of the network, you likely have a passing knowledge of the show's conceit and typical real estate tropes that are presented. You may have encountered a meme from the show while surfing the internet, watched another home and garden–related show that has been shaped by its popularity, or talked about a recent episode with your mother-in-law. This is important to note because, even if you do not read a home and garden magazine or watch HGTV, you may well be influenced by the narrative and design trends prevalent in these sources.

HISTORY OF HOME AND GARDEN SOURCES

Since its founding, the United States has been a country of do-it-yourself (DIY) individuals. Robert Thompson, the director of the Bleier Center for Television and Popular Culture at Syracuse University, has helped explain the popularity of HGTV through the lens of the American ethos, saying, "The history of the United States is one big makeover show. The pilgrims came here to annihilate their history, to create a new and improved life. That . . . theme hums loudly under the surface of American life, and HGTV has managed to turn all the do-it-yourself stuff into entertainment, based on the theme of before and after."[29] It is no wonder that the history of media in the United States has prominently featured material about home and garden information. This section briefly covers the history of home and garden–related information sources in both magazine and television, closing with the contemporary media landscape.

Magazine History

Since before the founding of the United States, magazine publications were a popular means of transmitting a wide variety of information to the literate elites. American magazine publishing began on February 13, 1741, with the publication of the lengthily titled *American Magazine, or A Monthly View of the Political State of the British Colonies*, published by Andrew Bradford.[30] Bradford bested Benjamin Franklin to become the first American magazine publisher by three days, although many believe Franklin to have been the first. As literacy rates increased in the United States, so did magazine readership, and the publishing industry grew and diversified like their more established publishing contemporaries in England.

Home and garden information first appeared in the form of homemaking and household economics content in early American women's magazines of the 1790s, although the material was not common.[31] The first home-focused magazine, *House and Home* (1892–1905), was published more than 150 years after American magazine publishing began. *House and Home* began after the Philadelphia monthly building and woodworking–focused magazine *Builder, Decorator, and Woodworker* (1883–1891). The 1890s saw the creation of a new category of magazines that addressed "house planning, interior decorating, furnishings, and landscape gardening."[32] The most notable magazines to come out of this category were *House Beautiful* (1896–present) and *House and Garden* (1901–1993, 1996–2007).[33]

While *House Beautiful* and *House and Garden* helped popularize home and garden–themed magazines, the zenith of this genre became *Better Homes and Gardens (BHG)* (1922–present).[34] *BHG* began as a trial, spin-off magazine of the agricultural monthly *Successful Farming* (1902–present), published by Edwin Thomas Meredith, the founder of Meredith Corporation. The magazine began as *Fruit, Garden, and Home* before changing its name in 1924. *BHG* was notable at the time for soliciting reader feedback and acting as a forum for readers to share practical information. It was also a bit of a novelty for the time as a nationally popular magazine that did not contain fiction, fashion, or sex.[35] Practicality was the distinguishing characteristic of *BHG*, and it positioned itself as a home and garden magazine that appealed to middle-income men and women alike.

In addition to *BHG*, other home and garden or "lifestyle" magazines became popular throughout the twentieth century. Lifestyle magazines provided information on food, fashion, and vacations as well as home and garden information. *Sunset* (1898–present) is the oldest regional magazine in the United States. It was created by the Southern Pacific Railroad to promote western travel.[36] *Sunset* evolved from a promotional tool to a literary magazine, which was largely unsuccessful, to its current iteration as "the ultimate western lifestyle" magazine when it was purchased by Laurence Lane, who had previously worked for *BHG*.[37] Following the model of Lane's success with *Sunset*, *Southern Living* was founded in 1966.[38] A few years later, in 1987, *Country Living* was founded as a spin-off of *Good Housekeeping* and focused on bringing "the country look home."[39]

When magazine publishing began in the United States, before the founding of the country, the variety of sources most Americans were exposed to were few, and their access was limited by their abilities to read and afford print materials. Since then, many technological advances have shaped the media landscape to shift many individuals' source preferences away from magazines and newspapers toward cheaper and easier-to-understand forms of information. In fact, in 1956, when more and more American families began purchasing television sets for their homes, a research study found that individuals who read the most magazines were also the first to buy televisions.[40] Other studies conducted around the same time also found that television watching led to a decrease in magazine readership. Although magazines are still a major source of home and garden information, television has become the primary place to get ideas for decorating, buying, and selling your home.

Television History

While magazines predate the United States, in many ways, America created television. The first working television was demonstrated to a small group of American dignitaries, including Secretary of the Navy Curtis Wilbur on June 13, 1925, in Washington, D.C. Although several companies, including RCA (Radio Corporation of America), were working to build the first television, Charles Francis Jenkins, an independent inventor, beat them to it.[41] Once the television was successfully working, it took a few years for consumer models to make it to market and many more for them to become mainstays in most American homes. In January 1928, RCA and General Electric held the first public demonstrations of home televisions, and those companies were selling televisions for $75 each later that year. In order to provide content for early television broadcasts, popular radio shows of the time were filmed and simulcast as both radio and television broadcasts. Still, RCA and other companies struggled to popularize television. The Great Depression dramatically slowed television adoption and innovation in the United States, while Great Britain and Germany developed prospering television industries at the time. The

Nazi Party in Germany used television broadcasts to spread propaganda and boost soldiers' morale throughout the war.

After World War II, American television adoption skyrocketed when the first large batch of consumer television sets came off the assembly lines in September 1946.[42] In 1949, advertisers began shifting their focus away from radio programs toward television, a trend that would continue as television overtook radio as the preferred American broadcast medium through the present day. The growth of television also led to a growth in types of television programs. For the past forty years, home and garden television programs have been welcomed into American homes while also shaping them.

The cultural understanding of making over one's life and one's home has been present on American television since 1979 with the premier of *This Old House*, starring Bob Villa on PBS. Unlike most other shows of that era, it is still on the airwaves today in several forms, including as a spin-off (*Ask This Old House*), a magazine, and a website.[43] *This Old House* is widely credited as beginning the trend of home and garden television. The show's creator had been involved in previous lifestyle programs on PBS, including *The French Chef* with Julia Child and *The Victory Garden*.[44] The show has evolved over the years to follow many of the trends that emerged from the popularity of other, similar programs. In the first season, the show focused on the restoration of a vacant and dilapidated Victorian home in Dorchester, Massachusetts. Eventually, the show came to focus on a home and the home owners and their journey learning to renovate their home with a team of knowledgeable tradesmen led by the show's host. While some things never changed, including most of the cast, the level of detailed information presented, and the format of focusing on a single property renovation over many episodes, *This Old House* may have helped start the popularity of home renovation programs, but it is still unique even in today's crowded home and garden television landscape. The show is also still quite popular, with 2.043 million households watching and another 1.876 million watching *Ask This Old House* in the first quarter of 2019 sitting atop their television program category.[45]

The impact of *This Old House* is present throughout home and garden television. For example, the show's original host, Bob Vila, became a prominent spokesman and handyman icon. His workman-style of flannel, jeans, and work boots has come to define the contractor aesthetic that has been picked up to great success by Jonathan Scott of *Property Brothers* and Chip Gaines of *Fixer Upper*.

When *This Old House* attracted tens of thousands of regular viewers on PBS, other networks and programming executives began to take notice. On December 30, 1994, the television network HGTV began as the first cable network devoted entirely to home and garden information.[46] The network was the brainchild of Kenneth Lowe, a Scripps executive and do-it-yourselfer who opined to his wife about the lack of home and garden how-to information on television, saying, "Why doesn't somebody do more television programming in this area? Someday I'm going to create this network."[47] Shortly after the network's launch, the *New York Times* published an article about the network, calling it "the first full-service shelter magazine of the airwaves."[48] At the time, few others saw the need for twenty-four hours of home and garden television. An HGTV executive joked at the time that cable providers were not interested in adding a network to their lineup of "paint drying and grass growing."[49] Despite the initial hesitance, HGTV quickly proved to be just what many Americans wanted to watch, climbing the cable ratings and becoming profitable after just three years.

Early HGTV programming was filled with how-to shows on transplanting a rosebush or reupholstering an old chair. The shows focused on being thrifty and crafty and featured regional celebrities doing small craft projects with silk flowers or helping you select attractive yet affordable flooring.[50] For some viewers, HGTV replaced the home and garden magazines they enjoyed. In 1995, a viewer remarked, "On one show, they changed a light fixture, which I think is valuable information. I don't have a lot of time to read magazines, but if I'm doing something else, I can keep HGTV on and listen for tips."[51] In the early years of HGTV, all of their programming fit into five categories: gardening, remodeling, crafts, decorating, and at home.[52] While these early programs found an audience, the network became a cultural touchstone with the launch and immensely popular for what has become the network's flagship program: *House Hunters*.

In 1999, *House Hunters* premiered on HGTV. The show was created by Tara Sandler and Jennifer Davidson, creators of popular documentary series *A Baby Story* and *A Dating Story* on TLC.[53] *House Hunters* follows a potential home buyer or a couple as they look at three options comparing the price, location, and design. The early seasons of the show were filled with more pitfalls of the home-buying process than today. One early episode featured a couple delaying purchasing their home for a year to improve their credit and followed them cashing out their retirement funds.[54] While these issues are not the focus of later seasons of the show, *House Hunters* does present a great variety of home-buying experiences. From $150,000 budgets in the Midwest to multi-million-dollar homes in the San Francisco Bay Area, there have been hundreds of different American real estate stories told on the show over the years. In addition to the ratings success and longevity, *House Hunters* is a show that has cultural resonance with countless online memes, drinking games, jokes on shows such as *30 Rock*, and a skit on *Saturday Night Live*.

HGTV AND THE HOUSING CRISIS

As HGTV grew in viewership and cultural clout, it also became a target of many during the housing crisis. *House Hunters* not only changed popular culture but also changed HGTV. After the show became the network's most notable show, it began a trend on the network of focusing less on cheap crafting projects and more on home buying, selling, and eventually flipping. This new focus at the network was popular among viewers, but during and after the housing crisis, it seemed to some to be glamorizing home ownership and home makeovers in many ways that obscured the financial risks associated with taking on a mortgage or home improvement loans.

On January 3, 2009, the *Wall Street Journal* featured an opinion piece titled "Blame Television for the Bubble," which outlined a powerful narrative about how HGTV and home makeover shows more broadly were responsible for the housing crisis.[55] The essay begins,

> So now we know what happens when too many people who have too few assets buy too much house with the help of too many risky mortgage products and too little oversight. And while there's plenty of blame to go around—unethical mortgage brokers, greedy bankers and irresponsible homeowners—one culprit continues to get off scot-free: HGTV.[56]

The essay goes on to argue not only that HGTV oversold the dream of home ownership but also that it did so while also making viewers, no matter their living situation, feel bad about it. "You couldn't watch these shows without concluding that you must be an idiot and a loser if you lived in a house you could actually afford."[57] The essay also rather adeptly explains how each of the different types of HGTV programming delivers the message that your home is not good enough in notably different ways:

> You can loathe your current domicile 24/7 with programs such as "Stagers" (move a few things around and double the value of your home); "Designed to Sell" (you can sell your house, even if the house next to yours is in foreclosure); "Design on a Dime" (see, it's cheap); and "Property Virgins" (losing your virginity was fun, wasn't it?) Every show features highly attractive hosts who show you how to "unlock the hidden potential" in your home, how to turn a $10 thrift-store table into a "wow" media center, and how to make everything "pop."[58]

Now, in truth, there were much larger and more direct factors that led to the housing crisis, but for many readers, this essay struck a nerve. Home and garden programming, like the home and garden magazines before them, were trying to profit off providing all types of home owners and apartment dwellers with information on how to make the most of their living space. To do that, they had to continue presenting content, highlighting new trends, and keeping the reader or viewer interested in the material. To do that, your home can never be finished. There must always be another DIY project or improvement, another planting season and holiday get-together to style, and the next level of the American dream to strive for. In a lot of ways, the housing crisis should have been bad business for home and garden information. But as the home experts featured in these sources often do, they turned lemons into lemonade, performed a quick makeover, and helped their bottom line and their viewers fall back in love with their houses after the Great Recession.

DATA COLLECTION AND ANALYSIS

In order to explore popular home and garden–related sources, I examined the most prominent popular press and broadcast sources that address home and garden information. In the United States after the housing crisis, two of the most prominent home and garden sources are home and garden magazines and the HGTV television network.

Magazines

To understand the narratives present in home and garden magazines after the housing crisis, I examined the table of contents of a sample of issues of the top five home and garden magazines.[59] See figure 5.1 for the

Media Property	Parent Company	City	State	Type	Report Date	MagCirc
Better Homes And Gardens	Meredith Corporation	Des Moines	IA	MAG	12/2018-PS	7,628,025
Good Housekeeping	Hearst Magazine Media, Inc.	New York	NY	MAG	12/2018-PS	4,232,948
Southern Living	Meredith Corporation	Homewood	AL	MAG	12/2018-PS	2,856,164
HGTV Magazine	Hearst Magazine Media, Inc.	New York	NY	MAG	12/2018-PS	1,318,881
The Magnolia Journal	Meredith Corporation	Des Moines	IA	MAG	12/2018-PS	1,317,478
Country Living	Hearst Magazine Media, Inc.	New York	NY	MAG	12/2018-PS	1,306,790
Sunset	Sunset Publishing Corporation	Oakland	CA	MAG	06/2018-PS	1,268,196
Family Handyman	Trusted Media Brands, Inc.	Eagan	MN	MAG	12/2018-PS	1,237,926
Birds & Blooms	Trusted Media Brands, Inc.	Milwaukee	WI	MAG	12/2018-PS	1,120,376
Traditional Home	Meredith Corporation	Des Moines	IA	MAG	12/2018-PS	869,949
House Beautiful	Hearst Magazine Media, Inc.	New York	NY	MAG	12/2018-PS	810,103
Architectural Digest	Advance Magazine Publishers Inc.	New York	NY	MAG	12/2018-PS	807,915
This Old House	This Old House Ventures, LLC	Stamford	CT	MAG	12/2018-PS	792,517
Elle Decor	Hearst Magazine Media, Inc.	New York	NY	MAG	12/2018-PS	555,014
Veranda	Hearst Communications Inc.	Charlotte	NC	MAG	12/2018-PS	477,458
Dwell	Dwell Life, Inc.	San Francisco	CA	MAG	12/2018-PS	256,587
Land Line	Owner Operator Services, Inc.	Grain Valley	MO	MAG	12/2018-PS	216,018

Figure 5.1. Home Magazine Circulation from December 2018. *Alliance of Audited Media, "Magazine Circulation Report for 12/2018," Alliance of Audited Media: Media Intelligence Center, December 2018, https://auditedmedia.com/data/media-intelligence-center.*

full list of the top "home" magazines by circulation as of December 2018. I excluded any magazines that are categorized as women's magazines, although they may have home and garden content, to focus on home and garden and lifestyle magazines. Home and garden and lifestyle magazines are sometimes interchangeable and can even change throughout the history of a magazine. The top five home and garden magazines I examined were *Better Homes and Gardens (BHG), Southern Living, HGTV Magazine, Country Living,* and *Sunset.*

To compare the magazines, I sampled the same four issues (February, May, August, and November) for 2008–2018. *HGTV Magazine* was started in 2011 but was still included because of its popularity throughout its run, consistently being a top home and garden magazine. Some issues may have represented two months (January/February) but included one of the sampling months. I examined the table of contents of twenty-seven issues for *HGTV Magazine* and forty-four of each of the other four for this analysis. The table of contents provides a snapshot of the full contents of the magazine. I read through each table of contents from the sample of each magazine for 2008–2018 one at a time with an iterative coding strategy. The tables of contents sometimes contained only a title for an article, while other times, they had short descriptors of the article. For example, the May 2009 issue of *BHG* included an article listed as "Tent Show—A Deck Canopy Creates an Outdoor Living Room."

There were several similarities across the magazines, including having multiple articles in each issue about decorating, gardening, and cooking. For this analysis, I coded articles related to decorating, gardening, home renovation, real estate, and related topics. Table 5.1 shows the list of codes as well as their frequencies across all five magazines.

Three codes, (budget, quick, and increase value) were added to the main codes to note when the article emphasized a certain aspect of the topic. For example, budget referred to an article about decorating or gardening on a budget.

HGTV

To examine the narratives present on HGTV, I collected the brief show description from the HGTV website for all 313 of the shows that I could determine aired on the network from 2008 to 2018.[60] HGTV, like many specialty networks, have a lot of short-lived shows and special programming that was excluded from this analysis because it was difficult to determine how frequently it was broadcast. To be considered a show for this analysis, a program had to have either a minimum of eight unique episodes or a short yet complete run, such as the four-episode competition show *Brothers Take New Orleans,* where the popular Property Brothers

Table 5.1. Code Frequencies by Magazine

Code	Better Homes and Gardens	Country Living	HGTV Magazine	Southern Living	Sunset	Totals
Bargain Issue	0	6	0	0	0	6
Budget*	23	61	75	6	6	171
Decorating	322	483	434	220	135	1,594
Furniture Renovation	2	9	17	0	3	31
Gardening	150	27	18	199	176	570
Green Living	9	2	0	3	10	24
Home Construction	0	8	1	17	8	34
Home Information	0	0	14	0	0	14
Home Renovation	19	21	14	15	11	80
Home Repair	1	0	14	0	1	16
Increase Value*	0	0	1	0	0	1
Landscaping	9	0	2	4	6	21
Organization	25	5	13	2	0	45
Other	0	0	2	2	2	6
Quick*	5	3	1	4	0	13
Real Estate	0	38	19	0	11	68
Room Renovation	16	2	7	9	0	34
Totals	581	665	632	481	369	2,728

*Denotes a modifier code.

compete against each other to renovate similar houses in New Orleans. An exception to this rule are long running series of annual home giveaway shows, such as *HGTV Smart Home*, that, while consisting of only a single episode, recur every year with much fanfare on the network and online. I also excluded any shows that specifically mentioned a holiday in their title or specials about HGTV talent or that featured mostly "behind the scenes" content. To determine if a show was on the air from 2008 to 2018, I used the Internet Archive to review previous iterations of the HGTV website, which included network program guides.

To code the programs, I looked up the short descriptions from HGTV about the show. For example, *House Hunters*, a perennial HGTV hit, is described as follows:

> House Hunters takes viewers behind the scenes as individuals, couples and families learn what to look for and decide whether or not a home is meant for them. Focusing on the emotional experience of finding and purchasing a new home, each episode shows the process as buyers search for a home.

Descriptions were coded for concepts related to home and gardening topics as well as popular HGTV trends, including decoration, home buying, home renovation, home selling, flipping, and DIY/home improvement. Modifier codes were also used on this sample; these codes include

Table 5.2. HGTV Show Codes and Frequencies

Code	Total Frequency
Decorating	127
Home Buying	83
Home Renovation	64
Home Selling	39
Competition*	36
Budget*	32
Increase Home Value*	28
Flipping	25
DIY/Home Improvement	24
Unusual Homes	19
Quick*	17
Landscaping	16
Home Restoration	13
Home Construction	10
Home Repair/Inspection	8
Renting	6
Other	6
Crafts/Knitting	6
Furniture Repair/Restoration	5
Antiques/Salvage	5
Organization/Cleaning	5
Green Building/Design	4
Gardening	3
Total	581

*Denotes a modifier code.

competition, budget, increase home value, and quick. Table 5.2 lists all of the codes applied to this sample as well as their frequencies.

FINDINGS: MAGAZINES

When looking at all five magazines over time, several trends began to emerge. First, all of the magazines went through clear changes in their content, including the number of articles about real estate and home decorating. Second, there was not a strong influx of material that focused on keeping to a limited budget, and the content that emerged eventually dwindled. Third, there was a brief appearance of green living content.[61] In this section, I describe each of these trends in detail and provide some other notable differences among the magazines.

From 2008 to 2018 (2012–2018 for *HGTV Magazine*), the number of stories about home and garden material decreased in all five magazines.

For example, *BHG* had the most coded stories in the May and November 2008 issues, with thirty-two stories, and the least in February 2018, with only six. Other magazines had similar maximums and minimums: *Country Living*, max of thirty in May 2009, minimum of six in August 2016; *HGTV Magazine*, maximum of thirty-seven in February 2012, minimum of thirteen in November 2018; *Sunset*, maximum of fifteen in August 2008 and February and August 2009, minimum of three in November 2010 and 2012; and *Southern Living*, maximum of thirty-four in May 2008, minimum of two in November 2017 and 2018. As a share of total articles appearing in each magazine, home and garden–specific material stayed largely consistent. For example, the February 2008 issues of *BHG* and *Southern Living*, the two most popular magazines, both contained forty-four articles listed in the table of contents. Of those forty-four, fourteen articles in *BHG* and sixteen articles in *Southern Living* were coded as dealing with home and garden material. The February 2018 issues of each of the magazines contained only twenty-two articles each, and six articles in *BHG* and seven in *Southern Living* were coded.

The decrease in home and garden content appears to be tied to a general decrease in articles featured in each magazine. This trend can be explained largely by the cost-cutting measures many magazines have been adopting over the past several years to make up for advertisers moving their ads to more online platforms.[62] It seems unlikely that regular readers of these magazines were abandoning their magazine subscriptions over this period of time for other online or television sources. Subscription rates for these magazines were largely consistent from 2008 to 2018. For example, *BHG* had an average of 7,655,500 subscribers in 2008 and an average of 7,636,964 in 2018, a difference of 18,536 subscribers, or a .002 percent drop in circulation.[63] *Sunset* and *HGTV Magazine* gained subscribers over this time. *Country Living* had the largest decline in subscribers, going from an average of 1,626,279 in 2008 to 1,342,839 in 2018, a decrease of 17 percent.

Due to the housing crisis and the Great Recession, I was expecting to see home and garden magazines presenting more content about decorating and home renovation on a budget. But this was largely not the case. The magazine with the most budget-friendly related content was *HGTV Magazine* with seventy-five articles, followed by *Country Living* with sixty-one, *BHG* with twenty-three, and *Southern Living* and *Sunset* each with six. *HGTV Magazine* contained consistent content about decoration, renovation, and even home buying on a budget throughout its issues. For example, regularly occurring articles, such as "The High/Low List" and "Bang for Your Buck," highlight home decor items that are "paycheck friendly" and fit "every budget." *Country Living* also briefly featured a regular "Bargain Issue" in May 2009 and 2011–2014 and in

May 2017 renamed it "The $100-and-Under Issue." *BHG*, unlike *Country Living* and *HGTV Magazine*, did not have regularly occurring articles or special issues but featured several one-off articles about budget-friendly home and garden information. The frequency of these articles over time demonstrates that the housing crisis did not lead to a large and consistent growth in budget-friendly content. In 2008, the May issue of *BHG* contained no articles about budget issues, while the other issues that year included in the sample featured only one or two. From November 2009 until November 2018, twenty-eight of the thirty-seven issues contained no budget-friendly content, although the issue with the most budget-friendly articles, four, was for August 2013. *BHG* demonstrates that although there may have been an initial push for budget-friendly material after the housing crisis, the content was not very common or consistently produced aside from a few regularly occurring articles in *HGTV Magazine* and a few special issues of *Country Living*.

The last trend that stuck out of the magazine article data was the brief presence of green living material. Articles coded as dealing in some way with green living were present in four of the five magazines; *HGTV Magazine* had no green living content. The most articles, ten, were in *Sunset*. There were nine green living articles in *BHG*, three in *Southern Living*, and two in *Country Living*. Most of the articles come before 2011: nine out of ten in *Sunset* and eight out of nine in *BHG*. This establishes a green living trend that came and went during and in the immediate aftermath of the housing crisis. This trend is similar to a trend in the HGTV show data discussed below.

In addition to these overriding trends among all three magazines, each was also distinct in a few notable ways. When looking at the total number of articles and the average number per issue presented in table 5.3, it is clear that some of these lifestyle magazines are more focused on home and garden information than others. It is not surprising that *HGTV Magazine* has the largest percentage of home and garden articles per issue because even though only twenty-seven issues were included in the sample (because the magazine launched in 2012), it still had the second-largest

Table 5.3. Totals of Codes, Issues, and Average Number of Codes per Issue by Magazine

Magazine	Total Number of Codes	Number of Issues	Average Number of Codes per Issue
Better Homes and Gardens	603	44	13.7
Southern Living	484	44	11
HGTV Magazine	635	27	23.52
Country Living	675	44	15.34
Sunset	376	44	8.55
Totals	2,773	203	13.66

total number of relevant articles. *Sunset* had the least number and the lowest average, most likely because it has a larger focus on more lifestyle topics, including many articles on camping and other outdoor activities compared to the other magazines.

The magazines also varied quite a lot in terms of the amount of real estate–specific content presented in each one. *Country Living* had the most material with thirty-eight articles, mostly a regular article called "Real Estate Sampler," which was eventually changed to "Country Listings." After *Country Living*, *HGTV Magazine* had nineteen articles and *Sunset* eleven, while *BHG* and *Southern Living* had none. Like *Country Living*, *Sunset* has a regularly occurring article titled "Best Places to Live," which highlights different real estate markets in the western United States. *HGTV Magazine* has by far the largest variety of real estate–related content. The articles feature house hunting tips and tricks, listings, price-guessing games, and "ask a real estate expert" features.

FINDINGS: HGTV

Throughout its time on air, HGTV has changed from a network notable for its thrift and homely design to one of the most popular cable networks that features stars that host their own celebrity cruises (the Property Brothers) and launch their own television network (Chip and Joanna Gaines).[64] In 2018, HGTV was the ninth most watched network among cable and broadcast in America, and its popularity grew throughout the housing crisis and recovery.[65] When reviewing the programming on the network from 2008 through 2018, several trends emerged. First, the focus of shows shifted over time with the loss of more varied home and garden content to the deluge of house-flipping shows. Second, the network developed several shows that dealt directly with the housing crisis, some of which continue on today with a change in direction. Third, green building, like green living in the magazine data, was a short-lived trend that has passed.

HGTV began as a network for the do-it-yourselfer, a place to gain useful information about home and garden projects that you could realistically accomplish with a modest budget. Some of the early programming was still on the air in 2008 more than a decade after the network began. Two trends nicely denote the changes in the network during and after the housing crisis: the loss of programming about crafts and gardening and the precipitous rise in house-flipping shows. All of the programs that I coded as dealing with gardening (three shows) began in the 1990s and ended in 2008 or 2009. The longest-running gardening show, *Gardener's Diary*, ran from 1994 until 2009. Crafting shows (six shows) outlasted their gardening counterparts by a few years, with the last standing crafting show, *That's Clever*, ending in 2011 after a six-year run. All of the other crafting shows ended in 2008 or 2009.

The house-flipping trend began in 2010 with *The Vanilla Ice Project*, a show about Vanilla Ice, a musician turned home renovator flipping one house over a season and a different room in each episode. The flipping trend did not really start filling the prime-time HGTV block until 2013, when several notable shows, including *Brother vs. Brother*, featuring the Property Brothers, and *Flip or Flop* began. There were two other flipping-focused shows that launched that year: the short-lived *Renovate to Rent* and the DIY Network competition show *Texas Flip and Move*. After 2013, HGTV added more house-flipping shows every year with two in 2014, eight in 2015, two in 2016, six in 2017, and two in 2018. Over this time, the hit *Flip or Flop* spawned spin-offs in Atlanta, Fort Worth, Nashville, and Las Vegas.

HGTV also added and changed some of its previous shows in 2008 and 2009 to address the changes caused by the housing crisis.[66] The network added to its lineup shows that specialized in sharing information relevant to the changing housing market with the shows *Real Estate Intervention* (2009–2013) and *Income Property* (2008–2016). *Real Estate Intervention* features a real estate expert and a home stager to help sellers understand their local markets better and how to make small cosmetic home upgrades to help the home stand out on the local market. *Income Property* helped home owners convert portions of their homes into apartments to bring in additional income. This show is notable because it emphasizes very different parts of real estate than other HGTV shows that sell the ideal of home ownership with minimal focus on how individuals and families are actually able to pay their mortgage and play counter to the idea of the traditional single-family home.

The trend of shows dealing directly with the housing crisis continued through 2013 with one notable standout, *Flip or Flop*, a flipping show about a married couple of real estate agents struggling to make ends meet after the housing crisis that has transformed over the years into a high-end flipping show that features million-dollar homes. One aspect of the show that emphasizes its change over time is the audio that plays over the show's title sequence. When the show began in 2013, the opening titles included the star of the show, Tarek El Moussa, saying, "I'm Tarek, and this my wife Christina. We're real estate agents. Ever since the market crashed, it's been a rocky road. With a family to support, we're starting a new business, and we're flipping houses."[67] Starting in season 5, the episodes begin, "Flipping houses is a risky business. I'm Tarek, and this is my wife Christina. We buy the ugliest, the nastiest, the most run-down houses that we can find, and we transform them into beautiful homes that every buyer dreams of."[68] This subtle change removes reference to the market crash and the origin story of one of HGTV's most popular flipping pairs and refocuses the show's aim on the flipping business in general. In researching for this chapter, I had difficulty finding the show's original opening sequence because through HGTV's official streaming platform, all episodes now begin with the most recent season's introductory language. I was able to find the original opening sequence on episodes streaming on Hulu.[69]

Other, similar new shows that addressed the changing housing market include *The Unsellables* (2009–2012), *Power Broker* (2013), *Staged to Perfection* (2013), and *Rent or Buy* (2013–2014). In addition to these new programs, the network also increased production and focused on some of the more escapist fare, including doubling production on the popular *House Hunters* spin-off *House Hunters International*,[70] a show that often features Americans typically renting but sometimes purchasing homes in exotic locations around the world.

The final trend I want to note about HGTV programming after the housing crisis is the disappearance of green building or green living programming that matches a similar trend in home and garden magazines. There are only four shows that aired on HGTV from 2008 to 2018 that featured some note about green living or green building in their show synopsis. Those four shows are *Carter Can* (2007–2010), *Red Hot & Green* (2008), *Pure Design* (2008–2010), and *HGTV Green Home* (2009–2012). *Carter Can* features home improvement expert Carter Oosterhouse, who helps home owners with their home improvement projects while highlighting green building solutions. *Red Hot & Green* also features Oosterhouse along with a designer to make over rooms with a green twist. *Pure Design* is a similar green-themed makeover show. The most interesting show for considering how HGTV has changed is the *HGTV Green Home*. HGTV began giving away beautifully designed and appointed homes in 1997 and have had several different titles for their giveaways as well as different annual shows that highlight the homes' features and design. In 2008, HGTV began its *HGTV Green Home* show and giveaway with a home in Hilton Head, South Carolina. Homes designed to emphasize green building and design were featured in the annual giveaway and special until 2013, when HGTV rebranded this annual tradition as *HGTV Smart Home*, shifting the focus away from green building and design toward a "smart" emphasis on new home technology and trends. By 2013, none of the programs reviewed for this study had any description of a focus on green building, design, or living.

CONCLUSIONS

Both home and garden magazines and HGTV shows changed after the housing crisis in ways that likely impacted the way readers and viewers considered their homes and the housing market. While home and garden magazines presented minimal material about the new realities of the housing market and wider economy, HGTV shifted the focus on some of their shows and created new ones that directly dealt with the financial side of real estate. These changes likely reflect the differences in these sources and the ways people view them. Magazines are something that people must go out of their way to acquire through subscriptions or by picking them up at a newsstand, while HGTV is included in the cable or satellite packages of millions of Americans. Television is the more widely consumed source, and it dealt with the crisis head-on. One similarity in both mediums is that after it was clear that the housing crisis recovery was working and that many people were again buying and selling homes with fewer foreclosures and short sales, things went back to the way they were. It is interesting that flipping shows that began in the aftermath of the housing crisis (due in part to a large inventory of homes created by foreclosures and short sales) are still popular when the next housing crisis may be caused by a housing shortage.[71] Flipping shows persisted even without the large amounts of inventory caused by the crisis and the focus shifted to design trends, what these sources have always been about.

The housing crisis impacted millions of Americans, but ten years later, its impact on the view of home ownership does not seem to be lasting. This may be in part because even when our homes are the cause of chaos and uncertainty in our lives, the ideals of home and home ownership presented in beautiful magazine photo spreads and featured on *House Hunters* are still comforting. It is nice to know that recently married couples are buying their first homes, new parents are decorating nurseries, and empty nesters are relocating to a condo with a view. These tropes and the DIY ideology are embedded in American culture in the same way that home ownership is a cornerstone of the American dream. While the level and type of change presented above in both mediums of home and garden sources are different, their continued focus on home is what makes them the comfortable content that Americans yearn for even after a financial crisis that centered on the home.

NOTES

1. Madeleine Shufeldt Esch, "A Nation of Cocooners? Explanations of the Home Improvement TV Boom in the United States," in *Exposing Lifestyle Television: The Big Reveal*, ed. Gareth Palmer (Burlington, VT: Ashgate, 2008), 164.

2. In 2018, HGTV was the ninth most watched network among cable and broadcast; Michael Schneider, "Most-Watched Television Networks: Ranking 2018's Winners and Losers," *IndieWire*, December 27, 2018, https://www

.indiewire.com/2018/12/network-ratings-top-channels-espn-cnn-fox-news-cbs-nbc-abc-1202030597.

3. Esch, "A Nation of Cocooners?," 165.

4. Esch, "A Nation of Cocooners?," 164–65.

5. Richard Huff, "TV'S New Subdivision: Fixer-Uppers—Home Shows Really Rate," *Daily News*, September 30, 2002, Lexis Nexis, para. 7.

6. William Rohe and Mark Lindblad, "Reexamining the Social Benefits of Homeownership after the Housing Crisis," Harvard University: Joint Center for Housing Studies, August 2013, https://www.jchs.harvard.edu/sites/default/files/hbtl-04.pdf.

7. Eric S. Belsky, "The Dream Lives On: The Future of Homeownership in America," Harvard University: Joint Center for Housing Studies, January 2013, https://www.jchs.harvard.edu/sites/default/files/w13-1_belsky_0.pdf.

8. Becky Sullivan, "10 Years after Housing Crisis," *NPR.org*, April 28, 2018, https://www.npr.org/2018/04/28/603678259/10-years-after-housing-crisis-a-realtor-a-renter-starting-over-staying-put.

9. Douglas Holtz-Eakin and Andrew Winkler, "Boom, Bust, and Beyond: A Look at Housing Market Data in Florida," American Action Forum, November, 2012, https://www.americanactionforum.org/wp-content/uploads/sites/default/files/final%20paper%20FL.pdf.

10. Sarah Mikhitarian, "How the Housing Bust Widened the Wealth Gap for Communities of Color," *Zillow Research*, April 25, 2019, https://www.zillow.com/research/housing-bust-wealth-gap-race-23992.

11. A recession is defined as two consecutive financial quarters of economic decline, typically represented as a decline in the gross domestic product of a country; Jim Chappelow, "Recession Definition," *Investopedia*, February 27, 2020, https://www.investopedia.com/terms/r/recession.asp; Robert Rich, "The Great Recession," *Federal Reserve History*, November 22, 2013, https://www.federalreservehistory.org/essays/great_recession_of_200709.

12. Rich, "The Great Recession."

13. Annie Lowrey, "The Great Recession Is Still with Us," *The Atlantic*, December 1, 2017, https://www.theatlantic.com/business/archive/2017/12/great-recession-still-with-us/547268.

14. Rohe and Lindblad, "Reexamining the Social Benefits of Homeownership after the Housing Crisis."

15. Rohe and Lindblad, "Reexamining the Social Benefits of Homeownership after the Housing Crisis,"12.

16. Belsky, "The Dream Lives On," 4.

17. Kari Paul and Jacob Passy, "A Decade after the Housing Crisis, Foreclosures Still Haunt Homeowners," *MarketWatch*, September 30, 2018, https://www.marketwatch.com/story/a-decade-after-the-housing-crisis-foreclosures-still-haunt-homeowners-2018-09-27.

18. Paul Davidson, "Boomerang Buyers," *USA Today*, May 21, 2019, https://www.usatoday.com/story/money/2019/04/25/housing-market-2019-more-who-lost-homes-crisis-buying-again/3535675002.

19. Elizabeth Renter, "2019 Home Buyer Report," *NerdWallet*, February 26, 2019, https://www.nerdwallet.com/blog/2019-home-buyer-report.

20. Paul and Passy, "A Decade after the Housing Crisis, Foreclosures Still Haunt Homeowners."

21. Calvin Schnure, "The Long Tail of the Housing Crisis," *Morning Consult*, August 8, 2019, https://morningconsult.com/opinions/the-long-tail-of-the-housing-crisis.

22. Paul and Passy, "A Decade after the Housing Crisis, Foreclosures Still Haunt Homeowners."

23. Drew Desilver and Kristen Bialik, "Blacks and Hispanics Face Extra Challenges in Getting Home Loans," *Fact Tank (Pew Research Center)*, January 10, 2017, https://www.pewresearch.org/fact-tank/2017/01/10/blacks-and-hispanics-face-extra-challenges-in-getting-home-loans.

24. Davidson, "Boomerang Buyers," "Losing the American Dream" section.

25. Belsky, "The Dream Lives On," 16.

26. Donald O. Case and Lisa M. Given, *Looking for Information: A Survey of Research on Information Seeking, Needs, and Behavior*, 4th ed. (Bingley: Emerald, 2016), 375.

27. James Krikelas, "Information-Seeking Behavior," *Drexel Library Quarterly* 19, no. 2 (1983): 14–15.

28. Reijo Savolainen, "Elaborating the Sensory and Cognitive-Affective Aspects of Information Experience," *Journal of Librarianship and Information Science*, August 21, 2019; Melissa Ocepek, "Sensible Shopping: A Sensory Exploration of the Information Environment of the Grocery Store," *Library Trends* 66, no. 3 (2018): 371–94.

29. Cathy Lubenski, "Home Improvement Network Has Built Quite a Following in 10 Years," *San Diego Union-Tribune*, May 8, 2005, Access World News, paras. 13–14.

30. John William Tebbel and Mary Ellen Zuckerman, *The Magazine in America, 1741–1990* (New York: Oxford University Press, 1991), 3.

31. Tebbel and Zuckerman, *The Magazine in America, 1741–1990*, 37.

32. Frank Luther Mott, *A History of American Magazines*, vol. 4 (Cambridge, MA: Harvard University Press, 1957), 324.

33. Elliott and Pérez-Peña, "Publication to Cease for House & Garden."

34. Frank Luther Mott, *A History of American Magazines*, vol. 5 (Cambridge, MA: Harvard University Press, 1968), 36–48.

35. Tebbel and Zuckerman, *The Magazine in America, 1741–1990*, 191.

36. Tebbel and Zuckerman, *The Magazine in America, 1741–1990*, 259.

37. Sunset Magazine, "About Us," https://www.sunset.com/general-about-us, "About Sunset" section (accessed February 21, 2020); Peggy Bernal and Victoria Bernal, "Sunset Magazine: The Bible of Western Living," *KCET*, March 14, 2012, https://www.kcet.org/history-society/sunset-magazine-the-bible-of-western-living.

38. Tebbel and Zuckerman, *The Magazine in America, 1741–1990*, 259.

39. Rachel Hardage Barrett, "Greetings from the Country," *Country Living*, August 7, 2014, https://www.countryliving.com/life/a5634/editors-letter-rachel-hardage-barrett/.fig. (the first issue of *Country Living*).

40. Tebbel and Zuckerman, *The Magazine in America, 1741–1990*, 245.

41. Harry Castleman and Walter J. Podrazik, *Watching TV: Four Decades of American Television* (New York: McGraw-Hill, 1982), 5.

42. Castleman and Podrazik, *Watching TV*, 27.

43. Ronda Kaysen, "'This Old House' Turns 40," *New York Times*, July 5, 2019, "Real Estate" section.

44. Kaysen, "'This Old House' Turns 40."

45. Kaysen, "'This Old House' Turns 40."

46. Lubenski, "Home Improvement Network Has Built Quite a Following in 10 Years."

47. Lubenski, "Home Improvement Network Has Built Quite a Following in 10 Years," para. 19.

48. Mitchell Owens, "Is America Ready for All-Home TV?," *New York Times*, January 5, 1995, https://www.nytimes.com/1995/01/05/garden/is-america-ready-for-all-home-tv.html, para. 4.

49. Meredith Blake, "HGTV Builds into a Top Cable Network on Foundation of No-Frills Shows," *Los Angeles Times*, July 18, 2014, https://www.latimes.com/entertainment/tv/la-et-hgtv-cable-network-20th-anniversary-20140720-story.html, "Useful Escapism" section.

50. Caitlin Flanagan, "HGTV Is a Never-Ending Fantasy Loop. Look Deeper, and It Gets Pretty Ugly," *Vulture*, September 20, 2017, https://www.vulture.com/2017/09/the-ugliness-behind-hgtv-never-ending-fantasy-loop.html.

51. Owens, "Is America Ready for All-Home TV?," para. 13.

52. Anna Everett, "Trading Private and Public Spaces @ HGTV and TLC: On New Genre Formations in Transformation TV," *Journal of Visual Culture* 3, no. 2 (2004): 157–81.

53. Blake, "HGTV Builds into a Top Cable Network on Foundation of No-Frills Shows."

54. Flanagan, "HGTV Is a Never-Ending Fantasy Loop."

55. Jim Sollisch, "Blame Television for the Bubble," *Wall Street Journal*, January 3, 2009, Eastern edition, ABI/INFORM Collection.

56. Sollisch, "Blame Television for the Bubble," para. 1.

57. Sollisch, "Blame Television for the Bubble," para. 5.

58. Sollisch, "Blame Television for the Bubble," para. 6.

59. Alliance of Audited Media: Media Intelligence Center, "Magazine Circulation Report for 12/2018," December 2018, https://auditedmedia.com/data/media-intelligence-center.

60. This information was determined using HGTV.com via the Internet Archive as well as tvguide.com, which lists air dates for television episodes.

61. Green refers to environmentally sustainable practices.

62. Sydney Ember and Michael M. Grynbaum, "The Not-So-Glossy Future of Magazines," *New York Times*, September 23, 2017, https://www.nytimes.com/2017/09/23/business/media/the-not-so-glossy-future-of-magazines.html, "Business" section.

63. Alliance of Audited Media, "Publisher's Statement," https://auditedmedia.com (accessed March 9, 2020)

64. Flanagan, "HGTV Is a Never-Ending Fantasy Loop"; Claire McNear, "Lost at Sea with the Property Brothers and Their Legion of Superfans," *The Ringer*, December 13, 2018, https://www.theringer.com/tv/2018/12/13/18138222/property-brothers-cruise-superfans; Michelle Profis, "Chip and Joanna Gaines

Announced Their New TV Network and Fans Went Nuts," *Country Living*, November 11, 2018, https://www.countryliving.com/life/entertainment/a24926271/chip-joanna-gaines-new-tv-network-fan-reactions.

65. Schneider, "Most-Watched Television Networks: Ranking 2018's Winners and Losers"; Michael Schneider, "Most Watched Television Networks: Ranking 2015's Winners and Losers," *TV Insider*, December 28, 2015, https://www.tvinsider.com/62572/most-watched-tv-networks-2015.

66. Blake, "HGTV Builds into a Top Cable Network on Foundation of No-Frills Shows."

67. "Flip or Flop," *Cracked Flip*, HGTV, October 7, 2014, https://www.hulu.com/series/flip-or-flop-2605c6ae-7f2f-4ef1-97d8-d0a8902a44b0.

68. "Flip or Flop," *Down to the Studs*, HGTV, June 9, 2016, https://www.hulu.com/series/flip-or-flop-2605c6ae-7f2f-4ef1-97d8-d0a8902a44b0.

69. This change may also be due to the recent divorce of the two stars, as the current opening season has removed the reference to Christina as Tarek's wife.

70. Blake, "HGTV Builds into a Top Cable Network on Foundation of No-Frills Shows."

71. Felix Salmon, "America's Housing Shortage Is Getting Worse," *Axios*, January 30, 2020, https://www.axios.com/us-housing-shortage-crisis-prices-17eba84d-6ad4-4860-9fa1-34b00b22e08f.html.

Six

A Community Responds to Growth

An Information Story about What Makes for a Good Place to Live

Hannah Weber, Vaughan M. Nagy,
Janghee Cho, and William Aspray

Most literature about where to live is written from the perspective of the individuals seeking a place to live or the perspective of the stakeholders, such as mortgage brokers and real estate agents, who facilitate finding a place to live. However, this chapter considers the narrative from the point of view of the community. It explores factors that make a community an attractive place to live and identifies stakeholders involved in the process. The chapter examines these issues through a case study of Arvada, Colorado, a suburb of Denver.[1]

Located approximately twelve miles northwest of downtown Denver (i.e., the capital and largest city of Colorado) and twenty miles southeast of Boulder (i.e., the home of the main campus of the University of Colorado, the state's largest university), Arvada had humble beginnings as a small gold-rush establishment known as Ralston Point. The first documented discovery of gold in Colorado occurred on June 22, 1850, in the same area.[2] By 1870, the town had been established and was named after the brother-in-law of the city's founder, Benjamin Wadsworth. Arvada was then incorporated in 1904 and would grow substantially.[3]

By the 1920s, the initial seeds of suburbia had been planted in the areas surrounding Denver. In 1925, the first concrete road was constructed in Arvada and ran all the way to Denver. Arvada grew after World War II, when the GI Bill stimulated the construction of mass-produced housing in Arvada.[4] As a result, the city experienced an increase in both the local economy and the population. This growth continued until the 1980s, when an economic downturn hit the entire Denver region.[5] Since the turn of the present century, however, Arvada has experienced high rates of both population and economic growth, part of a widespread migration to Colorado's Front Range.[6] In recent years, Denver has experienced a population boom, partially because of an abundance of job opportunities.[7] This change has led Arvada to a rapid influx of people and a steady rise in the cost of housing.

Arvada is currently home to just over 120,000 residents (the eighth-largest city in Colorado).[8] Despite being a part of the larger metropolitan area, the city has its own distinctive character that differentiates it from neighboring towns. It has a mix of rural land, older communities, new developments, and a historic Olde Town district. Arvada continues to enjoy a small-town atmosphere made possible through effective civic initiatives to preserve its historic character as well as through its strong community engagement. Figures 6.1 and 6.2 and tables 6.1 to 6.3 present additional background information about Arvada.

Arvada provides an interesting case study of how a community experiencing a rapid population increase comes together to work to remain an attractive place to live. During the summer of 2019, the authors conducted extensive research on the city. We examined City of Arvada documents (e.g., city council minutes, policy proposals, documentation of city initiatives, and urban renewal documents), local news stories, state and federal archives, advocacy group and corporate (e.g., real estate development) websites, and social media. The goal was to assess the role that information plays in community issues, stakeholder interactions, and policy

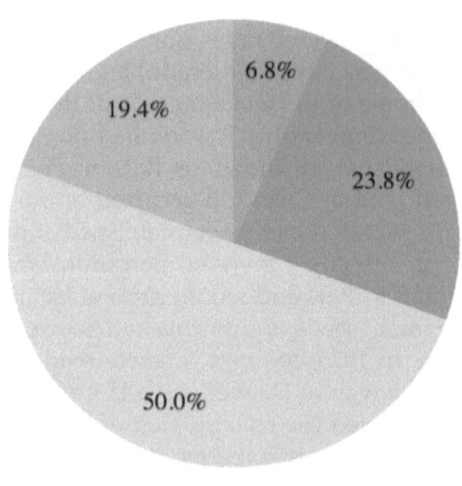

● Persons under 5 years, percent   ● Persons under 18 years, percent
● Persons 18-65 years, percent   ● Persons 65 years and over, percent

Figure 6.1. Arvada, Colorado, Age Breakdown. *United States Census Bureau.* "U.S. Census Bureau QuickFacts: Arvada City, Colorado." *2018. Accessed November 21, 2019, https://www.census.gov/quickfacts/fact/table/arvadacitycolorado/PST045218.*

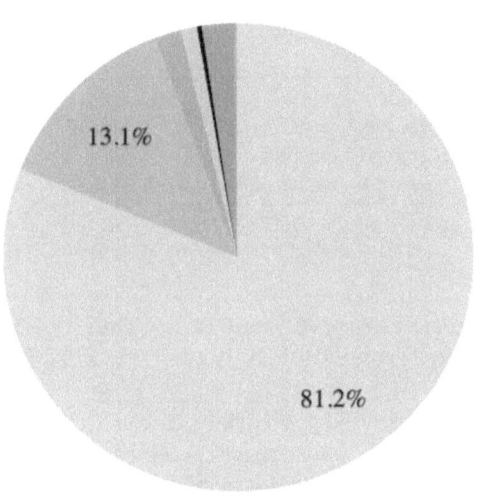

● White ● Hispanic ● Asian ● Black/African American
● Native American/Pacific Islander ● Two or More Races ● Other

Figure 6.2. Arvada, Colorado, Ethnicity Breakdown. *United States Census Bureau. "U.S. Census Bureau QuickFacts: Arvada City, Colorado." 2018. Accessed November 21, 2019, https://www.census.gov/quickfacts/fact/table/arvadacitycolorado/PST045218.*

Table 6.1. Arvada, Colorado: Income and Employment Information

Income and Poverty	Arvada	National
Unemployment rate	2.7%	3.5%
Median household income	$75,640	$57,652
Percentage below poverty line	6.9%	11.8%

Source: U.S. Census Bureau, "U.S. Census Bureau QuickFacts: Arvada City, Colorado," 2018, https://www.census.gov/quickfacts/fact/table/arvadacitycolorado/PST045218 (accessed November 21, 2019); U.S. Department of Labor, Bureau of Labor Statistics, "Databases, Tables & Calculators by Subject," https://data.bls.gov/timeseries/LNS14000000 (accessed November 21, 2019).

Table 6.2. Arvada, Colorado: Households

Household Type	Number of Households	Average Number of People per Household	Percentage of Owned Households
Married	24,707	3.10	86.7%
Male	2,005	3.12	59.0%
Female	4,083	3.23	62.3%
Nonfamily	16,237	1.28	58.8%
Total	47,032	2.48	73.8%

Source: U.S. Census Bureau, "U.S. Census Bureau QuickFacts: Arvada City, Colorado," 2018, https://www.census.gov/quickfacts/fact/table/arvadacitycolorado/PST045218 (accessed November 21, 2019).

Table 6.3. Arvada, Colorado: School Information

Number of schools	155
Total enrollment	86,131
Number of teachers	4,700
Student-to-teacher ratio	18:1

Source: Jefferson County, "Jeffco Public Schools," http://jeffcopublicschools.org (accessed November 21, 2019).

decisions affecting the attractiveness of a community. Our analysis here focuses on population growth, which is currently affecting many areas in the United States.

Population growth provokes a variety of reactions from the community's stakeholders relating to whether it is seen as an opportunity for economic development or a threat to a way of life. The community can be regarded as a complex network of interests, interactions, and collaborations among stakeholder groups, acting across multiple platforms. Through these platforms, information is produced, distributed, and consumed by stakeholders. This information is then used to discover, communicate, and advocate for various positions and actions affecting the community.

Table 6.4 summarizes the information and communication technologies (ICTs) used by stakeholders in the Arvada community. Note that none of the ICTs are used exclusively to produce and distribute information. One key benefit of modern ICTs is their ability to facilitate multidirectional flows of information through built-in interaction mechanisms (e.g., the city government uses its website primarily to produce and distribute information, but it is also able to collect information from its website through the comments and feedback posted by users).

The remainder of this chapter is structured into two main sections. The first focuses on Arvada's issues related to traffic, land development, affordable housing, and schools. The second examines the impact of growth-related development through a cultural lens by exploring a controversial urban renewal project. The chapter concludes with a discussion of how this case study contributes to the overall understanding of what makes for an attractive place to live. We also make suggestions for future research drawing on two areas of information science: computer-supported cooperative work and community informatics.

ADJUSTING TO GROWTH

In this section, we focus on how stakeholders in Arvada have responded to issues regarding a proposed parkway, affordable housing, the controversial

Table 6.4. Stakeholders and Information and Communication Technologies[a]

Information and Communication Technologies	Stakeholders									
	1	2	3	4	5	6	7	8	9	10
Social media	C	C	B	B	B	B	B	B	B	
Mobile applications	C	C	P							
City of Arvada website	C	C							B	
Developer websites	C	C	B							
Real estate websites		C		B	B					
Advocacy websites	C	C				B				
Nonprofits websites	C	C								
News websites	C	C					B			
Government-owned databases	C	C							B	
Privately owned databases		C	B	B						
Podcasts	C	C								
Radio	C	C			P					
E-mail/listservs	C	C	B	B	B	B	B	B	B	B
Newspapers	C	C			P			P		
Books	C	C								
Television news programs	C	C					P			
Places of worship	C	C				B				
Libraries	C	C								

Legend

Does not use information and communication technologies
Use only to produce/distribute information
Use only to consume information
Use to produce/distribute and consume information

Key to Major Stakeholders

1	Arvada Residents
2	Prospective Homebuyers and Renters
3	Real Estate Developers
4	Real Estate Companies
5	Real Estate Agents
6	Olde Town Arvada District
7	Jefferson County Public Schools
8	Arvada Emergency Services
9	City of Arvada Government
10	Arvada City Council

a. The table above presents eleven important stakeholders in Arvada and nineteen communication sources available to them. For each stakeholder, we researched the communication sources they utilize for information production and consumption.

use of land, and the increase in demand for public educational facilities. All of these issues have emerged because of Arvada's population increase.

Traffic

Traffic issues, such as congestion, car accidents, car pollution, and deteriorating road conditions, have been prominent among Arvada's growth-related concerns.[9] In some cases, these issues have been resolved or mitigated by policy decisions to make physical changes to the road infrastructure. Examples include the construction of an overpass to reduce traffic delays caused by a railroad crossing during heavy traffic periods, widening of an overpass to eliminate a traffic pinch point, the construction of an underpass to increase safety for bikers and pedestrians, and the addition of a tolled express lane on a major highway to both generate revenue and improve traffic flow.[10] These were effective resolutions to some of the traffic issues in Arvada; however, not all traffic issues have been resolved so successfully.

The Denver metropolitan toll roads were a response to growing traffic levels corresponding with a population boom in the area during the 1960s. Gradually, a beltway of toll roads was constructed around the perimeter of most of the metropolitan region, with one major exception.[11] The exception was the Jefferson Parkway project, which was intended to serve as the northwestern quadrant of the metropolitan beltway. The planned highway would run northeast through Arvada and the neighboring towns of Westminster and Broomfield. The Jefferson Parkway would be the final connecting link to complete the beltway surrounding the entire Denver metropolitan area (see figure 6.3).[12]

Unlike previous road construction projects in Arvada, which were achieved through collaborative effort, the Jefferson Parkway has resulted in ongoing conflict and legal action.[13] Leyden Rock, a community in northwest Arvada, has been especially affected, as the proposed tollway would be built as little as sixty feet away from homes in the neighborhood. Residents of Leyden Rock have voiced numerous concerns regarding the proximity of the parkway. Their concerns regard the dangers of fire, pollution, road debris, the safety of their children and pets, a decrease in property values, traffic congestion, and a lack of local access to the tollway for emergency vehicles and residents despite its passing directly through their community.[14]

Advocacy groups formed by residents play an important role in bringing attention to community issues. These groups give increased structure to residents' concerns and ensure that their voices are heard. The most effective means of protest for Leyden Rock residents has been a neighborhood advocacy group named the Movement to Stop Jefferson Parkway

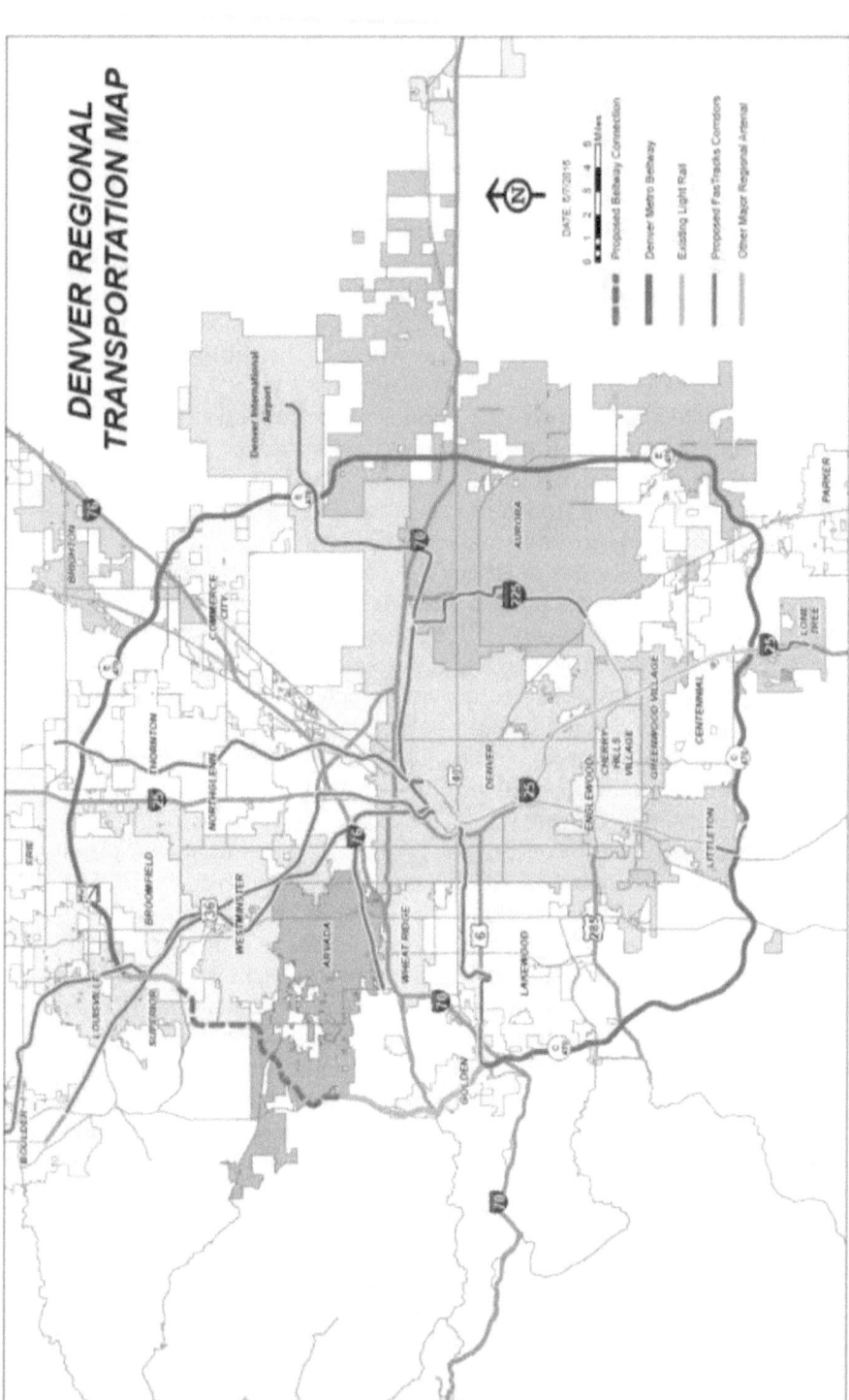

Figure 6.3. The Denver Regional Transportation Map. Jefferson Parkway Public Highway Authority. "Jefferson Parkway Public Highway Authority." Accessed November 21, 2019, https://www.jppha.org.

(MSJP).[15] Founded in January 2019, it began in an effort to preserve the current living conditions of residents in the area. By joining and supporting the group, residents can unify their voices and appeal to the city government to stop construction of the Jefferson Parkway.

MSJP has raised awareness for its cause by attending community events and city council meetings in addition to maintaining a significant online presence. MSJP tailors information to appeal to the logical minds and emotional hearts of city council members by strategically presenting testimonies and other information related to the concerns of both the affected residents and the community as a whole.[16] The group also maintains a presence on local news, which makes it possible for MSJP to share information related to its positions with a wider audience. The MSJP website also serves as an educational and mobilization platform. In addition to presenting facts related to the potential problems of the Jefferson Parkway, the website lists upcoming meeting dates to encourage those interested in joining the group to make their voices heard.[17]

In opposition to MSJP is the Jefferson Parkway Public Highway Authority (JPPHA), whose mission is to "design, build, finance, operate and maintain the Jefferson Parkway."[18] JPPHA was formed in conjunction with the project to secure funding and handle the bureaucratic processes. The group also serves as a liaison through which involvement with and interactions between stakeholders can be facilitated.

As the administrative group in charge of the Jefferson Parkway, JPPHA has public-, financial-, and business-related interests concerning the completion of the project. While the executive director of JPPHA, Bill Ray, acknowledges the concerns of Leyden Rock residents, he plans to continue the construction of the Jefferson Parkway. Initially, JPPHA worked with Leyden Rock developers to provide land for the housing development on the condition that the tollway could be built through the neighborhood. Ray claims that without the Jefferson Parkway project, the Leyden Rock community would not exist.[19] He also argues that JPPHA provided adequate information to prospective home owners about the construction of the tollway. For example, his organization installed signs every 500 feet along the route announcing the construction of Jefferson Parkway. Additionally, he made every original home owner sign a waiver affirming their awareness of the highway development plan.

JPPHA works in conjunction with city officials to secure permissions and funding for the project. In principle, the city council represents the interests of all Arvada residents. The city council has received repeated pleas from residents to reconsider the highway construction. Nevertheless, the city council has fully supported JPPHA and voted 5–1 to allocate funds to move forward with the Jefferson Parkway project.[20]

Many people in the metropolitan area do not work in the town in which they live. In particular, there is much commuting for work into Denver and Boulder. One of the Arvada city council's primary goals is to alleviate traffic on key commuter roads running through their town, and the Jefferson Parkway represents a viable way to do so.[21] In the 2019 Arvada State of the City address, Mayor Marc Williams emphasized the project's importance in removing traffic from local secondary roads.[22] By approving the Jefferson Parkway project, the city council acted in what it believed to be the community's best interests, achieving both traffic alleviation and economic advancement through increased commercial development.

The final hurdle remaining prior to construction of the Jefferson Parkway is the approval of funding by the neighboring city of Broomfield. However, Broomfield's approval for the project has recently been revoked because a soil sample drawn from a site nearby the proposed tollway showed elevated levels of plutonium.[23] (See the discussion of Rocky Flats below.) Although their concerns have not been resolved by Arvada city officials, the residents of Leyden Rock have a respite, knowing that Broomfield's city council is unlikely to fund the project as long as there is the potential to expose residents to hazardous material.

Construction of New and Affordable Housing

The availability of new and affordable housing is a crucial component of Arvada being considered a desirable place to live. The goal for the Arvada housing market is to develop a sustainable and diverse community of neighborhoods where quality housing is attainable for people across income classes.[24] The housing market has been affected by the rapid increase in population, and stakeholders, such as developers and advocacy groups, have worked to accommodate the surge of new residents. With the existing housing market being in high demand, housing and rental prices have increased substantially.[25] Finding affordable housing options has become a greater challenge for both existing and prospective residents. The city is constrained in its growth on the east side due to saturated use of its existing land and the proximity to other communities. The landscape on the west side of Arvada, which includes numerous open spaces, would appear ideal for the construction of new developments. However, there have been challenges with developing on this land, due primarily to Rocky Flats.

Development of Open Land on the West Side of Arvada

The underdeveloped land on the west side of Arvada has attracted both residential and commercial developments to accommodate the growing population and supplement Arvada's economy.[26] In 2004, land on Arvada's west side was designated for development under the Jefferson Center Urban Renewal Plan.[27] A key component of this plan was the construction of the Candelas community. Candelas features 3,030 family households, 619 nonfamily households, and a total population of more than 10,000 residents.[28] It includes a variety of housing types, ranging from condominiums to custom luxury single-family homes. The median listing price for a home in the Candelas community is approximately $200,000 higher than the average price of a home in Arvada.[29]

To illustrate the role of developers in Arvada's growth, we profile Lennar, one of the nine developers working in the Candelas community. It is an established national company involved in the construction and sale of single-family detached homes in the Candelas area. Lennar is a vertically integrated company able to handle many aspects of the home construction process, from land development to home building to sales. We examined Lennar's website to gain a better understanding of the information and communications technology used by these stakeholders.

Lennar uses multiple media types to generate awareness of its homes in Candelas. On social media, it uses a uniform structure to present similar messages across multiple platforms, such as posting an original blog post from its website on Facebook.[30] Lennar's website offers customers an in-depth experience by serving as a platform for initiating transactions. With an intended principal target audience of prospective home buyers, Lennar's website touts the company's ability to meet the needs of the community while also addressing the desires of individual home owners.

In order to facilitate the sales process, Lennar's website has adopted the standard features of online real estate services such as Zillow (e.g., interface with a map feature, pictures of the home, and basic information about the listing and surrounding community). Through the conscious design of the website, Lennar has made its homes, as well as the community of Arvada, look inviting to prospective home buyers. Before available listings are displayed on the website, Lennar provides access to important information for prospective residents, such as lists of nearby amenities, schools, and services. The layout of information on the website provides potential home buyers with the convenience of not having to search for this information while simultaneously advertising Arvada as a desirable place to live.[31]

Lennar lists on its website only homes that have never been occupied. By doing so, it can focus on promoting housing features that most influence buyer appeal, such as the opportunity for customization. When navigating the website, customers are presented with options regarding the configuration of interior spaces and opportunities for incorporating various in-home technologies. Customization is facilitated by Lennar's business partnerships with various product and service companies, such as Amazon, Samsung, and Baldwin, all of which produce smart home features that Lennar makes directly available to prospective buyers.[32]

Although many prospective residents are knowledgeable about the place to which they are looking to move, some people may be uncertain as to which location is going to best meet their needs. For this reason, developers and real estate websites strategically list properties to highlight the location's appeal. Prospective residents consult these platforms to become informed on the "quick facts" regarding a particular listing, such as listing pricing, square footage, and number of bedrooms and bathrooms. In addition, prospective residents want to ensure that they are within an acceptable distance from amenities such as shopping centers, health resources, schools, and other community resources. They also want to ensure that they have ready access to public utilities such as garbage collection and gas, electric, and water services. Lennar's website provides access to this type of information on the overview page for its Candelas homes, signifying the importance of this information to the decision-making process of home buyers (and an implicit statement of Lennar homes being a desirable place to live).[33]

Lennar intentionally avoids adding information to its website (e.g., photos showing people in their homes) that would suggest any one particular group of people (based on class, race, gender, and so on) as its target audience of home buyers. The company presents customer feedback and testimonials on its website from a diverse range of people. By doing so, Lennar is implicitly sending the message that its homes are designed for all people, even though the price of the homes is affordable to only a limited demographic.[34] Lennar's website also includes a tool allowing users to compare information about up to three Lennar homes in the Candelas neighborhood. This tool provides potential Arvada home buyers with information on the home's listing price, square footage, special features, amenities, nearby schools, and home availability.

Affordable Housing

Population growth in the Denver metropolitan area has resulted in a high demand for housing and a surge in housing prices, especially in Arvada. Between 2009 and 2019, the average price of a home in Arvada increased more than 90 percent, and the rental price increased more than 62 percent. (In comparison, during this same period, Denver's housing and rental prices increased 28 and 39 percent, respectively.[35]) Arvada defines "affordable" as housing that meets the needs of the household without costing the resident(s) more than 30 percent of its monthly income.[36] Considering that Arvada's average monthly income in 2017 was

$6,300, the average rental fees should have been less than $1,890 to meet the definition of affordable. However, the actual average monthly rental fee was slightly higher—at $1,937. According to a 2017 survey, 62 percent of residents believed that the housing costs were a deterrent to prospective Arvada home buyers. Of the residents of middle to low incomes, 71 percent of people "somewhat" or "strongly" agreed that Arvada's housing costs were difficult for them to afford.[37]

The rising cost of living in Arvada is particularly concerning for lower-income residents. If Arvada ceases to become affordable for them, they could be forced to move away. Some of these concerns have been expressed in community surveys:[38]

> There is such a high turnover of residents in Arvada. You get to know your neighbors, and then they have to move somewhere more affordable. There used to be better housing for young families in Arvada.

> Everyone is moving away or having to find roommates. I'll be moving to Greeley [in northern Colorado] next month. But I love Arvada. It's my home. I grew up here.

The City of Arvada provides financial assistance programs for people struggling to pay their rent. These programs are listed on the city's website, along with information on how to apply.[39] The city plans to make housing more affordable by working with developers and by approving funding and designating land for affordable housing projects. The new affordable housing developments will include both nonfamily (a "nonfamily household" consists of a householder living alone or where the householder shares the home exclusively with people to whom he or she is not related[40]) and multifamily housing.

Construction of multifamily housing, such as apartments and townhomes, is controversial across the United States due to issues such as parking and declining property values.[41] Although many cities have developed multifamily housing to provide affordable options to lower-income families, approximately one-third of Arvada residents are opposed to increasing this type of housing. By contrast, most lower-income and minority residents of Arvada "somewhat agree" or "strongly agreed" that the city should build more affordable multifamily housing developments.[42]

Nonfamily housing in Arvada is projected to see a 48 percent increase by 2035; however, only 9 percent of these houses will be considered affordable, according to the city's definition.[43] To address the lack of affordable housing, the city council has adopted a mixed new housing plan that incorporates a variety of housing types and styles in order to better accommodate diverse housing needs.[44]

Arvada has also instituted a series of housing development plans focused on affordable housing for the elderly.[45] City planners anticipate that the number of older adults will continue to rise over the coming years given the current size of the baby boomer (ages 45 to 64) and senior (age 65 and over) populations.[46] The city believes that it is increasingly important to provide affordable housing to the growing population of senior citizens. In response, the Attainable Senior Housing Development Program was launched in 2016 with the objective of developing at least fifty units of affordable senior housing by 2019.[47]

To gauge the need for senior housing in Arvada, the city launched a survey of older adults that was posted in various places, including the City of Arvada website and Arvada's Apex Senior Center. From the survey results, the city was able to determine that, although many seniors own the homes in which they currently live, seniors are nevertheless highly concerned with the availability of affordable options if they were to transfer to an assisted-living facility. Many respondents fear that they will have to leave Arvada due to the lack of affordable options. The survey also asked seniors about their preferences for housing and community resources. Proximity to grocery stores and medical services were among the top priorities. As a result, the city is ensuring that future development of affordable senior housing will be within walking distance of important amenities, and the council is implementing public transit stops at key locations throughout Arvada.[48]

Rocky Flats

The physical landscape of northwest Arvada, consisting of 6,240 acres of uncompromised land, would appear to be perfect for development; however, it contains hidden dangers in its soil. From 1952 until 1989, the land was home to the Rocky Flats Plant, a facility run by Dow Chemical and Rockwell International on behalf of the U.S. Department of Energy that manufactured nuclear bomb triggers. Due to manufacturing processes, spills, fires, and improper waste management at the plant, the land became highly contaminated. In 1989, the site was subject to extensive government cleanup efforts removing more than 500,000 cubic meters of radioactive waste. Every five years, the Environmental Protection Agency (EPA) visits the Rocky Flats area to assess the contamination levels. In 2005, the EPA determined that remaining contaminants in the soil no longer posed significant risk to human health.[49]

Despite the EPA determination that the land was safe for development, controversy arose with the construction of the Candelas community, which directly borders the Rocky Flats Wildlife Refuge, an area of land that occupies the site of the former weapons plant. Many Candelas home owners were distraught to learn that their homes bordered one of the most expensive hazardous materials cleanups in U.S. history. Many home owners did not know about their close proximity to Rocky Flats because developers are not required under law to disclose to home buyers details regarding the history of the land on which their homes are built.[50]

The concerns regarding the location of the new housing development were brought to light in part by the advocacy group Rocky Flats Right to Know. It is dedicated to educating residents about the history of the Rocky Flats Plant. It wants to ensure that Arvada residents, especially those living near the site, are informed about the remaining contaminants in the area. Some people still believe that the cleanup was rushed and negligent.[51] Like other advocacy groups in Arvada, Rocky Flats Right to Know relies heavily on in-person outreach through public meetings.[52] It also maintains an extensive online presence through an educational website and social media.[53]

One of the main goals for developers and real estate companies, of course, is to generate profit for its owners and shareholders. As a result, the new housing near Rocky Flats needs to be presented as an attractive place for residents to live. Because developers are not legally required to disclose information on Rocky Flats, they typically remain silent on this issue because it would likely decrease the appeal in the area.

This silence highlights the conflicting goals between developers and advocacy groups. At the center of this controversy is the notion of selective information sharing, as stakeholder groups reveal only the information that aligns with their personal interests. Selective information sharing directly impacts prospective home buyers, who are forced to consult multiple sources if they want to make knowledgeable decisions. The most readily available sources are sometimes biased, giving one-sided accounts. While ultimately the decision-making power is in the hands of the buyer, the decision may be influenced by the most readily available information. As a result, advocacy groups seek to have multidimensional outreach strategies to ensure that their concerns are heard by prospective residents, who may otherwise see only the flashy billboards and model homes of the Candelas developers.

Educational Facilities

The quality of the local school system is an important issue for prospective residents with children or those planning to have children when deciding where to live. It is also important for parents to find a school that best suits the learning style of their children to maximize their short- and long-term educational success. When looking for potential areas to live, parents will typically consult the information provided by real estate websites regarding the local schools. The west side of Arvada is experiencing rapid growth with the construction of multiple residential developments, such as Leyden Rock and Candelas. This construction has increased student enrollment numbers in public schools faster than what the Jefferson County (Jeffco) Public School District had expected.

Despite efforts to establish additional classroom space, the lack of educational infrastructure has become a significant issue for Arvada. It is projected that new developments will generate an additional 8,000 homes in western Arvada alone in the near future. With an estimate of one student per home, the area should expect an approximate increase of 8,000 students. To address the population increase, Jeffco Public Schools opened the Three Creeks K–8 School for the 2017–2018 academic year in the Candelas community. The school was designed to accommodate 800 students at full capacity, but by the end of its second academic year, it had already enrolled 750 students. Due to Arvada's growth projections, the developer designed the school to be able to expand by an additional 20,000 square feet. Three Creeks K–8 is a recipient of the Jeffco measures 5A and 5B funding and already plans to expand the building. The Jeffco measures are also providing funding for the development of another K–8 school in northwest Arvada.[54]

ENRICHING COMMUNITY AND ENVIRONMENT

In this section, we examine the impact of growth-related development through a cultural lens. We discuss a controversial development project within Arvada's historic district, the Olde Town Residences, initiated through a collaborative effort between Arvada's Urban Renewal Authority and developer Trammel Crow.

Arvada Urban Renewal Authority

The Arvada Urban Renewal Authority (AURA) is a city organization partnering with developers to reinvigorate blighted and underutilized areas in Arvada. While its primary objective is not fiscally related, the organization's new developments have a history of positively impacting the local economy. In 2017, AURA constructed 1,185 new households in the Arvada area. Multiplying the number of new households by the average household taxable spending, one finds that these developments added an estimated $12 million to Arvada's total taxable household base. In addition, AURA estimates that its activities in the commercial sector contributed to more than $3.5 million in new city revenues and fees.[55]

AURA's success demonstrates that it is in the city's best interest to develop strong partnerships with developers so as to both expand and improve Arvada's infrastructure. However, the development process is filled with constraints. Developers must undergo a comprehensive review process to gain permission to build in Arvada. First, they submit an initial proposal containing information related to the site plan, necessary materials, and other reports regarding the infrastructure. These developer plans are then subject to a review process by different bureaucratic entities within the city and the state (e.g., the planning division, ground engineering, parks and urban design committee, traffic engineering, fire protection, and the Colorado Department of Transportation). Next, the reviewed material containing the comments from each reviewing party are returned to the developers. After revisions are made to address the comments, the proposal goes through the reviewing process again. There may be several iterations.[56] Once the proposal is finalized, it must be reviewed by the city council and presented in a public hearing for any concerned residents to make their voices heard. Then the city council must vote to approve the development and its allotted funding. Only at the conclusion of this multistage process can a development project be initiated in Arvada.[57]

AURA serves as the liaison between residents and developers. It holds monthly meetings to review logistical procedures and discuss updates on the ongoing developments in the city. Similar to city council meetings, AURA's meetings are open to public comment, which enables developers to hear any concerns expressed by citizens directly. The goal of the AURA meetings is to reach outcomes that reflect the interests of the whole community. Even though AURA serves as the liaison to foster collaborative relationships, there is still a potential for conflict, as discussed in the following section.

Reimagining Olde Town

Located in the heart of the city, the historic district of Olde Town Arvada serves as a locus of the city's culture and small-town atmosphere. Olde Town has become a tourist attraction as well as a place for Arvada residents to enjoy a casual outing.[58] In addition to a walkable, compact area filled with restaurants, bars, and retail stores, Olde Town features a tree-covered park, a public library, a town square that hosts community events, and a recently opened commuter light rail system with service to Denver.[59] Despite Arvada's growth, Olde Town has maintained its small-town feel with a modest population of 1,500 people distributed across 883 households.[60] The businesses are mostly independently owned rather than national chains, and the neighborhood has a year-round schedule of community events.[61]

Many of Arvada's residents want to maintain Olde Town's historic character; however, this presents a challenge for the city. In response to population growth, an initiative was introduced to develop affordable housing for diversified residents across the city.[62] As a result, Arvada has instituted numerous affordable housing projects, including a controversial development in Olde Town.[63] In 2017, AURA worked the Regional Transportation District[64] to sell a nine-acre plot of land near the light rail system in Olde Town to developer Trammel Crow. The light rail is an eleven-mile stretch of track running from Arvada to Denver.[65] AURA wanted to sell this land to the developer for just $30 even though the land was valued at more than $6 million.[66] The city reported that the low selling price, together with a sales and property tax rebate until 2034, represented a concession of $13 million.[67] In return, the developer agreed to build a dense, affordable, transit-oriented housing development in Olde Town.[68] The Olde Town Residences, a 252-unit apartment complex and parking garage, are also planned to include a park, dog park, and streetscape.[69] A later phase of the project would include 40,000 square feet of retail space.[70]

The Olde Town Residences project has met with substantial resistance from citizens, who believe that it will compromise the character and charm of Olde Town Arvada.[71] One of the leaders of this resistance is a grassroots organization, Arvada for All the People (AAP). The organization's goal is to ensure that the city council makes decisions that represent the best interests of Arvada's residents. Many of the items on AAP's action agenda are directly related to issues of growth in Arvada.

AAP has recently addressed the Olde Town Residences and the alterations to the historic district initiated by the AURA.[72] AAP is concerned that the new development will require the demolition of several historic buildings and introduce a tall residential structure into an area filled with historic stone and brick, low-rise structures.[73] They also argue that the development will not promote the light rail system or increase civilian use but instead will cause greater traffic and pollution in the area and increase the rent and cost of living for residents.[74]

The controversy surrounding the Olde Town Residences has been debated primarily during community gatherings, including city council meetings, and through legal action.[75] While developers work on a contractual basis with AURA and the city, advocacy groups use city council meetings to air their concerns. News media have also played a significant role in how residents produce, distribute, and consume information related to the Olde Town Residences project. For example, when the $30 Land Deal was finalized, it became a major news story broadcast across local and regional media. Arvada's mayor, Marc Williams, expressed support for the project, which was widely recorded and televised.[76] Although advocacy groups, such as AAP, continue to oppose the development in the historic district, their efforts have largely been unsuccessful. The Olde Town Residences project was approved with a plan to break ground in 2019.[77]

FINAL WORDS

This chapter examined the issue of where to live from the perspective of a community rather than from the viewpoint of an individual or an organization. It explored the issues facing the city of Arvada as a result of a rapid increase in population. Altering aspects of a community is a complicated process because of the multiple stakeholders involved, each possessing different values, motives, and objectives regarding the community. Many of Arvada's issues are directly connected to the impact that population growth has on the demand for housing, facilities, and infrastructure.

From a business perspective, the increasing demand provides an opportunity for developers to make an immense profit and for the city to expand its economic base. The use of ICTs by developers is largely commercial, as they often have a product (i.e., a housing development) to sell. Developers strategically tailor their websites to appeal to the values of prospective home buyers by listing options for customization as well as information on the nearby amenities and resources.

Economic booms resulting from increased demand have incentivized the city to foster a positive relationship with developers. It is also beneficial for city officials to become information liaisons between residents and developers to ensure that all stakeholder voices are heard. One of the main goals for the local city government is to provide a hub of information and resources for residents and community stakeholders. Having easy access to important information regarding the community is crucial in terms of developing an attractive place to live.

Concerned citizens have formed advocacy groups to collectivize individual voices and produce a larger and more impactful opposition regarding community issues. City council meetings continue to be an integral part of both the information acquisition and the dissemination strategies of advocacy groups. Social media and their personal websites enable these groups to distribute information to a wider audience. Advocacy groups also benefit from news media coverage, which can quickly spread their messages beyond the confines of the community. This wide-scale recognition is necessary to both increase support bases and disincentivize controversial developments.

Demand is invariably tied to location. As a result, schools are being built and expanded near new housing developments, and senior housing is being built near to amenities and light rail routes. However, the relationship between demand and location can also have negative consequences. The construction of a trendy, convenient, affordable housing base in historic Olde Town Arvada, the Olde Town Residences, has evolved into a community-wide controversy. Another negative consequence was exposed when it became public that the Candelas developers did not disclose information about the Rocky Flats Plant to prospective home buyers. Instead, prospective buyers had to consult other information sources to make an educated decision on whether to buy a home in the Candelas community. As suggested by our discussion in this chapter, effective communication between stakeholders is crucial to ensure that the community remains an attractive place to live.

Directions for Future Research

This chapter presents an empirical case study focused on understanding what makes a community an attractive place to live. Although the main contributions of this research are situated in everyday information behavior, our work also provides opportunities for future studies drawing on the methods and approaches of two other well-established fields of information science known as computer-supported cooperative work (CSCW) and community informatics.

CSCW is a research field exploring "the technical, social, material, and theoretical challenges of designing technology to support collaborative work and life activities."[78] It is concerned with the design and use of technologies affecting groups, organizations, communities, and networks. Recent studies in CSCW, for example, have considered how government data can be made more accessible to residents through participatory infrastructural design and open-source platforming.[79]

Community informatics examines the potential of ICTs to impact the social and economic development of communities.[80] The goal of community informatics is to overcome barriers in a community by using information technology to facilitate connections between stakeholders.[81] Previous studies in community informatics, for example, have examined the potential of ICTs to improve communication between residents in a community. In addition, they have studied how data, information, and ICTs are used differently, depending on the characteristics of the people, communities, and societies.[82] Community informatics has the potential to mediate conflict through the creation of digital environments in which stakeholders can share different perspectives, reach agreements, and create sustainable plans.[83]

We do not have space here to explore the use of CSCW or community informatics. However, there are many questions that can be addressed in future research. These questions include the following:

1. How are the concerns of stakeholders in a community addressed or mirrored in the designs of various city-provided resources?
2. How can existing resources be used to more effectively involve the relevant stakeholders in important community decisions? How can these resources be used more efficiently to facilitate discussion among stakeholders?
3. Does the way in which ICTs are used by stakeholders align with the intended purpose of the ICTs? How does the use of ICTs differ among stakeholders for different issues? What are the implications for the developers of ICTs?

NOTES

1. This chapter is based, in part, on a much longer white paper written by the authors titled "Understanding Living in a Bedroom Community: A Case Study from the Denver-Boulder Metropolitan Region" (2019). A link to the white paper can be found at https://justcode.cbi.umn.edu/william-aspray.

2. City of Arvada, "Colorado's First Documented Gold Strike," n.d., https://arvada.org/about/our-community/colorado-s-first-documented-gold-strike.

3. City of Arvada, "The Founding of Our Community," n.d., https://arvada.org/about/our-community/the-founding-of-our-community.

4. History.com, "G.I. Bill," May 27, 2010, https://www.history.com/topics/world-war-ii/gi-bill.

5. Lyman Stone, "A Population History of Denver—In a State of Migration," August 18, 2016, https://medium.com/migration-issues/a-population-history-of-denver-8a6804e3dac5.

6. "Arvada, Colorado Population 2019," n.d., http://worldpopulationreview.com/us-cities/arvada-co-population; Grand Park, "Why Is Everyone Moving to Colorado?," https://www.grandparkco.com/why-is-everyone-moving-to-colorado (accessed April 26, 2019).

7. Grand Park, "Why Is Everyone Moving to Colorado?"

8. U.S. Census Bureau, "U.S. Census Bureau QuickFacts: Arvada City, Colorado," 2018, https://www.census.gov/quickfacts/fact/table/arvadacitycolorado/PST045218 (accessed November 21, 2019).

9. City of Arvada, "Speak Up Arvada December 2018 Report," https://arvada.org/source/Speak%20Up/FINAL%20SpeakUpArvadaReport_withAppendix_jan1 0%202.pdf (accessed November 21, 2019); Anthony Downs, "Why Traffic Congestion Is Here to Stay . . . and Will Get Worse," *ACCESS Magazine*, October 1, 2004, https://escholarship.org/uc/item/3sh9003x; Law Offices of George Salinas, "San Antonio's Rapid Population Growth May Lead to More Traffic Accidents," https://www.salinastriallaw.com/san-antonios-rapid-population-growth-may-lead-to-more-traffic-accidents (accessed July 16, 2018); Movement to Stop Jefferson Parkway, "Join Our Movement Now! No Political Position, Just the Facts," https://stopjeffersonparkway.com/parkway-history (accessed November 21, 2019).

10. City of Arvada, "Dec 9, 2008: Grandview Overpass Opens over Wadsworth," https://arvada.org/about/news-events/dec-9-2008-grandview-overpass-opens-over-wadsworth (accessed November 21, 2019); Hamon Infrastructure, "Wadsworth By-Pass Grade Separation," https://hamoninfrastructure.com/project-details/wadsworth-by-pass-grade-separation/ (accessed November 21, 2019); Sarah Kutah, "Enforcement in Focus on U.S. 36 Toll Lanes," *Daily Camera*, October 7, 2016, http://www.dailycamera.com/ci_30447179/enforcement-focus-u-s-36-toll-lanes.

11. Movement to Stop Jefferson Parkway, "Join Our Movement Now!"

12. Jefferson Parkway Public Highway Authority, "Jefferson Parkway Public Highway Authority," https://www.jppha.org (accessed November 21, 2019).

13. Joe Rubino, "Federal Judge Dismisses Suits Blocking Jefferson Parkway Land Swap Deal," *Daily Camera*, December 22, 2012, https://www.dailycamera.com/2012/12/22/federal-judge-dismisses-suits-blocking-jefferson-parkway-land-swap-deal (accessed November 21, 2019).

14. Movement to Stop Jefferson Parkway, "Join Our Movement Now!"

15. Movement to Stop Jefferson Parkway, "Join Our Movement Now!"

16. Movement to Stop Jefferson Parkway, "Join Our Movement Now!"

17. Movement to Stop Jefferson Parkway, "Join Our Movement Now!"

18. Jefferson Parkway Public Highway Authority, "Jefferson Parkway P3 Project Request for Qualifications," September 7, 2018, https://static1.squarespace.com/static/5982321ecd0f68fa59f9fd97/t/5baa92dc7817f7d61464863e/1537905373916/Original+RFQ+plus+addendum+%231+redline+version.pdf (accessed November 21, 2019).

19. Michael Abeyta, "Some Neighbors Unhappy with Planned Jefferson Parkway: 'What They Are Doing Is Wrong,'" *CBS Denver*, March 3, 2019, https://denver.cbslocal.com/2019/03/03/neighbors-unhappy-jefferson-parkway (accessed November 21, 2019).

20. City of Arvada, "Summary of Minutes of the Meeting of the Arvada City Council Held March 18, 2019," https://library.municode.com/co/arvada/munidocs/munidocs?nodeId=14bfcf8c81bfd (accessed November 21, 2019).

21. Jefferson Parkway Public Highway Authority, "Executive Summary," July 20, 2009, https://www.jppha.org/wp-content/uploads/2019/08/2009-System-Feasibility-Study.pdf (accessed November 21, 2019).

22. Shanna Fortier, "Safety, Infrastructure, Community Focuses of Arvada State of the City Address," *Arvada Press*, April 22, 2019, https://arvadapress.com/stories/safety-infrastructure-community-focuses-of-arvada-state-of-the-city-address,279531 (accessed November 21, 2019).

23. Jennifer Kovaleski, "Broomfield City Leaders Say Jefferson Parkway Will Not Be 'Moving Forward,'" *The Denver Channel*, September 2, 2019, https://www.thedenverchannel.com/news/our-colorado/broomfield-says-jefferson-parkway-is-not-moving-forward (accessed November 29, 2019).

24. City of Arvada, "City Council Strategic Plan 2020–2025," September 16, 2019, https://arvada.org/source/Focus/COA%20Council%20Strat%20Plan%202019.pdf (accessed November 29, 2019).

25. Jennifer Black, "A 10 Year Look at the Denver Real Estate Market," *USAJ Real Estate*, September 4, 2019, https://blog.usajrealty.com/posts/a-look-at-the-denver-real-estate-market (accessed November 29, 2019).

26. City of Arvada, "Arvada 2005 Comprehensive Plan," https://static.arvada.org/docs/City-of-Arvada-2005-Comprehensive-Plan-Final-1-201410271311.pdf (accessed November 21, 2019).

27. The west side of Arvada (Candelas, Leyden Rock, and Whisper Creek areas) was called Jefferson Center before. This development plan has been called by different names—such as the Jefferson Center Urban Renewal Plan, the Northwest Arvada Urban Renewal Plan, and Candelas development—but these plans covered the same area at the intersection of Highway 93 and Highway 72 and along Indiana Street.

28. Point 2 Homes, "Candelas Demographics," https://www.point2homes.com/US/Neighborhood/CO/Candelas-Demographics.html (accessed December 9, 2019).

29. Candelas, "Candelas—A Master Planned Community in Arvada, CO," https://www.candelaslife.com (accessed November 21, 2019); Zillow. "United States Home Prices and Values," https://www.zillow.com/home-values (accessed November 29, 2019).

30. Lennar, "Lennar," *Facebook*, https://www.facebook.com/Lennar (accessed November 29, 2019).

31. Lennar, "Candelas," https://www.lennar.com/new-homes/colorado/denver/arvada/candelas (accessed November 29, 2019).

32. Lennar, "Everything's Included in Your New Dream Home," https://www.lennar.com/ei (accessed November 29, 2019).

33. Lennar, "Candelas."

34. While these prices are much higher than they are in eastern Arvada, they are substantially less than in nearby communities of Boulder and Louisville or in the higher-end neighborhoods of Denver.

35. Zillow, "Zillow: Real Estate, Apartments, Mortgages & Home Values," https://www.zillow.com (accessed November 21, 2019).

36. City of Arvada, "Attainable (Affordable) Housing," https://arvada.org/residents/city-neighborhoods/attainable-housing (accessed November 30, 2019).

37. Northwest Research Group, "2017 Arvada Community Survey Final Report," December 21, 2017, https://arvada.org/source/Arvada_2017_Community_Survey_Final_Report_12-21-2017_Final.pdf (accessed November 30, 2019).

38. City of Arvada, "Speak Up Arvada December 2018 Report," https://arvada.org/source/Speak%20Up/FINAL%20SpeakUpArvadaReport_with Appendix_jan10%202.pdf (accessed November 21, 2019).

39. Arvada, "Attainable (Affordable) Housing."

40. U.S. Census Bureau, "Subject Definitions," https://www.census.gov/programs-surveys/cps/technical-documentation/subject-definitions.html (accessed December 4, 2019).

41. Mark Orbinsky and Debra Stein, "Overcoming Opposition to Multifamily Rental Housing," Harvard University, Joint Center for Housing Studies, March 2007, https://www.jchs.harvard.edu/sites/default/files/rr07-14_obrinsky_stein.pdf (accessed November 30, 2019)

42. Northwest Research Group, "2017 Arvada Community Survey Final Report."

43. City of Arvada, "Comprehensive Plan 2014," September 16, 2014, https://static.arvada.org/docs/Arvada_2014_Comprehensive_Plan_(Full_version)-1-201706071308.pdf (accessed November 30, 2019).

44. City of Arvada, "Growth and Development," http://arvada.clearpointstrategy.com/growth-and-development/housing-in-mixed-use-areas (accessed June 15, 2019).

45. City of Arvada, "Housing Programs," https://arvada.org/residents/city-neighborhoods/housing-programs (accessed November 21, 2019).

46. City of Arvada, "Comprehensive Plan 2014."

47. City of Arvada, "Attainable (Affordable) Housing."

48. City of Arvada, "Senior and Workforce Housing in Arvada, December 2016," https://arvada.org/residents/city-neighborhoods/attainable-housing (accessed December 10, 2019).

49. State of Colorado, "What Is the History of Rocky Flats?," https://www.colorado.gov/pacific/sites/default/files/HM_sf-rocky-flats-exposures-study-history-of-site.pdf (accessed November 21, 2019); U.S. Environmental Protection Agency, "Superfund Site: Rocky Flats Plant (USDOE) Golden, CO," https://cumulis.epa.gov/supercpad/SiteProfiles/index.cfm?fuseaction=second.cleanup&id=0800360 (accessed November 29, 2019).

50. Candelas Concerns, "About Candelas," http://www.candelasconcerns.com/about-candelas (accessed November 29, 2019).

51. Rocky Flats Right to Know, "Rocky Flats History," https://www.rockyflatsrighttoknow.org (accessed November 29, 2019).

52. Rocky Flats Right to Know, "Calendar," https://www.rockyflatsrighttoknow.org/calendar (accessed November 29, 2019).

53. Rocky Flats Right to Know, "Home," Facebook, https://www.facebook.com/ROCKYFLATSRIGHTTOKNOW (accessed November 27, 2019).

54. Hord I Coplan I Macht, "Three Creeks K–8 School," https://www.hcm2.com/projects/three-creeks-k-8-school (accessed December 9, 2019); Jefferson County Public Schools, "Future Funding: Growing Pains in Jeffco Schools," YourHub, October 22, 2018, https://yourhub.denverpost.com/blog/2018/10/jeffco-schools-technology-use-three-creeks/228472 (accessed November 29, 2019).

55. Arvada Urban Renewal Authority, "Economic and Fiscal Benefits of the AURA Projects and Activities," February 2018, http://arvadaurbanrenewal.org/about-us/economic-impact-report (accessed December 13, 2019).

56. Project Search, "Project #DA2019-0034," City of Arvada, eTRACKit, https://www.arvadapermits.org/etrakit3 (accessed December 10, 2019).

57. Municode Library, "Arvada, CO Munidocs," https://library.municode.com/co/arvada/munidocs/munidocs (accessed December 10, 2019).

58. City of Arvada, "Olde Town Arvada," https://arvada.org/explore/olde-town-arvada/olde-town-arvada (accessed November 21, 2019).

59. Realtor.com, "Olde Town Arvada Area, Arvada, CO Real Estate & Homes for Sale," https://www.realtor.com/realestateandhomes-search/Olde-Town-Arvada-Area_Arvada_CO (accessed November 27, 2019).

60. Statistical Atlas, "The Demographic Statistical Atlas of the United States," https://statisticalatlas.com/neighborhood/Colorado/Arvada/Historic-Olde-Town/Population (accessed November 27, 2019).

61. City of Denver, "Olde Town Arvada," https://www.denver.org/about-denver/neighborhood-guides/olde-town-arvada (accessed November 27, 2019).

62. "Based on similar initiatives in nearby cities such as Loveland, Lafayette, and Longmont, Colorado, as well as on information mined from extensive city documents, the Arvada Arts and Culture Master Plan includes three major ideas addressed in its framework: openness; being welcoming towards diversity, social offerings; town-offered amenities that people enjoy, and aesthetics; how the town manages a physically-pleasing atmosphere. The plan features four general stages which the city believes will promote their leadership in creating a welcoming environment for arts and culture. They are outlined here: 1. The first of these highlights the creation of places that instill feelings of attachment to the community through environmental and historic preservation, as well as the creation of an arts district. 2. This stage looks further into the creation of an arts district in Arvada, outlining a two-mile corridor between the Arvada Center and Olde Town (included with the plans for linkage addressed above) that would promote cultural activities and events, as well as the work of various artists. 3. This stage looks to create new events that are friendly to every generation. 4. This stage will use the insights of local artists to determine the barriers to this group in living and functioning within the city and then effectively work to eliminate these barriers to facilitate these artists' accommodation (includes adding affordable housing options). See City of Arvada, "Arvada Arts and Culture Master Plan," 2018, https://arvada.org/source/AACC%20Master%20Plan%202018.pdf (accessed November 29, 2019).

63. Arvada Urban Renewal Authority, "Development Areas," http://arvadaurbanrenewal.org/aura-development-areas (accessed November 27, 2019).

64. Colorado Community Media, "The Truth about the Olde Town Residences Development," May 23, 2018, http://coloradocommunitymedia.com/stories/the-truth-about-the-olde-town-residences-development,262438 (accessed November 27, 2019).

65. Regional Transportation District—Denver, "G-Line," https://www.rtd-denver.com/fastracks/g-line (accessed November 27, 2019).

66. Rob Low, "City Council Kills $30 Land Deal in Arvada," Fox 31 Denver, January 28, 2018, https://kdvr.com/2018/01/23/city-council-kills-30-land-deal-in-arvada (accessed November 29, 2019).

67. Low, "City Council Kills $30 Land Deal in Arvada."

68. Transit-oriented development is a relatively new phenomenon of housing developments centered around high-quality railroad-based transportation systems. It focuses on condensing housing (often through apartment complexes) and amenities into walkable communities while reducing the need for reliance on cars by residents. See Transit Oriented Development Institute, "Home," http://www.tod.org (accessed November 29, 2019); Angie Schmitt, "Why Affordable Housing Is So Important for Development Near Transit," Streetsblog USA, June 20, 2018, https://usa.streetsblog.org/2018/06/20/why-affordable-housing-is-so-important-for-development-near-transit (accessed November 29, 2019); and Jana

Lynott, "Transit-Oriented Housing Helps Older Adults Live Independent Lives," AARP Livable Communities, September 2017, https://www.aarp.org/livable-communities/getting-around/info-2017/transit-oriented-development-senior-housing-denver.html (accessed November 29, 2019).

69. Colorado Community Media, "The Truth about the Olde Town Residences Development."

70. Arvada Urban Renewal Authority, "Olde Town Residences TOD," http://arvadaurbanrenewal.org/projects/9-acre-tod-site (accessed November 27, 2019).

71. Arvada for All the People, "Action Agenda for Arvada," https://www.arvadaforallthepeople.com/action-agenda-for-arvada.html (accessed November 27, 2019); City of Arvada, "Summary of Minutes of the Meeting of the Arvada City Council Held March 19, 2018," https://library.municode.com/co/arvada/munidocs/munidocs (accessed November 27, 2019).

72. Arvada for All the People, "Action Agenda for Arvada."

73. Save Arvada Now, "Park Place Olde Town Is a Threat to Olde Town Arvada," https://www.savearvadanow.info/park-place-olde-town-is-a-threat-to-olde-town-arvada (accessed November 27, 2019).

74. Arvada for All the People, "Action Agenda for Arvada."

75. Arvada Urban Renewal Authority, "Summary of Minutes of Regular Meeting Arvada Urban Renewal Authority Board of Commissioners Wednesday, May 2, 2018," http://arvadaurbanrenewal.org/calendar-meetings/meeting-minutes (accessed December 10, 2019); City of Arvada, "Summary of Minutes of the Meeting of the Arvada City Council Held January 22, 2018," https://library.municode.com/co/arvada/munidocs/munidocs (accessed December 10, 2019).

76. Low, "City Council Kills $30 Land Deal in Arvada."

77. Arvada Urban Renewal Authority, "Olde Town Residences TOD."

78. ACM CSCW, *CSCW '20: 23rd Conference on Computer Supported Cooperative Work and Social Computing: Introduction*, 2019, https://cscw.acm.org (accessed December 5, 2019).

79. Aare Puussaar, Ian G. Johnson, Kyle Montague, Philip James, and Peter Wright, "Making Open Data Work for Civic Advocacy," *Proceedings of the ACM on Human-Computer Interaction* 2, no. CSCW (2018): 143; Miriam Redi, Luca Maria Aiello, Rossano Schifanella, and Daniele Quercia, "The Spirit of the City: Using Social Media to Capture Neighborhood Ambiance," *Proceedings of the ACM on Human-Computer Interaction* 2, no. CSCW (2018): 144; Ronald Schroeter, "Engaging New Digital Locals with Interactive Urban Screens to Collaboratively Improve the City," in *Proceedings of the ACM 2012 Conference on Computer Supported Cooperative Work*, 227–36 (New York: Association for Computing Machinery, 2012); Nick Taylor, Loraine Clarke, Martin Skelly, and Sara Nevay, "Strategies for Engaging Communities in Creating Physical Civic Technologies," in *Proceedings of the 2018 CHI Conference on Human Factors in Computing Systems*, 507 (New York: Association for Computing Machinery, 2018).

80. Michael Gurstein, "Introduction Community Informatics: Enabling Community Uses of Information and Communications Technology," 2000, https://www.igi-global.com/chapter/community-informatics-enabling-community-uses/6702 (accessed December 20, 2019).

81. Michael Gurstein, "What Is Community Informatics (and Why Does It Matter)?," ArXiv:0712.3220 [Cs], December 19, 2007, http://arxiv.org/abs/0712.3220 (accessed December 20, 2019).

82. Information School | University of Washington, "Information and Society | University of Washington," https://ischool.uw.edu/research/areas/information-society (accessed December 20, 2019); University of Michigan School of Information. "Citizen Interaction Design | University of Michigan School of Information," https://www.si.umich.edu/node/12166 (accessed December 20, 2019).

83. Arizona State University, "Center for Policy Informatics | Arizona State University," https://policyinformatics.asu.edu (accessed December 20, 2019); Arizona State University, "Synthetic Empathy | Center for Policy Informatics," https://policyinformatics.asu.edu/content/synthetic-empathy (accessed December 20, 2019).

Seven

The Valley between Us
The Meta-Hodology of Racial Segregation in Milwaukee, Wisconsin

Judith Pintar

> Boundaries are only of interest because they define the limits of regions. But precisely because of this, boundaries can acquire a life of their own. The existence of a boundary can have a palpable effect on the behaviour of objects and people in its vicinity. Disputes over territory automatically become focussed into disputes over boundaries, and the boundary itself can become a symbol for the territory it delineates.[1]

> We got a couple of threatening telephone calls saying that if we march on the South Side we're going to march in blood. And I thought it was an open city. Everybody says Milwaukee's an open city and you can walk any place you please, but it seems like that 16th Street Viaduct is the "Mason Dixon Line" so now we're going to march across that and walk around on the South Side a little bit and go out to [Kosciusko Park] and have a little Black Power picnic out there and see what the people out there think about it, especially that Mayor Maier.[2]

In 1967, African American civil rights activists in Milwaukee, Wisconsin, led a march for fair housing across the 16th Street Viaduct, one of eight long bridges that span the Menomonee River Valley. This nonviolent march, which included many children from Milwaukee's chapter of the NAACP Youth Council, was met by openly racist counterprotest. The violence of the white response shocked the city and brought its racial problems to the attention of the nation. Two hundred consecutive days of marching by the activists led to the 1968 passage of a local open housing ordinance, the same year that the federal Fair Housing Act became law. These positive legislative movements did not, however, lead to housing integration across the valley; more than half a century later, the city of Milwaukee remains one of the most racially segregated cities in the United States and the single most segregated metropolitan area.³

In trying to understand the real estate processes that created racialized neighborhoods and cities, researchers have looked to the maps made in the 1930s by the Home Owners Loan Corporation (HOLC), an agency formed during the Roosevelt administration. Among the economic consequences of the 1929 Wall Street crash was widespread unemployment. The federal government acted to protect home owners from foreclosure through a variety of means, including refinancing. The HOLC maps were intended to guide the standards used by private lenders as well as decisions made by the Federal Housing Administration (FHA). Between the 1930s and the early 1970s, millions of homes were purchased with help of the FHA. These loans and the home owners' insurance necessary to receive them were overwhelmingly made to white families that desired to move outside city centers. In effect, the FHA incentivized a suburbanization process that shifted the *white* middle class out of urban areas, with deleterious consequences for inner-city neighborhoods.⁴

Milwaukee, like many other American cities, was mapped by the HOLC. These maps were based on systematic data collection that operationalized the imprecise concept of "risk" in real estate investment, making it appear to be empirically measurable by the same standards nationwide. The instrument crafted for the data collection used demographic variables, including race, income, and immigration status, to assign risk values to each surveyed neighborhood. The most homogeneously white, desirable neighborhoods were rated A, "Best," and colored green. Homogeneously white, racially unchanging neighborhoods in less prosperous areas were rated B, "Still Desirable," and colored blue. Racially or ethnically mixed "at-risk" neighborhoods were rated C, "Definitely Declining," and colored yellow. The neighborhoods with the largest numbers of nonwhite residents and most new immigrants were rated D, "Hazardous," and colored red. People living in "C" and "D" neighborhoods could be denied the insurance and the loans needed to buy a home as a result of their residence in high-risk neighborhoods and not, ostensibly, because of their race or ethnicity. This disingenuous practice came to be known as redlining.⁵

Whether and to what degree HOLC maps are responsible for *causing* the redlining that occurred throughout the twentieth century and into the twenty-first has been an issue of contention.⁶ Because both the term and the practice had existed in the real estate industry prior to the making of the HOLC maps, the data that created them can also be understood as a snapshot of the racial views that already had influenced the housing industry when HOLC entered the scene. To assess the social impacts of the HOLC maps, it is necessary to examine the embedded narratives that shaped them. What can be found there is evidence of a systematic plan for the maintenance of racial segregation across urban centers in the United States; the HOLC maps were one tool applied toward that end.

In this chapter, I argue that the federal government and a complex network of actors connected to the real estate industry, including lending agencies, insurance companies, and urban policymakers, fostered racial and ethnic segregation by systematically encouraging disinvestment in neighborhoods where African Americans and immigrants resided. Their policies and practices resulted in an enduring disenfranchisement of African Americans but not white immigrants in Milwaukee and across the United States. I understand redlining as racial bias in practice, a kind of data storytelling that is best understood as narrative manipulation—as propaganda.

THE HOLC MAPS

When they were commissioned, the HOLC maps were intended to be a forecasting tool to guide real estate practitioners. Their purpose was to assess "stability," a projection of whether credit risk would increase or decrease in given neighborhoods. Stability was based on a simple racial metric, as the FHA handbook laid it out in 1938: "If a neighborhood is to retain stability, it is necessary that properties shall continue to be occupied by the same social and racial classes. A change in social or racial occupancy generally contributes to instability and a decline in values."[7] By equating stability with racial homogeneity and credit risk with racial integration, they produced a powerful self-fulfilling prophecy; home owners' insurance and loans flowed to segregated white communities at the expense of nonwhite, integrated, integrating, neighborhoods, or those perceived to be at risk for future integration.

Academic awareness of redlining began in earnest with the work of historian Kenneth Jackson, who discussed redlining in the context of a larger argument regarding the federal government's support for white suburbs and its sacrifice of urban and increasingly African American city centers.[8] When Jackson's research on the HOLC maps went public, the HOLC data collectors' use of unapologetically racist language to record the "infiltration" of African Americans and the "encroachment" of Jews, Italians, and Slavs seemed to many to be a smoking gun. Had the HOLC maps *caused* redlining and the racial segregation that was its direct result? There were empirical reasons why this appeared to be so.

In a sample of fifty-two cities mapped in 1940, despite African Americans making up only 8 percent of the sampled population, 86 percent lived in redlined neighborhoods, compared to white people who represented 90 percent of the sample population, with only 35 percent living in redlined areas.⁹ The correlation between the HOLC maps and discriminatory real estate practice is also clear: denial of access to home loans to members of redlined communities was endemic across the United States in the twentieth century, and the effects have lingered. Fair housing laws have been on the books for half a century, but the negative effects on neighborhoods redlined in the 1940s, in terms of housing supply, density of population, and economic activity, have continued.¹⁰ In Milwaukee neighborhoods lying within ZIP code 53206, for example, one of Milwaukee's redlined areas, the poverty rate in 2017 was six times greater than in the city's white suburbs.¹¹ A study that looked at housing discrimination in relationship to racial cancer disparities found that rates of African American cancer mortality correlate with residence in areas with higher levels of mortgage discrimination.¹²

A renewed interest in HOLC maps, which are housed at the National Archives, has followed their digitization by a team at the University of Richmond's Digital Scholarship Lab. Led by Robert K. Nelson, the lab created interactive versions of the maps, linking them directly to the collected information used to construct them.¹³ Data collectors were asked to rate the security of neighborhoods through a specific set of criteria. The "Area Description—Security Maps" forms collected data that included residents' race, ethnicity, and social class as well as real estate values. As had been done in other cities based on census data and other records, the researchers filled them out neighborhood by neighborhood from field observation as well as from their own personal and local knowledge.

The "Area" data collected for each neighborhood included a narrative: "Description of the Terrain" and the "Favorable" and "Detrimental Influences" on it. The section on "Inhabitants" included composite information regarding residents' occupation; income; percentage of foreign-born residents with reference to predominant areas of origin; percentage of "Negroes" and families receiving "relief" payments; whether the population was increasing, decreasing, or remaining static; and what type of people were "infiltrating" each neighborhood. A long section included information about building types, age, condition, occupancy, ownership, price range over time, rental cost over time, demand, and activity. The general availability of mortgage funds was noted.

A final section titled "Clarifying Remarks" invited the data collectors to provide narrative explanation for their ratings, comments that include descriptive and at times almost ethnographic depictions of neighborhoods and the people who lived in them. These notes inadvertently captured the bias of those who did the collecting. The fact that the research instrument did not flag racialized language as problematic is an indication that the HOLC and the federal government that created the agency did not find it so. The word "infiltration," for example, is printed on the form itself.

Despite the bias of the HOLC data collection and evidence of long-term economic and social damage associated with redlining, the direct influence of the maps has been contested by scholars over the past few decades. Examining residential mortgages in Philadelphia in the 1930s, Hillier did not find that the HOLC grade explained differences in lending patterns over time since real estate practices that discriminated against immigrants and African Americans were in place before the HOLC maps were made. She suggests that they may have reflected rather than influenced the urban housing policy in the residential real estate market. The maps were also not the only available information that lenders used to determine neighborhood risk, and evidence suggests that they were not much in use outside of HOLC, limiting their direct influence. Despite Jackson's claim that the FHA made free use of the HOLC maps, Hillier found no specific evidence to back up the assertion. She says that researchers building on Jackson's work "took for granted" that this was so, inferring causality. She notes that the HOLC never distributed the maps outside federal agencies and that they recalled them in 1941.[14] In 1942, the maps not already archived were destroyed.[15]

Other scholars, not discounting the negative effect of redlining or the intent of the HOLC maps to encourage the practice, likewise suggest that the causality is more complex. Crossney and Bartelt argue that reducing emphasis on the HOLC allows for an understanding of the complex interaction between federal agencies and other actors—appraisers, brokers, lenders, investors, and insurance companies—and how they "interact with each other and with the nation's broader sociopolitical context."[16] There are significant barriers that have to be crossed even before a prospective home owner goes looking for a loan, and bias can enter the process at any stage. Gregory Squires has looked at redlining in the property insurance industry as well as the effects of discrimination practiced by individual real estate agents and home appraisers.[17] Examination of the various actors working through interlinked institutions and industries reveals a network of interlinked discriminatory housing practices.

Clearly, the HOLC must bear some responsibility for the disastrous disinvestment in African American communities that occurred in the decades that followed the creation of their maps. The enforced segregation of African Americans in blighted neighborhoods produced significant negative social consequences that even the passage of civil rights legislation could not prevent. Assessing the HOLC's specific influence on these negative social phenomena, however, is not a straightforward task.

It has been persuasively argued that the HOLC research mapped only the social geography as it observed it, but that does not mean that the HOLC did not participate in an effort to *reproduce* what it found. The construction of its research instrument, with data fields collecting information on racial "infiltration" and the racial color coding of its redlined maps, is evidence that it supported segregation both philosophically and in its policies and recommendations and that it wished to encourage real estate practices that would maintain it. I would argue that the HOLC's desire to encourage the real estate industry to maintain a racialized status quo in American cities is significant in itself. But how did such a massive data visualization project become a cog (if not an engine) in a social machine intended to maintain segregation through racist housing practices? In attempting to answer this question, the role of the physical maps themselves must be considered.

META-HODOLOGY

David Turnbull's work on indigenous mapmaking has led him to view maps, like other artifacts of knowledge production, as performative and inherently narratological. He connects the act of storytelling with the act of following a path, referring to them as cognate activities in which events and actions are ordered "hodologically" in space and time:

> The somewhat obscure, but freshly emergent term hodology neatly links space, knowledge and cognition. In geography, hodology is the study of paths, in philosophy, the study of interconnected ideas, and in neuroscience, the study of the patterns of connections in the white matter of the brain.[18]

Critical geographers view maps as social constructions that both represent and act on the world by encoding the biases, ideologies, and ontological assumptions of their makers. It is their agency in the world that makes them "performative":

> It is the hodological emphasis on the concept of trails that is central to a performative understanding of the coproduction of knowledge and space. Performativity has two facets; one is that meaning, understanding, and knowledge are based in embodied practices. The other is that the performance of knowledge practices and their attendant knowledge spaces and artefacts simultaneously structure and shape our socio-cultural world in a process of coproduction. We make our world in the process of moving through and knowing it.[19]

In taking hodology to broadly describe the study of trails in both maps and the complex social and geographic networks that they represent, I have coined the term "meta-hodology" to refer to the study of the narrative logics and values that are invisibly at work inside maps, guiding their application in the world, the same way that algorithms run inside a piece of digital software or that capitalism operates inside the board game

Monopoly.[20] I view the analytical work of meta-hodology to be the task of putting the complexity back into a knowledge artifact that has been stripped of its historical context and its narrative intentions.

Maps can also be productively analyzed as *boundary objects* as theorized by Susan Leigh Star, informational artifacts that move through a network, linking disparate communities together.[21] The HOLC maps black-boxed the narratives that had shaped interpretation and analysis of neighborhood data, making invisible the process of data collection and how the information was visualized in maps. The effect was to make the social prescriptions that followed seem to flow naturally from the world and not from the intentions of the makers of the maps. A physical map that is innocent of its making is much like a myth, which Roland Barthes understood as transformed and depoliticized speech: "myth is constituted by the loss of the historical quality of things: in it, things lose the memory that they once were made. . . . In passing from history to nature, myth acts economically: it abolishes the complexity of human acts, it gives them the simplicity of essences, it does away with all dialectics, with any going back beyond what is immediately visible, it organizes a world which is without contradictions because it is without depth, a world wide open and wallowing in the evident, it establishes a blissful clarity; things appear to mean something by themselves."[22] Maps, like myths, abolish the complexity and contradiction of the world they represent. Their visual clarity necessitates the forgetting of the contexts through which they were made. Maps encode narratives other than racial ones, of course. The idea of private ownership replaced indigenous understandings about land and resources as European social hierarchies were inscribed on natural boundaries of mountains and rivers. Two dramatically different understandings of the narrative meaning of mapped land are today playing out in battles between indigenous people and big oil across the Americas.[23]

The complexity of the lived world, in contrast to the shallowness of its mapped representations, seems to be a key to explaining how a map can end up dominating what it represents. This is a puzzle that Bruno Latour has addressed in reference to the political power of documents within a bureaucracy: "a man is never much more powerful than any other—even from a throne; but a man whose eye dominates records through which some sort of connections are established with millions of others may be said to dominate."[24] Along these lines, Manuel Aalbers's work on redlining rests on of a line of thinking about mapping as a practice of power and knowledge acting on and producing social space.[25] A political agenda, once it is encoded in a map, appears to be representing the reality and needs of the physical world and not the desires of human actors.[26] This is a fair description of what happened in the creation of the HOLC maps.

In redlined maps, racist narratives of invasion, contamination, and the inevitability of urban decay were naturalized. The real estate industry then shaped white people's expectations through specific suggestions about what would happen to them and to their property values should they remain in an integrating city rather than moving to a homogeneously white suburb. Correspondingly, the HOLC maps should be understood not only as real estate instruments that may have been shaped by the racial bias of their historical moment. They are only one of an arsenal of real estate tools developed beginning in the 1930s that disseminated an ideology in which whiteness was equated with creditworthiness. The persuasive power of this narrative influenced real estate policies and practices and perpetuated racial segregation across the United States. In what appears, retrospectively, as less a social experiment than a national tragedy, the HOLC, the FHA, and other real estate professionals successfully routinized their data collection practices so that they could be reproduced in city after city. Redlining maps then operated destructively on the real world and its lived human relations, preventing communities from devising creative responses to the "problem" of racial integration.

The U.S. racial map might look quite different today had local communities been left alone; unique solutions might well have emerged idiosyncratically from local cultures, characters, and complexities. Thomas Hantchett's work on redlining practices in Charlotte, North Carolina, for example, clarifies the method through which redlined maps mechanized previously informal real estate practices: "As long as bankers and brokers calculated creditworthiness according to their own perceptions, there was considerable flexibility and a likelihood that one person's bad risk might be another's acceptable investment. The HOLC wiped out that fuzziness by getting Charlotte's leading real estate agents to compare notes, and then publishing the results. The handsomely printed map with its sharp-edged boundaries made the practice of deciding credit risk on the basis of neighborhood seem objective and put the weight of the U.S. government behind it."[27]

Jackson had earlier argued that the contribution of the HOLC to the real estate industry was not the *concept* of appraisal, a long-standing real estate practice, but the "formal and uniform system of appraisal, reduced to writing, structured in defined procedures, and implemented by individuals only after intensive training. The ultimate aim was that one appraiser's judgment of value would have meaning to an investor located somewhere else."[28] In the interests of efficiency and standardization, the FHA *Underwriting Manual* set up a similar system that collected specific data and from it created categories for rejection. The intent was to make field appraisals unnecessary.

This efficient strategy required that the pertinent values be black-boxed; the perception that the maps were scientifically objective freed the users of the maps from having to recognize the racist logic that lay behind them. As Jennifer Light explains, "By understanding federal officials' ties to a research tradition whose practitioners imagined themselves as pioneers of a quantitative science of cities—a professional identity these policymakers craved—we can see more clearly how the discriminatory values embedded in the agency's model of mortgage risk represented for federal officials measurable social facts from which scientific housing policies followed."[29] Light describes the federal mortgage insurance system of the 1930s meta-hodologically when she explains that FHA officials who presided over programs that systematically employed redlined risk rating may not have viewed what they were doing as discriminatory. On the contrary, they may have believed that they were raising their industry above politics by creating computational mechanics that could improve on the subjective human judgment used in the making of mortgage insurance decisions in the field.[30]

This insight is key to understanding how structural racism in housing operates. Real estate professionals using redlined maps do not need to acknowledge their own racism or even to be a racist person at all to facilitate racist practices. By focusing on neighborhood risk, using tools that hide race as a factor in determining that risk, real estate policies can have "an adverse racial effect, even though no racial animosity may be intended and no violation of law may occur."[31] A redlined map appears, as Barthes would say, to mean something by itself.

A meta-hodological understanding of the HOLC maps requires an analysis of the discriminatory values baked inside of them. What were the narratives that moved through real estate networks, carried by the boundary objects that the HOLC maps and other FHA resources became? Federal and private housing and real estate professionals were not social scientists and did not research or invent the theories and values that they embedded in their practices. They adopted their ideology from work being done by sociologists at the University of Chicago.

Beginning in the 1920s, sociologists, including Robert E. Park, began developing their "social ecology" model of society. Based on a metaphorical rather than an empirical assertion that society operates just like physical environments do, they theorized that human communities resemble plant and animal ecologies that experience "natural" cycles of growth, decay, and renewal. Sociologist Ernest Burgess hypothesized a "zonal theory" on urban growth and change in which different types of neighborhoods were imagined as different ecologies, territories that were vulnerable to invasion.[32] The racist practices of Jim Crow were depoliticized as they were interpreted through this theoretical lens. According to Burgess,

> Negro occupancy is an unmistakable symptom of depreciation—an indication that the value of property has fallen to their economic level as well as an aid to depreciation in its last stages.[33]

Likewise, in a report to the FHA, Homer Hoyt, a colleague of Burgess's, ranked ethnic groups by their impact on property value, with English and Germans at the top and "Negroes" and Mexicans at the bottom.[34]

Failing to observe that empirical correlations between race and real estate might have resulted from racial discrimination directed *toward* the groups rather than emanating *from* them, these pronouncements frame white supremacist ideas as social science. Such assumptions, taken as scientific fact, have tremendous power to shape social policy. The ecological metaphors provided by the Chicago school, which influenced thinking about urban neighborhoods and the way that they change, can be directly detected in development of federal housing policy at both the HOLC and the FHA. The FHA *Underwriting Manual* rested on an uncritical belief in the decline of urban areas as part of a natural life cycle in which racial change in a neighborhood leads to urban blight, decadence, and the rapid decline of property values.[35] The FHA handbook of 1933 provides their value-laden description of the connection between race and risk quite plainly:

> Areas surrounding a location are to be investigated to determine whether incompatible racial and social groups are present, for the purpose of making a prediction regarding the probability of the location being invaded by such groups.[36]

That presumption—that the races cannot peaceably commingle and that the disruption of racial homogeneity in a neighborhood is a dangerous intrusion—consists of narrative ideologies that throughout the twentieth century gained acceptance through self-fulfilling practice.

John Metzger details the 1942 Chicago Land Use Survey created by Homer Hoyt, who had worked for the FHA, and James Downs of the Real Estate Research Corporation (RERC). Hoyt's urban planning study looked at racial changes in Chicago neighborhoods block by block rather than neighborhood by neighborhood. His study was used by the mortgage banking industry to continue to redline African Americans even after judicial decisions had reduced their ability to use municipal racial zoning.[37] Downs's son, Anthony Downs, an economist, was responsible for much of the racialized framing of urban housing that laid the groundwork for policies that have proved to be extremely damaging to African American communities. These policies include "planned shrinkage," "benign neglect," and "urban triage,"[38] ideas that justified the abandonment of African Americans neighborhoods, deliberately allowed to decay. Available resources were simultaneously shifted to suburban areas where people of color did not (and in many cases could not) live because of racial covenants—legally enforceable contractual agreements that restricted the sale, lease, or occupation of property in a given neighborhood according to race.

Hillier, whose criticism of Jackson set off the academic debate on the culpability of the HOLC maps, believes that the maps have been misunderstood: "Rather than being the primary cause of redlining, these sources point to a more complicated story that involves a much wider cast of characters."[39] Her meta-hodological conclusion is that "ecological and infiltration theories, racial prejudice, and real estate and appraisal industry codification of all these sentiments in combination with federal endorsement and promotion of them—not the maps, themselves—caused urban decline."[40] Focusing on the HOLC as the sole bad actor correspondingly distracts from the complicity of the FHA in the segregationist policies that it supported as well as the actions of individuals in the real estate industry who could hide personal bias and discriminatory acts behind the plausible deniability of the redlined maps and handbooks that they used to make their decisions. Hillier insists that responsibility must be attributed to a wide range of networked actors; if we focus only on the actions of federal agencies, "we assign relatively passive roles to the thousands of appraisers, realtors, and lenders who decided where to make loans."[41]

Squires likewise argues that we must take into account "more subtle forms" of racial discrimination. He notes that discriminatory housing practices did not significantly decrease after the passage of civil rights legislation, including the federal Fair Housing Act, the Equal Credit Opportunity Act, and the Community Reinvestment Act, and points to failures in enforcement. In the years following the passage of fair housing legislation, members of regulatory bodies were often drawn, problematically, from the insurance industry, and the resources allocated for the investigation of complaints were inadequate.[42] The reliance of the Department of Housing and Urban Development on voluntary compliance to housing regulations, combined with an unwillingness to pursue complaints, seems to have encouraged (or at least did not deter) real estate actors from breaking fair housing laws.[43]

Although a regulatory agency that processed consumer complaints regarding racial bias in lending received 37,000 such reports between January 1987 and August 1989, they found there to have been no violations of the law. Chairman of the Senate Subcommittee on Consumer and Regulatory Affairs Senator Alan J. Dixon, at a hearing on mortgage lending discrimination, remarked that he found it "incredible" that the agency could claim that there were no violations when the evidence was so overwhelming that violations were taking place: "Well, I'm not a statistician, but when Blacks are getting their loan applications rejected twice as often as whites and, in some cities, it's three and four times as often, I conclude that discrimination is part of the problem."[44]

All across America, discriminatory practices in the real estate industry operated in the open, following real estate guidelines created by the FHA. Decades of urban policy helped to maintain racial segregation of American cities, protecting the homogeneity and prosperity of middle- and upper-class white neighborhoods and suburbs at the expense of African American and other minority residents of inner cities. In Milwaukee, the social costs of these practices and policies have been immense.

REAL ESTATE BIAS IN MILWAUKEE

The terms "north sider" and "south sider" in Milwaukee parlance refer to residents on each side of the Menomonee River Valley, the city's most characteristic geographic feature. This long and broad swath of land stretches from the city's western edge to the shores of Lake Michigan. Once a fertile river plain at the confluence of the Menominee, Kinnickinnic, and Milwaukee rivers, the valley was home to diverse indigenous inhabitants at the time of European settlement. The Potawatomi tribe predominated, but the richness of the river plain drew a unique multiethnic community that included various times members of the Ottawa, Ojibwe, Ho-Chunk, Mascouten, and Sauk and Meskwaki tribes.[45] Through the eighteenth century, these communities were involved in a complex fur trade network that stretched from Montreal to New Orleans. Their populations were decimated by smallpox and by the chaotic violence of the wars between European colonial powers into which they were drawn. As European settlers flooded into the area, indigenous tribes ceded territories and fled or were removed to the Missouri River valley, to elsewhere in Wisconsin, or to Canada. By the late nineteenth century, the descendants of the colonial-era settlers in Milwaukee had completely displaced its indigenous population.[46]

The modern city of Milwaukee was formed from three rival European settlements that had been established on different banks of the rivers at the east end of the valley. The first was founded by a French Canadian fur trader, Solomon Juneau, in 1818; the next in 1834 by Byron Kilbourn, a surveyor from Connecticut; and the last by George Walker, a trader from Virginia. The three settlements grew together contentiously, incorporating as one city in 1839 but retaining a stubborn sense of geographic difference that may have lingered in Milwaukeeans' attachment to neighborhood identities. The Bridge War of 1845, in which competing bridges across the rivers were destroyed and rebuilt, permanently inscribed itself on the layout of streets and bridges that still, to this day, do not line up.[47]

During the late nineteenth and early twentieth centuries, the once fertile wetland had been transformed into an "industrial valley," a swath of odiferous, smoke-belching factories, rail yards, and warehouses within which successive waves of arriving European immigrants labored. German Catholics were the first to arrive and remained the largest, most prosperous and influential ethnic group in the city through much of the twentieth century. A steady influx of southern and eastern European immigrants labored in breweries, stockyards, and foundries, working as tanners and machinists and in other skilled trades, but they also found work as unskilled laborers and in service-sector jobs. By the relatively late arrival of African Americans to the city, the occupations that they had marked out in other northern areas, well established before great numbers of immigrants arrived, were closed to them in Milwaukee, as were higher-paying union jobs.[48]

The Menomonee River Valley came to be, over the course of the twentieth century, both a geographical and a symbolic barrier between the city's working-class, largely African American north side and its working-class, largely European immigrant south side. African American people in Milwaukee in 1967 lived north of the valley in a small segregated set of neighborhoods near the city center, the so-called inner core, while a wide patchwork of European immigrant communities settled in the lower-rent areas referred to as the near north and near south sides ("near" meaning "near to the valley") and then spread outward in an imperfect ring, being halted to the east by Lake Michigan. The industrial valley, that broad ribbon of mostly nonresidential land, acted as an effective boundary—and a barrier—between the two populations.

The near south side neighborhoods had ethnic churches, the greatest number being Catholic, which offered services in "old country" languages in close proximity to boarding houses, shops, and ubiquitous taverns catering to recent immigrants and their children. Polish Americans settled in the near south side in great numbers. A well-known local joke had it that the 16th Street Viaduct was the longest bridge in the world because it linked Poland to Africa. As immigrants flowed into the city, coloring its urban experiences, wealthier, nonimmigrant white citizens, who lived in neighborhoods on both the north and the south sides of Milwaukee, migrated steadily out of the city. Homogeneously white suburbs came to form what is colloquially described as an "iron ring" around the city's poor and working-class communities, both Black and white.

The difference between these two poor communities on opposite sides of the valley is that many white south siders aspired to and did eventually own their own homes. Their children had access to both public schools and Catholic ones in their own neighborhoods. Crucially, their skin color gave them the freedom to move out of the city into suburban areas with higher property values and even better public schools, facilitating their intergenerational mobility. African American neighborhoods, offering mostly rental housing—often horrendously neglected by white absentee landlords—became ever denser and more homogeneous, with substandard schools and high levels of unemployment, drug use, and crime. Even if residents of these blighted neighborhoods had the financial means to seek a better life in the suburbs, discriminatory lending policies, racial housing covenants, and threat of community-level and individual acts of race-based discrimination and harassment prevented them from moving anywhere at all.

A closer examination of Milwaukee's HOLC map offers some insight into the racial geography of the city. Milwaukee's map clearly shows the landscape of race and social class. Surrounding it, "near" north and south side neighborhoods all received ratings of "D," hazardous, and coded red. Around this red center of the map are areas colored yellow, with the rating of "C," definitely declining. The "B" and "A" neighborhoods appear around the edges of the city proper, on the north shore of Lake Michigan and in the suburban neighborhoods to the west and south, where a few less desirable neighborhoods also dot the landscape (see figure 7.1).

Geographical imagery and racial and ethnic imagery are superimposed on one another in the Milwaukee HOLC map in a particularly powerful way. The language used to describe the neighborhoods of Milwaukee in the collected data reflects the embedded narratives of the Chicago school social ecology model. Neighborhoods classified as "A" are highly rated not only because of their homogeneity but also because they are in some way safe from incursion because of either geographic or community restrictions on their inhabitants. For example, the Washington Highlands, a subdivision in Wauwatosa, a suburb on Milwaukee's west side, is recorded as having 0 percent foreign born or Negroes; its inhabitants are chiefly from a "business, professional, and executive" class, and it is described as "highly protected and restricted." The data collector goes on to explain its restrictions: "Plans and specifications for new building must be approved by the Washington Highlands Building Committee which permits a wide latitude of discrimination in accepting residents into the neighborhood." Geography is also on their side: "The small portion of the area south of Milwaukee Avenue, joined on the east and west by 'C' sections, is in a deep ravine. High ground along the southern boundary of this area fronting on Milwaukee Avenue forms a natural barrier so that C-17 on the south offers no adverse influence on this area."

Besides geographical barriers to unwanted incursions, neighborhoods designated as "B" are sometimes described as protective of "A"-rated

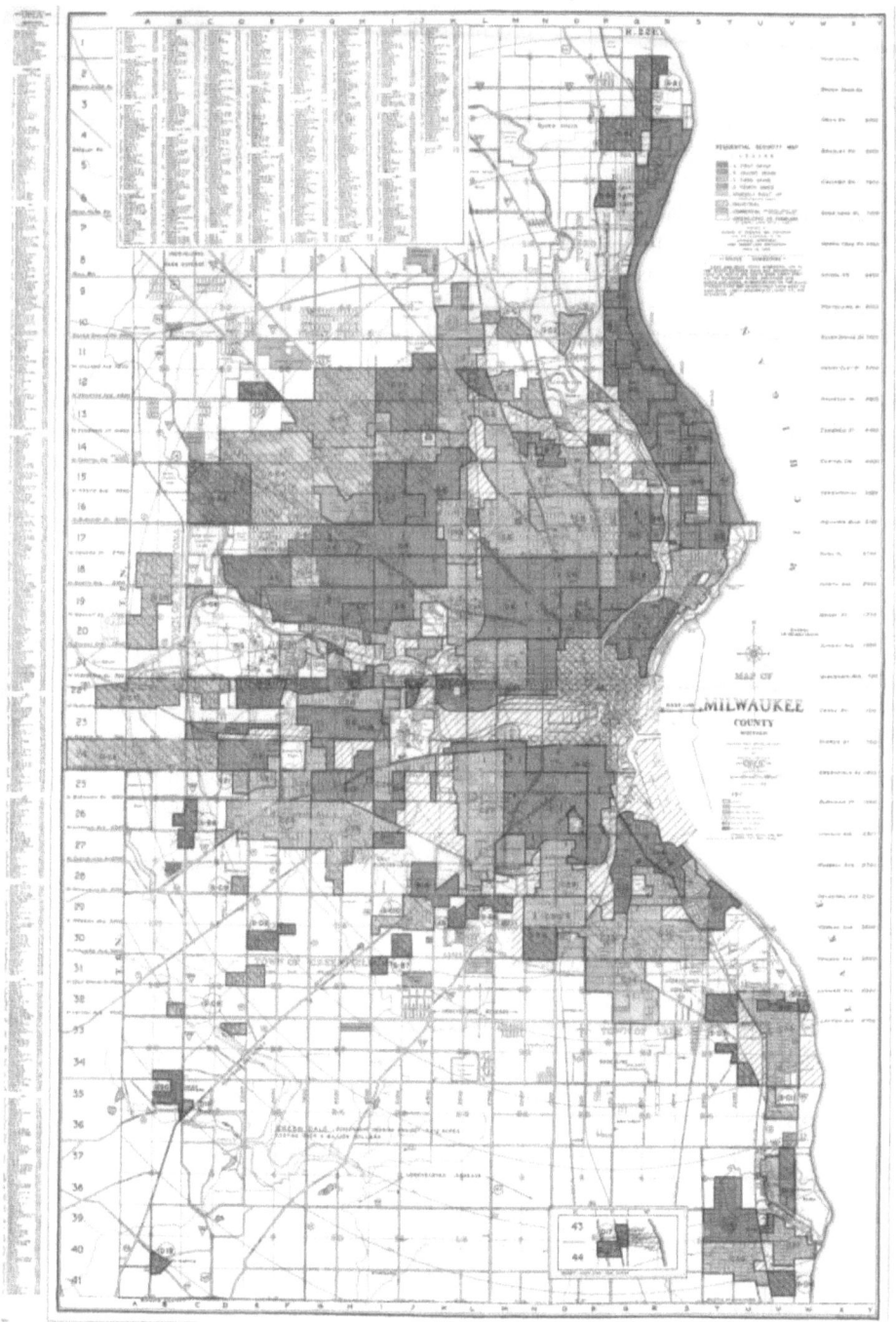

Figure 7.1. Home Owner's Loan Corporation Map of Milwaukee, Wisconsin, 1938. *HOLC Map of Milwaukee Wisconsin, 1938*, National Archives; image retrieved from Mapping Inequality, University of Richmond, https://dsl.richmond.edu/panorama/redlining/#loc=11/43.03/-88.196&city=milwaukee-co.-wi.

neighborhoods nearby. One "B" neighborhood on the northeastern side of the city, for example, inhabited by businessmen and "high class mechanics," was noted to have 50 percent Polish, German, and Austrian residents, with 5 percent of families receiving relief, and no Negroes. The data collector recorded that it was being further infiltrated by the "better class of Polish." Some older houses do not "warrant a second grade rating. However, they constitute a good buffer to the better class of houses to the east."

A "C"-rated neighborhood on the far north side of town, inhabited by "clerical, skilled and common laborers," with 20 percent foreign born (German, Polish, and Russian), many relief families, but no Negroes, reflects the city's bias toward the older immigrants from western Europe over the more recent immigrants to the city from eastern and southern Europe. "This large area, while declining due to age, will sustain values for some time chiefly because of the conservative German influence. It is occupied by wage earners, Germans of the first, second, and third generation predominating overwhelmingly."

Another "C" neighborhood, directly to the west of the industrial valley, with most residents being working laborers, is recorded as 20 percent foreign born, with Yugoslav and southeastern Europeans mixed with German and Austrians, many relief families, but no Negros, Characterized more by class than by ethnic origin, it is described as a "working man's area" with a "haphazard and cheap subdivision" at one end but the "new building of good houses" on the other. In contrast, a "D" neighborhood on the near northeast side, which lists "Polish infiltration" as its main detrimental influence, has 80 percent foreign born (Polish, Russian, and German). Germans are also listed as "infiltrating," but this is not considered to be a detrimental influence. The clarifying remarks tell us that this is a "typical Polish district—railroad runs diagonally through section." It follows up with a pseudoethnographic detail: "Many of these people would not live elsewhere."

In the HOLC model, it is not the existence of Polish people in a neighborhood that is detrimental but rather the movement of ethnic groups from one area to another. The description of Milwaukee's predominantly Polish neighborhood on the south side, the area that was aroused to action by the NAACP Youth Council march across the 16th Street Viaduct, reflects the density of immigrants in the area: "This is Milwaukee's heaviest Polish concentration. Throughout the area there are many so-called 'Polish Flats' wherein basements have been converted into one and two and sometimes three small apartments.... Many of the institutions are either owned or managed by Polish or cater to Polish trade." A hazardous white neighborhood could become even riskier through racial mixing, as the researcher noted: "Mexicans are encroaching in the northeast."

Another "D" neighborhood on the south side near the lake with 25 percent foreign born, many relief families, but no Negroes notes, "The area around the northwest portion of Conway and South Bay was formerly identified with the bootlegging industry. There are many Italians in this section." The ethnic stereotype here is hidden in the juxtaposition of observations, but the researcher took no such pains to hide his opinion of African Americans. The inhabitants of a "D" neighborhood on the near north side of Milwaukee are described as "Laborers and Ne'er-do-wells" with 65 percent "Negro" and 25 percent foreign-born Russian Jews: "This is the Negro and slum area of Milwaukee. It is old and very ragged. Besides the colored people, a large number of lower type Jews are moving into the section. This section housed Milwaukee's wealthiest families seventy years ago."

The lament for the loss of Milwaukee's "Gold Coast" neighborhoods to urban blight—because of the arrival of non-white residents—is the Milwaukee version of the embedded narrative that underlies the entire HOLC project. The arrival of nonwhite people and immigrants is inevitably a destructive force. Even the proper application of real estate practices cannot prevent the inevitable decay. Fortunately, the narrative goes, the damage to white residents can be alleviated through racial covenants and processes of suburbanization. In this worldview, there is no hope to improve the lot of those who constitute the threat.

The purpose, in practice, of the HOLC maps was to guide lending toward the support of homogeneous white neighborhoods; evidence that they did so in Milwaukee can be found in their data. An "A" neighborhood in the northwestern suburb of Wauwatosa, which boasts no foreign born or Negroes and no relief families, is described in the remarks as having the advantage of a country club and exclusive girls' school. It also informs us of the FHA's involvement in the neighborhood: "Virtually all of the houses herein have been built during the last three or four years and financed chiefly through FHA loans." The idea that this investment might have shaped the worth and prospects of this neighborhood or that such loans might have a similar positive effect in less racially homogeneous neighborhoods is nowhere in evidence.

Looking at the neighborhoods mapped by the HOLC, it is clear that their estimation of the chances for prosperity on the one hand and blight on the other is almost entirely predicated on characteristics of the residents despite their collection of other data. Social class also plays a part; there are better classes of Poles and Jews, but there is no "better class of Blacks," referenced in the data, despite the existence of middle-class Black people. And that defines the problem. There was no neighborhood in Milwaukee that people who could afford to leave Milwaukee's "inner core" would find welcoming. The resemblance between maps showing

194 Judith Pintar

the racial makeup of Milwaukee neighborhoods today and the residential security map of Milwaukee created by the HOLC is immediately apparent (see figure 7.2).

Arguably, however, the real smoking gun in the case of Milwaukee is not to be found in the HOLC maps but rather in the rigid determination of its metropolitan suburbs to remain segregated, as evidenced by the use of racial covenants. These legally binding contracts made integration

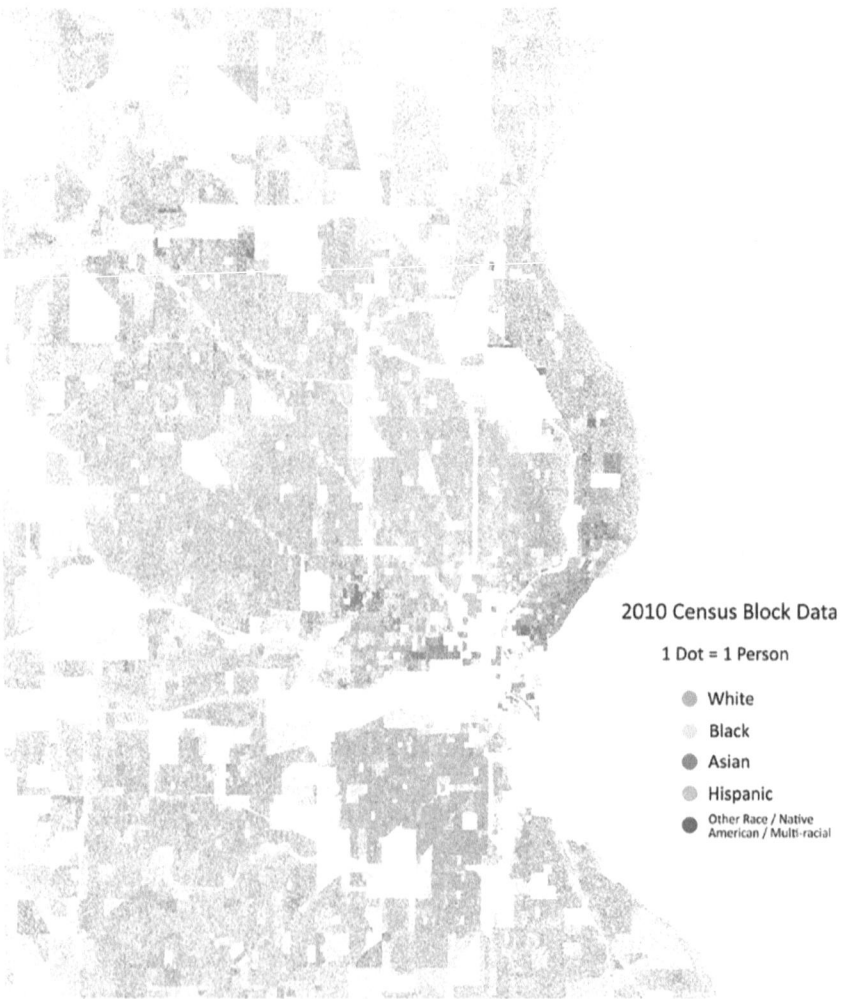

Figure 7.2. Racial Dot Map of Milwaukee based on 2010 U.S. Census Bureau population data. *Image Copyright, 2013, Weldon Cooper Center for Public Service, Rector and Visitors of the University of Virginia (Dustin A. Cable, creator), https://demographics.coopercenter.org/racial-dot-map.*

impossible. In a report prepared in 1979 for the Metropolitan Integration Research Center, Lois Quinn documented the fact that, by the 1940s, sixteen of the eighteen suburbs in the Milwaukee metropolitan area had restricted African Americans from residing within them through the use of racial covenants. White home owners who sold their property to Black families could be fined by the court. The FHA supported such covenants, and despite the U.S. Supreme Court ruling in 1948 in *Shelley v. Kraemer*—that judicial enforcement of racial covenants is unconstitutional—Milwaukee county continued to register them.[49]

The text used in these suburban covenants is quite similar, though it is possible to detect class differences between the versions used by different communities. Consider the legalese employed in the northeast suburban Shorewood subdivision of Lake Bluff #2:

> At no time shall any portion of said Subdivision or any improvements erected thereon, be occupied by, or sold, conveyed, mortgaged, pledged, rented or leased in whole or in part, to any person of Negro or Ethiopian descent, provided, however, this is not intended to include or prevent occupancy by such person as a domestic servant or while actually employed in or about the premises by the owner or occupant thereof.

The contrasting blunt tone of West Milwaukee's Orchard Hill subdivision's covenant may reflect the fact that servants would have been far less commonly found there: "These premises shall never be occupied or conveyed to a colored person or persons." The terms of these documents ranged from a few decades, sometimes with automatic renewal, to much longer periods; in the case of George T. Hansen's subdivision in the suburb of South Milwaukee, the covenant registered in 1937 was set to expire on January 1, 2024.[50]

Many suburban racial covenants were active during the dramatic events of 1967–1968 that brought housing discrimination out of the shadows and into the streets. African American nonviolent activists from the NAACP Youth Council were led by their militant wing, the Commandos, organized to protect their younger and more vulnerable members. The Commandos operated under the principle of "not-violence." This meant that they would not instigate violence but would not hesitate to fight if they were attacked.[51]

The Youth Council and the Commandos marched peacefully into white neighborhoods in the company of non–African American allies, including, most conspicuously, an Italian American Jesuit priest, Father James Groppi. The social justice wing of the Catholic Church emerged as a player in the civil rights movement in Milwaukee despite such activity being actively resisted by its conservative wing. In a representative 1963 speech, sociologist Charles T. O'Reilly addressed a Catholic Conference on religion and race, identifying poverty in the African American community as a reflection of inequalities in employment, education, and housing, which were themselves a product of white racism.[52] The understanding of social and racial justice to be a proper expression of church teaching is what brought Father Groppi to the civil rights movement.

A fair housing ordinance proposed by Alderwoman Vel Phillips, the only African American and the only woman on the Common Council, Milwaukee's lawmaking body, would be voted down four times over six years, beginning in 1962. In a speech given in Dubuque, Iowa, on July 12, 1968, Groppi recalled one of those council meetings and its connection to the fair housing protests:

> We went to the Common Council, we brought the Episcopal Bishop, we brought the clergymen, white and Black, we brought the people, rich and poor. We filled the Common Council chambers and began to speak about the immorality of discrimination and about the necessity for a fair housing bill. We talked about Black soldiers going over to Vietnam and dying for this country and then coming back here and not being able to live where he chooses. We practically begged them, we pleaded for a fair housing bill. We filled the council with people standing all over the place. When the vote was taken in Milwaukee for the fair housing bill, and it was defeated 19 to 1 and all we got out of that meeting was our pictures taken by the Milwaukee police department. We were suspects. We were involved in some kind of subversive activity.[53]

Frustration within the African American community toward the city's inaction on fair housing steadily rose:

> The bill was given to the Common Council on three other occasions and on three other occasions it was again defeated. It was then that the Youth Council began to demonstrate and come to the conclusion, after a while, you know, that the white man doesn't have a conscience. There is no sense trying to bring about civil rights legislation, of gaining one's rights to the law by persuasion, because the man doesn't listen.[54]

On August 28, 1967, the NAACP Youth Council, led by the Commandos, marched across the 16th Street Viaduct into the heart of a predominantly Polish American working-class community (see figure 7.3). They intended to gather in Kosciuszko Park to read a Declaration of Open Housing, a symbolic response to the Common Council's refusal to enact fair housing laws in the city.[55] The 100 people who met on the steps of St. Boniface Church, Father Groppi's north side parish, had planned a peaceful crossing across the bridge. Groppi's old south side parish of Saint Veronica sent a small group of white parishioners carrying "welcome" signs to join them on the north side of the bridge.

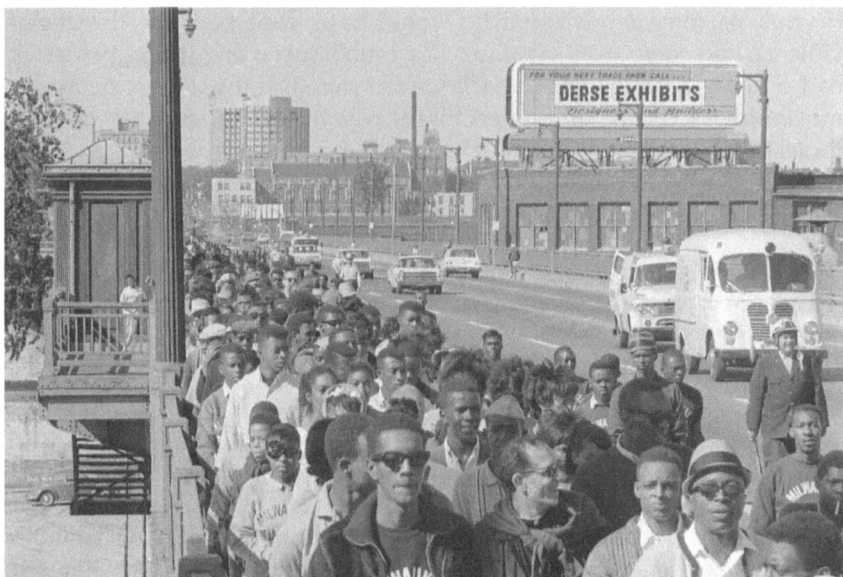

Figure 7.3. Crossing the 16th Street Viaduct, Father James Groppi in center front. *Photo credit: Milwaukee Journal-Sentinel, https://projects.jsonline.com/topics/50-year-ache.*

The organizers of the march anticipated push-back—even hoped for it in the interest of media attention—but they (and the city as a whole) were shocked by what was waiting for them on the other side of the bridge. A crowd of 3,000 white people met them there, some waving signs with messages of quite a different kind: "White Power," "Niggers go home," and "Sich Heil." As Groppi recalled the scene,

> It was something to see, you know. A man holding a girl in his arms, three or four years old, pointing at myself or pointing at the Black people in the line, you know, saying "Nigger, Nigger Nigger!" A little kid looking at you with hate in his face, three, four, five, six, seven years old, "Nigger! Nigger!" The father and the daughter both reach out and pick up a brick and begin to throw it at you.[56]

The crowd blocked their way, threatening violence. The Milwaukee police force had to form a wedge to allow them to progress toward Kosciuszko Park. There, another 5,000 white counterprotesters had gathered in wait. Violence erupted as they fled back across the bridge, pelted by rocks and debris.

The police prevented a south-to-north crossing of the 16th Street Viaduct by angry white south siders intent on destruction of north side African American homes and properties. Mayor Henry Maier considered but stopped just short of calling in the National Guard. He was criticized for this, as some opined that he would have done so if the threatened violence had come from an angry *Black* mob. Just a few weeks before, he had ordered a curfew after Black youths rioted in the inner city. Such a move now would have implied that it was the white response to Black protest that was the problem. It was the free housing activism that was being framed as the instigator of all the violence, both Black and white. The activists pushed the mayor on the point to no avail:

> After that first march on the southside, I called up the mayor's office and said, "Well, we want protection. We want you to give us the National Guard. We're exercising our American constitutional rights for protesting. A man got killed on the southside last night and we think we deserve protection." The governor's office said, "No, the governor is out of town." The mayor's office said, "Well we just can't call out the National Guard for anything." I told the mayor, I said "If one youth Council member sheds his blood on the southside tonight, that blood is going to be on your hands."[57]

Despite the possibility of increased danger from the police decision not to allow marchers to walk in the street, the activists were determined to return to the south side the following night. They were forced to march on sidewalks, making confrontation with the south siders who blocked their way inevitable:

> The Commandos marched in front of the Youth Council line and the police in front of them almost like a snow shovel, snowplow, you know, just pushing people off the sidewalk all the way down, all the way down. We go down to Tenth and Lincoln. The crowd was so great, you know, it wreathed into road. It was like a football [game] being let out. It pushed the policemen back. It pushed the Commandoes back. It started to corner us, you know, and a few of the Youth Council members broke down and began to cry and you know, I thought we were all going to get killed.[58]

The police threw tear gas to disperse the crowd and then offered to send the protesters back to the north side in buses. Groppi recalled Lawrence Friend, the president of the Youth Council, responding, "We asked for the National Guard. You wouldn't give them to us. We are marching to the park whether you like it or not. Dead or alive."[59] The protesters arrived at a park where they sat and sang "We Shall Overthrow" to the tune of "We Shall Overcome" until a firebomb was thrown at them, badly burning one of the protesters. After the young woman, a white south sider, was taken away in an ambulance, the marchers made another harrowing run back to the north side, again being pelted by stones and bricks. They gathered at the Freedom House, a community house used by the NAACP Youth Council, established in 1968. Groppi describes what happened next as "a little rumpus" during which the police threw an incendiary tear gas canister into the house and set it ablaze.

The protesters believed this was done intentionally by the police, who denied this, claiming there had been a sniper in the house, a fact the protesters in turn dispute. Regardless, the response to the fire was slow. According to Groppi,

> The policemen held the fire truck back. It came around the corner with its lights off, very slowly and we were shouting at them to hurry up, but they took their time. The house got a good start, a real good start. In fact, it got such a good start, it started the house on fire next door to ours.[60]

Undeterred by the threat of white violence, the lack of support from the mayor, and the hostility of the police, the protesters would meet on the steps of the burned house and continue to march. For 200 consecutive days, they protested, demanding the enactment of fair housing laws in the city. Four people would die, 100 injured, and 1,740 arrested.[61]

Arguably, the African American protesters and their allies were intent on something more threatening to the white people of Milwaukee than property damage when they crossed the 16th Street Viaduct. They demanded access to home loans and home owners' insurance and to the safer neighborhoods and better schools that came along with living in neighborhoods with higher levels of home ownership, more single-family homes, and the resulting tax revenue these provided. Most important, they wanted the freedom to live where they wished. A few years earlier, a resident from Milwaukee's inner core, interviewed by the *Milwaukee Star*, an African American newspaper, had clarified their intent:

> Living next door to white neighbors is probably the furthest thing from our minds. We wish only to live where we choose in an environment conducive with our economics. This is what whites are fighting. They are fighting to keep us huddled together in the vilest ghettos possible. Won't someone please inform them we don't give a tinker's damn about living next door to them? All we want is our constitutional right to live wherever our money affords us![62]

Similar discriminatory housing practices made home ownership difficult for lower-class immigrants to attain as well, but these difficulties eased over time for those whose skin color and their abandonment of certain ethnic identities, customs, and neighborhood belonging allowed them to melt into white racial identity in the suburbs.

Milwaukee was not the only city in the United States where African Americans were protesting for fair housing, but it became one of the most iconic. The dramatic events of 1967 and 1968 in Milwaukee are remembered for rioting by African American youth, police brutality, and violent white counterdemonstrations. These protests became national news because they were occurring in an economically liberal, northern city as opposed to the southern hot spots of civil rights activity:

> Many of us looked at what was going on in Selma, Alabama as the Southern problem and then we came back to Milwaukee. Many of the white liberals and many of the clergymen who participated in the demonstrations there came back home and refused to demonstrate in their own backyards. They didn't want to disrupt the comfort that they lived in in their own rectory. At any rate, when we came back home and we marched in Wauwatosa, Wisconsin, we marched on the southside of Milwaukee. We found that the old word "racism" that we thought was merely a Southern problem was a problem in the North as well.[63]

As days of fair housing protests turned to weeks and then to months, the African American protesters were joined by significant numbers of white Milwaukeeans as well as civil rights activists from out of state; these might constitute up to 40 percent of the marchers on any given night.[64] Over time, sympathy for the protesters and for the cause of fair housing grew both locally and nationally. Groppi occupied a controversial limelight. As a white leader within a Black movement, his speeches received media coverage and national attention when the words of the young African American leaders had not. Accounts of this time suggest a complicated process of decision making in which African American leaders from among the Commandos worked closely with Groppi to plan their daily actions. Groppi's interviews and speeches brought desired media coverage to the movement, and through them, he directly challenged the racial map of Milwaukee.[65]

By referring to the 16th Street Viaduct as the "Mason-Dixon" line, the housing protesters said out loud what was rarely publicly acknowledged but was no real secret to anyone in the city: African Americans in Milwaukee were not free to live anywhere other than their blighted north side ghetto. Crossing the bridge was a meta-hodological act. An invisible barrier became visible through the act of transgressing it, but what also became visible were the narrative values of racism and white supremacy that lay beneath the real estate map of Milwaukee and its traditional geography. In one interview, Groppi tellingly declared, "We are coming off the reservation."

The outcome of the Milwaukee housing protests was positive, as both local and national legislation pertaining to housing was passed. Yet more than half a century later, Milwaukee remains a profoundly segregated city, with a densely homogeneous African American community surrounded by the same iron ring of racial exclusion. Milwaukee's suburbs remain astonishingly white.[66] The Polish neighborhoods that rose up against the fair housing protesters, which the HOLC maps noted were being infiltrated by Mexicans, now have a Latin American majority population. Whether the maps predicted this demographic change or were complicit in shaping it by enabling white flight out of the near south side and into the suburbs is beside the more important point. When all the complexity is returned to the map of Milwaukee, the bottom line is that racial segregation greatly benefited its white residents, who gained wealth through home ownership and passed that wealth and its advantages to their children.

From that point of view, the real estate practices and urban policies followed in Milwaukee were completely successful. Squires points out the irony that redlining is *ethical practice* in an industry that sees its purpose to be generating profit. The National Association of Real Estate Boards declared in its national code of ethics, "A realtor should never be instrumental in introducing into a neighborhood a character of property or occupancy, members of any race or nationality, or any individual whose presence will clearly be detrimental to property values in the neighborhood."[67] The ecological models of urban decay rested on cultural narratives of white supremacy, but they also reflect deeper ideological assumptions about the inevitability of social hierarchies and the inequalities that "naturally" result. In this view, the reproduction of racial segregation in housing can appear to be a basic good, a simple expression of the spirit of capitalism and the workings of the free market.

Analyzing the real estate industry meta-hodologically may help to explain why real estate professionals failed to acknowledge the existence of racial discrimination in their practices despite the blatant demonstrations of white racism in response to fair housing activism in the 1960s. In the 1970s, two studies on redlining in Milwaukee had no discussion of racism as an underlying cause of discriminatory lending.[68]

Deanna Schmidt argues that a triage narrative inspired urban planning policies in Milwaukee in the post–civil rights era and that the adoption of this ideology bears responsibility for the city's continuing segregation following the passage of fair housing legislation.[69] In 1977, a planning map known as the Relative Residential Status (RRS) map distinguished between Milwaukee neighborhoods that were savable and those that supposedly could not be saved. They enacted policies that deliberately disinvested from the neighborhoods most critically in need, spending available resources on "better" neighborhoods. This resulted in a systematic disenfranchisement of areas where African Americans lived and a concentrated investment in white middle-class neighborhoods. Schmidt argues that the RSS plan was calibrated for cities at greater economic distress than Milwaukee, resulting in an abandonment of areas that in other cities would have been judged savable. She concludes that disastrous patterns of disinvestment, combined with shared social consensus about neighborhoods' relative values, created a self-fulfilling prophecy that exacerbated racial injustice in Milwaukee as a result.[70]

In a speech regarding the RRS plan, Mayor Maier opened his speech with reference to the transformative power of mapping: "Today, we are drawing a map. We must all use it together to reach the goal of a great city." The people included in that "we" would not all fare the same. It was not until well into the 1980s that there was any substantive change of policy from disinvestment to reinvestment in Milwaukee's African American neighborhoods.[71] However, a second round of resistance to civil rights gains by a resurgence of a "culture of poverty ideology" also arose in that decade, blunting the positive effects of reinvestment. This narrative blames African Americans for their existential circumstances, suggesting that social interventions will only promote "dependency," one of the cultural values that supposedly keeps them poor. This view came to rest as accepted wisdom on the political right; it continued to affect urban housing policies through the 1990s and into the present despite empirical study that can document the continuance of redlining and other racial bias in practice in the real estate industry.[72] A 2019 study, for example, found that in Milwaukee, overcharging relative to the market value of a property is more likely to occur in poor neighborhoods and in those with a large concentration of African Americans.[73]

To date, the cumulative social effects of housing discrimination in the city of Milwaukee are sobering. The study of the redlined Milwaukee neighborhood contained in ZIP code 53206 describes an "enduring ecosystem of disadvantage" in the area of Milwaukee's inner core, where 95 percent of the residents are African American. Half the children there live in poverty; children born there thirty-five years ago have no intergenerational economic mobility, in sharp contrast to the gains made by white males in the metropolitan area; and 15 percent of Black males in their twenties and thirties born into low-income households in the area were or had been incarcerated. The research concludes that "no matter what variable we examine—employment, earnings, income, poverty, education, housing, or incarceration—the data confirm the persistence of concentrated disadvantage in 53206."[74] African Americans living in other, less blighted parts of the city still face persistent housing inequalities and not just in the buyer's market. Comparing African American experiences to those of white suburban residents, it is found that while 20 percent of 53206 reported incomes of under 10,000, only 3.8 percent of suburban residents did, while 3 percent of 53206 residents reported income above $100,000 between 2013 and 2017, and 33.5 percent of suburban Milwaukeeans did so.[75]

The economic recovery of Milwaukee's downtown neighborhoods is today clearly visible to the eye. The city has sought to create affordable middle-class housing on both sides of the Menomonee River Valley under the positive influence of new urbanism, a design movement dedicated to reinvigorating cities. Kenney and Zimmerman describe the new urbanists celebration of Milwaukee's "fine architecture and walkable streets" and a nostalgia for the past in which "the streets were supposedly full of life, civic-minded progress dominated urban politics, people relied on their own capabilities (rather than handouts from the government) and 'genuine' community was rooted in the humanly scaled streetcar neighbourhood." The problem with this vision of the past, they argue, is that it willfully forgets "white flight, redlining, block busting, the decline of the public schools and the attending capital drain and depreciation of the central city," not to mention the fact that "the city's small African American population was restricted to a tightly bound ghetto, where overcrowded housing and a restricted participation in the local labour market were the order of the day."[76] There seems to be an unwillingness among Milwaukee's new urbanists to acknowledge the racist history that created the social structural problems that make Milwaukee's economic recovery racially inequitable.

In 2020, it is still headline news for Federal Reserve Chair Jerome H. Powell to testify to the U.S. Senate that lack of adequate employment, rather than dependence on "welfare," is what is keeping Americans poor.[77] The belief that the poor are responsible for their own poverty is a narrative that politicians resuscitate whenever they wish to use the human capacity to discriminate for their own political gain. But when this belief guides housing policy, discrimination can become systematic, automated, and structural, giving individual actors plausible deniability for the bias hidden in their professional acts. These beliefs affect individuals' personal choices as well, including their claim that a decision to move out of the city and into a homogeneous white suburb has nothing at all to do with race. And indeed, they may feel certain that it does not. A feeling, however, is not an empirical test of reality. The HOLC map, viewed beside the racial map of Milwaukee today, provides more reliable witness.

CONCLUSIONS

Where we choose to live is constrained by where we are able to live, which is dictated by financial means but also involves issues of identity, custom, and belonging. These values are powerfully inscribed on the geography of the physical world and naturalized on its maps. They appear at first blush to be positive values, but they are double edged. Some Americans hold racist beliefs about those with whom they do not identify, they feel intolerant toward the customs of social groups other than their own, and they wish to keep out those they believe do not belong in the physical spaces that they themselves inhabit. As the dramatic events of 1967–1968 in Milwaukee can attest, they also become angry when symbolic boundaries are transgressed.

We are not born with identities, customs, and belongings; these are delivered to us through socialization and are therefore vulnerable to manipulation. The meta-hodological work that many researchers who have analyzed the HOLC maps have done is to call out the narratives that were transmitted around the country through risk assessment maps. Understood as boundary objects traveling across the network of real estate agencies, organizations, and individuals, they proliferated racist assumptions, values, and ideologies. I have argued that the information tools used in real estate practice operated as racial bias in practice, energized by a kind of data storytelling that can be appropriately analyzed as propaganda.

African American economist Robert C. Weaver, the first secretary of Housing and Urban Development and the first African American to be appointed to a cabinet-level position in the federal government, wrote about the social psychological process underlying flight of white people to homogeneous, segregated suburbs. He describes it as the product of a deliberate disinformation campaign. The process could sometimes be overt and undeniable, as in the deliberate fearmongering tactics known as blockbusting: a few African Americans would be brought into a neighborhood and then used to frighten white residents into selling their houses at a loss and moving to neighborhoods "protected" by racial covenants. But it could also be connected to more subtle social psychological processes, as Weaver explains:

> It seems apparent, in retrospect, that the rise of racial covenants and other instruments of enforced segregation was more the result of manipulation than the reflection of a spontaneous movement. Intense resistance to the concept of Negro neighbors was usually concentrated in given neighborhoods. It became widespread only after the professional advocates of enforced residential segregation had spent much time and money to propagandize its necessity and desirability. The fact that many of those to whom the propaganda was addressed were insecure whites intent on and anxious in effecting social and economic mobility assured a responsive audience.[78]

Father Groppi also reflected on social mobility in his 1968 speech. He understood, meta-hodologically, that it was not simple hatred that caused white south siders to throw stones at innocent children. By transgressing the invisible boundaries controlling housing in the city of Milwaukee, those who marched across the Menomonee River Valley revealed to the light of day the racial anxiety hidden inside the city's map:

> These white Polish Christians on the southside, you know, got a terrific security problem. Hanging on to one thing in life and that is the color of their skin. They've got nothing else. They don't live in affluent white America, I can assure you of that, for the one form of his security is his white skin. You see, it is an outlet. There is a chance in life because I have got this color. It is the identity problem in the white community that causes white people to step upon Black people and has caused him to look at himself, to wonder, you know.[79]

Groppi never says what it is exactly that white people wonder. He seems to be implying that the south siders' rage arose from the repressed knowledge that their supremacy was a lie, that the valley between north and south, between white and Black, was never as wide as it appeared.

I began this chapter by citing Antony Galton, who analyzes the ontology of geographical borders and the representation of boundaries in information systems. The fuzzy distinction between a region and the boundary around that region grants a kind of agency to geographical boundaries. Gaining a "life of their own," boundaries can have a powerful social effect, becoming a focus for a dispute and coming to represent the distinctness of the territories that they divide.[80] Certainly for Milwaukeeans, the geographic boundary of the Menomonee River Valley has come to represent a historical racial conflict, but it remains a social psychological as well as a geographic barrier to this day. Narratives are naturalized within knowledge artifacts, after which embedded ideologies can work silently and invisibly in the world. Maps and the ontologically problematic boundaries inscribed on them have forgotten that once they were made. Taken to be objective reflections of the world, they are powerful tools in the hands of social actors. The work of meta-hodology is to bring the narratives, concealed inside such maps, to light.

NOTES

1. Antony Galton, "On the Ontological Status of Geographical Boundaries," in *Foundations of Geographic Information Science*, ed. Matt Duckham, Michael F. Goodchild, and Michael Worboys (London: CRC Press, 2003), 151.

2. Civil rights activist Prentice McKinney in an interview aired by Milwaukee radio station WTMJ on August 23, 1967, WTMJ-TV Film Archive, cited in Patrick D. Jones, *The Selma of the North: Civil Rights Insurgency in Milwaukee* (Cambridge MA: Harvard University Press, 2009), 182.

3. Andrew Mollica and Ashley Luthern, "How We Measure Segregation and What the Numbers Actually Tell Us," *Milwaukee Journal Sentinel*, July 10, 2019,

https://www.jsonline.com/story/news/special-reports/milwaukee-violence/2019/07/10/milwaukee-segregation-how-we-measure-and-define/1523075001.

4. Kenneth T. Jackson, "Race, Ethnicity, and Real Estate Appraisal: The Home Owners Loan Corporation and the Federal Housing Administration," *Journal of Urban History* 6, no. 4 (1980): 433.

5. Jackson, "Race, Ethnicity, and Real Estate Appraisal," 423.

6. See, for example, Amy E. Hillier, "Redlining and the Home Owners' Loan Corporation," *Journal of Urban History* 29, no. 4 (2003): 394–420.

7. U.S. Federal Housing Administration, *Underwriting Manual: Underwriting and Valuation Procedure under Title II of the National Housing Act* (Washington, DC: U.S. Federal Housing Administration, 1938), para. 937. See also Brian J. L. Berry, *The Open Housing Question: Race and Housing in Chicago, 1966–1976* (Cambridge, MA: Ballinger, 1979), 9.

8. Kenneth T. Jackson, *Crabgrass Frontier: The Suburbanization of the United States* (Oxford: Oxford University Press, 1987).

9. Jacob Krimmel, "Persistence of Prejudice: Estimating the Long Term Effects of Redlining," SocArXiv, March 2, 2018, 2, doi:10.31235/osf.io/jdmq9.

10. Krimmel, "Persistence of Prejudice," 3.

11. Marc V. Levine, "Milwaukee 53206: The Anatomy of Concentrated Disadvantage in an Inner City Neighborhood, 2000–2017," Center for Economic Development Publications 48, 2019, 5, https://dc.uwm.edu/ced_pubs/48.

12. Kirsten M. M. Beyer, W. Laud Purushottam, Zhou Yuhong, and Ann B. Nattinger, "Housing Discrimination and Racial Cancer Disparities among the 100 Largest US Metropolitan Areas," *Cancer* 125, no. 21 (2019): 3824. See also Zhou Yuhong, Amin Bemanian, and Kirsten M. M. Beyer, "Housing Discrimination, Residential Racial Segregation, and Colorectal Cancer Survival in Southeastern Wisconsin," *Cancer Epidemiology, Biomarkers & Prevention* 26, no. 4 (2017): 561–68, and D. Phuong Do, Lindsay R. B. Locklar, and Paul Florsheim, "Triple Jeopardy: The Joint Impact of Racial Segregation and Neighborhood Poverty on the Mental Health of Black Americans," *Social Psychiatry and Psychiatric Epidemiology* 54, no. 5 (2019): 533–41.

13. See "Mapping Inequality: Redlining in New Deal America," https://dsl.richmond.edu/panorama/redlining/#loc=5/39.1/-94.58.

14. Hillier, "Redlining and the Home Owners' Loan Corporation," 414.

15. Forrest R. Holdcamper, *Preliminary Inventory of the Records of the Federal Home Loan Bank System*, NC 94 (March 1965), supplement in the National Archives Microfiche Edition of Preliminary Inventories, Record Group 195, National Archives, Washington, DC, cited in Kristen B. Crossney and David Bartelt, "The Legacy of the Home Owners' Loan Corporation," *Housing Policy Debate* 16 (2005): 549.

16. Crossney and Bartelt, "The Legacy of the Home Owners' Loan Corporation," 571.

17. Gregory D. Squires, "Racial Profiling, Insurance Style: Insurance Redlining and the Uneven Development of Metropolitan Areas," *Journal of Urban Affairs* 25, no. 4 (2003): 391–410.

18. David Turnbull, "Maps Narratives and Trails: Performativity, Hodology and Distributed Knowledges in Complex Adaptive Systems—An Approach to Emergent Mapping," *Geographical Research* 45, no. 2 (2007): 142.

19. Turnbull, "Maps Narratives and Trails," 142.

20. See Christian Sandvig, Kevin Hamilton, Karrie Karahalios, and Cedric Langbort, "Automation, Algorithms, and Politics | When the Algorithm Itself Is a Racist: Diagnosing Ethical Harm in the Basic Components of Software," *International Journal of Communication* 10 (2016): 4972–90, and Benjamin J. Darr and Alexander H. Cohen, "The Rules of the Game: Experiencing Global Capitalism on a Monopoly Board," *Journal of Political Science Education* 12, no. 3 (2016): 268–81.

21. Susan Leigh Star, "The Structure of Ill-Structured Solutions: Boundary Objects and Heterogeneous Distributed Problem Solving," in *Readings in Distributed Artificial Intelligence*, ed. M. Huhns and L. Gasser (Menlo Park, CA: Kaufman, 1988); Susan Leigh Star and James R. Griesemer, "Institutional Ecology, Translations and Boundary Objects: Amateurs and Professionals in Berkeley's Museum of Vertebrate Zoology, 1907–39," *Social Studies of Science* 19, no. 3 (1989): 387–420. See also chapter 8 in this volume.

22. Roland Barthes, *Mythologies*, trans. Annette Lavers (1957; reprint, New York: Hill and Wang, 1972), 141–43.

23. See Tara L. Joly, Hereward Longley, Carmen Wells, and Jenny Gerbrandt, "Ethnographic Refusal in Traditional Land Use Mapping: Consultation, Impact Assessment, and Sovereignty in the Athabasca Oil Sands Region," *The Extractive Industries and Society* 5, no. 2 (2018): 335–43.

24. Bruno Latour, "Visualization and Cognition," *Knowledge and Society* 6, no. 6 (1986): 32.

25. Manuel B. Aalbers, "Do Maps Make Geography? Part 1: Redlining, Planned Shrinkage, and the Places of Decline," *ACME: An International E-Journal for Critical Geographies* 13, no. 4 (2014): 525–56. See also Michel Foucault, *Power/Knowledge: Selected Interviews and Other Writings 1972–1977*, ed. Colin Gordon (New York: Pantheon, 1980); Michel De Certeau, *The Practice of Everyday Life* (Berkeley: University of California Press, 1984); and Henri Lefebvre, *The Production of Space* (Oxford: Blackwell, 1991).

26. Nadine Schuurman, "Reconciling Social Constructivism and Realism in GIS," *ACME: An International E-Journal for Critical Geographies* 1 (2002): 80, cited by Aalbers, "Do Maps Make Geography?," 529.

27. Thomas W. Hanchett, *Sorting Out the New South City: Race, Class, and Urban Development in Charlotte, 1875–1975* (Charlotte: University of North Carolina Press, 2017), 231.

28. Jackson, "Race, Ethnicity, and Real Estate Appraisal," 422.

29. Jennifer Light, "Discriminating Appraisals: Cartography, Computation, and Access to Federal Mortgage Insurance in the 1930s," *Technology and Culture* 52, no. 3 (2011): 520.

30. Light, "Discriminating Appraisals," 485. See also T. M. Porter, *Trust in Numbers: The Pursuit of Objectivity in Science and Public Life* (Princeton, NJ: Princeton University Press, 1995).

31. Gregory D. Squires and Charis E. Kubrin, "Privileged Places: Race, Uneven Development and the Geography of Opportunity in Urban America," *Urban Studies* 42, no. 1 (2005): 47–68.

32. Aalbers, "Do Maps Make Geography?," 541.

33. Ernest W. Burgess, "Residential Segregation in American Cities," *Annals of the American Academy of Political and Social Science* 140, no. 1 (1928): 113–14, cited in

Gregory D. Squires, "Community Reinvestment: An Emerging Social Movement," in *From Redlining to Reinvestment: Community Responses to Urban Disinvestment* (Philadelphia: Temple University Press, 1992), 4.

34. Homer Hoyt, *One Hundred Years of Land Values* in *Chicago* (Chicago: University of Chicago Press, 1933), 315–16, cited in Squires, "Community Reinvestment," 5.

35. Frederick Morrison Babcock, *The Valuation of Real Estate* (New York: McGraw-Hill, 1932), 91, cited in John T. Metzger, "Planned Abandonment: The Neighborhood Life-Cycle Theory and National Urban Policy," *Housing Policy Debate* 11 (2000): 8.

36. U.S. Federal Housing Administration, *Underwriting Manual*, para. 937.

37. Davis McEntire, *Residence and Race: Final and Comprehensive Report to the Commission on Race and Housing* (Berkeley: University of California Press, 1960), cited in Metzger, "Planned Abandonment," 11.

38. Metzger, "Planned Abandonment," 16.

39. Hillier, "Redlining and the Home Owners' Loan Corporation," 414.

40. Hillier, "Redlining and the Home Owners' Loan Corporation," 413.

41. Hillier, "Redlining and the Home Owners' Loan Corporation," 415.

42. Hillier, "Redlining and the Home Owners' Loan Corporation," 401–2.

43. Squires, "Community Reinvestment," 14.

44. Subcommittee on Consumer and Regulatory Affairs, "Discrimination in Home Mortgage Lending," in *Hearing before the Subcommittee on Consumer and Regulatory Affairs of the Committee on Banking, Housing, and Urban Affairs* (Washington, DC: U.S. Government Printing Office, 1990), 118, cited in Squires, "Community Reinvestment," 15.

45. Robert F. Sasso and Dan Joyce, "Ethnohistory and Archaeology: The Removal Era Potawatomi Lifeway in Southeastern Wisconsin," *Midcontinental Journal of Archaeology* 31, no. 1 (2006): 186.

46. John Gurda, "The Menomonee Valley: A Historical Overview," 2003, https://static1.squarespace.com/static/5b1738a7f8370aa49cd05cf8/t/5bc75d8c652deab42f75fbdf/1539792269161/131-4gurdavalleyhistory6000wordversion.pdf.

47. Goodwin Fauntleroy Berquist and Paul C. Bowers, *Byron Kilbourn and the Development of Milwaukee* (Milwaukee, WI: Milwaukee County Historical Society, 2001).

48. Hannah Walker and Dylan Bennett, "The Whiteness of Wisconsin's Wages: Racial Geography and the Defeat of Public Sector Labor Unions in Wisconsin," *New Political Science* 37, no. 2 (2015): 188.

49. Lois M. Quinn, "Racially Restrictive Covenants: The Making of All-White Suburbs in Milwaukee County," 1979, https://dc.uwm.edu/eti_pubs/178.

50. Quinn, "Racially Restrictive Covenants," 7.

51. Patrick D. Jones, *The Selma of the North: Civil Rights Insurgency in Milwaukee* (Cambridge MA: Harvard University Press, 2009), 133–34. For firsthand accounts of Milwaukee's fair housing marches, see "Fifty Year Ache: How Far Has Milwaukee Come since the 1967 Marches," https://projects.jsonline.com/topics/50-year-ache.

52. Steven Avella, *Confidence and Crisis* (Milwaukee, WI: Marquette University Press, 2014), 92. See also Jones, *The Selma of the North*, 93–95.

53. Cited by Thomas R. Feld, "The Rhetoric of Father James Groppi in the Milwaukee Civil Rights Movement: A Study of the Rhetoric of Agitation," master's thesis, Northern Illinois University, 1968, 35–36.

54. James Groppi, 1968 speech, cited in Feld, "The Rhetoric of Father James Groppi in the Milwaukee Civil Rights Movement," 36.

55. Jones, *The Selma of the North*, 169.

56. Groppi, cited in Feld, "The Rhetoric of Father James Groppi in the Milwaukee Civil Rights Movement," 36–37.

57. Groppi, cited in Feld, "The Rhetoric of Father James Groppi in the Milwaukee Civil Rights Movement," 37.

58. Groppi, cited in Feld, "The Rhetoric of Father James Groppi in the Milwaukee Civil Rights Movement," 38–39.

59. Groppi, cited in Feld, "The Rhetoric of Father James Groppi in the Milwaukee Civil Rights Movement," 39.

60. Groppi, cited in Feld, "The Rhetoric of Father James Groppi in the Milwaukee Civil Rights Movement," 33–34.

61. For a detailed description of the fair housing marches, see Jones, *The Selma of the North*, 169–209.

62. Janis Carter, Milwaukee resident interviewed in the *Milwaukee Star*, July 6, 1963, 122, cited in Jones, *The Selma of the North*, 182.

63. Groppi, cited in Feld, "The Rhetoric of Father James Groppi in the Milwaukee Civil Rights Movement," 22–23.

64. Jones, *The Selma of the North*, 200.

65. Jones, *The Selma of the North*, 201–2.

66. Andrew Mollica and Ashley Luthern, "How We Measure Segregation and What the Numbers Actually Tell Us," *Milwaukee Journal Sentinel*, July 10, 2019, https://www.jsonline.com/story/news/special-reports/milwaukee-violence/2019/07/10/milwaukee-segregation-how-we-measure-and-define/1523075001.

67. This statement remained in the handbook from 1924 to 1950. For discussions, see Dennis R. Judd, *The Politics of American Cities: Private Power and Public Policy* (Boston: Little, Brown, 1984), 284, and Squires, "Community Reinvestment," 4.

68. Michael L. Glabere, "Milwaukee: A Tale of Three Cities," in Squires, *From Redlining to Reinvestment*, 152.

69. See Deanna H. Schmidt, "Urban Triage: Saving the Savable Neighbourhoods in Milwaukee," *Planning Perspectives* 26, no. 4 (2011): 569–89.

70. Schmidt, "Urban Triage," 585–86.

71. For a discussion of reinvestment strategies in Milwaukee through the 1980s, see Squires, "Community Reinvestment," 19, and Glabere, "Milwaukee," 155–63.

72. See Gregory D. Squires and William Velez, "Insurance Redlining and the Process of Discrimination," *Review of Black Political Economy* 16, no. 3 (1988): 63–75. See also Sunwoong Kim and Gregory D. Squires, "Lender Characteristics and Racial Disparities in Mortgage Lending," *Journal of Housing Research* 6, no. 1 (1995): 99–113.

73. See Matthew Desmond and Nathan Wilmers, "Do the Poor Pay More for Housing? Exploitation, Profit, and Risk in Rental Markets," *American Journal of*

Sociology 124, no. 4 (2019): 1090–124. See also Adam Travis, "The Organization of Neglect: Limited Liability Companies and Housing Disinvestment," *American Sociological Review* 84, no. 1 (2019): 142–70.

74. Levine, "Milwaukee 53206," 61.

75. Levine, "Milwaukee 53206," 30.

76. Judith T. Kenny and Jeffrey Zimmerman, "Constructing the 'Genuine American City'": Neo-Traditionalism, New Urbanism and Neo-Liberalism in the Remaking of Downtown Milwaukee," *Cultural Geographies* 11, no. 1 (2004): 92–93.

77. Heather Long and Andrew Van Dam, "Why Aren't More Americans Working?," *Washington Post*, February 15, 2020, https://www.washingtonpost.com/business/2020/02/15/powell-labor-force.

78. Robert C. Weaver, *The Negro Ghetto* (New York: Harcourt, Brace and Company, 1948), 39.

79. Groppi, cited in Feld, "The Rhetoric of Father James Groppi in the Milwaukee Civil Rights Movement," 62.

80. Galton, "On the Ontological Status of Geographical Boundaries," 151.

Eight

Modeling Hope

Boundary Objects and Design Patterns in a Heartland Heterotopia

David Hopping

This chapter tells the story of how a naive but compelling new housing project broke with conventional practice in multiple domains and carved out a unique and precarious position within the larger ecologies of child welfare, supportive housing, retirement, and intentional community. The program was designed to achieve a simple overarching purpose: to embed foster children into adoptive families and families into supportive multigenerational networks of intentional neighbors.

Woven into this narrative is a second thread that retraces how three formalisms—Michel Foucault's *heterotopia,* Leigh Star and James Griesemer's *boundary objects,* and the concept of *pattern language* proposed by Christopher Alexander—helped a team of colleagues from sociology and information science get a handle on what had been achieved and how it might be done again in other places.

The original "pilot" site for this innovation opened in 1994, utilizing repurposed military housing on the former Chanute Air Force Base in Illinois. The basic plan for Hope Meadows was to invite retirees to live alongside families who were adopting children from the foster care system, and the vision was to cultivate an open-ended, long-term network of supportive and durable relationships spanning multiple generations.

This story is thus a natural sequel to chapter 11 in this volume on where to live in retirement, in which the author identifies one of the more emotionally powerful questions facing retirees making this decision: "Will they be able to be the person they want to be in retirement?" Retirees at Hope Meadows have responded to this question by helping to cocreate the very place they want to live, organized around the difference they want to make in the world.

Even in its earliest years, Hope Meadows found itself inspiring similar efforts around the country, and new initiatives continue to emerge to address new challenges. While some have pursued the same original objective of supporting foster-adoptive families (East Hampton, Massachusetts; Seattle, Washington; Portland, Oregon; and Tampa, Florida), others have worked to adapt or extend the model's focus to groups such as "wounded warriors" and their families (New Orleans, Louisiana), families of adults with developmental disabilities (Hardeeville, South Carolina, and Spokane, Washington), and unmarried teen mothers (Washington, D.C.).

I joined in efforts to formally model the program fairly soon after its launch, just as it began to be deluged by requests from across the country and abroad for "replication manuals" or other formal guidelines for reproducing the program. Most of us initially working on this modeling agenda were affiliated in one way or another with the Department of Sociology at the University of Illinois at Urbana-Champaign, and most of us were or had been students of Norm Denzin, Susan Leigh Star, and Clark McPhail—which partly explains both the interpretive ethnographic flavor of our early work and the information-theoretic turn it soon took.

Our earliest attempts to develop theory from interview data was, not surprisingly, replete with metaphors, such as "webs of relationship" and "networks of care." McPhail suggested that we approach this more formally in terms of social network analysis, and Star encouraged us to expand our sense of what such networks were composed of by adopting the more capacious lens of actor–network theory, which systematically incorporates other kinds of (nonhuman) objects and entities into its scope. We found ourselves attending to how information moved through the networks we traced and how certain key social objects translated and propagated such information in ways that were critical to the functioning of the networks themselves.

Even as our initially ad hoc modeling grew more sophisticated, new replication initiatives were cropping up around the country, challenging us to adapt our formalisms to accommodate a stream of exceptions and further innovations. And as benevolent funders began to step up and offer major investments to some of these projects, we found ourselves routinely being asked whether this or that prospective new initiative actually held real promise.

EPIPHANY

In the late 1980s, the child welfare system in Illinois had begun placing some of its "older" foster care wards (meaning older than infants) in adoptive homes. It was an experimental program. At that point in time, "long-term foster care" was still the normal case-planning goal for children whose prospects of ever returning to their parents' custody had vanished, so most could expect to remain "in the care of the state" until they reached adulthood.

University of Illinois researchers Brenda Krause Eheart and Martha Bauman Power described this pilot adoption effort as earnest and well intentioned but ultimately ill fated. Power and Eheart followed a dozen of the earliest adoptive families for several years and found a recurring pattern of disjuncture between cultural expectations and the reality of experience. They theorized this in terms of Denzin's interpretivist approach to the study of emotion. "Culture-making institutions," writes Denzin, "create emotional needs and fantasies, and often lead persons to judge their own lives in terms of the emotional fantasies given in these larger than life social texts."[1] Power and Eheart found that parents in their study operated under the assumption that they would quickly and easily resemble a "normal" family both interactionally and emotionally. When their expectations of early normalization were not met, they became frustrated, angry, and disillusioned.[2]

As a consequence, parents also came to experience a growing sense of isolation and helplessness that, in some cases, ultimately led to the "undoing" of an adoption, with devastating effects on the children who found themselves back in foster care. Already disembedded from networks of family and friends and community, these children now had to cope with yet another deep and isolating rejection. Power and Eheart frequently found themselves wondering how their own children would fare in such a system.

It had become clear that in order for foster adoptions to work, adoptive parents would need not only much more preparation and professional assistance but also a much less isolated social context. Perhaps, Eheart reasoned, if several foster-adoptive families lived together in one neighborhood, they could render each other practical and emotional support, disentangle themselves from limiting cultural myths, and better understand and cope with the challenges of incorporating "special needs" children into their families.[3] And if service professionals could visit an entire caseload by simply walking around the block, perhaps they could better understand and meet the needs of the children and families.

The complete initial vision for Hope Meadows also included a large contingent of retirees, approximately four times as many senior households as adoptive families. This was not initially part of Eheart's vision but was necessitated by the conditions of the transfer of military housing: it was either eighty-six units as a package or nothing at all. Eheart had been musing over a talk by Gray Panthers founder Maggie Kuhn that outlined a program that matched college students with elderly home owners needing a tenant/companion who could help them with daily activities. Eheart recognized what would become one of the guiding principles of the eventual program, that what is good for children is frequently very good for everyone: a safe and supportive neighborhood with space and opportunities to connect and grow.

The program and property were managed by the staff of a new licensed foster-adoption agency, headed by Eheart, with its own innovative way of working. Their broader goal was to cultivate a natural web of supportive relationships around the adoptive families, thus decentering and (after adoption) actually superseding the authority and control of the state.

Carving out space, both figuratively and literally, in which this comprehensive vision could be realized was daunting and would entail renegotiating rules and boundaries across multiple agency domains and realms of professional practice. Eheart first had to buffer the disciplinary grip of state supervision to allow parents wider autonomy, clearing away obstacles to regarding their adoptive children as their own. She negotiated with the Department of Children and Family Services, for example, a reimbursement protocol that intercepted conventional per-diem-per-child payments for foster care and provided parents instead a flat stipend during (typically) eighteen to twenty-four months of "pre-adoptive" foster care while adoptions moved through the court system. The goal of this intervention was to short-circuit any unconscious tendency to regard children still in foster status as calculable assets and (in that sense) different from siblings who had been born into the family.

She also had to bootstrap the reframing of roles and expectations of retirees and in this task found allies within a new national movement that recast them as "untapped resources" and "experts in the use of unstructured time."[4] Just as adoption was intended to provide a child with a "forever family," Hope seniors would be available as potential companions without a programmatic expiration date. This sounds deceptively natural and sensible, but at the time, the largest national "foster grandparent" program actually prohibited elder mentors from spending any time with their assigned children outside of allotted program hours. Similarly, foster care caseworkers would often pull children from an assigned foster family if the worker felt they were "getting too close."

Acquiring the former military base housing required months of negotiation (and an eventual intervention from the White House) since this was one of the earliest base closures and there was no precedent to follow. By 1993, the property had at last been acquired and a million-dollar grant from the State of Illinois secured, and in mid-1994, the program began bootstrapping itself into existence.

Eheart's guiding principle was simple and unwavering: to ensure that children being adopted from foster care would achieve the same embeddedness in family and kin-like relationships that we would want for our own children.

"SO OLD-FASHIONED IT'S, WELL, NEW"

Eheart's founding principle provided an intuitive guide star, but the actual program would require several more years to fully invent itself. But even as it was developing, it found itself, almost immediately, in the media spotlight.

Perhaps the most insightful coverage was a segment on ABC's *Nightline* in 1996 featuring candid interviews with a number of families, seniors, and staff along with several other key figures in the larger ecosystem of the program. "It begins," Ted Koppel teased in the introductory block, "with a whole bundle of problems which, because of the vision of one remarkable woman, were put together and appear to have created a whole bunch of solutions."

He described the plight of children who had arrived, sometimes in sibling groups as large as four, "from tragic backgrounds." One seven-year-old, who had never in his life held a pencil, was now being regularly tutored by a retired schoolteacher: Miss Irene had effectively become part of his new Hope Meadows family and had in turn brought him informally into her own extended family of rural Illinois farmers.

Koppel summed up the program with an apparent paradox: "It all adds up to a community so old-fashioned it's, well, new."

This *Nightline* episode is also how I first learned of the project. It appeared to be the perfect sociological puzzle, and I was startled to realize that it was happening only fifteen miles away. Within a year, I had been introduced to Eheart, conducted interviews with several residents, represented the program at a conference in Croatia, and begun outlining a dissertation.

One cannot, of course, just concentrate intractable problems and expect new solutions to emerge. By itself, such an approach leads only to competition for resources, aggravation of underlying issues, and panicked objections from policymakers along the lines of "more for the children just means less for the elderly." In principle, however, and even in formal justice theory, this does not have to be the end of the story. As Norman Daniels points out, over the course of a lifetime, most of us can expect to be children and adults and elderly, and this simple perspective switch unlocks new angles on seemingly intractable problems. With regard to the allocation of health resources, for example, the task of determining what is fair between age-groups can thus be recast as that of "discovering what it is prudent to do between stages of life, over the whole lifespan."[5] Daniels's reframing brings the perspectives of children and seniors into consideration not as separate constituencies but rather as inalienable aspects of each person, as common denominators of every deliberation.

And if we are willing to take Eheart's particular leap of moral imagination, even this reframing can be broadened, yielding even more room for innovation. What she was implicitly proposing was to extend our frame of reference for defining what a social problem actually is—and on two dimensions at once: temporally to encompass the entire life course and socially to encompass a critical mass of potential human connections. More specifically, that meant roughly 100 age-diverse, ethnically diverse, and class-diverse residents, all "bundled" into an intricately woven network of long-term, geographically proximal neighbors.

The next step is to look for how multiple problems may be interrelated and how people who have become identified *as problems* may actually prove to be "untapped resources"—families, elderly neighbors, and the kids themselves—people who have been excluded in various ways from normal flows and circuits of care.

And this begs the next question: Under what specific conditions does this transformative synergy, this "super-optimal" solution[6] to a "bundle of problems" become possible and viable? And, following on this, how might we appropriately formalize[7] our emerging understanding of these conditions and dynamics to help guide the efforts of others to replicate this approach?

COMMUNITY AS INTERVENTION

Hope Meadows had achieved significant notoriety even before the *Nightline* segment aired, with stories hitting the front pages of the *Chicago Tribune* and the *New York Times*. Requests for assistance with new local replication efforts across the country began trickling and then pouring in. Initially, staff simply shared literal details of Hope's implementation, eventually creating handbooks that simply transcribed policies and described specific program components, such as the Intergenerational Center and the schedule of community events.

Not surprisingly, these products proved to be of limited practical use to projects working to "replicate" the program, as local circumstances typically diverged from Hope's in multiple ways. Requests nevertheless continued to mount, delegations of visitors arrived monthly, and it became clear that we needed to go beyond literal plans and manuals and codifications. We needed to sort the essential innovations from dumb luck or idiosyncrasy and to articulate our tacit knowledge as shareable information.

Eheart had set up a very competent agency, adept at shepherding adoptions through the courts, supporting kids and families, cultivating a network of relationships, and even generating policies, reports, and rich ethnographic and statistical data on pretty much everything. Analysis, however, typically had to wait until the pace of activities would abate, and given their intense legal and social service agenda, this rarely occurred. In spite of these pressures, Eheart's staff pushed hard to compile detailed reviews every six months, documenting a bustling neighborhood and embedded agency in which scores of routine and special activities transpired each month and hundreds of hours of "volunteer" activity were logged.

As I watched the *Nightline* episode, I began to conceive of Hope Meadows as a space of deliberate liminality and open-endedness where a tacit moratorium held regarding ordinary expectations for all the conventional social roles, such as "foster child" and "retiree" and "adoptive parent." Within this exceptional space, new structures and identities were emerging. Some, such as "Hope Senior," had come about spontaneously, as if created out of whole cloth. Others, such as the simulacrum of "old-fashioned community," were being consciously enacted in thousands of routine gestures and acts of care, creating a paradoxically natural yet intentional normality.

All of it, in fact, was paradoxical, and the paradoxes seemed to be floating for the time being without needing any immediate resolution, as if held in creative suspension. Some examples:

- Professionals (therapist, caseworker, and adoption specialist) provided support and guidance as well as backup in emergent crises but in a "domesticated" fashion reminiscent of the early settlement house movement. Their offices were simply rooms upstairs in what is literally just another neighborhood house. Staff would regularly convene training and support sessions for parents, but the parents would arrive at the neighborhood guest apartment set aside for this as if simply neighbors casually gathering for coffee.
- Children would come to the office for appointments with the staff psychologist, but they would meet in what (to the casual observer) was just another basement playroom, indistinguishable from any other family basement playroom in the neighborhood. The playroom itself, as well as the toys and other affordances there, also illustrate a wider pattern of multiple superimposed purposes, as the dollhouse and the sand tray and a very punchable Bobo doll serve both playful and therapeutic ends.

- The Intergenerational Center took the paradigm of superimposed purposes even further. Eheart had been insistent from the outset that there be no special structures dedicated to only one category of resident, so the inevitable suggestion to create a "senior center" was recast as "intergenerational center," and the spaces within it were designed to accommodate any kind of activity drawing any mix of residents. On a typical afternoon, you might see tutoring happening in the large main open space, which would be reconfigured later for a potluck supper; the following morning, seniors would gather there for coffee before welcoming a mid-morning cohort of preschoolers into the "enrichment" program they had designed for the neighborhood children, partly as a way of providing parents with a couple of hours of respite but also as a renegotiation of parents' requests for "babysitting" into something more robust and proactive.

By 2001, Eheart had secured funding for a small program within the University of Illinois Institute for Government and Public Affairs, which became the first formal home for our efforts at theory and modeling. We applied, adapted, and invented our first formalisms and conceptual models, trying to make sense of a wealth of ethnographic and administrative data and struggling to improve our response to requests for replication advice.

Our first pass at an overall model began with inverting a familiar paradigm—that of intervening in community to fix or enhance deficits—to focus instead on how community itself might be deployable as a first-line intervention in social challenges. In this "inversion of control" the professional experts yield (sometimes reluctantly) direct authority or control over outcomes.

We began to tease out layers of structure within Hope Meadows and to trace the emergent neighborhood relationship network, eventually putting together a fairly straight-up sociological model and coining the term "community as intervention" to characterize it. One objective was to explore how such a network could be leveraged in pursuit of more proximal "service goals," such as securing foster adoptions or getting children's socioemotional development back in sync with their physical age.

Another task was to trace the programmatic "scaffolding" through which the hoped-for relational network would emerge. We imagined this scaffold as a metaphorical trellis supporting the vine of emergent community, which, as it grows, contributes to the strength of the trellis itself. We traced this scaffolding process on both material and organizational levels.

Materially, the scaffolding consists of the program infrastructure and its manner of usage: the physical layout and architecture of the neighborhood, the interspersing of family and senior units, the unassuming intergenerational center, the extensive green space and playground, and so on. Relationships may precipitate out of innumerable casual meetings of neighbors and the general circulation of children at play.

On the organization/program level, emergent relationships were being scaffolded in at least two ways: through the planning and convening of routine (daily, weekly, monthly, and annual) and special events and through the management of the senior volunteer "economy." Data from both these areas were naturally suited to a network-analytic approach that enabled us to augment our ethnographic inquiry with computational methods that fed new empirical questions back into the research cycle.

THE SCAFFOLDING FRAMEWORK

All these scaffolding layers exist within and together constitute the substance of the overall *space of exception* in which the life of the program/community unfolds.

Layer 1—Architecture and Site Design

The exquisite suitability of the base housing was in some ways a matter of luck but not entirely of coincidence. In the 1950s, military planners could implement then cutting-edge ideas about street layouts and the design and arrangement of structures, prerogatives that would become available to municipal jurisdictions decades later only with the advent of local zoning commissions. Secondary and tertiary streets could create coves sheltered from through traffic where young children could safely ride bicycles, new residents could become quickly acquainted with their neighbors when front doors faced one another across common carports, and children could run freely between unfenced backyards that merged into fields and playgrounds.

Layer 2—Routine and Special Events

Social events draw different people at different times into different gatherings for different purposes, and our earliest network visualizations suggested a metaphor for how they function: they look very much like "quilting points" in the social fabric. Each gathers multiple residents and punctuates the course of their relationships, and the overall pattern can be seen operating on multiple levels.

Community events are scheduled as either routine or special. Daily after-school tutoring or morning coffee at the Intergenerational Center are routine, as are the annual Easter Egg hunt and the Fourth of July barbecue.

Special events are one-off gatherings, sometimes novel, but in some cases may also become a recurring part of the community's routine and self-identity. A classic example is the Young Ladies' Formal Tea, which began as a spontaneous project of a few "Red Hat Society" residents in the neighborhood ("When I am old, I shall wear purple . . .") and quickly became an established annual event.

Layer 3—Volunteer Engagement

Retirees were offered reduced rent for their apartments in tacit exchange for their organized contributions to the community and agency, a softly compulsory engagement requiring them to engage with one another on tasks that really do need to be done, providing a natural way to get acquainted and stay connected while also adding instrumental value to the program.

Layer 4—Roles and Expectations

The active presence of multiple seniors, available to assume multiple roles as friends, mentors, tutors, neighbors, and so on, can mitigate the risks and difficulties entailed in the adoption process, which in the case of a large sibling-group adoption actually involves a melding of different family systems.

Newly arriving children pick up very quickly on what sorts of interactions and relationships are possible, suddenly finding themselves with a wealth of opportunities for (re)building a personal network of care and support. This is particularly remarkable given that children in foster care have very few if any opportunities for exercising this kind of proactive agency in their lives and too often reach adulthood without basic social skills.

Figure 8.1 reveals the implicit subnetwork of close senior–child relationships that had developed over the first fifteen years of operation, and the active agency of the children in building up this network is evident in a couple of ways: they had become some of the most highly connected individuals in the network, and each would frequently bring multiple new senior residents into the fold, so to speak.

Subgroups within this senior–child system are also detectable (figure 8.2). But given this clustering by natural affinity, what is striking is the degree of interconnectivity of the whole. Through the larger network that contains this analytical slice, knowledge and understanding of the complex developmental challenges facing these foster-adoptive children and information about their progress and achievements can propagate rapidly.

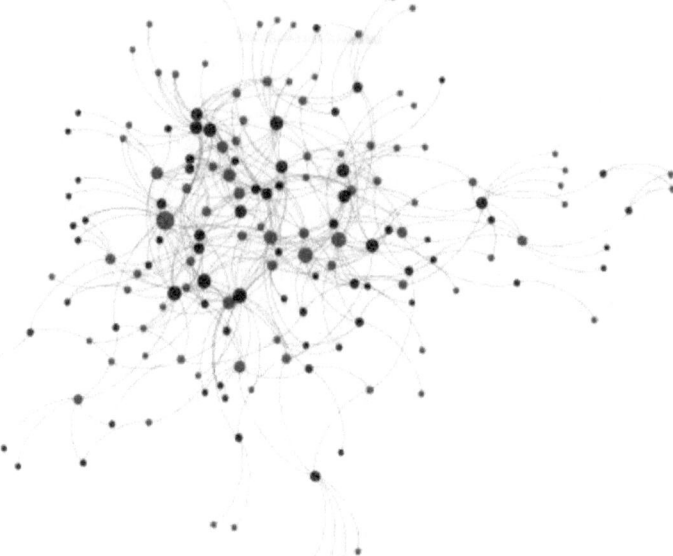

Figure 8.1. Implicit network of close senior–child relationships (mentor, "grandparent") as they accumulated over the first fifteen years of the neighborhood's history. Multiple seniors (gray dots) connect with multiple children (black dots) in multiple ways. Larger dots indicate more connections. Recently arrived residents tend to be located on the periphery of the graph. Note how multiple seniors tend to be brought into the larger network by individual children, while new children often connect as a sibling group to individual seniors.

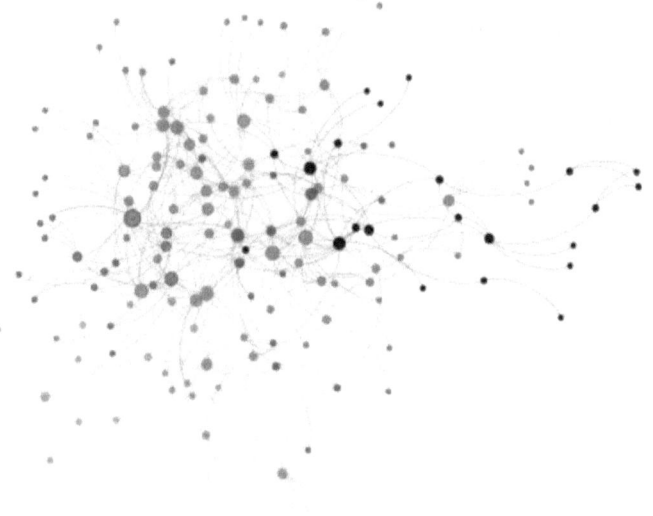

Figure 8.2. The same graph as in Figure 8.1 but with shades now indicating groups of people that are more connected to one another than to the rest of the network (modularity = 0.548). These implicit groupings conform with observations on an ethnographic level, but it is the emergent picture of the interconnective whole that is especially striking. The average distance between any two individuals in this diagram is less than four steps.

Layer 5—Communication

While events and volunteering and even the fortuitous design of the housing all contributed to informal flows of information and circuits of trust and affinity, more formal channels for reliable communication were also crucial. The weekly *Seedlings* newsletter was established at the inception of the program in 1994, designed not only for delivering practical information such as calendars and announcements but also for floating requests and extending appreciation among residents, sharing ideas, and (most strikingly) elevating the achievements of children who had never experienced positive recognition before in their lives.

Layer 6—Professional Services and Material Supports

Finally, there are the professional services themselves, delivered unobtrusively from an office that is indistinguishable from any of the homes. There is a pastoral flavor to the professional service roles at Hope Meadows that is absent from the conventional service industry with its "field visits" (as if clients lived out in the wilderness) and fifty-minute hours.

The Generations of Hope Community Model

We developed the overall conceptual framework in the early 2000s, and some early formalisms were already present—the idea of program *scaffolding*, for example, began as a metaphor that was subsequently stylized and specified and would eventually become formally prescriptive. We also adopted the name "Generations of Hope" for a new legal entity through which to support "replication" initiatives and so began to refer to our new conceptual framework as the Generations of Hope Community model. We described its implementation as

> an intentionally created, geographically contiguous intergenerational neighborhood, where some of the residents are facing a specific challenge around which the entire community organizes.

We also carefully stated the "program theory" aspect of it, building on broadly recognized service-intervention goals in similar (but more targeted) programs and proposing that

> purposeful engagement and intergenerational relationships, developing over decades within a contiguous neighborhood, can *sustain transformative gains* and *support lifecourse transitions*, producing new kinds of organizational capacity.

This statement of the model helps to make some sense of the Hope Meadows phenomenon, indicating how creative tensions are held in suspension. But the actual pathways through which such tensions resolve still remained paradoxical, and while our formalisms had begun to mature, they were still largely bound up with the idiosyncrasies of Hope Meadows. Our statements had become more concise and our theoretical claims more specific, but we still needed to distinguish essential features from incidental ones and explicitly open up more space for the model to adapt to local situations in order for it to help guide parallel attempts toward parallel objectives in parallel places.

We were also acutely aware of Leigh Star's admonition that much of the actual work being captured in a model gets deleted from view when formalisms are created and must somehow be restored when it comes time to actually implement a formalism in a new setting. It seemed that the only way through this was to somehow induce each local initiative to actually generate its own model and implementation while staying tethered to the underlying paradigm.

In working through these challenges, some new formalisms would prove especially useful both for advancing our own understanding and for articulating and communicating the elements and informational flows of this striking but, in many ways, stubbornly puzzling innovation.

HETEROTOPIA

In 1975, Michel Foucault delivered an invited lecture to a group of architects in Paris on the subject of space. After briefly discussing the concept of *utopia*, he then contrasted it with the strange and perhaps somewhat whimsical notion of *heterotopia*.

He had actually coined the term earlier in *The Order of Things* as a purely abstract and semantic concept,[8] but for this audience, he adopted an anthropological frame of reference and, playfully and poetically, extended it. A heterotopia, he offered, differs from a utopia in that it is a "way of appropriating space" that is actually implemented, whereas utopias are strictly imaginal sites with no real place. He went on to distinguish two major categories of heterotopia, the first being oriented toward resolution of a *crisis*. This might be a normally occurring crisis but one still in need of rules and boundaries, such as a rite of passage or childbirth. He noted that such "crisis heterotopias" seem to be disappearing, persisting mainly in institutions such as the boarding school or military service.

The second type of heterotopia he called the "heterotopia of deviation." Rest homes, prisons, and psychiatric hospitals are classic examples, and retirement villages are on the border since old age is in a sense a crisis, while leisure or idleness is seen as a deviation. These heterotopias, he suggested, seem to be on the rise.

Two of the most important characteristics of heterotopias (he names at least six) are that they "always presuppose a system of opening and closing that both isolates them and makes them penetrable" and that they can "juxtapose in a single real place several spaces, several sites that are in themselves incompatible." Moreover, it is not only multiple *places* but also multiple *times* that may be emplaced, producing what he called a *heterochronic* dimension.

Foucault's illustrations of these last points are striking, and his observation about their capacity to "superimpose meanings" adumbrates Star's seminal studies of heterogeneous objects that share "coincident boundaries" and are able to merge diverse streams of information into coherent wholes. "Thus it is," he explains,

> that the theater brings onto the rectangle of the stage, one after the other, a whole series of places that are foreign to one another; thus it is that the cinema is a very odd rectangular room, at the end of which, on a two-dimensional screen, one sees the projection of a three-dimensional space; but perhaps the oldest example of these heterotopias that take the form of contradictory sites is the garden.
>
> We must not forget that in the Orient the garden, an astonishing creation that is now a thousand years old, had very deep and seemingly superimposed meanings. The traditional garden of the Persians was a sacred space that was supposed to bring together inside its rectangle four parts representing the four parts of the world.[9]

This nuanced formalism, with its clever distinctions between crisis and deviation, offered an intriguing framework for describing the multifaceted spaces and flexible artifacts proliferating within the Hope Meadows space of exception and for distinguishing this innovative leap from other superficially similar phenomena. Foster care itself, for example, was originally imagined as an exceptional space of protection and security, but in practice, it all too often lingers (through neglect or inertia) into a de facto heterotopia of deviation.

Chanute Air Force Base would seem to have been a perfect example of Foucault's crisis heterotopia. As a training-focused heterotopia within a larger military-service heterotopia, its mission was to transform recruits into airmen and airmen into experts in various domains, often by delivering real-world flight experiences through mechanical flight simulators—an intriguing nesting of multiple heterotopian contexts.[10]

The *heterotopia* formalism nicely captures the boundary work and negotiation entailed in bootstrapping Hope Meadows as a space of exception within an otherwise dysfunctional but well-established way of doing things. On the broadest level, the entire community and program functions as a heterotopia, specifically a version of "crisis" heterotopia in which transformation is sought and expected—in this case the reembedding of tragically disembedded children into new extended-family networks. And in the process, it also functions the same way for many older adults, with their own complex histories.

A chronically "siloed" service industry is simply blind to the synergies that can come from connecting different "problematic" populations because it is blind (and/or resistant) to the very possibility of any heterotopia that might merge services across siloes. At Hope Meadows, the potential upside of such merging is vividly illustrated by the cases of seniors who themselves grew up in foster care or residential institutions.

Loralee Peña, for example, was able to recognize the anger and frustration that shadowed many of the children arriving at Hope Meadows, having spent her own childhood in long-term foster care and having spent years trying to understand why.[11] "In my mind," she says,

> I was always waiting for my real family to show up.... Anger wells up unexpectedly to me. For a child, it's probably like that, and it probably goes further than they expect, so it's scary.

When this does happen to kids at Hope Meadows, says Peña, "I want to be there."[12] Hope senior Bertie Leavitt told a similar story: she and her older brother were taken from their parents when they were nine and ten and would grow up in institutional foster care. "I was rebellious and ornery," she says. "We didn't get attention and love at the children's home; we got discipline, schooling, and food. We worked every night after school." Leavitt well understood the resulting dynamics:

> When kids first get here, I can see they are rebellious. They hold stuff inside. They don't want anyone to touch them and reach inside them. They hide their feelings. You know when not to touch them by the look in their eyes. I've seen it in a lot of kids who don't know how to show affection. They don't want to be touched. They are scared. But eventually they come out of that, and then they look so peaceful.[13]

BOUNDARY OBJECTS

Heterotopias can be large or small. Toward the small end, the sand tray device widely used in play therapy offers a fascinating study, being a kind of miniature theater in which the child's imaginative microdramas transpire in the guise of figures and toy structures, narrated spontaneously and autonomously by the child and investigated together with the therapist, and through these narratives and gentle guidance, critical information is disclosed and narratives are rewoven into healing patterns.

This imaginal space exists not only in the here and now of the holding environment and special therapeutic relationship but also in the there and then in the past and in multiple implicit possible futures.

The sand tray is also a classic example of a *boundary object*—a powerful formalism introduced by Leigh Star and James Griesemer in 1989 in their study of how the Museum of Vertebrate Zoology at the University of California came to be established.[14] Their research focused on the extensive network of diverse players involved and on the complex artifacts or "boundary objects" that mediated and facilitated cooperation among very different groups of actors with different interests and concerns.

In the evolution of the museum, such actors included not only philanthropists and scientists but also amateur collectors wanting to conserve native flora and fauna, professional trappers wanting to earn money, and even farmers who had been recruited as fieldworkers. Boundary objects included diagrams; ideal-type concepts, such as *species*; "coincident boundaries," such as the outline of the state of California (within which very different maps were drawn for different purposes); and standardized forms, such as those developed to get all the various contributors (farmers, amateur collectors, and trappers) to report the "same" information. Interestingly, the museum itself can be regarded as a huge boundary object, containing and organizing the juxtaposition of specimens and a range of subordinate boundary objects.

Perhaps the most important feature of boundary objects is that they facilitate cooperation without necessarily requiring consensus. Different social/professional worlds may be coordinated via multiple boundary objects. Each object will have different meanings for each group, and each group will have some partial jurisdiction over the information that flows into and through it.

Since almost any object or formalism might exhibit some qualities of a boundary object, the inevitable question arises: What is *not* a boundary object? Star answers by noting that the concept really works best at the level of organizations.[15] Importantly, the boundary objects that make it possible for Hope Meadows to function as an agency and housing provider often also extend (by design) into the neighborhood community as well, collating potentially problematic information flows in sometimes very clever ways.

Tutoring sessions, for example, originally instituted by seniors themselves as a "volunteer" activity, were also typically memorialized by the tutors in brief semiformal reports that often also captured other relational insights about a child's traumatic past or current concerns, or joys, or accomplishments. This stream of information, appropriately filtered and contextualized, fed forward into therapy plans, casework reviews, parent consultations, and even planning and management of volunteer resources.

Multiple such informational streams were prismed through similar boundary objects, creating standing waves of patterned interaction that served to distribute information, prompt reflection, and bridge the very different internal logics and dynamics of organizational structure and natural community.

THE "VEIL OF INTERVENTION"

If the sand tray stands, in many ways, as the quintessential "boundary object," it also contains and reflects another critical feature that is a little trickier to describe—a sort of *barrier* behind which the intimate therapeutic work on relationships—exploring, negotiating, and distinguishing from old traumatic versions and patterns—can be partly shared in confidence with the therapist while also unfolding inscrutably on its own. The child has to do this work autonomously, with assistance but not direction, immune to being disciplined and managed by other adults and professionals.

In parallel fashion, the Hope Meadows community itself had to discover and develop its own relational capacity—spontaneously, serendipitously, and autonomously—in a realm that actually lies just beyond the direct reach of professionals and staff. The formal purview of the program ultimately does not extend across what we came to refer to as a "veil of intervention."

The question for theory and modeling, for refining this "veil" notion as a useful new formalism, is just how permeable should this veil be? This then leads to a cascade of further questions:

- What are the optimal roles of professional staff versus organic community processes?
- How can deliberations be conducted and decisions made that appropriately respect this (potentially frustrating) boundary?
- How can information move across this boundary and be gathered and appropriately shared to shape those deliberations and decisions?

Hope Meadows did not definitively resolve these questions, but it did initiate a life-size experiment that put new options and opportunities on the table.

Strictly from the perspective of the state's fiduciary mandate, professional staff (especially caseworkers and therapists) must ensure children's *safety*, *permanency*, and *well-being*, with the last item typically defined in medical and physical terms. Beyond this, the Generations of Hope Community model specifies that a network of relationships will emerge to augment or "potentiate" conventional counseling and casework and (beyond this) that eventually it will be the community itself that takes the lead in "sustaining transformative gains" and "supporting life course transitions" as a natural part of its own mandate.

In getting the conventional side of casework done, many boundary objects come into play, particularly during the transitional phase from foster to adoption when the program is acting as a licensed agent of the state for a particular child or sibling group. These boundary objects align the efforts of dozens of different actors and agencies and institutions, appearing in the form of reports and records and conversations and memoranda that channel information from multiple sources and perspectives into often stylized narratives and statistics. Their combined effect is to fasten the child/ward into a standard trajectory through the larger bureaucratic system, and the objects are crafted largely for the convenience and smooth functioning of the system itself.

Niranjan Karnik has noted how a folklore effect often weaves through a child's case record. For example, an offhand observation about hyperactivity made by one worker becomes the basis for a probable diagnosis of attention-deficit/hyperactivity disorder for another and then a salient or even defining characteristic of the child later on; meanwhile, the child's natural anger about his or her situation and history is "transformed into the experience of hyperactivity, and his history of [having suffered] violence is slowly erased." The result is that the child gets constructed at the lowest common denominator of understanding, and as the case record accumulates cardboard stereotypes and meaningless jargon, the actual child disappears.[16]

One can recognize the children themselves as boundary objects in this broader choreography, sometimes with strange results. There was for a while serious discussion at the Department of Children and Family Services about implanting them with subdermal microchips to carry identification and medical information, thus making their disembeddedness from family and community simply moot for at least one vector of state care and responsibility.

By contrast, while the Hope Meadows program also comprises complex assemblages of boundary objects, many are woven across multiple program layers and even serve, at the furthest remove from professional direct intervention, to cultivate and sustain the sensitive, intimate, formative ground of new relationships. Multiple roles and expectations, for example, converge in the formalisms of "Hope senior" and "Hope child," offering a template for the emergence of multistranded relationships as children and seniors enact these patterned roles in recurring encounters and contexts.

Routine and special events bring different constellations of individuals together around various agendas. Tutoring, for example, has obvious instrumental value in different ways for the child and for the program, for the senior, and for the senior–parent and senior–child relationships, while a tutoring report may inform a therapy strategy, mark a stage of learning progress, and offer an ethnographic glimpse into an emerging kin-like relationship.

All the various communications channels at Hope Meadows are examples of multipurpose, synergizing boundary objects. More intricate is the patterned multiplicity of volunteering tasks, which can be seen (through correspondence analysis) to generate an "ecology of engagement" in which program and community purposes are aligned while conserving individual autonomy.[17]

And most concretely, the architecture and the overall neighborhood site function in classic boundary-object fashion to provide mutable yet consistent physical containers for interaction, spaces of exception supporting a multiplicity of focused purposes. The Intergenerational Center is perhaps the preeminent example, designed to host a broad range of activities and thus to combine and recombine opportunities for meaningful connection and interaction across all resident groups, frequently including professional staff.[18]

THE PATTERN LANGUAGE OF INTENTIONAL NEIGHBORING

> It is impossible, utterly impossible, to make a building or a town which is alive by control from above. And it is impossible for the people to make the town for themselves with the ashes of the dead language which they now have.
>
> —Christopher Alexander, *The Timeless Way of Building*

We searched for years for a neologism that could capture, in the abstract, our concrete goal of realizing the elusive conditions first achieved at Hope Meadows. We settled, very late in the game, on "intentional neighboring." To oversimplify, you could say that *heterotopia* makes intentional neighboring possible, while *boundary objects* make it work, but neither make it good or even a good idea. For this, we needed another level of formalism that could shepherd things into an arc that bends toward living community.

Foucault's formalism does distinguish "crisis" from "deviation" heterotopias, and clearly Hope Meadows is distinguishable from retirement homes that warehouse the elderly or from residential foster care institutions that warehouse "orphans of the living."[19] To recap in terms of Eheart's original vision, the "crisis" or transformation being sought at Hope is the emergence of an extended network of relationships—extended socially to as many as 120 persons and temporally to (in principle) the entire life course. The notion of *boundary object* further helped in detailing the mechanisms through which these transformative aspirations were to be realized through coincident layering of purposes and functionality and the coincident channeling of information and knowledge.

All this was helpful, moving us toward a clearer formal language for identifying critical features and propagating them more widely. As an overall model, though, it remained incomplete by leaving us entirely in charge. When asked, for example, about how to arrange structures in a site layout, we often found ourselves falling back on sheer intuition and authority. In an early site plan for Bridge Meadows in Portland, architects from the seasoned firm of Carleton-Hart had initially concentrated "senior housing" in a single structure on the edge of the property. We said no, that types of housing should be interspersed as they would in a "normal" neighborhood (as we imagined it). And because we controlled the flow of predevelopment loan funds, our intuitive objections had to be taken into account.

Fortunately for everyone, Brian Carleton returned very quickly with a redesign, cleverly interspersing some units while still retaining a more sheltering common block of apartments that could accommodate mobility-restricted residents, connect seamlessly with other affordances of the site, and also realize some economies of scale. They had, we would eventually recognize, introduced into the site plan elements drawn from their wealth of knowledge of "living patterns," in effect proposing a coherent "language" for the project that was largely composed of those patterns.

Architect Christopher Alexander popularized this "pattern language" idea in the late 1970s, having developed it in the course of a deep inquiry into the nature of generativity in architectural design. The "patterns" in question are ways of resolving tensions or cross-purposes in a design—repeatable solutions that work, for example, to bring light into a room to resolve shadows just enough to clarify unambiguously who else is present and perhaps infer what they might expect of us. To this particular pattern, he gave the name "light on two sides of every room"; other examples include "entrance transition" and "sheltering roof" and "sleeping to the east."[20]

Patterns can be composite, and the pattern of their composition is what matters most of all. Each pattern that comes into play in some larger context (such as a room, a house, or a village), he explains,

> depends both on the smaller patterns it contains, and on the larger patterns within which it is contained ... [each] sits at the center of the network of connections which connect it to certain other patterns that help to complete it.... And it is the network of these connections between patterns which creates the language.[21]

The unfettered functioning of a coherent "pattern language," applied throughout the course of a project's design and construction, can lead to buildings and neighborhoods that are "alive" in ways that more severe environments, such as manufactured tract houses and steel and glass high-rises, simply cannot be.

In many ways, architects are the heroes of this Hope Meadows story, having more than once inspired breakthroughs in our modeling journey. We consciously adopted the *pattern language* formalism, for example, which had been floating in the background of our conversations with architects for years, when it was brought to bear on a difficult design problem by architect Andrew Alden.

In 2009, we had begun eliciting design ideas for a new structure at Hope Meadows that would be optimized around the needs and limitations of aging seniors. We were still limited by a number of common conventions to which the term *antipattern* aptly applies.[22] These included an initial impulse to provide shelter and care for the frail elderly at physical margins of the neighborhood, away from the bustle and near to the office and potential assistance. In retrospect, we had been on the verge of implementing a miniature deviance heterotopia right within the Hope Meadows neighborhood.

As we mused together over a map of the neighborhood, Alden described a project he had recently worked on for a Native American tribe that had insisted on keeping elders at the physical heart of their community. "So, where," he asked rhetorically, "would you say is the heart of this neighborhood?" He then drew two bright red dotted lines crossing at the actual geographic center, which, of course, is where we eventually built it.

Alden also inverted another antipattern, the conventional assisted-living layout with its central station and wings of "double-loaded corridors." In the design of our new "Hope House" (as it became known), residents' front doors are on the periphery, while kitchen doors connect to a central commons with a large hearth and fireplace (the only one in the neighborhood) with space to host intimate gatherings and an unostentatious door providing separate access from the neighborhood. Some of the oldest seniors live there now, and the Hope board of directors meets regularly in the central living room.

The kind of information brought to bear on housing design in this way is subtle, relational, and difficult (but not altogether impossible) to capture and codify, residing largely in the realm of tacit folk knowledge and material practices and often disclosing itself only as an emergent effect of getting multiple things right. Architectural practice has developed what might be described as a special heterotopic boundary object designed to assemble such multiple perspectives and produce a full set of models and planning documents and other subordinate boundary objects. The *charrette* is usually a multiday session of intensely focused planning activities with a broad range of stakeholders providing input and deliberation.

The charrette became a cornerstone of Generations of Hope's practical consultations with client projects, which continued through 2015. By then, the influence of intentional neighboring as an intuitive and formal model had spread so widely and become so robust in its various local incarnations that a separate national organization was no longer required to promote it.

LEGACY

As Star observes, while formalisms can solve lots of problems, they can also create them.[23] Among the most problematic for us were the countless antipatterns embedded in conventions that commanded way too much formal authority, such as standard architectural designs that isolate and concentrate vulnerable populations or nearly good (or frankly bad) patterns that remain mired in limiting assumptions. All of these patterns are part of a secondary consulting and evaluation industry that, with the very best of intentions, often worked to blunt the innovative thrust of our work and channel it into more conventional paths. Experts urged us to certify replication efforts—to "police the brand" and "control the excellence"—and evaluation consultants advised us to establish the value of the program through a proposed controlled trial that would assign children randomly to adoptive families.

Ironically, this obtuse and relentless emphasis on freezing innovation in order to establish an "evidence-based brand" actually undermines any effort to sustain open-ended reflection on formalisms and conceptual models, distorts the information-gathering and knowledge-building process, and ultimately short-circuits the very innovation it seeks to support.

In our case, with our particular mission, formalisms were an obligatory part of the work of modeling and communicating. The most fortunate effect of developing them in just the ways that we did was that we were eventually forced to delegate authority to the various entailed boundary objects and the partners involved in making and using them and to afford others with local knowledge and growing experience a path to make new and unanticipated contributions, thus building up a deeper pattern language for wider use and collective benefit.

Our early ad hoc formalizations, deriving mostly from insightful but mostly tacit intuitions, gradually gave way to better arguments, more capacious boundary objects and heterotopian spaces, and more coherent flows of information within these new state/civil/neighborhood hybrid organizations.

The first adapters of this model are now themselves centers of replication and expansion, generating their own guidance for their own satellite initiatives and further refining the model within their own specific domains. Bridge Meadows in Portland and The Treehouse Foundation in Easthampton are now national leaders in the foster care and adoption space and are working to address the next-level challenges of broader system reform.

The Bastion Community of Resilience in New Orleans has been supporting returning warriors and families through their transition from military service and beyond through creative adaptation of intentional neighboring. Bastion's model is closely articulated with Veterans Administration and other medical and rehabilitation services, and the program is moving to leverage the stability of the core neighborhood program as an anchor for extended outreach to other veterans living with brain or spinal cord injuries.

Perhaps the most ambitious adaptations are those that focus on another often overlooked vulnerable population, adults with developmental disabilities and their families, whose needs for village-scale support and opportunities can be overwhelming. Osprey Village in Hardeeville, South Carolina, and Building Ohana in Spokane, Washington, are in active planning with the aspiration that when such special-needs adults outlive their caregiving parents, the intentional neighboring community will continue to be their home.[24]

The Osprey and the Ohana projects will embed housing for intentional neighboring into larger mixed-use developments that will include other components, such as retail and other public-facing amenities, which could offer a sheltered environment for adults with disabilities to be employed and/or interact with the wider community in multiple ways. In the case of Ohana, the plan may even encompass a second neighborhood of conventional single-family housing.

At this scale, the number of stakeholders increases dramatically, and the complexity of keeping them all on the same page intensifies. Such initiatives could thus offer extraordinary opportunities for research and design efforts to further develop models of the systems of boundary objects that manage information flows across distinct sectors of society (private, civil, services, market, and government) as they are channeled and brought to bear on the task of supporting and empowering the most vulnerable among us.

For such vulnerable individuals, the question of "where to live" is not so much a matter of having good information about housing options as of having any options at all. Similarly, the prospect of being able to "age in place" within a close-knit neighborhood community while continuing to contribute actively to its life and substance remains stubbornly out of reach for most retirees. It need not be so.

NOTES

1. Norman Denzin, "On Understanding Emotion: The Interpretive-Cultural Agenda," in *Research Agendas in the Sociology of Emotions*, ed. T. D. Kemper (New York: State University of New York Press, 1990), 103.

2. Martha Bowman Power and Brenda Krause Eheart, "Adoption, Myth, and Emotion Work: Paths to Disillusionment," *Social Perspectives on Emotion* 3 (1995): 97–120.

3. "Special-needs" criteria included being part of a sibling group or member of a minority or having a physical, developmental, or emotional condition requiring treatment. But simply being "in the system" for an extended length of time was also strongly associated with the exacerbation of emotional and psychological difficulties and tended to move children into the special-needs category. A panel study from a few years earlier had found that at the time of foster placement, nearly 80 percent of children had severe psychological disturbances, and more than 10 percent were psychotic; after five years in foster care, the rate of disturbance rose to more than 90 percent and psychosis to nearly 30 percent. See G. Frank, "Treatment Needs of Children in Foster Care," *American Journal of Orthopsychiatry* 50 (1980): 256–63.

4. Marc Freedman, *Prime Time: How Baby Boomers Will Revolutionize Retirement and Transform America* (New York: Public Affairs, 1999).

5. Norman Daniels, "A Lifespan Approach to Health Care," in *Aging and Ethics*, ed. Nancy S. Jecker (Totowa, NJ: Humana Press, 1991), 237.

6. Stuart S. Nagel and Sarah Eckart, *Handbook of Win-Win Policy Analysis: Basic Concepts of Win-Win Analysis*, vol. 1 (Hauppauge, NY: Nova Science Publishers, 2001).

7. Susan Leigh Star, "The Politics of Formal Representations: Wizards, Gurus, and Organizational Complexity," in *Ecologies of Knowledge: Work and Politics in Science and Technology* (Albany: State University of New York Press, 1995), 92.

8. Michel Foucault, *The Order of Things* (London: Routledge, 1970).

9. Michel Foucault, "Of Other Spaces," *Diacritics* 22, no. 27 (1986): 22–27.

10. Hope Meadows resident Jim Saunders had not only lived and worked as a civilian on the same base years before but had actually occupied the very same duplex apartment. Now retired from a service role that had included packing parachutes for airmen, he now found himself fixing bikes for children, still in service simply in the role of himself: an elder and an available "grandparent."

11. Rob Gurwitt, "Fostering Hope," *Mother Jones*, March–April 2002, 52.

12. Wes Smith, *Hope Meadows: Real Life Stories of Healing and Caring from an Inspiring Community* (New York: Berkley Books, 2001), 10.

13. Smith, *Hope Meadows*, 90–91.

14. Susan Leigh Star and James R. Griesemer, "Institutional Ecology, Translations, and Boundary Objects: Amateurs and Professionals in Berkeley's Museum of Vertebrate Zoology, 1907–39," *Social Studies of Science* 19, no. 3 (1989): 387–420.

15. Susan Leigh Star, "This Is Not a Boundary Object: Reflections on the Origin of a Concept," *Science, Technology, & Human Values* 35, no. 5 (2010): 604.

16. A student and advisee of Leigh Star, Karnik was one of the earliest investigators of the Hope Meadows project and in fact facilitated my own involvement.

See Niranjan S. Karnik, "Foster Children and ADHD: Anger, Violence and Institutional Power," *Journal of Medical Humanities* 21(2000): 199–214.

17. David Hopping, "Thinking Further outside the Box: Can Program Evaluation Keep Up with Program Innovation?," in *Changing Welfare: Implications for Children and Youth*, ed. Rachel Gordon and Herbert J. Walberg (New York: Kluwer, 2003), 179–99.

18. David Hopping, *Architecture and Site Design Guidelines* (Champaign, IL: Generations of Hope Development Corporation, 2010).

19. Jennifer Toth, *Orphans of the Living: Stories of America's Children in Foster Care* (New York: Touchstone Press, 1998).

20. Christopher Alexander, *A Pattern Language* (New York: Oxford University Press, 1977).

21. Christopher Alexander, *The Timeless Way of Building* (New York: Oxford University Press, 1979), 312–313.

22. Andrew Koenig, "Patterns and Antipatterns," *Journal of Object-Oriented Programming* 8, no. 1 (1995): 46–48.

23. Star, "The Politics of Formal Representations."

24. See https://www.treehousefoundation.net (Treehouse Foundation), https://www.bridgemeadows.org (Bridge Meadows), https://www.joinbastion.org (Bastion), http://www.ospreyvillage.org (Osprey), and https://www.buildingohana.org (Ohana).

Nine

Home Buying in Everyday Life

How Emotion and Time Pressure Shape High-Stakes Deciders' Information Behavior

Carol F. Landry

Wow, I am buying a house! For many people, this is a monumental decision. As we move through our everyday lives, we make decisions. They can be routine and involve little risk. We know what to expect.[1] For example, choosing to order Chinese takeout from a favorite restaurant represents such a decision, as the outcome is predictable with the food's quality being equivalent to previous meals. Other decisions, however, embody risk and present uncertain outcomes. Opting to forgo a youngster's vaccinations represents such a decision since the child's health may be influenced by future events. Such decisions are referred to as "high stakes."[2] More specifically, a high-stakes decision is characterized by the potential for a damaging financial and/or emotional outcome with the probability of great expense to reverse the decision once it is made. Regardless of the decision type, decisions frequently involve a need for information; thus, decision makers proceed to conduct one or more information behaviors: seeking, using, managing, avoiding, sharing, or destroying information. Moreover, each method of behavior typically requires that a choice be made, and such choices can be shaped by many factors.[3] Of interest to this chapter are the factors of emotion and time pressure. Given the large financial commitment associated with purchasing a home, I anticipated that home buyers experienced myriad emotions, such as excitement, fear, frustration, or delight, and I envisioned time constraints to attend to aspects of the decision process, such as having scant few minutes to decide on making a home-buying offer. In view of these considerations, home buying qualifies as high-stakes deciding.

The objective of this study was to contribute to and expand the body of knowledge on information behavior by providing insights into how time pressure and emotion affect people's information behavior when making high-stakes decisions. To test these fundamental concepts, I conducted an exploratory field study using qualitative methods within the home-buying domain. The research included participation in a mock home-buying experience, semistructured interviews using a time line approach, and participant observations. This approach permitted me to discover the rich, multiple perspectives embraced by home buyers, real estate agents, lenders, and escrow agents.

A COMPETITIVE MARKET

The following discussion of the domain of inquiry presents a snapshot of Seattle's competitive, residential real estate market from April 2012 through March 2013. Previously, U.S. home prices soared nearly 90 percent in the first six years of the twenty-first century.[4] As annual gains on property value surpassed the value of interest on a loan, people jumped into the housing market. Contributing to this boom was the loosening of loan underwriting standards, thereby making financing easily attainable.[5] High-risk borrowers were extended nontraditional mortgages in the form of subprime and near-prime mortgages. In other words, people who could not afford homes were given loans that were unsustainable in the long term. Such conditions contributed to the creation of a "housing bubble." In 2006, residential asking prices exceeded new buyers' available resources, and the prevailing housing bubble burst.[6] Home values dropped over the next two years,[7] foreclosures skyrocketed,[8] and the economy took a downturn. Thus, the Great Recession was born.

In 2012, the state of residential real estate began to change as low interest rates and a recovering economy reawakened Seattle metropolitan home buyers' interest in the market.[9] Demand for houses increased, and competitive situations arose due to record low inventory. On December 31, 2012, 46 percent fewer homes were available than the year before.[10] As a result, undesirable homes now looked attractive and were highly sought after. According to the Northwest Multiple Listing Service, multiple offers on a house became the "new normal" for Seattle.[11] Bidding wars ensued as home buyers upped the ante by offering above list prices, including escalation clauses, making extralarge deposits, paying cash, forgoing inspections, writing personal letters to tug at sellers' emotions, or allowing a seller to remain in the home once the deal closed. Yet, despite these tactics, many home buyers lost their bids and were forced to compete for other houses over and over. Buying a Seattle home was not easy.

THE APPEARANCE OF EMOTION

Emotion is a part of our everyday lives. We laugh and cry or become angry or feel joyful many times throughout our daily activities. Emotion signifies specific states (e.g., fear, anger, or happiness) that are "more intense, short-lived and usually have a definite cause and clear cognitive content."[12] Experts in the presentation of information, such as authors, marketers, and filmmakers, know this; they "want us to 'feel' their message."[13] Because emotion is such a presence in our daily lives, it is conceivable that emotion also appears within the scope of our information behavior and decision making.

Emotion has not always been a significant component of information behavior. In the 1980s, a cognitive approach informed information behavior research, such as human-centered information retrieval scholar Nicholas Belkin's anomalous states of knowledge.[14] During the 1990s, however, a focal shift to information in context was noted,[15,16] but it was not until the new decade of the twenty-first century that emotion came into its own, as evidenced by the book *Information and Emotion*.[17] Researchers, however, did include reference to emotion in earlier work; for example, well-known information behavior scholar Carol Kuhlthau noted that students doing research for a high school term paper experienced feelings of uncertainty, anxiety, and confusion during their early search stages[18] while optimism and confidence presented during later phases of the project. A scholar known for his information behavior models, Thomas D. Wilson, observed that monitoring or blunting information were coping techniques when people were faced with stressful situations.[19] Diane Nahl, an affective researcher, suggested that emotion is significant to information behavior since it provided motivation to satisfy an information need.[20] With such a backdrop, emotion clearly has a bearing on information behavior.

Regarding decision making, emotion had been disregarded by rational choice researchers;[21] however, others had recognized it as an important element in the decision process.[22,23] Despite this reluctance to consider emotion in decision theory, it became mainstream. Illustrating this point was the *Journal of Behavioral Decision-Making*, which devoted an entire issue to the topic in 2006. Perhaps the most compelling argument for the influence of emotion on decision making comes from the neurologist Antonio Damasio,[24] who used case studies to investigate the role of emotion in decision making of patients with prefrontal brain damage (the emotion center of the brain). For example, a patient with such an injury was asked to choose between two alternative dates for his next appointment. Referring to his calendar,

The patient enumerated reasons for and against each of the two dates: previous engagements, proximity to other engagements, possible meteorological conditions, virtually anything that anyone could think of . . . he was now walking us through a tiresome cost benefit analysis, and endless outlining of the fruitless comparison of options and possible consequences.[25]

The episode continued for half an hour with no date selected. The issue was finally resolved when the patient was told to return on the second of the two days.

Given that emotion is a component of decision making, the question of its influence on information behavior associated with high-stakes deciding was of interest for this inquiry.

THE PRESENCE OF TIME PRESSURE

Like emotion, time pressure has become a presence within the field of information behavior.[26,27] Defined as the discrepancy between what one would like to do and what one can actually do before time runs out,[28] research has approached the notion of time pressure as a significant contextual factor of information behavior.[29,30] Within the concept of context, time is viewed as both a resource[31] and a stressor.[32] For resource, Thomas D. Wilson suggested that time as a limited supply presented a barrier to obtaining information once a need had been identified. Similarly, everyday life information–seeking scholar Reijo Savolainen submitted that scant amounts of time act as a qualifier to accessing information.[33] As a result, people are limited in their choice of information sources to that which can be attained quickly and easily. This applies to both objective and subjective deadlines. As such, deadlines act as stressors since people can feel less capable assessing whether they have enough information.[34] Conversely, when time is not an issue, people approach information seeking in a different manner, such as pursuing information that is not urgently required.[35]

Like information behavior, time pressure is accepted as a significant aspect of decision making. Demonstrating this is the work *Time Pressure and Stress in Human Judgment and Decision-Making*,[36] which examined the effect of time stress and constraints on judgments and deciding. Time pressure in this field involves two considerations: making the right choice and doing so in a limited time frame.[37] Time stress can be produced by real-time constraints, such as a deadline, or by self-imposed limitations.[38] Moreover, individuals react to time stress differently wherein some perform better when challenged by a deadline, while others find time limits debilitating.

In sum, emotion and time pressure present as noteworthy dynamics in the fields of both information behavior and decision making. As such, the two factors are likely to influence the information behavior of high-stakes deciders.

RESEARCH IMPLEMENTATION

People buy homes for many reasons, such as needing a starter home, trading up, downsizing, making an investment, or simply being "fed up" with paying rent. Furthermore, home buyers apply certain criteria when shopping for homes.[39] Examples included property location, the size of a house, being close to jobs, house amenities, having a view, being near public transportation, or residing in specific neighborhoods. Closely associated with the home-buying process are stakeholders, such as lenders, real estate agents, home inspectors, escrow agents, attorneys, or title insurance agents. To gain a more complete understanding of the home-buying experience, it was necessary to talk with stakeholders. Therefore, I conducted an exploratory investigation with both home buyers and stakeholders.

All participants were recruited from the Seattle area using such standards as being eighteen years of age or older, having purchased a home, being on the cusp of making a purchase offer, or having helped someone buy a home within the previous six months. The sampling strategy for home buyers encompassed referrals from acquaintances, recruiting flyers posted on the University of Washington campus, and a paid advertisement placed on Craigslist. Stakeholders recruitment involved asking for referrals from other stakeholders and connecting with them in person at open houses or home-buying classes. Using this approach, I recruited twenty-two home buyers and twelve stakeholders who met study conditions and provided information-rich data regarding the phenomena under study.

The Mock Home-Buying Experience

I am a home owner, which means that I personally experienced the home-buying process. Despite this background, my house was purchased more than twenty-five years ago. Given the tumultuous changes that have occurred in the residential real estate market in recent years, my familiarity with home buying was akin to that of a novice buyer rather than an expert. As such, I needed to learn about home buying again. To educate myself, I examined various real estate–related websites, such as Zillow.com, Redfin.com, and ForSaleByOwner.com. These sites provide information about listed homes so that knowledgeable choices can be made regarding houses of interest. Next, I investigated mortgage information online. E-loan.com as well as real estate–related websites offer tools and calculators for determining how much home one can afford as well as mortgage term comparisons. Unlike financing, where a lender is necessary, having a real estate agent is not required. Homes are available on Craigslist, or one can approach a seller directly through sites such as ForSaleByOwner.com. However, agents can be found on websites, open houses, or word-of-mouth referrals. Interviewing a prospective realtor is recommended to ensure that the person is a good fit for the home buyer. Additional steps in the mock process were learning about inspections, appraisals, escrow services, title insurance, and closing the property transaction.

Online research was useful, but to obtain a deeper understanding of the complexities and nuances of the process, I attended free home-buying classes. Lenders and agents facilitated the classes and provided in-depth information on a variety of issues, such as credit history and credit scores, types of mortgages, home inspections, property taxes, and closing costs.

The final piece of the mock experience involved attending open houses. This exercise was a valuable part of the experience, as it allowed me to look at properties like a prospective home buyer, interact with real estate agents, and view available printed material about the homes.

Overall, the mock home-buying experience armed me with the language of home buying, such as dual agency, being under contract, and loan preapprovals. Further, the experience permitted me to discover the rich, multiple perspectives embraced by home buyers, real estate agents, escrow agents, and lenders. Finally, each aspect of the exercise complemented the others and prepared me for data collection.

Semistructured Interviews

To further understand how emotion and time pressure impacted home-buying behavior, thirty-three interviews employing a time line approach were conducted with home buyers and stakeholders, such as lenders, real estate agents, and escrow agents. Interviews allowed participants to reconstruct the past while expressing their thoughts, feelings, and opinions regarding the home-buying experience. Key to obtaining high-quality data was the incorporation of a time line into the interview protocol. The time line served to establish the specifics of the process from the home buyers' and stakeholders' perspectives while detailing the step-by-step nature of their situations.[40] Moreover, the time line acted as an event history calendar, as it relied on sequential and topic-driven information[41] while permitting the resurrection of home-buying memories along with their attendant emotions, sense of time stress, instances of information behavior, and decision making.

Participant Observation

Additionally, participant observation was employed to obtain firsthand information about people and places within the context of their circumstances.[42] Eight observations were conducted, including one open house, two property showings, one initial client meeting with a real estate agent, and four home-buying classes. Observations noted what was said and how it was said as well as body language, tone of voice, and nonverbal language for evidence of emotion and time stress.

By using the above methods, this exploratory inquiry took a broad, holistic approach to understanding the information behavior of high-stakes deciders.

EXPERIENCING INFORMATION

As discussed above, information behavior encompasses many facets, such as information use, needs, seeking, sharing, managing, and so on, and associations can be drawn between various forms of information behavior and emotion or time pressure

The Dimensions of Emotion and Information Behavior

Emotion is relevant to information behavior,[43] and it was no less significant to home buyers and stakeholders. Interviews and observations identified ten information behaviors and nineteen emotions (table 9.1). Further, the emotions were experienced at varying levels of intensity: strong, medium, or light. For example, strong fear was deemed as alarmed or panicky, medium fear as worried or nervous, and light fear as uneasy or wary. A dictionary and thesaurus were employed to help define the levels of emotion.

How Information Use Affects High-Stakes Decision Makers

Home buyers and stakeholders revealed that *information use* was the most prevalent behavior present in the home-buying process, and such emotions as joyful, fear, love, hate, and sadness attended the use of information. Exemplifying the medium level of joyful (which includes feelings

Table 9.1. Co-Occurring Information Behavior and Emotion

Emotion	Info Use #	(%)	Info Use by Proxy #	(%)	Info Share #	(%)	Info Seek #	(%)	Info Need #	(%)	Info Avoid #	(%)	Info Security #	(%)	Info Create #	(%)	Info Mgmt #	(%)	Info Monitor #	(%)	Total #	(%)
Joyful	120	(13.2%)	—		15	(1.6%)	8	(0.9%)	2	(0.2%)	—		—		—		—		—		**145**	**(15.9%)**
Fear	85	(9.3%)	—		17	(1.9%)	20	(2.2%)	22	(2.4%)	1	(0.1%)	—		1	(0.0%)	1	(0.1%)	—		**147**	**(16.2%)**
Love	69	(7.6%)	—		5	(0.5%)	5	(0.5%)	—		—		1	(0.1%)	1	(0.1%)	—		1	(0.1%)	**82**	**(9.0%)**
Anger	52	(5.7%)	—		22	(2.4%)	12	(1.3%)	10	(1.1%)	2	(0.2%)	1	(0.1%)	1	(0.1%)	—		—		**100**	**(11.0%)**
Confident	46	(5.1%)	1	(0.1%)	7	(0.8%)	7	(0.8%)	3	(0.3%)	—		—		—		—		—		**64**	**(7.0%)**
Hate	42	(4.6%)	—		8	(0.9%)	1	(0.1%)	—		1	(0.1%)	—		1	(0.1%)	1	(0.1%)	—		**54**	**(5.9%)**
Sad	39	(4.3%)	—		5	(0.5%)	2	(0.2%)	0	(0.0%)	1	(0.1%)	—		—		—		—		**47**	**(5.2%)**
Doubtful	30	(3.3%)	—		6	(0.6%)	3	(0.3%)	2	(0.2%)	1	(0.1%)	—		—		—		—		**42**	**(4.6%)**
Calm	29	(3.2%)	1	(0.1%)	4	(0.4%)	3	(0.3%)	1	(0.1%)	1	(0.1%)	—		—		—		—		**39**	**(4.3%)**

Indifferent	27 (3.0%)	—	2 (0.2%)	1 (0.1%)	—	—	—	—	—	—	30 (3.3%)
Surprised	25 (2.7%)	1 (0.1%)	—	1 (0.1%)	—	—	1 (0.1%)	—	—	—	28 (3.1%)
Trusting	25 (2.7%)	6 (0.6%)	4 (0.4%)	7 (0.8%)	1 (0.1%)	4 (0.4%)	2 (0.2%)	—	—	—	48 (5.3%)
Appreciative	17 (1.9%)	—	4 (0.4%)	1 (0.1%)	—	—	—	—	—	—	22 (2.4%)
Judgmental	9 (1.0%)	—	4 (0.4%)	—	1 (0.1%)	—	1 (0.1%)	—	1 (0.1%)	—	14 (1.5%)
Caring	8 (0.9%)	—	10 (1.1%)	2 (0.2%)	2 (0.2%)	—	—	—	—	—	22 (2.4%)
Ambivalent	7 (0.8%)	—	—	—	—	—	—	—	—	—	7 (0.8%)
Offended	7 (0.8%)	—	2 (0.2%)	—	—	—	—	—	—	—	9 (1.1%)
Shame	4 (0.4%)	—	—	—	—	—	—	—	—	—	4 (0.4%)
Helpless	2 (0.2%)	1 (0.1%)	1 (0.1%)	—	2 (0.2%)	—	—	—	—	—	6 (0.7%)
# (%) Total	643 (70.7%)	10 (1.0%)	116 (12.7%)	73 (8.0%)	46 (5.0%)	11 (1.2%)	5 (0.5%)	4 (0.4%)	2 (0.2%)	1 (0.1%)	910 (100%)

of happy, like, pleased, and relieved) is Duke, a repeat home buyer who desired a view home. Due to Seattle's geography, view homes look on mountain ranges, water vistas, or the Seattle cityscape. Duke found a place with a spectacular water view; however, the house was built on a steep slope, and this was of concern to him. Several years previously, Seattle had experienced an exceptionally wet winter, resulting in a major landslide that compromised the structure of a lifeline community bridge. Working as a photojournalist at the time, Duke documented the massive landslide and worried that such an eventuality could happen to his desired property. After consulting with his real estate agent, several geotechnical engineers were contacted:

> So, this one geotech engineer I talked to . . . the main things he wanted to do was go through all the data and historical stuff that's online and available at city hall. . . . He said the key thing is to figure out what has happened in the past. He goes "I don't need to take samples because they know exactly what these hills are made of." So, I felt better about that because I felt like other companies were trying to get me to pay for services that I didn't need.

Armed with this knowledge, Duke expressed relief and chose to hire the engineer to investigate slope stability for his prospective home.

Fear was also a common feeling among home buyers. Strong fear entailed intense feelings, such as alarm, panic, or fright. Lara, who was buying a home with her partner, used input from her agent to determine what to offer on a house. The suggested large sum engendered fear for Lara:

> It was really nerve wracking. I couldn't believe that we had found a house that we were willing to buy. I had never done anything so adult before. It felt like we didn't know what we were doing. My face was really hot. I was really nervous just looking at those numbers on the offer.

In contrast to fear, many people felt a sense of love associated with information use. Ann, a repeat home buyer, experienced medium love or liking with the location of her new home. "The neighborhood was lovely. It is kind of private. . . . They have covenants and restrictions. . . . We wanted to live somewhere that the houses are similar and have a neighborhood feel." Ann used the information about the neighborhood and attendant feelings in the decision to buy her home.

Representing strong emotion was anger. Rachel, an independent escrow agent, described her outrage and fury regarding a client who was both a reluctant home seller and a reluctant home buyer:

> I just felt bad in the reaction of the agents and it supported the fact that no one was listening to him. No one was caring about what he wanted because this

should have come up when he talked to his agent about putting his property on the market. . . . I don't see how it could have just come up with me. . . . But I can see the agent being a bit of a bully and saying "It's time. Your house is too small. . . . Here's this other beautiful house." She was looking at two commissions for the sale and for the purchase. A lucrative proposition for her.

Based on her feelings and the information provided by the client, Rachel decided to delay closing the deal until the client assured her that he wished to proceed with both real estate transactions.

Compelling Influence behind Emotion and Noninformation-Use Behaviors

Unlike information use, a significantly different effect presented with other information behaviors. Emotion drove information sharing, seeking, or management. Medium anger, such as irritation or exasperation, was felt by a lender when deciding to fire a client. "If the client is rude, I don't tolerate that at all. I simply suggest that we're not a values match, and my advice is to find someone else." Regarding information seeking, Genevieve, a single home buyer, worried that she would not be able to afford a house on her own. Consequently, she sought information showing that her income allowed for home ownership. Jo feared that "she would not have a place to live in a month," so she asked the manager if she could obtain an extension on her current lease.

David's panic, on the other hand, shaped his information management. Having obtained a remodel loan as part of his mortgage package, David explained that "for many estimates, contracts, permits, etc., we ended up piling them on any number of flat surfaces in our house. Every couple of weeks, I would freak out that I didn't know where everything was, then go through the piles and try to group things together by type." Angie felt an aversion to rehabilitating a foreclosed house, and this influenced her avoidance of information about such properties, while the lender felt nervous regarding his need for information from underwriters since "once you get to final underwriting, there are additional conditions needed. We may need another pay stub or explanation. What if I missed something in my write-up?"

Time Pressure and Information Behavior

Time pressure, like emotion, shaped high-stakes deciders' information behavior. When asked about time pressure, information use again represented the prevailing behavior, followed with fewer instances of noninformation-use behavior.

Information Use Generates Time Urgency

Home buyers and stakeholders indicated the time pressure was an important factor regarding their information behavior. As such, information use created a sense of time urgency for deciders. Joe, a property investor and part-time real estate agent, created self-imposed time pressure after viewing a condominium that he determined was "a good deal." Joe "decided there and then to go back home, draft it [the contract] up" and make an offer that very day. Molly, an escrow agent, experienced externally imposed time pressure when a document package arrived on Monday "and the signing and closing was on Tuesday. We have to make sure that there's enough time to get them signed, get them copied, and get half of the documents to the title company for recording and the other half back to the lender." Angie discussed how knowing that other people were interested in the same house as she was prompted her to draw up an offer within three hours of viewing the property. Previously, Angie allowed three to four days to pass before bidding on a home. Phil used information about lengthy short-sales transactions to decide against them, as Phil had a small window of time to buy a home and move into it. He recognized that short sales had long and indefinite closing times, which would not serve his needs.

Time Pressure Propels Noninformation-Use Behavior

Although less common than information use, people experienced time pressure in tandem with noninformation-use behaviors. In many instances, the sense of urgency to share information arose around financing. Jo "scrambled" to assemble and share preapproval documents with her banker, while the lender spoke of a client who entered a competitive home-buying situation on Sunday and urgently needed an updated loan approval letter that day. The lender explained that he could not provide the document but could contact the listing agent and "let him know the strength of the [client's] file immediately." Real estate agent Lilly spoke of time pressure's influence on sharing, "as time is of the essence" when it is crucial to get a client's contract to pending by sharing important documents with the listing agent and her managing broker.

Time pressure, too, was felt with information seeking. Like information sharing, financing prompted people to move quickly when seeking needed information. From a banker's perspective, Lois discussed the phenomenon; for example, when someone finds his house and he is under contract, "the clock ticks, and I've really got to have the stuff like yesterday." The information or "stuff" sought compromised a long list of documents that verify income or demonstrate the viability of a self-employed business. Moreover, the sense of urgency can be amplified by other factors. For Amy, communication difficulties with her Israeli bank complicated seeking account information for a preapproval letter, as did the need for an English translation of the documents.

Needing information exhibited time urgency as well. Genevieve, a condominium buyer, explained that once her offer was submitted, she needed to know "right now" if her bid was accepted or rejected. Lara, on the other hand, needed information about available home inspectors, as "there was that whole time component, and the house needed to be inspected within a week." Consequently, the time stress shaped Lara's choice of inspectors.

The Interaction of Emotion and Time Pressure

Although less common than the stimulation of emotion or the creation of time pressure, the interaction of these two components was correspondingly significant to high-stakes decision makers. Additionally, emotion once again landed in the strong, medium, or light continuum.

INFORMATION USE INDUCES THE CO-OCCURRENCE OF EMOTION AND TIME PRESSURE

As with stand-alone emotion or time pressure, the co-occurrence of the two factors affected decision makers' information behavior, information use again presenting as the dominant behavior. Real estate agent Anna expressed medium anger or exasperation while simultaneously experiencing a time stress situation. When using information that her clients found a house that "just came on the market" and had "at least one other offer," Anna was compelled to write their offer quickly. At the same time, Anna acknowledged that "it can be really stressful for me. Real estate doesn't care about things like putting your son to bed or showing up at your mother's birthday party or that you haven't seen your husband for three days." For escrow agent Rachel, light anger or frustration occurred when other stakeholders create time stress issues through mistakes: Either they can't generate their documents in time to be signed, in time to get the documents back to review, to close. Or the appraisal isn't done, or it needs to be redone, or the file is stuck in underwriting. Very frustrating because then, no matter how organized we are, no matter how prepared we are, at the end of the day there is this made time crunch and it reflects poorly on us.

Similarly, after viewing a foreclosed home, Megan exclaimed, "Holy cow! This is everything we've looked for, and we didn't anticipate it being this good based on what we read on the Internet." Information about the property triggered Megan's strong love for the house while simultaneously generating "immediate time pressure" since she thought "there's got to be other offers, so we need to put in an offer now." For some home buyers, the housing market shifted during their home-buying experience. Illustrative of this change was Starr, who embraced a leisurely two-week time frame before deciding to place an offer on a first house. Conversely, following the market shift, Starr took one day to submit an offer on a second home. Starr was excited about this property, as she "didn't realize that there was going to be something of this quality at that price. When I first saw the house, I said 'we have to make an offer right now.'"

NONINFORMATION USE IS PROPELLED BY THE INTERACTION OF EMOTION AND TIME URGENCY

Unlike information use, the interaction of time pressure and emotion motivated high-stakes deciders' need for information. Evidence of such impact came from home buyer Phil, who experienced both anxiety and a strong sense of helplessness in his urgent need for information along with the pressing requirement to share information. Phil explained that his situation revolved around such life events as defending his dissertation, attaining a PhD, and transitioning to a higher salary while also buying a home. More specifically, Phil had to share information showing that he earned doctorate-level income rather than the pay of a graduate student. Because of this requirement, a cascade of time sensitive behaviors was set in motion, beginning with the need for feedback on his dissertation:

> I was expecting to get all of my feedback on the written part of my dissertation on the same day [Friday], and then make corrections and submit all of that to the grad school . . . but one of the people from my reading committee didn't give me comments until Sunday. He looked through all that [corrections] and got back to me on Tuesday.

In this instance, Phil's need for information, along with his obligation to share information, engendered feelings of anxiety, as one behavior was dependent on the other. Consequently, when Phil received his final feedback, he submitted his dissertation to the university graduate school, prompting additional time pressure episodes of information needing and sharing. Phil stated,

> I submitted my information to the grad school, and then I waited some time and never heard anything back from them, I ended up talking to the grad advisor to my department. She called the school and got them to process my paperwork so I could get documents back to my department and so I could transition to my new salary.

Phil then discussed the emotions he felt during this time sensitive process. "I just didn't have any control of the situation. . . . I needed everything done by a certain time, but I didn't see anything that I could do to speed the process. So, I felt helpless . . . anxious."

With reference to information seeking, home buyer Angie suffered the interaction of time urgency and worry as her apartment lease was set to expire. Therefore, Angie was motivated to ask her landlord about extending her current lease. "I was so worried about trying to get moved in a three-day period, so I e-mailed our landlord." In Jo's situation, because "time was an issue," strong trust in her real estate agent encouraged Jo to solicit recommendations for a mortgage lender. Molly, however, felt both time urgency and concern as she endeavored to create accurate escrow documents "as quickly as possible" for her clients.

The Role of Information Use by Proxy

As noted above, emotion can affect high-stakes deciders' information behavior when buying a home. Moreover, the people using the information and subsequently making the decisions are doing so by and for themselves. In some instances, however, emotion prompted home buyers to relinquish their information responsibilities and rely on trusted surrogates to use information to make decisions on their behalf. This emergent theme is referred to as "information use by proxy."[44] Such a phenomenon is not to be mistaken for lay information mediary behavior,[45] wherein one person seeks information for another's use. For example, a person finds diabetes information for a spouse. Nor should it be confused with asking someone to complete a task once needed information has been found, such as asking a friend to book an airline ticket based on flight information for a pending trip.

Information use by proxy was not a common practice for home buyers, but it did present. Veronica, a twenty-four-year-old first-time home buyer, "didn't understand half of what she [real estate agent] was telling me. I just went along with it." Trust was the motivating emotion for this behavior, as Veronica "felt that's what she did for a living, so I would trust her." For this reason, Veronica accepted her agent's choice for a lender: "She gave me the name and said, 'Hey, this person is going to be calling you to set up an appointment.'" In a like manner, Veronica accepted her lender's choice regarding the most appropriate loan for her mortgage. Genevieve, also a first-time home buyer, trusted her realtor to find property to show since "she had a better eye for what I like." Strong trust was apparent when Genevieve and her agent were putting together an offer on a condominium. She acknowledged that her real estate agent determined the amount offered since "I didn't have much to say in it. I just trusted her."

At age sixty-three, Mark admitted his inexperience with home buying, and thus he experienced numerous emotions, thereby triggering his information use by proxy. Mark explained that he feared that a "slick realtor" would sell him something he neither wanted nor could afford. Additionally, Mark worried that people would take advantage of him like "sharks circling in the water." As a result, he turned to a trusted cousin for help deciding the amount to offer on a house: "She's a millionaire. She has business sense. So, tell me exactly what to say, and I said exactly what she told me." Finally, Steven acknowledged that "I never made the decision to buy a house. Somebody made it for me." Steven referred to his wife's use of information regarding a house that met their family's needs, prompting her decision to begin the home-buying process. Steven trusted his wife's judgment about the house.

Altering Information Behavior

Study findings further revealed a second emergent theme, namely, that emotion, time pressure, and the co-occurrence of the two elements caused people to modify or abandon their typical information behaviors.[46] In some instances, the effect was positive, but more common was a negative outcome.

Emotion was clearly the primary factor altering one's information behavior. Megan demonstrated this shift in her home-buying journey. Initially, Megan took responsibility for all information seeking and sharing pertaining to an initial house of interest. However, the experience ended poorly, and Megan deemed that the negative result was demoralizing. When a subsequent house of interest became available, Megan elected to abandon all property-related information duties by shifting responsibilities to her husband. Megan noted that "yes, I let my husband do it all. . . . I'd get an e-mail and vaguely read it, and I'd push it aside because I knew he was going to take care of it." Similarly, On and Pon, a couple relocating from New Jersey, altered their behavior after an offer on a fifth property was rejected. On stated that she "was devastated. I was like 'Oh my gosh, not another one!' We lost the bid only because they were able to put down over $120,000. It's hopeless." Despairing and hopeless, On and Pon avoided home-buying information for some time: "I refused to look for about three weeks or so." Mark, on the other hand, moved in a positive direction from that of information use by proxy to using information by and for himself. He attributed this change in behavior to gaining confidence from his initial home-buying attempt. As a result, Mark used what he had learned previously to make an offer on another home, stressing that he "felt good because I wasn't just grabbing a number. I had something to rely on, experience. I was getting more self-confident. I was getting smarter."

Like emotion, time stress altered information behavior as people were not always allowed to act in an expected manner. Demonstrating this phenomenon was home buyer Angie, who needed information pertaining to a home's condition. Her predictable behavior was to obtain information by way of a home inspection; however, a two-day deadline to accept the seller's offer impeded Angie's typical information seeking. She was forced to decide on the offer minus needed information. Real estate agent Franklin substantiated this type of predicament, as "sellers are setting review dates, which create excitement and discourages contingencies based on inspections. So, you can do a pre-inspection, but often there isn't time to get one done before the review deadline." Consequently, home buyers were forgoing the procedure. In Phil's case, price was a significant consideration; thus, he looked for homes that fell within his pricing constraints. These encompassed move-in-ready, short-sales, and foreclosed properties. Yet, despite such a parameter, Phil altered his information-seeking behavior due to an expiring apartment lease and chose to view only homes engendering shorter closing times. Anna, a real estate agent, acknowledged that she changed her manner of information sharing due to time urgency. Anna indicated that "we wrote the contract differently than other times. Previously, we met face-to-face to get paperwork done, but in this case, we would have done everything by fax and e-mail. We're in such a tight deadline that we had to get things done quickly. There wasn't time to meet." Similarly, the interaction of emotion and time pressure affected people's information behavior. Home buyer David found that time stress and emotion collided when he needed to understand closing documents, leading to feelings of disapproval over the quick signing of important documents. He explained,

> I would have liked to at least understand what type of document I was signing at each step along the way. But I didn't have time for that. I think it's a failed, terrible process in the real estate system today, that you have to just blindly sign whatever they put in front of you or the deal doesn't go through. I would have liked to have had a week with that packet before going to signing.

Given the nature of the signing appointment, David surrendered to the co-occurring emotion and time pressure by vacating his need for information.

For Lara, the interaction of time pressure and emotion during her home-buying experience was described as "horrible," as she was compelled to abandon systematic control of her information behavior. Lara explained that she had thirty minutes in which to decide whether to make an offer on a house while also determining what amount to offer. Lara went on to describe her predicament:

> I am very methodical with my decision making. . . . I research every angle. I look into everything, and I need to have time to really look at everything. So, it felt just awful. Finally, I just had to go against my nature and say, "Let's just do this. I'm going to throw caution to the wind. There's only one way we can do this, and I'm going to have faith that it will work out somehow." But yeah, it was totally against my nature to do something like that.

CONCLUSION

The focus of this inquiry was on the information behavior of high-stakes decision makers in the home-buying domain, with an overarching attentiveness to the elements of emotion and time pressure. From this, a general picture of high-stakes deciders' information behavior materialized wherein information use represented the primary behavior. Further, findings show that decision makers' use of information precipitated emotion at varying levels, for example, strong anger/outrage, medium anger/irritation, or light anger/frustration. Along with triggering emotions, information use could produce a sense of time urgency as well as generating an interaction between the two factors. Despite its predominance, information use was not an exclusive behavior. People also revealed myriad noninformation use activities, such as information seeking, sharing, needing, and so on. However, unlike information use, emotion and time pressure functioned as motivators by propelling behaviors such as information avoidance, seeking, or sharing. As such, a notable divergence emerged between high-stakes deciders' information use and nonuse behaviors.

In addition to traditional forms of information behavior, the inquiry identified the emergent theme of the strategy of information use by proxy regarding high-stakes decision making. That is, home buyers relinquished their information responsibilities and engaged others to use information for making decisions on their behalf. Here, too, one finds evidence of emotion's influence, as feelings such as fear, uncertainty, or trust prompted people to rely on supportive family members or principled professionals to make home-buying decisions. This suggests, then, that emotion is a leading reason behind information use by proxy.

Findings also suggested that time pressure and emotion can alter high-stakes decision makers' information behavior. Deciders revealed that the presence of emotion, time pressure, and the interaction of the two elements triggered people to modify or abandon characteristic information behavior. In some instances, the effect was positive, for example, shifting from information use by proxy to using information by and for oneself. Less constructively, time urgency obliged home buyers to forgo systematic information seeking and use in favor of a more impulsive or arbitrary approach. Emotion derived from negative feelings, such as discouragement, can shift active information use to that of blunting or information avoidance. Home buyers indicated that behavior modifications induced by emotion or time pressure were generally unwelcomed and went against their very natures. In other words, they wanted control over their information behavior.

It is important to look for limitations while concomitantly considering contributions of the study. Two such limitations were noted. First, all participants originated from the Seattle metropolitan area. Large urban areas such as Seattle may present opportunities for information acquisition that are unavailable in small or remote communities. Regional differences, too, may influence information behavior, as social norms can enhance or hinder opportunities for information. Second, findings apply to this specific area. As naturalistic inquiries focus on people's understanding of their situations, such as social context, generalizing across context-specific situations is not possible. Nevertheless, findings can inform or encourage a working hypothesis for new inquiries and areas of study.

The home-buying experience represents a high-stakes decision-making situation that engenders many emotional responses. Time pressure, too, enters the home-buying equation. As such, the interactions of the two factors significantly affect one's information behavior. By understanding how people think and feel when experiencing stress, research can help them to make decisions, to make decisions less stressfully, and to work more easily with decision stakeholders. Moreover, study results offer transferability to other high-stakes contexts, such as making important medical decisions. Findings may also inform system design. Given that emotions are likely to influence information behavior associated with high-stakes deciding, system designers must attend to such a variable. Time pressure also must be considered in design, as high-stakes deciding may precipitate the use of new and unfamiliar technology when engaging in information behavior. Designers should embrace a user-centered attitude and create systems that do not require a large learning curve, as deciders may not have the luxury of time or the emotional resilience to learn how to operate them. Finally, social media could facilitate information behavior associated with rapid decision making and provide emotional support by establishing connections to appropriate support networks. Home-buying groups could fulfill this need, for example, sharing articles, blogs, or other relevant information. In a like manner, social networks could provide a platform for sharing applications for high-stakes-decision scenarios. For instance, a role-playing app has been created to simulate outcomes for various decision alternatives. By employing such an app, a decider may be better equipped to engage helpful information behavior associated with high-stakes deciding.

In sum, this study extends researchers' understanding of how emotion, time pressure, and the co-occurrence of the two can shape the information behavior of high-stakes deciders. The insights arising from the study are potential benefits to the information field, as systems can be developed to assist people's information behavior when decisions are emotionally charged or when deciders are compelled to make choices under severe time stress.

NOTES

1. A. John Maule and Ola Svenson, "Theoretical and Empirical Approaches to Behavioral Decision Making and Their Relation to Time Constraints," in *Time Pressure and Stress in Human Judgment and Decision Making*, 3–25 (New York: Plenum, 1993).

2. Howard Kunreuther, Robert Meyer, Richard Zeckhauser, Paul Slovic, Barry Schwartz, Christian Schade, Mary Frances Luce, et al. "High Stakes Decision Making: Normative, Descriptive and Prescriptive Considerations," *Marketing Letters* 13, no. 3 (2002): 259–68.

3. Karen Fisher and Heidi Julien. "Information Behavior," in *Annual Review of Information and Technology*, ed. Blaise Cronin, 317–58 (Medford, NJ: Information Today, 2009).

4. Mark Trumbull, "Housing: A Crisis with Staying Power," *Christian Science Monitor*, December 10, 2007.

5. Jay Rabideau, "What Do the Changes in the Housing Market Mean to Me?," *North Denver News*, 2008, https://northdenvernews.com/what-do-the-changes-in-the-housing-market-mean-to-me-5606.

6. Trumbull, "Housing."

7. Ruth Mantell, "Home Prices Off Record 18% in the Past Year, Case-Shiller Says," *Market Watch*, https://www.marketwatch.com/story/home-prices-off-record-18-in-past-year-case-shillers-says.

8. RealtyTrac, "1.9 Million Foreclosure Filings Reported on More Than 1.5 Million U.W. Properties in First Half of 2009," http://www.realtytrac.com/content/press-releases/19-million-foreclosure-filings-reported-on-more-than-15-million-us-properties-in-first-half-of-2009-5035.

9. Sanjay Bhatt, "Inventory Crunch Drives King County Home Prices Up," *Seattle Times*, March 5, 2013.

10. Eric Pryne, "Local Supply of Homes for Sale Hits Another Record Low," *Seattle Times*, January 7, 2013.

11. Ashley Van Sant, "Multiple Offers the New Normal for Seattle-Area Housing Market," Q13Fox.com, http://q13fox.com/2013/05/07/multiple-offers-the-new-normal-for-seattle-area-housing-market/#axzz2ZtLH7vVN.

12. J. P. Forgas, "Affect in Social Judgments and Decisions: A Multiprocess Model," in *Advances in Experimental Social Psychology*, ed. M. Zanna (San Diego, CA: Academic Press, 1992), 227–75.

13. Jennifer Preece, "Foreword," in *Information and Emotion*, ed. Diane Nahl and Dania Bilal (Medford, NJ: Information Today, 2007), xv.

14. N. J. Belkin, "Anomalous States of Knowledge as a Basis for Information Retrieval," *Canadian Journal of Information Science* 5 (1980): 133–43.

15. Elfreda A. Chatman, "Life in a Small World: Applicability of Gratification Theory to Information -Seeking Behavior," *Journal of the American Society for Information Science* 42, no. 6 (1991): 438–39.

16. Elfreda A. Chatman, *The Information World of Retired Women* (Westport, CT: Greenwood Press, 1992).

17. Diane Nahl and Dania Bilal, eds. *Information and Emotion* (Medford, NJ: Information Today, 2007).

18. Carol C. Kuhlthau, "Developing a Model of the Library Search Process: Cognitive and Affective Aspects," *Reference Quarterly* (1988), doi:10.9776/16139.

19. T. D. Wilson, "Information Behaviour: An Interdisciplinary Perspective," *Information Processing & Management* 33, no. 4 (1997): 551–72.

20. Diane Nahl, "Learning the Internet and the Structure of Information Behavior," *Journal of the American Society for Information Science* 49, no. 11 (1998): 1017–23.

21. George E. Marcus, W. Russell Neuman, and Michael Mackuen, *Affective Intelligence and Political Judgment* (Chicago: University of Chicago Press, 2000).

22. I. L. Janis and L. Mann, *Decision-Making: A Psychological Analysis of Conflict, Choice and Commitment* (New York: Free Press, 1977).

23. R. B. Zajonc, "Feeling and Thinking: Preferences Need No Inferences," *American Psychologist* 35, no. 2 (1980): 151–75.

24. Antonio R. Damasio, *Descartes' Error* (New York: G. P. Putnam's Sons, 1994).

25. Damasio, *Descartes' Error*, 193.

26. Heidi Julien and David Michels, "Intra-Individual Information Behaviour in Daily Life," *Information Processing & Management* 40, no. 3 (2004): 547–62.

27. Diane Nahl, "Measuring the Affective Information Environment of Web Searchers" (paper presented at the 67th annual meeting of American Society for Information Science and Technology, Providence, RI, November 12–17, 2004).

28. A. John Maule and Ola Svenson, eds., *Time Pressure and Stress in Human Judgment and Decision Making* (New York: Plenum, 1993).

29. Jennifer Berryman, "What Defines 'Enough' Information? How Policy Workers Make Judgments and Decisions during Information Seeking: Preliminary Results from an Exploratory Study," *Information Research* 11, no. 4 (2006), http://informationr.net/ir/13-4/paper356.html.

30. Reijo Savolainen, "Time as a Context of Information Seeking," *Library & Information Science Research* 28, no. 1 (2006): 110–27.

31. Wilson, "Information Behaviour."

32. Berryman, "What Defines 'Enough' Information?"

33. Savolainen, "Time as a Context of Information Seeking,"

34. Berryman, "What Defines 'Enough' Information?"

35. Debra J. Slone, "The Impact of Time Constraints on Internet and Web Users," *Journal of the American Society for Information Science* 58, no. 4 (2007): 508–17.

36. Maule and Svenson, *Time Pressure and Stress in Human Judgment and Decision Making*.

37. Eric J. Johnson, John W. Payne, and James R. Bettman, "Adapting to Time Constraints," in Maule and Svenson, *Time Pressure and Stress in Human Judgment and Decision Making*, 103–16.

38. Haleh Rastegary and Frank J. Landy, "The Interactions among Time Urgency, Uncertainty and Time Pressure," in Maule and Svenson, *Time Pressure and Stress in Human Judgment and Decision Making*, 217–39.

39. Carol F. Landry, "The Impacts of Time Pressure and Emotion on the Information Behavior of High Stakes Decision Makers: The Home Buying Experience." PhD diss., University of Washington, 2014.

40. Brenda Dervin, "A Theoretic Perspective and Research Approach for Generating Research Helpful to Communication Practice," in *Sense-Making Methodology Reader: Selected Writings of Brenda Dervin*, ed. Brenda Dervin, Lois Foreman-Wernet, and Eric Lauterbach, 251–68 (Cresskill, NJ: Hampton Press, 2003).

41. Robert F. Belli, "The Structure of Autobiographical Memory and the Event History Calendar: Potential Improvements in the Quality of Retrospective Reports in Surveys," *Memory* 6, no. 4 (1998): 383–406.

42. John W. Creswell, *Educational Research: Planning, Conducting, and Evaluating Quantitative and Qualitative Research* (Upper Saddle River, NJ: Merrill, 2005).

43. Karen E. Fisher and Carol F. Landry, "Understanding the Information Behavior of Stay-at-Home Mothers through Affect," in Nahl and Bilal, *Information and Emotion*, 211–33.

44. Landry, "The Impacts of Time Pressure and Emotion on the Information Behavior of High Stakes Decision Makers."

45. J. A. Abrahamson and K. E. Fisher, "What's Past Is Prologue: Towards a General Model of Lay Information Mediary Behaviour," *Information Research* 14, no. 4 (2007), http://informationr.net/ir/12-4/colis/colis15.html.

46. Landry, "The Impacts of Time Pressure and Emotion on the Information Behavior of High Stakes Decision Makers."

Ten

In Search of Home

Examining Information Seeking and Sources That Help African Americans Determine Where to Live

Jamillah R. Gabriel

There are many hidden (and not so hidden) challenges that come with not only selecting and securing a place to live but also finding a safe location that has the potential to become a nurturing home where each member of the household can thrive and prosper. One can assume that there are people throughout the country currently engaged in the process of determining where to live. Any given number of life events can lead one to search for a new place to live, whether it is relocation for a new job, graduation from college, returning to one's hometown to be closer to aging parents, or the desire to start anew in an unknown place. For these reasons and more, and at some point in our lives, many of us will be faced with circumstances in which we will have to determine where we should live. Such is the case particularly when looking at African Americans[1] and the numerous impediments that can prevent them from finding an adequate place to live. From a historical perspective, many of these obstacles emerged after Reconstruction and as part and parcel of Jim Crow legislation first implemented in the 1870s and 1880s that was intended to control, restrict, and eliminate the constitutional rights of African Americans. But even after the end of the Jim Crow era, there continue to be various laws, policies, and regulations that negatively impact the lives of African Americans and impede their ability to find suitable places to live. In order to navigate these barriers, African Americans might turn to information sources that can both provide specialized knowledge about a place and directly address concerns of safety, employment, and diversity, among others. While people we know, such as family and friends, are often a primary information source, the internet is another source that people turn to for reliable information that can also influence how one searches for information regarding where to live. In turn, the search for information sources is a necessary step for considering the mitigating factors that African Americans find important in selecting a place to settle in. This chapter explores both historical and contemporary issues preventing African Americans from finding places to live, examines information sources and strategies that play a role in the search for home, and discusses the factors that influence the decision making in determining where to live.

THEORETICAL PERSPECTIVE

In this examination of how African Americans decide where to live, it is important to understand the social situations in which this decision making takes place and the ways in which race plays a role. Therefore, this work is grounded in critical race theory (CRT),[2] which is employed in an effort to expose the dominant power structure that exists within housing policies and regulations as a racist hegemonic system that permeates every facet of the real estate industry. First emerging as a theory developed by law scholars, CRT is a theoretical model used by cross-disciplinary scholars and activists that challenges the white-normative power structure present in society. As explained by Delgado and Stefancic, there are several basic tenets that CRT is comprised of, some of which are addressed here:[3]

- Racism is ingrained in the way society does business and is part of the common, everyday experience of most Black, Indigenous, and people of color (BIPOC)[4] in this country.
- Racism goes unacknowledged in favor of the adoption of "color-blindness," both of which are considered normal and ordinary by societal standards, making it increasingly difficult to address or cure. Additionally, racism advances the interests of white people via material determinism, leaving little incentive to abolish it.
- Race is a social construct and product of social thought and relations where racial categories are invented by society for the purpose of manipulating the system.
- BIPOC are uniquely qualified to communicate issues of race and racism because of their personal experiences in ways that white people cannot.

As it pertains to this study of the relationship between race, racism, and power within discourses around real estate and information, CRT is used toward a critique of the racist and discriminatory practices and policies of the housing industry and the subsequent impact on the information behavior of African American house searchers.

HISTORICAL OVERVIEW

To understand the many motivating factors that lie at the heart of decision making of African Americans searching for a place to live, an overview of the historical context is necessary to undergird issues of housing and race as experienced by Black people. While this overview is by no means exhaustive, it does aim to provide a general understanding of key components that have irrevocably shaped the discussion of race-based exclusions from home ownership and housing that Blacks, particularly those of a lower socioeconomic status, have faced.

Shortly after the end of the Civil War in 1865, Jim Crow laws were enacted throughout the South as a means for white southerners to enforce the racial segregation of African Americans from the rest of southern society. The first act was actually passed in the North when Massachusetts created a law that required Blacks to ride in a separate railcar from whites.[5] Soon after, southern states began enacting legislation with laws first emerging in Florida, Mississippi, and Texas. There was a brief period during the Reconstruction era when many of these early Jim Crow laws were repealed. But after Reconstruction ended, effectively placing white southerners back in political power, Jim Crow laws were reinstated and remained so up until 1965, although the repercussions of these laws continue to be felt today. The laws were a way of controlling and restricting the movements and mobility of African Americans who remained in the South after the end of slavery, with some laws eventually affecting northern Blacks as well. Jim Crow laws outlawed Blacks from sitting next to whites, eating in the same restaurants, drinking from the same water fountains, and walking on the same sidewalk, among other restrictions. In fact, "by 1915, Black and white textile workers in South Carolina could not use the same 'water bucket, pails, cups, dippers or glasses,' work in the same room, or even go up or down a stairway at the same time."[6] The laws were invasive, permeating every aspect of society and affecting every aspect of African American lives and livelihood. While Jim Crow was legally dismantled by the *Brown v. Board of Education of Topeka* U.S. Supreme Court case in 1954, the Civil Rights Act of 1964, and the Voting Rights Act of 1965, its legacy continues and is evidenced by the systemic racism that still exists in the legislation, policies, and attitudes of today.

The Great Migration refers to the phenomenon taking place between 1915 to 1975 when an exodus of African Americans left the South for cities in the North and the West. The migration was not just one event but rather a steady flow of people leaving home in search of a better home. Many southern Blacks could no longer bear the oppression of Jim Crow and out of desperation sought freedom, adventure, and prospects in other places. Like other migrations, migratory patterns developed that could practically predict the trajectory of migrants from one region to the next. Wilkerson describes how the migratory currents of the Great Migration functioned:

> The Great Migration ran along three main tributaries and emptied into reservoirs all over the North and West. One stream . . . carried people from the coastal states of Florida, Georgia, the Carolinas, and Virginia up the eastern seaboard to Washington, Philadelphia, New York, Boston, and their satellites. A second current . . . traced the central spine of the continent, paralleling the Father of Waters, from Mississippi, Alabama, Tennessee, and Arkansas to the industrial cities of Cleveland, Detroit, Chicago, Milwaukee, Pittsburgh. A third and later stream carried people . . . from Louisiana and Texas to the entire West Coast, with some Black southerners traveling farther than many modern-day immigrants.[7]

Wilkerson goes as far as to compare southern Black migrants to refugees who have come to America seeking asylum, only in this case, the "refugees" never leave the continent. Fernández-Kelly makes a similar comparison to immigrants, stating that internal Black immigrants, much like international immigrants, "were propelled by aspirations similar to those of European Americans," and the two groups shared many commonalities.[8] What is most relevant about this migration is the mass movement to the North, where thousands of African Americans arrive unwanted. This, in turn, prompted northern cities to begin implementing measures to increase residential segregation in hopes of staving off the migration of Blacks to their cities and subsequently provoking white flight from urban cities to the suburbs. With this comes the beginning of other racist and discriminatory practices meant to exclude Black people from white communities.

While Jim Crow was the equivalent of racial segregation enforced by law, residential segregation was exemplary of de facto segregation, which was not always necessarily mandated by law but definitely by practice. Racially segregated neighborhoods were initially self-imposed with whites deciding that Blacks would be allowed to live only in separate areas of town or sometimes in entirely separate towns altogether. Later, government policies were implemented to ensure that Blacks stayed in their designated areas. This separation, according to place stratification theory as explained by Williams and Collins, is a product of "an institutional mechanism of racism that was designed to protect whites from social interaction with Blacks."[9] These actions can be characterized as what Sewell calls the "structural reality of race and racism," which is "a concept that captures the ways that institutional and environmental mechanisms work together and autonomously to undergird racial inequality independently of the individuals affected by it."[10] Policies included racial zoning where ordinances were passed regulating who could live in designated neighborhoods and public housing that could be constructed only in areas with high concentrations of minorities, particularly of a lower class. The rationale behind "these ordinances was that residential segregation would preserve the peace, maintain property values, and even prevent miscegenation."[11] Racial zoning came under fire when the court case *Buchanan v. Warley* ended up before the U.S. Supreme Court in 1917 as a result of the questionable constitutionality of a Louisville, Kentucky, ordinance meant "to create and maintain racially segregated settlement spaces."[12] The practice of racial zoning was eventually deemed unconstitutional out of a concern for the rights of white private property owners, an action that ultimately left racial covenants as a preferred method and the only *legal* option for enforcing residential segregation.

Racially restrictive covenants were first implemented in the later nineteenth century for the purpose of restricting who could sell or occupy a residence. Rose and Brooks explain,

> But soon after the twentieth century, the packages of deed restrictions in new subdivisions often began to include racial covenants, the most common being a requirement that the residence be owned or occupied by "Caucasians only," often with an exception for servants. Here is an example, taken from an early 1900s deed in a Los Angeles development: "It is hereby covenanted and agreed by and between parties hereto and it is a part of the consideration of this indenture, . . . that the said property shall not be sold, leased, or rented to any persons other than of the Caucasian race, nor shall any person or persons other than of Caucasian race be permitted to occupy said lot or lots." Although this particular deed does not reflect it, on the West Coast, racial restrictions were likely to extend to Asians as well as African Americans.[13]

Although racial zoning had been outlawed, the courts doubled down on racial covenants and considered them to be both constitutional and an effective tool for ensuring the property rights of white property owners, mainly because they could be used "to enforce segregated living spaces in a way that was beyond public scrutiny or legal challenge by the courts."[14] This led to the wholesale adoption of racial covenants and a professionalization of its use and implementation, eventually leading to a provision added to the "Realtor's Code of Ethics" that mandated that realtors not introduce into a particular neighborhood "members of any race or nationality, or any individuals whose presence will clearly be detrimental of property values in that neighborhood."[15] Realtors viewed this mandate as part of their obligation to the public, and this would persist into the 1960s.

One prime example of how racial covenants were implemented is that of Levittown, Pennsylvania, a planned community that was founded by William Levitt and his family company, Levitt & Sons, and the second of several communities the company created. At the town's inception was a policy of racial segregation as evidenced by the housing agreements that "included specific policies barring anyone but individuals from the 'Caucasian race' from living there."[16] Ironically, Levittown was built for World War II veterans, yet African American soldiers were turned away and were not allowed to use the GI bill to purchase homes in the community.[17] Potential buyers were required to meet with Levitt & Sons management in person to ensure that buyers were white. This and other methods were used by Levitt for decades after exclusionary practices had been ruled unconstitutional by the U.S. Supreme Court.[18] Levitt, however, was not able to control who home owners subsequently sold their homes to, which is how a Black family was able to move into town in 1957. William and Daisy Myers purchased the home from its previous owners, a Jewish couple that had decided to relocate to Philadelphia. Suddenly, Levittown had become integrated, ushering in riots and years of harassment that the Myers endured at the hands of the community's white residents, including tactics such as cross burning, threatening phone calls, protests on the Myers' lawn, rock throwing, and other acts of intimidation, forcing the Myers to secure constant protection in their own neighborhood.[19]

In addition to covenants, zoning, and public housing developments, yet another practice was implemented at the federal level. Redlining[20] was a practice of the Federal Housing Administration (FHA) that was used to block the movement of African Americans into white suburbs and was part of an agenda to dismantle ethnic enclaves and discourage the development of interracial neighborhoods.[21] More specifically, "redlining was related to the practice of surveying and mapping neighborhoods to determine and to indicate their worthiness for government-backed mortgage," and in 1933, it "became the official policy of Franklin Delano Roosevelt's New Deal."[22] For decades, the FHA's redlining practices meant that African Americans applying for home loans would be denied, ensuring that they could not move out of Black neighborhoods and into white suburbs and often having the added effect of pushing potential home buyers into public housing projects.[23] In later years, redlining would give way to the passage of fair housing policies and usher in reverse redlining, or predatory inclusion, and the increased disenfranchisement of would-be African American home owners.

Predatory inclusion is a term coined by Keeanga-Yamahtta Taylor to describe "how African American homebuyers were granted access to conventional real estate practices and mortgage financing, but on more expensive and comparatively unequal terms."[24] Effectively the opposite of redlining, or reverse redlining as some scholars like to call it, it was essentially a practice that inordinately targeted Black women in a money-grab opportunity where everyone involved in the deal would profit except for the home buyer. African American home buyers were now eligible for FHA loans, but traditional lenders still would not back their mortgages, using markers such as physical condition and geography as proxies for race in their decisions for rejecting loan applications. This caused potential buyers to seek loans from unregulated mortgage banks, resulting in riskier loans with higher fees and interest rates and, ultimately, greater debt. These buyers were selected precisely because they were of a low-income status and "because of the *likelihood* they would fail to keep up their home payments and slip into foreclosure."[25] Once this happened, mortgage and bank lenders knew they were guaranteed payment in full by the Department of Housing and Urban Development/FHA, which "transformed risk from a reason for exclusion into an incentive for inclusion."[26] This loophole is what created the ideal situation for predatory lending practices that would disproportionately impact African Americans, particularly poor Black women, leaving shattered credit and ruined neighborhoods in its wake.

This combination of historical events, regulatory policies, and government laws have allowed for a massive disenfranchisement of potential African American home buyers that continues to reverberate in Black communities across the nation. Black people have been forced to find alternative means for mitigating a housing system that has been rigged against them for many decades. Ultimately, and in the wake of navigating the inherent pitfalls and obstacles of an inequitable and racist system that has deemed them unworthy of living in or owning adequate housing, African American house searchers have had to seek out resources and employ strategies that might enable them to make the best housing choices for themselves and their families.

THE INFORMATION BEHAVIOR OF HOUSE SEARCHING

Decision making in determining a place to live arguably begins with information seeking, where the seeker initiates the house (or home) search process. Krikelas's model of information seeking[27] describes this search as an information activity that is in response to what an individual perceives as an information need, and in this instance, that need is to find an adequate place to live.[28] He further expands on the idea of the information source, making a distinction between internal and external sources that ultimately has an impact on source selection. While internal sources are characteristic of an individual's reliance on oneself and one's own experience gleaned from memory or personal observations, external sources make use of resources outside of the individual, such as books and materials or relatives and friends. Furthermore, Krikelas finds that in the case of the external source, human sources, or face-to-face contact, are preferred.[29] This would explain why many African Americans, as well as house searchers of other races to a lesser degree, often rely on social networks consisting of relatives and friends for information[30] who can be highly influential in the selection of potential neighborhoods[31] to live in. Henefer and Fulton discuss Krikelas's assertion of an order of preference in source selection:

> In analyzing the motives for source selection in information seeking, Krikelas develops an order of preference, with convenience, as opposed to accuracy, being the underlying principle. Information seekers prefer to obtain their information from an individual who they know, who can be consulted with a minimum of effort, and who is believed to have the requisite knowledge. . . . Should this type of personally acquainted, direct source be unavailable, the information seeker will ty to find an individual who is recognized by others as someone who will have the information. Krikelas contends that, in most cases, it is only when these two direct, personal approaches to information seeking are unsuccessful that the information seeker turns to the impersonal, material resources to satisfy his or her information need.[32]

This brief analysis explains how the information seeker, or house searcher, might begin the process by asking relatives and friends for advice but eventually move to the internet for more resources beyond the information provided by one's social network. To better understand the information behavior of African Americans looking for homes, an examination of search strategies used in the process of information seeking is necessary, followed by an analysis of information sources, such as ranking lists and their usefulness in the house-searching process.

Information Seeking and Search Strategies

During the information-seeking process, search strategies are developed by the seeker in an attempt to find the resources needed to facilitate information gathering. House searchers, regardless of race, are then developing strategies that allow them to do things such as narrow down locations, make decisions to either rent or buy, find potential homes, and assess various other factors that make a particular place more desirable than the next. For the African American house searcher, however, there may be even more to consider when determining where to live. Krysan argues that "mechanisms of segregation play themselves out through the strategies, experiences, and decisions people make" in their search for housing and that these mechanisms are likely the result of discriminatory practices in the housing market.[33] Even in their attempt to navigate these obstacles and despite residential mobility, it is highly possible that neighborhood disadvantage can still follow African American house searchers who are actively searching for "stable, racially integrated, and middle-class neighborhoods."[34] African American house searchers are having to maneuver around various impediments based on the racial discriminatory practices that are perpetuated throughout the housing industry, resulting in search strategies that are adapted to these circumstances.

In her exploratory study on race and search strategies, Krysan determined that there were three primary search strategies (networks, own research, and professionals) with house searchers' own research being the most popular search strategy. Search strategies were generally the same across white buyers and Black buyers although not as much for renters, a distinction that points to an intersection of both race and class differences. With Black renters, the study indicates significant racial differences in search strategies that Krysan suggest are effects of racial segregation and discrimination that persists in U.S. cities. As was mentioned earlier, one such difference is that Black renters were more likely to use informal strategies and networks in their searches for places to live. This often meant taking precautions to avoid "all-white communities out of concerns for potential discrimination" or encounters with discriminatory landlords.[35] Other notable strategies included an increased likelihood of African American searchers to secure an African American real estate agent, a decreased likelihood of obtaining a mortgage through an existing relationship with a company or bank rather than their own research or advertisements, and an increased use of community organizations for help with securing a home. Krysan concludes not only that "African Americans face more hassles and have to put more effort into securing a place to live" but also that they suffer a greater financial and a psychic cost to difficult house searches.[36]

Taplin-Kaguru's investigation of search strategies takes a different approach in its focus on search strategies employed by African American home buyers for the purpose of neighborhood selection, which the author states can be understood as a two-part filtering process in which home searchers narrow down the options from an initial set of choices of where one might live. The basic premise of this study is that while African Americans employ various strategies in choosing a neighborhood with the most desirable characteristics, the heuristics (or strategies) within the search process often ensured that the results would lead to racially segregated neighborhoods that ultimately did not meet the criteria. While the first-order process is simply an imposition of limitations based on factors such as geography or transportation, among other things, it is second-order filtering that determines the actual strategies. In a close examination of the filtering process, Taplin-Kaguru explains what search strategies emerge from second-order filtering:

Within the imagined set of potential neighborhoods, homebuyers use heuristics to guide them in selecting neighborhoods that they hope will maintain or gain the ideal qualities that interest them. Homebuyers have three main strategies for the search process: avoiding decline, searching for improvement, and searching for stability.[37]

Avoiding decline is described as a strategy applied for the purpose of avoiding neighborhoods with an overabundance of renters and voucher recipients. Some African American home buyers use this strategy on the basis of class as opposed to white home buyers, who use race as the primary criterion for eliminating potential neighborhoods from consideration. These home searchers typically look for information about the number of apartment buildings in a neighborhood or the maintenance of public buildings. The second heuristic, searching for improvement, is a strategy that looks at up-and-coming neighborhoods that have the potential for improving in the near future. African American home buyers who have the mobility to move to a chosen neighborhood search for communities with the potential for gentrification and economic development and will rely on informal networks and real estate agents for information about such neighborhoods. The last search strategy, searching for stability, refers to the home buyer's desire to live in a stable neighborhood that does not need improvements. Here, home buyers employ the idea of "satisficing," first introduced by Herbert Alexander Simon, in which they searched for just enough information that confirmed the desirable features they sought in a neighborhood, including housing values, demographics, and amenities.[38] Taplin-Kaguru found that home searchers were viewing stability "from the lens of a particular racialized mental map of the city" where more familiar areas were deemed more stable.[39]

These studies, when taken together, provide a very broad perspective on the search strategies that African American home searchers apply in determining a place to live. While one study focused on the actionable things that home searchers would do to find information, the other study highlighted the strategies used to eliminate unsuitable places from a list of potential communities to live in. The approaches were different, but each provides a better understanding of the search process used by African Americans looking for homes.

Information Sources and Ranking Lists

Although the focus of the previously mentioned studies was on illuminating the search strategies of African American house searchers (renters and buyers), the Krysan study also provided insight into the kinds of information sources these same house searchers were using for the purpose of finding information about places to live. As determined by Krysan, the sources used were grouped together based on the various strategies employed by the searchers. Sources for networks were friends and relatives; sources for house searchers' own research were newspapers, the internet, yard signs, and open houses; and sources for professionals were real estate agents, property management firms or rental agents, community or church organizations, and apartment locator services. Of the various information sources, African American house searchers were most likely to use a real estate agent (40 percent), read yard signs (40 percent), talk to friends (38 percent), and read newspapers (36 percent) to determine the best places to live.[40] These findings confirm Krikelas's information-seeking model and his assertion that most information seekers prefer to rely on internal resources but will obtain information from external resources when necessary, preferably someone they know and can consult with minimal effort, followed by a person who is recognized as being knowledgeable about a particular topic.

Of note is the finding that only 16 percent of African Americans surveyed in the Krysan study indicated that they use the internet as an information source when deploying search strategies. It was determined that when African American house searchers did use the internet, it was for the purpose of searching for home listings, mortgages, and information about communities. Yet one such internet resource that goes unmentioned in the study is the use of ranking lists frequently published by media outlets giving readers an idea of the best geographical places to live in the United States. It is unclear how useful these lists have proven themselves to be; however, a close reading of them can give some indication of what information they provide to the prospective African American house searcher.

One of the most recognized of these ranking lists is one published every few years by *Forbes* magazine called "The Cities Where African-Americans Are Doing Best Economically."[41] The latest iteration of this top ten ranking was published in 2018 and is developed by the Center for Opportunity Urbanism, a Houston-based think tank specializing in urban growth. Its rankings are "based on three critical factors that [they] believe are indicators of middle-class success: the home ownership rate as of 2016; entrepreneurship, as measured by the self-employment rate in 2017; and 2016 median household income."[42] Additionally, demographic trends were added as a fourth category to measure "the change in the African American population from 2010 to 2016 in these metro areas." A lesser-known list, "Ten Best Cities in America for Black Families to Live 2020," was compiled by media outlet *That Sister,* which specializes in news by and about Black women.[43] It is unclear how these rankings were compiled, but emerging themes included diversity, employment, schools, entertainment, housing market, cost of living, and quality of life. A third list, "The Worst Cities for Black Americans," brings a different perspective by compiling statistics on the top fifteen worst places for African Americans to live.[44] The list is compiled by *24/7 Wall St.*, a financial news and opinion site, and has been published annually for the past three years. The rankings were created based on an index "of eight measures to assess race-based gaps in socioeconomic outcomes in each of the nation's metropolitan areas . . . [ensuring] that cities were ranked on the differences between Black and white residents and not on absolute levels of socioeconomic development."[45] These measures included median household income, poverty, adult high school attainment, bachelor's degree attainment, home ownership, unemployment rates, incarceration rates, and mortality rates. The information gleaned from the ranking lists show emerging themes and factors of importance for African Americans to consider when deciding where to live.

Given the numerous obstacles African Americans contend with in determining a place to live, it becomes obvious that there can be real consequences if one does not choose carefully. As noted by Nareissa Smith in her critique of mainstream ranking lists, location is everything and is perhaps the most important factor for Black home searchers,[46] for whom safety and well-being are of utmost importance, particularly in an age where Black lives are constantly in jeopardy even, at times, within their own neighborhoods.[47] So what unique and immediate factors do African Americans consider when looking for a place to live? A brief discussion of the ranking lists[48] and a few select studies can provide an idea of what factors might be important to African American house searchers.

Each of the ranking lists by *Forbes*, *That Sister*, and *24/7 Wall St.* approached the endeavor of assessing the best (or worst) cities for African Americans to live in from different angles, yet what is clear is a universal emphasis on income and home ownership. These are clearly important factors, but each list considered a variety of factors that were not shared across all of the lists, making it potentially difficult to assess ranking lists on the whole as effective information sources. The list created by *24/7 Wall St.* appears to be the most thorough of the three with its eight measures attempting to envision a complete picture of what makes a place desirable for African Americans. But according to Smith, there are other things to consider that cater to the specific and unique needs of African Americans seeking places to live. She highlights how "racism affects the objective and subjective factors that may make a city desirable" and that these types of rankings do not always take overlooked and equally important factors into account.[49] For example, rankings are not considering issues around public transportation, police presence and brutality, food insecurity, or general Black well-being, all of which are heavily impacted by the racial disparities that exist in society and are certainly primary considerations of African Americans looking for the best place to live.

Table 10.1 is a compilation of lists that provide recommendations for African Americans on the best or worst places to live. While there is some variation, two of the lists agree on a few of the best places to live, those being Raleigh, San Antonio, Richmond, and Washington, DC. The 24/7 *Wall St.* list is unusual in that it documents the worst places to live (many of them in the Midwest), but in doing so, it highlights the many disparities (housing, income, education, poverty, race, and so on) that exist as a result of racist and discriminatory practices and policies that have ushered in the divestment of resources from predominantly Black communities.

Factors Affecting Decision Making

There are many factors to consider when selecting a place to live, and these factors are undoubtedly compounded for African Americans by issues of race and racism. For example, diversity is often a major factor for determining where to live and will often influence decision making toward communities that are racially diverse. According to Krysan, African Americans search for communities that have a variety of racial compositions, which is indicative of the importance of living in a place that is racially diverse. Taplin-Kaguru reinforces this importance of diversity for African American house searchers, stating that many of the respondents in her study "felt that racial diversity was a nice attribute to have in a neighborhood for their own sake but, more important, for properly raising children" and that racial diversity has intrinsic value.[50] Yet, related to this idea is the fear of living in a neighborhood that is racially hostile and uninviting to African Americans. As a result, house searchers must balance the desire to live in a diverse area with the fear of negative treatment from neighbors or discrimination by landlords and realtors.[51] Unfortunately, situations like these ultimately perpetuate segregation, as prospective renters and buyers might attempt to avoid these types of experiences in favor of predominantly Black neighborhoods, where racial discrimination is not a concern.

In other studies, issues around health disparities in African American children have proven to be related to racial segregation,[52] and questions have been raised about the health concerns of residents in communities of color where racist housing practices have been connected to redlined neighborhoods that are affected disproportionately by environmental factors, such as heat and climate change.[53] This is not to say that African Americans cannot or do not thrive in predominantly Black communities, but many of these communities are often at such a disadvantage that there

Table 10.1. Recommended Best and Worst Places for African Americans to Live in the United States

Source	Best Place	Worst Place
Forbes[a]	Washington, DC (District of Columbia, Maryland, and Virginia area)	
	Atlanta, GA	
	Austin, TX	
	Baltimore, MD	
	Raleigh, NC	
	Charlotte, NC	
	San Antonio, TX	
	Houston, TX	
	Miami, FL	
	Richmond, VA	
That Sister[b]	Raleigh, NC	
	Orlando, FL	
	Richmond, VA	
	Lansing, MI	
	San Antonio, TX	
	Washington, DC	
	San Diego, CA	
	Columbus, OH	
	Dallas, TX	
	Seattle, WA	
24/7 Wall St.[c]		Milwaukee, WI
		Racine, WI
		Waterloo, IA
		Cedar Falls, IA
		Minneapolis, MN
		St. Paul, MN
		Bloomington, MN
		Danville, IL
		Niles, MI
		Benton Harbor, MI
		Peoria, IL
		Rockford, IL
		Springfield, IL
		Rochester, NY
		Syracuse, NY
		Kankakee, IL
		Jackson, MI
		Atlantic City, NJ
		Hammonton, NJ
		Erie, PA

a. Joel Kotkin and Wendell Cox, "The Cities Where African Americans Are Doing the Best Economically," *Forbes*, January 15, 2018, https://www.forbes.com/sites/joelkotkin/2018/01/15/the-cities-where-african-americans-are-doing-the-best-economically-2018/#7a91455e1abe.
b. "10 Best Cities in America for Black Families to Live 2020," *That Sister*, 2019, https://www.thatsister.com/best-cities-in-america-for-black-families-to-live.
c. Evan Comen, "The Worst Cities for Black Americans," *24/7 Wall St.*, November 5, 2019, https://247wallst.com/special-report/2019/11/05/the-worst-cities-for-black-americans-5.

are adverse effects that can and do affect the overall quality of life of Black people. Education is yet another prominent factor with educational attainment and school systems being used as markers for stable communities, as is evident in criteria implemented for compiling the ranking lists. In fact, a study linking the academic performance of African American adolescents to low-income urban neighborhoods further demonstrates that education is as important a consideration as diversity and health in choosing a place to live.[54] In addition to diversity, health, and education, Taplin-Kaguru's study of search strategies and the first-order filtering process describes this stage as one in which a variety of factors or limits determine the set of choices that home buyers use to assess neighborhoods. These initial limits run the gamut from financial resources, transportation, and employment restrictions to housing values and geography. The study also identifies the ideal characteristics of a community, including "rising housing values, respectable and polite neighbors, low crime, access to a variety of amenities, and [of course] racial diversity."[55] These are the characteristics that African American house searchers are actively searching for and the factors that ultimately impact decision making about where to live.

In the case of a Milwaukee native and former Chicago resident, Kristin Ware, who in the process of looking for a home in North Carolina, cited better schools, more opportunities, and lower cost of living among her reasons for searching for a new home. She was able to find these things in Charlotte, a place she feels will provide the best opportunities for her son, including exposure and proximity to affluent and successful African Americans.[56] Ware is not alone, as she is part of what some are calling a "reverse Great Migration" or "Black flight" with many African Americans leaving northern cities in favor of southern ones in the past twenty years.[57] While there are many reasons for why this is happening, the end result is an increase of Black people searching for homes in areas that will provide financial stability and growth, good school systems, safe environments, and an overall improved lifestyle for themselves and their families.[58]

In terms of what Black people and people of color are generally searching for, Zillow is perhaps uniquely positioned to shed some insight. Its 2017 report speaks to the continued challenges faced by African Americans that figure heavily into the process of finding a home.[59] While the report addresses historical setbacks that have affected African Americans, including the housing bust as well as income and access to credit and their impact on renting or purchasing a home, there is little mention of the racist history ingrained in the housing industry—a missed opportunity to be sure. The report goes on to highlight the challenges that Blacks and people of color must navigate when entering the housing market, being first-time buyers who struggle to find the right real estate agents and desire to live in overpriced urban areas but are unable to secure financing for a home. This scenario is wrought with underlying circumstances that are not addressed in the report but still exist, such as the difficulty for African American home searchers in finding an agent who is fair and trustworthy, as Krysan discussed, or the housing discrimination preventing African Americans from even entering the housing market, as Taplin-Kaguru suggests. Overall, the Zillow report effectively describes the effects but fails to adequately explain the causes for the state of the housing industry as experienced by African Americans and people of color. Still, and despite the many obstacles African Americans face, the report remains optimistic about continued housing growth and a housing industry that "won't have a choice but to adjust to meet the needs of minority home seekers, as households headed by people of color will drive—and are currently driving—the future of household growth in America."[60]

Table 10.2 is a list of factors that were used by the lists to determine which cities were the best and worst places for African Americans to live. Many of these factors are also representative of what African Americans consider when choosing a place to live. Interestingly, there is very little overlap in what each list deemed to be the most important factors in assessing places to live.

CONCLUSION

The housing industry can be a field of land mines for African Americans in search of home. What might be a straightforward process for white Americans is not necessarily so for African Americans who are having to overcome the many extenuating circumstances that were put in place to prevent them from moving into white neighborhoods, buying homes, or even finding *any* adequate housing altogether. Resultantly, the information-seeking behavior of African American house searchers is complex and nuanced in direct response to seemingly insurmountable odds and a discriminatory and racially oppressive real estate industry whose many wrongs have yet to be righted. It goes without saying that the information search strategies and information sources that are needed to find a home, if you are a Black person, are instrumental and even detrimental to the success of securing a place in which one can not only live but also thrive. For African American house searchers, finding a suitable place to live also means having to consider a multitude of factors that ultimately have a significant impact on determining where that place should be, a fact that belies the importance of reliable search strategies and sources. Ultimately, the objective of this study was to both foreground the

Table 10.2. Factors That Determine Best and Worst Places for African Americans to Live in the United States

Factors	Sources
African American population/adequate representation	Forbes[a]
	That Sister[b]
Housing/home ownership	Forbes
	24/7 Wall St.[c]
	That Sister
Entrepreneurship	Forbes
Income	Forbes
	24/7 Wall St.
Disparities	24/7 Wall St.
Education	24/7 Wall St.
Health	24/7 Wall St.
Incarceration	24/7 Wall St.
Achievement gaps	24/7 Wall St.
Mortality rate	24/7 Wall St.
Poverty	24/7 Wall St.
Employment/unemployment	24/7 Wall St.
Segregation/diversity	24/7 Wall St.
	That Sister
Weather	That Sister
Entertainment	That Sister
Safety	That Sister
Cost of living	That Sister
Quality of life	That Sister
Location (suburban/urban)	That Sister
Food	That Sister
Other socioeconomic factors	24/7 Wall St.

a. Joel Kotkin and Wendell Cox, "The Cities Where African Americans Are Doing the Best Economically," *Forbes*, January 15, 2018, https://www.forbes.com/sites/joelkotkin/2018/01/15/the-cities-where-african-americans-are-doing-the-best-economically-2018/#7a91455e1abe.
b. "10 Best Cities in America for Black Families to Live 2020," *That Sister*, 2019, https://www.thatsister.com/best-cities-in-america-for-black-families-to-live.
c. Evan Comen, "The Worst Cities for Black Americans," *24/7 Wall St.*, November 5, 2019, https://247wallst.com/special-report/2019/11/05/the-worst-cities-for-black-americans-5.

historical considerations that undergird African American decision making in house searching and illuminate the information-seeking behavior that has resulted from those historical events.

Because there are very few studies that examine the information behavior of African Americans in relation to real estate (or any area outside of health information seeking), more research in this area would be helpful to understand explicitly the information-seeking behaviors African Americans exhibit in order to navigate around the obstacles set in place as a result of the discriminatory and racist practices discussed in this chapter that continue to impact the housing industry. Additionally, a study illuminating how African Americans interact with ranking lists and what information they glean from such lists could perhaps more definitively determine what factors influence decision making about where to live. Other information issues not addressed in this paper that warrant further research include Elfreda Chatman's theory of "information poverty" [61] to explain how self-protective barriers can hinder the house-searching (information-seeking) process or "information equity"[62] and "information privilege"[63] to address how Black people are not privy to or do not have access to the same information sources as white people, making house searching considerably more difficult. Certainly, a discussion about the digital divide[64] that many Black people face in accessing information technologies and how the impact of that could account for the low usage of the internet in the previously mentioned Krysan study would be useful. Simply put, we need more studies in the field of information behavior that specifically explore the narratives of Black, Indigenous, and people of color and that generally privilege marginalized voices and intersectional perspectives.

NOTES

1. For the purpose of this study, the term African Americans will be used interchangeably with Blacks or Black people.

2. Kimberlé Crenshaw, *Critical Race Theory: The Key Writings That Formed the Movement* (New York: New Press, 1995).

3. Richard Delgado and Jean Stefancic, *Critical Race Theory: An Introduction* (New York: New York University Press, 2001), 7–10.

4. See "About Us," The BIPOC Project, https://www.thebipocproject.org/about-us (accessed June 19, 2020).

5. Isabel Wilkerson, *The Warmth of Other Suns* (New York: Vintage Books, 2010), 41.

6. Wilkerson, *The Warmth of Other Suns*, 41.

7. Wilkerson, *The Warmth of Other Suns*, 178.

8. Patricia Fernández-Kelly, "Land, Race, and Property Rights in American Development," in *Race and Real Estate*, eds. Adrienne Brown and Valerie Smith (Oxford: Oxford UP, 2016), 7.

9. David R. Williams and Chiquita Collins, "Racial Residential Segregation: A Fundamental Cause of Racial Disparities in Health," *Public Health Reports* 116, no. 5 (2001): 404–16.

10. Abigail A. Sewell, "Real Estate and Racial Health Disparities," in *Race and Real Estate*, ed. Adrienne Brown and Valerie Smith, 87–107 (Oxford: Oxford University Press, 2016).

11. Carol M. Rose and Richard R. W. Brooks, "Racial Covenants and Housing Segregation, Yesterday and Today," in Brown and Smith, *Race and Real Estate*, 161–76.

12. Kevin Fox Gotham, *Race, Real Estate, and Uneven Development* (New York: State University of New York Press, 2002), 38.

13. Rose and Brooks, "Racial Covenants and Housing Segregation, Yesterday and Today," 162.

14. Gotham, *Race, Real Estate, and Uneven Development*, 38.

15. Rose and Brooks, "Racial Covenants and Housing Segregation, Yesterday and Today," 164–65.

16. Sarah Friedmann, "Trailblazers: The Story of the Myers Family in Levittown, Pennsylvania," *The Daily Beast*, July 25, 2019, https://www.thedailybeast.com/trailblazers-the-story-of-the-myers-family-in-levittown-pennsylvania.

17. Bruce Lambert, "At 50, Levittown Contends with Its Legacy of Bias," *New York Times*, December 28, 1997, https://www.nytimes.com/1997/12/28/nyregion/at-50-levittown-contends-with-its-legacy-of-bias.html.

18. Stephen Galloway, "The Real-Life Racial Battle That Inspired George Clooney's 'Suburbicon,'" *Hollywood Reporter*, September 1, 2017, https://www.hollywoodreporter.com/news/suburbicon-real-life-racial-battle-inspired-george-clooneys-film-1034430.

19. "Whites Riot in Response to Arrival of First African American Family in Levittown, PA," The History Engine, University of Richmond, https://historyengine.richmond.edu/episodes/view/5272 (accessed June 12, 2020).

20. For more on redlining, see chapter 7 in this volume.

21. Adrienne Brown, "My Whole Is Warm and Full of Light," in Brown and Smith, *Race and Real Estate*, 177–94.

22. K. Ian Grandison, "The Other Side of the 'Free' Way: Planning for 'Separate but Equal' in the Wake of Massive Resistance," in Brown and Smith, *Race and Real Estate*, 234.

23. Terry Gross, "A 'Forgotten History' of How the U.S. Government Segregated America," *NPR*, May 3, 2017, https://www.npr.org/2017/05/03/526655831/a-forgotten-history-of-how-the-u-s-government-segregated-america.

24. Keeanga-Yamahtta Taylor, *Race for Profit: How Banks and the Real Estate Industry Undermined Black Homeownership* (Chapel Hill: University of North Carolina Press, 2019).

25. Taylor, *Race for Profit*, 5.

26. Taylor, *Race for Profit*, 5.

27. James Krikelas, "Information-Seeking Behavior: Patterns and Concepts," *Drexel Library Quarterly* 19 (1983): 5–20.

28. Jean Henefer and Crystal Fulton, "Krikelas's Model of Information Seeking," in *Theories of Information Behavior*, ed. Karen E. Fisher, Sanda Erdelez, and Lynne McKechnie, 225–29 (Medford, NJ: ASIST, 2005).

29. Krikelas, "Information-Seeking Behavior," 15.

30. Maria Krysan, "Does Race Matter in the Search for Housing? An Exploratory Study of Search Strategies, Experiences, and Locations," *Social Science Research* 37 (2008): 581–603.

31. Nora E. Taplin-Kaguru, "Mobile but Stuck: Multigenerational Neighborhood Decline and Housing Search Strategies for African Americans," *City & Community* 17, no. 3 (2018): 835–57.

32. Henefer and Fulton, "Krikelas's Model of Information Seeking," 228–29.

33. Krysan, "Does Race Matter in the Search for Housing?," 583.
34. Taplin-Kaguru, "Mobile but Stuck," 835.
35. Krysan, "Does Race Matter in the Search for Housing?," 583.
36. Krysan, "Does Race Matter in the Search for Housing?," 598.
37. Taplin-Kaguru, "Mobile but Stuck," 844.
38. See Herbert Alexander Simon, *Administrative Behavior: A Study of Decision-Making Processes in Administrative Organization* (New York: Free Press, 1976).
39. Taplin-Kaguru, "Mobile but Stuck," 849–50.
40. Krysan, "Does Race Matter in the Search for Housing?," 590.
41. Joel Kotkin and Wendell Cox, "The Cities Where African Americans Are Doing the Best Economically," *Forbes*, January 15, 2018, https://www.forbes.com/sites/joelkotkin/2018/01/15/the-cities-where-african-americans-are-doing-the-best-economically-2018/#7a91455e1abe.
42. Kotkin and Cox, "The Cities Where African Americans Are Doing the Best Economically."
43. "10 Best Cities in America for Black Families to Live 2020," *That Sister*, 2019, https://www.thatsister.com/best-cities-in-america-for-black-families-to-live.
44. Evan Comen, "The Worst Cities for Black Americans," *24/7 Wall St.*, November 5, 2019, https://247wallst.com/special-report/2019/11/05/the-worst-cities-for-black-americans-5.
45. Comen, "The Worst Cities for Black Americans."
46. Nareissa Smith, "Are the 'Best Cities' in America Truly Best for Everyone?," *Atlanta Black Star*, May 3, 2018, https://atlantablackstar.com/2018/05/03/best-cities-america-truly-best-everyone.
47. Isabel Vincent, "Families of Ahmaud Arbery and Trayvon Martin Want to Meet," *New York Post*, May 16, 2020, https://nypost.com/2020/05/16/families-of-ahmaud-arbery-and-trayvon-martin-want-to-meet.
48. For more on ranking lists, see chapter 11 in this volume.
49. Smith, "Are the 'Best Cities' in America Truly Best for Everyone?"
50. Taplin-Kaguru, "Mobile but Stuck," 841.
51. Krysan, "Does Race Matter in the Search for Housing?," 583.
52. Diane Alexander and Janet Currie, "Is It Who You Are or Where You Live? Residential Segregation and Racial Gaps in Childhood Asthma," *Journal of Health Economics* 55 (2017): 186–200.
53. Meg Anderson, "Racist Housing Practices from the 1930s Linked to Hotter Neighborhoods Today," *NPR*, January 14, 2020, https://www.npr.org/2020/01/14/795961381/racist-housing-practices-from-the-1930s-linked-to-hotter-neighborhoods-today.
54. Samantha Francois, Stacy Overstreet, and Michael Cunningham, "Where We Live: The Unexpected Influence of Urban Neighborhoods on the Academic Performance of African American Adolescents," *Youth & Society* 44, no. 2 (2012): 307–28.
55. Taplin-Kaguru, "Mobile but Stuck," 841.
56. Jeremy Hobson, Chris Bentley, and Marcelle Hutchins, "Thousands of African-Americans Are Leaving Chicago Each Year. Why?," *WBUR*, February 28, 2019, https://www.wbur.org/hereandnow/2019/02/28/chicago-african-americans-leaving.

57. Patrick Sisson, "How a 'Reverse Great Migration' Is Reshaping U.S. Cities," *Curbed*, July 31, 2018, https://www.curbed.com/2018/7/31/17632092/black-chicago-neighborhood-great-migration.

58. Sisson, "How a 'Reverse Great Migration' Is Reshaping U.S. Cities."

59. Zillow Group, *Consumer Housing Trends Report: Explore the Ways Americans Rent, Buy, Sell and Think about Home* (Seattle, WA: Zillow, 2017).

60. Zillow Group, *Consumer Housing Trends Report*, 86.

61. See Elfreda A. Chatman, "The Impoverished Life-World of Outsiders," *Journal of the American Society for Information Science* 47 (1996): 193–206.

62. See Leah A. Lievrouw and Sharon E. Farb, "Information and Equity," *American Review of Information Science and Technology* 37, no. 1 (2003): 499–540.

63. See Char Booth, "On Information Privilege," *Info-mational*, December 1, 2014, https://infomational.com/2014/12/01/on-information-privilege.

64. Dana Floberg, "The Racial Digital Divide Persists," December 13, 2018, https://www.freepress.net/our-response/expert-analysis/insights-opinions/racial-digital-divide-persists.

Eleven

Where to Live in Retirement
A Complex Information Problem
William Aspray

Today's retirees want (and deserve) so much more than shuffleboard and early bird specials.[1]

If there was ever a subjective question, "what is the best state for retirement" must certainly rank right up there. After all it is a very personal question, almost as personal as your preference in mates or sports teams.[2]

The issue of where to live in retirement is a complex information problem, more so than in the past when a common default action was to move to "Heaven's Waiting Room" (a.k.a. Florida).[3] Approximately 10,000 people retire in the United States every day.[4] Retirement is an issue faced by an increasingly large number of people because the population of those age 65 or older is the fastest-growing sector in the United States.[5] As of 2016, 14.3 percent of the population was in this age-group, and that percentage was expected to exceed 20 percent in the 2020s as the 80 million baby boomers in America exigently age and move toward retirement.[6] It is an issue that may change over time: the newly retired individual who may be in good health has a different set of considerations from the person who has been in retirement for ten or twenty years and who may be facing more significant health issues.[7] In this chapter, we lay out the set of issues facing retirees about where to retire and address issues about sources and quality of information.

When do people retire? The median age for retirement in the United States is 62 years (mode 62, mean 59.88), and 63 percent retire between the ages of 57 and 66. However, people retire at widely varying ages.[8] The author once had a landlord who had made a fortune as a junk bond trader and retired at age 28. Career military personnel can retire with partial benefits after twenty years of service—thus as early as age 37—and with full pay benefits after forty years of service—typically in one's late fifties.[9] Average retirement age at most large corporations in the United States is 57.[10] Academics tend to work longer. In one longitudinal study of a single academic institution, the authors found that 60 percent of the faculty intended to work beyond age 70 and that 15 percent intended to work beyond age 80.[11] A study by Merrill Lynch and Age Wave indicated age 61 as a "freedom threshold" at which time people have fewer constraints about family or work responsibilities and so have more freedom to choose where they live.[12]

ISSUES FACING RETIREES ABOUT WHERE TO LIVE

Table 11.1 lists some of the questions that a retiree must consider about where to live after he or she retires. One of the important things to note is that the answers vary considerably from individual to individual, so the answers offered by the wealth of online articles about where to retire do not apply equally to any given person.

We begin to probe more deeply into these issues by first examining financial considerations. According to the 2014 Retirement Confidence Survey, only 20 percent of workers are "very confident" that they will have enough money to live comfortably in their retirement years.[13] Lifestyles vary considerably, as do living conditions, so there is no one ready answer a journalist or a retirement planner can offer to a family about how much money they will need in retirement. Does the retiree have a mortgage or extensive house maintenance and repair costs? Want to travel extensively? Face major health issues? Have responsibility for the upkeep of other family members? Have debts to pay off?[14]

Many people have saved little of their personal funds for retirement, and consequently they are heavily reliant on Social Security.[15] However, the average Social Security benefit in 2017 was $1,369 per month (or $16,428 per year for single people and $32,856 for couples), which is approximately $25,000 less than the median household income in the United States.[16] Rather than wait until their official retirement age of 66 or 67 (Social Security official retirement age depends on birth year), 57 percent filed before age 65, and approximately one-third of U.S. citizens retire at age 62, the first year most people are eligible for Social Security benefits.[17] For each year one begins taking Social Security benefits early, the monthly payout is reduced by 8 percent. For almost half of retirees, Social Security benefits represent 50 percent or more of their annual income. Unfortunately, this income stream does not match well with average living expenses for retirees, which are $4,300 per year for health expenses alone

Table 11.1. Issues to Be Considered in Where to Live in Retirement (Sample)[a]

1. How much money will I need in order to live in retirement? How does it compare to the amount I needed in order to live prior to retirement?
2. To what degree do these financial needs drive housing decisions? For example, do I save money by downsizing? Can I afford to move into some kind of assisted living facility?
3. Do I stay in the same location where I now live, where I have a social network and a familiarity with services, or do I move to some other location?
4. If I stay in the same geographic region, do I stay in the same house, move to a condo or apartment where the housing maintenance issues are reduced, or move to some other kind of living arrangement, such as a community or an assisted living facility for those age 55 and older, in anticipation of reduced self-sufficiency in the future?
5. If I decide to abandon a single-family home, can I handle the loss of privacy and control that may come with a different kind of housing arrangement?
6. If I decide to remain in my current home, how do I make it livable for me as I age? Is it practical from a building or financial perspective to undertake these changes?
7. If I decide to relocate, what are the major objectives in this move, for example, to live near friends and family, in a warm climate, in some place where I can be intellectually or culturally stimulated, or in a place that has sufficiently low costs that I can afford to live there in retirement without fear of running out of funds?
8. If I decide to relocate, which particular city, state, or country is best for me? What are the factors (e.g., taxes, housing costs, local services, cultural opportunities, work opportunities, crime, recreation, and proximity to friends and family) that I need to take into consideration?
9. How do I avoid making a costly mistake in deciding to move to another geographic region? Are there ways to mitigate the risks?

a. This table is based on culling issues from a wide reading in the literature and not from one or a small number of sources. The AARP Public Policy Institute has conducted a survey of 4,500 Americans age 50 and older about a closely related but not identical question: what aspects of community are most important to them. After considering some sixty possible factors, AARP identified seven categories of greatest importance: housing, neighborhood, transportation, environment, health, engagement, and opportunity. See "The Most Livable Places at 50+," AARP, https://www.aarp.org/home-family/your-home/best-places-to-live/?intcmp=AE-HF-YHOM-TERTNAV-BPLTOLIV (accessed June 25, 2019).

and $46,000 per year overall expenses.[18] Only 10 percent of Americans receive a private pension, and the average amount in a 401k personal retirement account—a program established in 1978 by Congress to encourage and enable personal retirement savings—is $103,866.[19]

Debt is a factor, too. Thirty-five percent of retirees age 65 to 74 are still holding a mortgage on their home.[20] Other barriers to a healthy financial situation for retirement include credit card debt, car loans, personal and payday loans, and student loans.[21]

Financial issues are more acute in retirement for women than for men. According to the National Institute on Retirement Security, women over 65 have incomes that are 25 percent lower than men over 65; women are 80 percent more likely than men to be at or below the poverty level than similarly aged men and three times more likely to be in poverty at age 75 to 79. Widowed women are twice as likely as widowed men to be living in poverty. The percentage of women working at age 55 to 64 increased between 2000 and 2015, perhaps to compensate for lower retirement savings during their working lives. In earlier times, women were less likely to qualify to participate in employer retirement plans, but this gender gap has been effaced over time. Women who worked in the health care, education, or public administration industries, where pension plans are more common, are generally better off than women who worked in other industries. Women overall have 26 percent less income in retirement than men. Women who are widowed, divorced, or over age 70 typically rely on Social Security for the majority of their income.[22]

Even when people have been careful financial planners throughout their working lives, there is uncertainty about the retirement years. According to a Gallup poll, 46 percent of those not yet retired anticipate that they will not be financially comfortable in retirement; however, about three-quarters of people actually in retirement reported adequate funds to live comfortably.[23] The fear is driven in part by the large number of people who do not have personal pensions, worries that the Social Security system will go under, or doubts about the nation's financial future. These people understand that the amount of income will be lower in retirement than it was in earlier years but are uncertain about how much less it will cost to live in retirement.[24] So it is hard for them to determine whether they will have adequate funds to support a reasonable lifestyle or that perhaps they will eventually run out of funds trying to maintain that lifestyle.

AGING IN PLACE—OR NOT

Another issue that people face is whether to remain in their home or downsize to another private residence that might be less expensive or easier to maintain. Approximately half of people downsize during the retirement years.[25] One thing that has made it possible for retirees to stay in their existing homes are reverse mortgages, which became available through the Federal Housing Administration only in 1989.[26] There is a literature that helps retirees decide whether to sell their home and relocate and another concerning the steps to take when one decides to downsize (e.g., things to ditch and things to save).[27]

One anthropologist, Robert Rubinstein, has provided insight into why the decision is difficult for retirees to sell their home, which they may have lived in for many years. He points to the emotional connection they may have to their home. They associate their home with important events from their lives even if those events are long past. The house is "an embodiment of themselves." Not only the home but also the personal possessions within the home help retirees "maintain their identity and a sense of continuity with their past." It is difficult to reproduce in an alternative living situation, such as a nursing home, a place with "our sense of individual rights," such as self-control and independence. For "having a home gives the power of say-so. You're the boss. When people are impaired or sick and can't get around, having power over their own space becomes even more important."[28]

Another study, by Bank of America's investment and wealth management organization Merrill Lynch, together with the think tank Age Wave, reinforces Rubinstein's observations. Their study found that one-third of retirees never intend to move away from their home, primarily because they love their home, are located close to family, or are afraid of losing independence when they move. The study showed that (in contrast to younger, working folks) for retirees in the 65–74 age-group, 56 percent found that the emotional value of their home was more important than its financial value, and this percentage was even higher for people over 75.[29]

For those who do decide to age in place in their existing home, there is a wealth of articles about how to do so. Some of these articles are about organizing the existing home better by removing clutter and hazardous items, such as throw rugs, and organizing medications, bills, documents, and regularly used kitchen items.[30] Another set of articles include changes to the house in order to make it more senior friendly, such as installing paddle-style light switches, widening door frames, installing additional handrails, adding grab bars in bathrooms, remaking bathtubs into zero-step showers, and providing at least one access to the house that does not involve steps.[31]

Various housing options are available to older Americans, depending on the amount of support services they need. One article identified the options described in table 11.2. These are in addition to aging in place in some location other than one's long-standing family home, such as moving to a townhouse or condominium community (where grounds and house exterior will be taken care of) or renting an apartment (where both inside and outside repairs and maintenance will be taken care of).[32] This wide range of options is another major decision that must be made by the retiree.[33]

In addition to the standard options in types of housing to live in during retirement—as described above—some more radical suggestions appear in the literature. One article claims that it provides greater location flexibility and is cheaper to live full-time in a hotel, especially with long-term-stay and senior discounts, than it is to live in a nursing home.[34] Another article suggests selling one's home, buying a recreational vehicle, and moving around to different campsites—traveling to a warm climate for the winter and picking up seasonal work if necessary.[35]

Table 11.2. Senior Housing Options[a]

Type	Description	Cost
Aging in place	Living in their own home or with family—best for relatively independent people; can have in-home caregivers, cleaning, and meals.	Low to medium but relies on some family assistance
Village concept[b]	Neighbors and businesses help people stay in their homes as they age—services provided by other members of the community.	Low, though there may be some fees for such items as transportation and yard care
Independent living	Housing designed exclusively for seniors, such as retirement communities and homes, and senior housing and apartments—designed for active seniors who want support for house maintenance, cooking, or housekeeping.	Medium
Residential care homes	Small facilities that offer personalized services to a small group of adults (a.k.a. adult family homes, board and care homes, personal care homes)—for those who need moderate help with lodging, meals, and daily activities.	Medium
Continuing care retirement community	Communities that are part independent living, part assisted living, part skilled nursing home—best for people who want to live in one location for the rest of their lives and can move within the community when their care needs increase.	High—both an entrance fee and increasing monthly fees when greater care is needed
Assisted living[c]	Communities that offer a wide range of services—good for somewhat active people who regularly need assistance in daily life, such as medical management, bathing, dressing, housekeeping, and transportation. Often have group dining and social and recreational activities.	High[d]
Nursing home or skilled nursing facility[e]	For people who need twenty-four-hour care with meals, activities, and health care—mainly for people with serious physical or mental health care needs; typically have a physician, nurse, and other medical service providers on-site.	High

a. "7 Senior Housing Options," *Daily Caring*, https://dailycaring.com/senior-housing-options-overview (accessed July 9, 2019). In fact, AARP and the National Association of Home Builders have developed a certificate program for builders, called the Certified Aging-in-Place Specialist program, to train the construction trade about the changing needs of people as they age.
b. Intentional living is one variety of the village concept. These communities have mostly begun only in the past decade. They include Beaver Meadows in Portland and Beaverton, Oregon; Hope Meadows in Rantoul, Illinois; Bastion in New Orleans, Louisiana; and Las Abuelitas in Tucson, Arizona ("Housing for Intentional Living," *AARP*, https://www.aarp.org/livable-communities/housing/info-2018/intentional-housing.html [accessed June 26, 2019]). For a detailed discussion of this topic, see chapter 8 in this volume.
c. For guidelines on how to choose an assisted living facility if you are vision impaired, see Barbara Beskind, "Retirement Living and Vision Loss," *Vision Aware*, https://www.visionaware.org/info/for-seniors/retirement-living/12 (accessed June 14, 2019).
d. While the costs of assisted living and other types of senior housing can be expensive, one senior living facility (Admiral at the Lake) pointed out that the cost of aging in place can also be expensive and involve maintenance and repairs that are too strenuous or dangerous for the retiree to do him- or herself. Modifications to the house, such as widening hallways and lowering cabinets, can cost as much $100,000 for the full set of changes. And do retirees really want to "tax" their friends and family to do household chores for them? (Admiral at the Lake, "The Hidden Costs of Aging in Place," April 17, 2019, https://blog.admiral.kendal.org/the-hidden-costs-of-aging-in-place?gclid=EAIaIQobChMIqK-J6cDN4gIVlbfACh1AbQV7EAAYAyAAEgKzifD_BwE [accessed June 13, 2019]).
e. Thirteen percent of U.S. retirees say that their greatest fear is having to move in to a nursing home; this is more than four times as many who say that their greatest fear is death.

MOVING WITHIN THE UNITED STATES

If a decision is made to sell one's house and move, the retiree faces the question of where the next lodging should be located.[36] It might be near the house being sold, but it also might be in another part of the country or even outside the country. There is a steady stream of articles appearing online providing recommendations about the best places for retirees to live. Many of these articles are driven by financial considerations because so many retirees live on limited incomes. These articles focus on either the low cost of living (in a particular town or city) or the issue of taxes (state and local taxes, individual income tax, pension tax, investment tax, capital gains, property tax, and estate tax).[37] These tax-oriented articles are focused more at the state level than at the city level. There is some consistency in the recommendations among these financial-driven articles because the tax situation in individual states is mostly clear and slow to change.[38]

There is much more variation, however, in the articles that focus on a wider set of criteria that, they argue, contribute to the desirability of a certain location for retirees. In addition to cost of living (food, housing, utilities, and so on) and taxes, factors taken into consideration include weather and natural disaster risk; crime and safety; quality, availability, and cost of health care; availability of recreational and cultural activities; shopping; public transportation; job opportunities and the health of the local economy; number of residents over 65; and even "hungry alligators." (The article that listed the alligators ranked Louisiana as the worst state to retire to, though it was impossible to determine the weighting given to the alligators.[39]) In cases where the news article is reporting on a study carried out using rigorous social science, the population surveyed may be mentioned, but one generally has to search for the original study in order to fully understand the details of how the results were arrived at. In many cases, these news articles seem to be less than "scientific" in the way they arrive at their recommendations (e.g., having lack of information about population surveyed, sampling techniques employed, ways of defining and measuring criteria, weighting of criteria, and so on). Some of the articles are slanted toward the target audiences of the publication; for example, *Southern Living* magazine focuses only on the best places to live in the South.[40]

Table 11.3 provides a sample of recommendations for the best places to live in the United States. You can see from this table that there is wide variation in the results. Some of the cities that appear on this list are expensive (e.g., Claremont and Kauai) and thus would not be a good choice for retirees on a budget. One trend is for college towns to appear on the lists: Madison, Iowa City, Ithaca, Claremont, Bloomington, Athens, and

Table 11.3. Recommendations about the Best Place to Live in the United States

Author/Title	Best Place
AARP, top-scoring communities[a]	San Francisco, CA (500,000+)
	Madison, WI (100,000–499,999)
	Fitchburg, WI (25,000–99,999)
Sauter[b]	Rochester, MN
Brandon[c]	Lancaster, PA
Retirement Living[d]	Bethel Park, PA
	Little Elm, TX
	Independence, KY
	Iowa City, IA
Barrett[e]	Asheville, NC
Livability[f]	Naples, FL
Brandon[g]	Pittsburgh, PA
	Minneapolis, MN
	Grand Rapids, MI
	Dallas, TX
	Fort Myers, FL
Caplinger[h]	South Dakota
	Florida
	New Hampshire
	Utah
	Idaho
Faris[i]	Alabama
	Florida
	Colorado
	Michigan
	Maine
Top Retirements[j]	Florida
Anderson[k]	Muncie, IN
Giffen[l]	Chicago, IL
	St. Louis, MO
	Philadelphia, PA
	Memphis, TN
	Minot, ND
	Tyler, TX
Tepper[m]	South Dakota
Economy Zoom[n]	Bellingham, WA
	Boise, ID
	Venice, FL
	Athens, GA
	Bartlesville, OK
	Ithaca, NY
	Claremont, CA
	Boulder, CO
	The Woodlands, TX
	Kauai, HI

Author/Title	Best Place
AARP, small cities[o]	Burlington, VT
	Athens, GA
	Bellingham, WA
	Portsmouth, NH
	Bloomington, IN
	Winchester, VA
	Corvallis, OR
	Springfield, MA
	Napa, CA
	Lewiston, ME

a. "Explore the Top-Scoring Communities in AARP's Livability Index," *AARP*, https://livindexhub.aarp.org/?intcmp=ae-hf-yhom-tertnav-livind-lvablidx (accessed June 19, 2019).
b. Michael B. Sauter, "Thinking about Where to Retire? Here Are 30 Great U.S. Cities for Older Americans," *USA Today*, May 6, 2018, https://www.usatoday.com/story/money/personalfinance/2018/04/26/best-us-cities-older-americans-retire/550108002 (accessed June 6, 2019).
c. Emily Brandon, "The Best Places to Retire in 2019," *U.S. News and World Report*, October 10, 2018, https://money.usnews.com/money/retirement/slideshows/the-best-places-to-retire (accessed June 6, 2019).
d. "4 Best Places to Retire in the U.S.," *Retirement Living*, February 11, 2019, https://www.retirementliving.com/5-best-places-to-retire (accessed June 6, 2019).
e. William P. Barrett, "25 Best Places to Retire in 2018," *Forbes*, https://www3.forbes.com/business/25-best-places-to-retire-in-2018/?utm_campaign=25-Best-Places-To-Retire-In-2018&utm_source=Adwords&utm_medium=ad87533d1us&lcid=ad87533d1us&utm_content=%7Bsite%7D&utm_term=%7Btitle%7D&gclid=EAIaIQobChMIs5SU9bjN4gIVRbnACh1LDw5gEAMYASAAEgL0gfD_BwE (accessed June 7, 2019).
f. "2018 Best Places to Retire," *Livability*, https://livability.com/top-10/retirement/best-places-to-retire/2018 (accessed June 7, 2019).
g. Emily Brandon, "10 Places to Retire on Social Security Alone," *U.S. News and World Report*, October 22, 2018, https://money.usnews.com/money/retirement/slideshows/places-to-retire-on-social-security-alone (accessed June 7, 2019).
h. Dan Caplinger, "The 5 Best States in Which to Retire in 2019," *The Motley Fool*, January 7, 2019, https://www.fool.com/retirement/2019/01/07/the-5-best-states-in-which-to-retire-in-2019.aspx (accessed June 7, 2019).
i. Stephanie Faris, "What Is the Cheapest State for a Retired Couple to Live In?," *Zacks*, December 6, 2018, https://finance.zacks.com/cheapest-state-retired-couple-live-in-8519.html (accessed June 7, 2019).
j. "What Are the Best States for Retirement?," *TopRetirements.com*, https://www.topretirements.com/blog/great-towns/what-are-the-best-states-for-retirement.html (accessed June 7, 2019).
k. Joel Anderson, "Best Places to Retire on a Budget of $1500 a Month," *Go Banking Rates*, April 12, 2019, https://www.gobankingrates.com/retirement/planning/best-cities-retire-budget-month (accessed June 10, 2019).
l. Peter Giffen, "20 Places Where You Can Buy a Retirement Home for Less Than $100,000," *MSN Money*, January 2, 2019, https://www.msn.com/en-us/money/realestate/20-places-in-america-where-you-can-buy-a-retirement-home-for-less-than-dollar100000/ss-BBNC5uE (accessed June 11, 2019).
m. Taylor Tepper, "These Are the Best and Worst States for Retirement," *Bankrate*, July 12, 2018, https://www.bankrate.com/retirement/best-and-worst-states-for-retirement (accessed June 11, 2019).
n. "10 Best Places to Live after Retirement in the US," *Economy Zoom*, https://www.economyzoom.com/retirement/10-best-places-to-live-after-retirement-in-the-us (accessed June 11, 2019).
o. "10 Great Small Cities for Retirement," *AARP Bulletin*, https://www.aarp.org/home-garden/livable-communities/info-10-2011/Great-Charming-Small-Cities-for-Retirement.html#quest1 (accessed June 13, 2019).

Boulder. The variation in these lists may be a good thing because individuals have different needs and interests, and there is no one-size-fits-all solution to this question of where to live.

MOVING OUTSIDE THE UNITED STATES

While the desire to experience another culture is an important driving force in deciding to move as a retiree outside of the United States, the financial dimension is also important. People who need to live on their Social Security benefits, possibly supplemented by modest private savings, often cannot afford to live a solid, worry-free, middle-class life in many places in the United States. However, living in another country—where the cost of living may be as little as one-fourth of the cost in the United States—is attractive.[41] Or for some, their dream home (e.g., a nice home on the beach) is affordable in a way that would have been impossible in the United States. The numbers of retirees moving out of the United States is sizable and growing. For example, more than a million Americans (and more than 500,000 Canadians) are currently living at least part of the year in Mexico.[42]

The tolerance for risk and unfamiliarity varies widely among U.S. retirees moving outside the United States. Some wish to live in an expatriate community of other Americans (with possibly a few Canadians and Brits sprinkled in) where they never have to speak a foreign language and can readily find most or all of the amenities they were accustomed to in the United States. But as James Michener said, "If you reject the food, ignore the customs, fear the religion and avoid the people, you might better stay home."[43]

Others are seeking a life-changing experience in a remote area where they can immerse themselves in the local culture. Clearly, there is no one-size-fits-all solution for American retirees living abroad.

All of the issues that were at play in moving within the United States remain at play when moving to other countries: cost of living; weather and natural disaster risk; crime and safety; quality, availability, and cost of health care; availability of recreational and cultural activities; shopping; public transportation; job opportunities and the health of the local economy; and the number of residents over 65. The tax issues can be complicated because of having to deal with both foreign and American taxes. Other questions that become more salient in living outside the United States include proximity and ease and cost of travel to return to the United States to see friends and family; local regulations about whether one can purchase a home; acquiring appropriate visas to stay for various lengths of time and residency requirements; whether to rent or buy; exit strategies that enable one to easily move back to the United States or to another country if desired;[44] comfort level living under the laws, regulations, and culture of the local community; costs of shipping household and personal goods across national boundaries; availability of English-speaking health care and other service professionals; currency exchange and banking issues; access to familiar American material goods; local and U.S. regulations about earning income while living outside the United States; and U.S. regulations about Social Security, Medicare, and Medicare supplement plans when living outside the United States.

Given that there are even more factors to consider for the retiree moving outside the United States compared to the retiree moving within the country, it is even less likely that news articles about where to live will fit every retiree's needs. Just as with the moves within the United States, authors of articles about where to live overseas often use different criteria from one another, weigh criteria differently, or are not rigorous in evaluating factors. Thus, as table 11.4 indicates, there is a wide range of findings about the best place for retirees to live outside the United States.[45]

There is also a subjective nature to these recommendations, a desire to let human feelings shape the data that go into the recommendations, as *Independent Living*'s Retirement Index (which the publication calls "the most comprehensive and independent study of its kind") baldly states:

> But don't think of it as a mere number-crunching exercise. At its heart lies the good judgement of our far-flung editors and correspondents. We didn't create this Index for it to be a purely objective resource. Yes, it is built on hard facts. But its power—its utility—lies in what we recommend you do with them. In other words, we bring our team's good judgement to bear on the question: Where should I go? We share with you their measured opinions and recommendations. We don't just tell you what the situation is on the ground—we help you figure out what it means for you.[46]

Chapter 1 has already discussed, in a general way, the variety of information sources used by home buyers and realtors, such as websites, apps, and published and self-published books. However, the retiree who is thinking of moving outside the United States faces an additional set of issues and needs information to make decisions about whether to move to another country and, if so, which one. Wikivoyage provides advice on searching for information about retiring in another country.[47] One can begin with a Web search, listing the name of a country and the word "expat" (a common nickname for the expatriates living abroad). As Wikivoyage cautions,

> The best of these are very good indeed, a prime information source. However, it takes some sifting to extract the good information; some are basically

Table 11.4. Recommendations on Best Places to Live outside the United States for Retirees

Source	Best Place to Live
International Living[a]	Panama
Live and Invest Overseas[b]	Algarve, Portugal
Trattner[c]	Costa Rica
Kuffel[d]	Portugal (no income taxes)
	Germany (best in Europe)
	Thailand (best in Asia)
	Spain (beaches and mountains)
	Costa Rica (low cost of living)
	Argentina (best in South America)
Max[e]	Algarve, Portugal
	Canggu, Bali
	Citta St. Angelo, Italy
	Cuenca, Ecuador
	Da Lat, Vietnam
The Street[f]	Switzerland
Holodny[g]	Algarve, Portugal
Drescher[h]	Coronado, Panama
	Penang, Malaysia
	Cascais, Portugal
	San Miguel de Allende, Mexico
	Killarney, Ireland
	Corozal, Belize
Wikivoyage[i]	Acapulco, Mexico
	Bali, Indonesia
	Belize
	Chiang Mai, Thailand
	Costa del Sol, Spain
	Canary Islands
	Cuenca, Ecuador
	Dumaguete, Philippines
	Greek Islands
	Mediterranean Turkey
	Penang, Malaysia

a. "The World's Best Places to Retire in 2019," *International Living*, https://internationalliving-magazine.com/best-places-in-the-world-to-retire/?utm_source=google&utm_medium=ppc&utm_campaign=one-step-best-places&utm_term=search&utm_content=PILVV5GA&gclid=EAIaIQobChMIs5SU9bjN4gIVRbnACh1LDw5gEAAYASAAEgKu_PD_BwE (accessed June 10, 2019).
b. "The World's Best Places to Retire in 2019," *Live and Invest Overseas*, https://www.liveandinvestoverseas.com/best-places-to-retire (accessed June 10, 2019).
c. Esther Trattner, "The Top Countries Where You Can Retire on $150,000," *MoneyWise*, https://moneywise.com/a/the-top-countries-retire-on-1 50000 (accessed June 10, 2019).
d. Hunter Kuffel, "The Best Places in the World to Retire," February 25, 2019, *Smart Asset*, https://smartasset.com/retirement/where-to-retire (accessed June 10, 2019).
e. Sarah Max, "5 Places You Can Retire Abroad on the Cheap," *Barron's*, June 9, 2019, https://www.barrons.com/articles/cheap-places-to-retire-abroad-51549049361 (accessed June 11, 2019).
f. The Street Staff, "The Best Countries to Retire In," *The Street*, October 2, 2018, https://www.thestreet.com/personal-finance/these-are-the-best-countries-to-be-retired-14729558 (accessed June 11, 2019).
g. Elena Holodny, "9 Cities in Europe Where Expats Are Happy, Housing Is Affordable, and Retiring Is Easy," *Business Insider*, December 5, 2017, https://www.businessinsider.com/best-places-europe-retirement-american-retirees-2017-12 (accessed June 11, 2019).
h. Cynthia Drescher, "The 10 Best Places in the World to Retire," *Conde Nast Traveler*, March 3, 2016, https://www.cntraveler.com/galleries/2016-03-03/the-10-best-places-in-the-world-to-retire (accessed June 13, 2019).
i. "Retiring Abroad," *Wikivoyage*, https://en.wikivoyage.org/wiki/Retiring_abroad (accessed June 14, 2019).

promotional sites for various businesses, loaded with biased information, some are one-person blogs which may have quite a limited scope, and even the good ones may have some clueless or crackpot participants. It's also good to be aware of when the person writing visited the location. No matter how good the information may be, if they haven't visited in years, it may be outdated and no longer reliable. This is particularly problematic in travel writings from developing countries where things are constantly changing.[48]

Wikivoyage also points to magazines and websites that have relevant information. These include ones for expats in general (*International Living, International Citizens, Escape Artist, Transitions Abroad,* and *Expat Exchange*) and ones specifically for retirees (*Retired Expat, Best Places in the World to Retire, Retirepedia, Retire Asia, Retire in Asia, Viva Tropical,* and *Retiring Singles*). The U.S. State Department publishes background notes on a number of countries. There are also numerous relevant statistical indices published by nonprofits, including Social Progress Index, Global Peace Index, Democracy Index, Corruption Perceptions Index, Press Freedom Index, Global Integrity Report, Gini Index, Mercer quality-of-living index, Expatistan cost-of-living index, and Human Security Index.

EXOGENOUS FORCES

In an essay titled "One Hundred Years of Car Buying in America," this author set out a framework for matching information history to everyday information behavior—a framework that was used by many of the authors in the book *Everyday Information*.[49] The paper argued that both endogenous and exogenous factors shape the questions of interest to someone in carrying out his or her everyday information behavior and may also shape the sources used to address those questions. For example, the cases of car buying, the rise of suburbs, women entering the workforce, and veterans returning from overseas after World War II were all exogenous factors that shaped the car-buying experience—the creation of a car culture that meant every family must have one or perhaps two vehicles, a need for reliable transportation rather than just a hobbyist purchase, and an openness to cars produced in other countries. Endogenous factors, such as the creation of the dealership system, also had impacts, such as relentless innovation from one model year to the next, even if the changes were primarily cosmetic. Progressivist sentiments that built up prior to World War II resulted in new sources and quality of information, such as *Consumer Reports*, which emphasized automobiles from its first issues, and mandated sales stickers on new automobiles, which emerged from the truth-in-advertising movement of the Progressives.

Table 11.5. Exogenous and Endogenous Factors That Shape Where People Live in Retirement

Exogenous factors

- Growing general economic wealth since World War II
- Increasing longevity of the American population and improved health in the older population
- Mobility of the society
- Enhanced education of the American population since 1945
- Changes in distance travel
- State and local tax structure
- Information and communication technologies
- 2007–2008 housing crisis
- Increasing specialization of place

Endogenous factors

- Lessening of control of the Multiple Listing Service system
- Relaxed rules about lending within the mortgage banking industry

How does this model work in the case of where to live in retirement? Table 11.5 summarizes some of the exogenous and endogenous forces that shape where Americans live in retirement. This list is not intended to be complete. We consider, in turn, the exogenous and endogenous factors discussed in table 11.5.

Let us briefly discuss items listed in table 11.5. One is the growing wealth in America since World War II. Indeed, the United States is wealthier today than it was in 1945. The gross domestic product in the United States rose from $14,655 in 1950 to $52,292 in 2015.[50] Greater wealth means that individual Americans are more likely to have the resources to relocate once they reach retirement age. There are more communities that are within their financial reach, so the range of options of where to live is broader. It also means that retirees may have the financial wherewithal to rent in a prospective location to check it out (without selling their home), and it may even mean that they can afford a second home.

A second exogenous factor is the increasing longevity of the American population and improved health in the older population. Americans are clearly living longer. Life expectancy at birth was 68.2 years in 1950 and 79.2 years in 2015.[51] This means that we anticipate living a long and active life in retirement, something that retirees in the 1920s or the 1950s could not count on.

Being more mobile today means that Americans are used to both traveling and relocating. They are more open to living in a variety of places and probably have visited some of them during their lives. A pattern of mobility enables one to break long-standing family expectations that retirees will age in place, move to where other family members are located, or make a traditional retirement choice, such as moving to Florida.[52]

Americans are also better educated today than they were immediately after World War II. In 1950, 51 percent of Americans ages 25 to 34 had not completed high school, 34 percent were high school graduates but had not pursued further formal higher education, 10 percent had received some college training or an associate's degree but had not completed a bachelor's degree or higher, and 6 percent had completed a bachelor's degree or higher. Compare that to 2009, when the respective figures were skewed to the higher-education categories: 12, 28, 28, and 32 percent.[53] The GI Bill had a significant role in democratizing higher education in the United States. This education made people generally more aware of and more open to different places and the lifestyles they offered. One other impact was the greater awareness of the resources and amenities that a college town has to offer and of college towns as increasingly popular relocation spots for retirees.

The creation of the interstate highway system,[54] the improvement in automobile reliability and safety,[55] and the democratization of airline traffic[56] means that people are able—by car or plane—to visit any place in North America relatively inexpensively. Long-distance travel is both more affordable and more prevalent. This means that retirees can more readily visit places they might like to live; also, that distance from friends and family is less of a barrier than it once was.

Personal finance magazines and websites, such as *Money*, *Kiplinger's*, and *The Motley Fool*, are peppered with stories about which states and cities are the best places to retire—based primarily on financial considerations, such as personal income tax and estate taxes for retirees.[57] As economic geographer Richard Florida notes, some of these specialty-focused regions cross city and state boundaries, making tax issues more of a question about where within a region to relocate rather than whether to move to that general region. Even the personal finance magazines recognize that financial issues are not the only consideration in selecting where to retire,[58] and many of these articles include other issues (weather, recreational opportunities, jobs, and so on) in addition to tax considerations.

The increased power and ubiquity[59] of information and communication technologies mean that we have tools (websites, social network groups, home-repair and home-buying television programs, and real estate apps) that we can use in our own homes both to imagine what it would be like to live in a particular place or kind of place (foreign city or oceanside village) and to look at properties without having the bother and expense to travel to these places and interact with a realtor. It provides us with powerful tools to imagine alternatives. (Note that this is also reliant on an endogenous force—changes in the way in which the real estate industry works, where the realtor and MLS are no longer so much in control of the information about houses and communities in which they are located. The past twenty years have witnessed a notable reduction in this information asymmetry.) Information and communication technologies also enable one to more readily work remotely if one needs to continue to work during retirement, so a retiree is partially or completely freed, in the case of certain types of jobs, about where to live and still work.

The 2007–2008 housing crisis meant that a number of people defaulted on loans and mortgages, making them credit-risky for future housing purchases. The wide availability of mortgages during that time led to many additional people entering the house-buying market, driving up prices and making housing less affordable. After the recession, almost 4 million homes were turned into rentals (many by large investors), and today there are fewer houses on the market than at any time since 1982. Scarcity of houses for sale drives up purchase prices, and higher purchase prices on sales drive up demand for as well as prices on rentals.[60] When the local real estate market dropped, as it did in many communities, many people had minimal or even negative equity in their homes, and it typically took them a long time to recover from this situation. Even today, more stringent borrowing guidelines are in place, including, for example, lower debt-to-income ratios to qualify for a mortgage, and these guidelines are problematic for people on a fixed income.[61]

Richard Florida argues that there is increasing specialization of place over time in the United States.[62] Particular cities or regions become known for some particular trait (e.g., Silicon Valley for high tech or New Orleans for jazz), and those places attract outsiders who have those talents or those interests, concentrating them even more than before. As individual regions become specialized, retirees have more real choices, and it is more valuable for the retiree to know this information in order to make informed decisions about what attributes a potential retirement community has. There is more diversity in regional life, Florida would argue.

FINAL WORDS

The purpose of this chapter has been to show some of the specifics concerning the complexity of the information search for retirees about where to live. The search involves both establishing criteria (e.g., do I want to live closer to relatives or in my dream home on the beach?) and then the effort to make a decision based on those criteria. There are multiple factors associated with these decisions: location, type of home, preferred lifestyle, affordability, and so on. This chapter has also suggested some of the exogenous factors that may shape a retiree's decision about where to live in retirement.

This chapter has not addressed the actions taken by an individual when seeking information about where to live—how one goes about searching for information. It is clear, however, that the information that informs a retiree's decision about where to live is gathered through simple exposure both to news stories and television shows and to comments from friends, families, and acquaintances as well as through active seeking of information.[63]

The information behavior literature includes a number of studies about information seeking that might be applied if one wants to go beyond the scope of this chapter. For example, one can imagine that the typical retiree might wish to rely on oral sources of friends and family more than on printed sources, as one might expect from Zipf's "principle of least effort," in which one chooses sources for their convenience (but also perhaps because the retiree might trust these people more or believe that they know his or her particular retirement needs better than a stranger).[64] One can imagine that most people will not want to take the time, trouble, and expense to visit a wide array of potential retirement locations but may be willing to visit or temporarily relocate to a place if it is one of a small number of top prospects for a long-term relocation. This approach is consistent with the "cost–benefit paradigm" and the various information behavior works that elaborate on this paradigm.[65] One might also believe that the retiree may play an active role in the selection of information sources after deciding what issues are most important to him or her. The mass communication theory of "uses and gratifications," which has been applied by information behavior scholars, may provide insight into the retiree's active process of information gathering.[66]

Whether the retiree has been active or passive in gathering and consuming information about where to live, at some point the retiree may make a decision about where to live. There are bodies of information behavior literature on making decisions,[67] satisficing,[68] unstructured searching,[69] and relevance and salience.[70] Also, making a decision about where to live is clearly not only cognitive but also affective. Will retirees be happy in a new location? Will they be able to be the person they imagine they want to be in retirement? Will they have the financial and physical resources to carry out their retirement plan? A body of information behavior literature on affective elements of decision making can inform issues that are a blend of the cognitive and the affective.[71] However, all of these issues are beyond the scope of this chapter.

NOTES

1. "2018 Best Places to Retire," *Livability*, https://livability.com/top-10/retirement/best-places-to-retire/2018 (accessed June 7, 2019).
2. "What Are the Best States for Retirement?," *TopRetirements.com*, https://www.topretirements.com/blog/great-towns/what-are-the-best-states-for-retirement.html (accessed June 7, 2019).
3. Barbara Corcoran, "Where Will You Retire?," *Today*, April 29, 2008, https://www.today.com/popculture/where-will-you-retire-wbna24341380 (accessed June 14, 2019). Actually, Florida has some problems, including high cost of storm insurance, increased housing costs, traffic congestion, lack of public transportation, and less-than-stellar health coverage that has caused some people to avoid or move away from Florida in their retirement years. As early as the 1960s, one can see journalists discussing substitutes for Florida, that is, places that are warm and low cost but not Florida. One article from that time recommends in addition to Florida retirement communities and Florida college towns the following places: Wilmington, Chapel Hill, and Tryon, North Carolina; Beaufort, Charleston, Columbia, and Clemson, South Carolina; Albany and Columbus, Georgia; Austin, Texas; and Tucson, Arizona (A. M. Watkins, "Where Can You Go for Low-Cost Retirement?," *Better Homes and Gardens* 43, no. 4 (April 1965): 136n). One can see journalists beginning to address radically different alternatives to Florida in the 1990s. For example, see Larry Van Dyne, "Will Senior Citizens Skip Florida to Live on a Washington Metro Line?," *Washingtonian*, September 1992. The importance of public transportation for seniors continues to be a theme in the journalistic literature today. See, for example, Jana Lynott, "Transit-Oriented Housing Helps Older Adults Live Independent Lives," *AARP: The Magazine*, https://www.aarp.org/livable-communities/getting-around/info-2017/transit-oriented-development-senior-housing-denver.html (accessed June 18, 2019).
4. Rebecca Lake, "Retirement Statistics," *Credit Donkey*, May 2, 2019, https://www.creditdonkey.com/retirement-statistics.html (accessed July 18, 2019).
5. Candice Reed, "We're Semi-Retired and Living in an RV. It's Not as Ghastly as It May Sound," *Los Angeles Times*, December 31, 2017, https://www.latimes.com/opinion/op-ed/la-oe-reed-rv-life-is-not-so-bad-20171231-story.html (accessed June 11, 2019).
6. Michael B. Sauter, "Thinking about Where to Retire? Here Are 30 Great U.S. Cities for Older Americans," *USA Today*, May 6, 2018, https://www.usatoday.com/story/money/personalfinance/2018/04/26/best-us-cities-older-americans-retire/550108002 (accessed June 6, 2019).
7. For a somewhat dated yet still useful academic literature review on the housing patterns for different ages of retirees in the United States, see Stephen Golant, "Deciding Where to Live: The Emerging Residential Settlement Patterns of Retired Americans," *Generations* 26 (2002): 66–73. On the "oldest old" and their housing choices, see a dated but useful academic study: Florian Heiss, Mike Hurd, and Axel Borsch-Supan, "Healthy, Wealthy and Knowing Where to Live: Projected Trajectories of Health, Wealth and Living Arrangements among the Oldest Old," NBER Working Paper No. 9897, August 2003, https://www.nber.org/papers/w9897.pdf (accessed June 14, 2019). Real estate broker Barbara Corcoran and War-

ren Berger have written a more popular sociological study, *Nextville* (New York: Springboard Press, 2008), in which they identify different patterns of housing for classes of retirees, such as "ruppies," who want the stimulation of living in urban environments; "zoomers," who want to zoom off to places across the globe; "huddlers," who are driven to find human contact and a sense of community; and "boomerangs," who go back and forth between the adventurous and the safety of a home base. For an excerpt of the book, see Barbara Corcoran, "Where Will You Retire?," *Today*, April 29, 2008, https://www.today.com/popculture/where-will-you-retire-wbna24341380 (accessed June 14, 2019).

8. "Average Retirement Age in the United States," *DQYDJ*, June 26, 2019, https://dqydj.com/average-retirement-age-in-the-united-states (accessed July 3, 2019).

9. "What Age Can You Retire from the Military?," *Online Military Education*, https://www.onlinemilitaryeducation.org/faq/what-age-can-you-retire-from-the-military (accessed July 3, 2019).

10. Felicity Duncan, "Retire at 55 and Live to 80; Work till You're 65 and Die at 67. Startling New Data Shows How Work Pounds Older Bodies," *Biz News*, September 10, 2013, https://www.biznews.com/thought-leaders/2013/09/10/retire-at-55-and-live-to-80-work-till-youre-65-and-die-at-67-startling-new-data-shows-how-work-pounds-older-bodies (accessed June 11, 2019).

11. Sharon L. Weinberg and Marc A. Scott, "The Impact of Uncapping of Mandatory Retirement on Postsecondary Institutions," *Educational Researcher* 42, no. 6 (2013): 338–48.

12. Steve Vernon, "Where Should You Live after Retirement?," *CBS News*, March 24, 2015, https://www.cbsnews.com/news/where-should-you-live-after-retirement (accessed June 11, 2019).

13. Michael Lewis, "6 Keys to a Comfortable and Happy Retirement," *Money Crashers*, https://www.moneycrashers.com/keys-comfortable-happy-retirement (accessed June 19, 2019). While the confidence is higher (35 percent claimed they were very confident) in more recent versions of the Retirement Confidence Survey (e.g., see the 2019 survey at https://www.ebri.org/docs/default-source/rcs/2019-rcs/2019-rcs-short-report.pdf), workers believe they are doing a good job saving for retirement but have neglected to do the calculations, and workers overestimate both the amount of money they will earn from working during retirement and the age at which they will retire. On the statistics on older workers in the United States, see Bureau of Labor Statistics, "Older Workers: Labor Force Trends and Career Options," https://www.bls.gov/careeroutlook/2017/article/older-workers.htm (accessed July 9, 2019).

14. This variation in monetary needs in retirement was the subject of a newspaper story about the differences in the needs of two couples in Canada, both of whom seemed typical in many respects but varied considerably in these needs: David Aston, "Two Retirement Couples, Two Different Budgets: How Much Are They Spending?," *The Globe and Mail*, March 19, 2018, https://www.theglobeandmail.com/globe-investor/retirement/retire-lifestyle/two-retired-couples-two-different-budgets-how-much-are-they-spending/article38234412 (accessed June 13, 2019).

15. For example, one study indicates that Americans age 55 to 64 have saved only 12 percent of what is needed to adequately fund retirement ("Retirement Is

on All of You," https://retirementisallonyou.com/retirement-statistics [accessed July 17, 2019]). For a more detailed study of beliefs about Social Security, see "Social Security," Gallup, https://news.gallup.com/poll/1693/social-security.aspx (accessed July 17, 2019). For a news analysis of reliance on Social Security, see Sean Williams, "American's Reliance on Social Security Is Near a Record High, Survey Shows," *The Motley Fool*, 2019, https://www.fool.com/retirement/2019/06/15/americans-reliance-on-social-security-is-near-a-re.aspx (accessed July 17, 2019).

16. Kenneth Kiesnoski, "Here Are the Best Places in Every State to Live in Retirement," *CNBC*, May 2, 2018, https://www.cnbc.com/2018/05/02/here-are-the-best-places-in-every-state-to-live-in-retirement.html (accessed June 7, 2019). For additional information about Social Security benefits, see "How Much Social Security Will I Get?," AARP Social Security Resource Center, December 17, 2018, Social Security Administration, SSA Publication No. 13-11785, September 2018, https://www.ssa.gov/policy/docs/chartbooks/fast_facts/2018/fast_facts18.pdf (accessed July 17, 2019); "Fast Facts & Figures about Social Security, 2018," https://www.ssa.gov/policy/docs/chartbooks/fast_facts/2018/fast_facts18.pdf (accessed July 17, 2019); and Emily Brandon, "How Much You Will Get from Social Security," *U.S. News and World Report*, February 21, 2019, https://money.usnews.com/money/retirement/social-security/articles/2018-08-20/how-much-you-will-get-from-social-security (accessed July 17, 2019).

17. For an interesting analysis of why people start Social Security benefits when they do, see Jeffrey R. Brown, Arie Kapteyn, and Olivia S. Mitchell, "Framing and Claiming: How Information-Framing Affects Expected Social Security Claiming Behavior," *Journal of Risk and Insurance*, 2013, https://onlinelibrary.wiley.com/doi/full/10.1111/j.1539-6975.2013.12004.x (accessed July 17, 2019). The article argues that people who frame the question about when to declare for Social Security benefits in terms of break-even analysis of total payout, they are likely to file early, while those who frame the question in terms of delay in filing leading to high monthly payments are more likely to delay filing. Moreover, people who are financially less literate, have credit card debt, or have lower earnings are more likely to be influenced by a framing scheme than others are.

18. "Retirement Is on All of You," https://retirementisallonyou.com (accessed August 4, 2020).

19. "Retirement Is on All of You." For an overall account of the general financial situation for retirees in the United States, see Nari Rhee and Ilana Boivee, "The Continuing Retirement Savings Crisis," *SSRN*, May 28, 2016, https://papers.ssrn.com/sol3/papers.cfm?abstract_id=2785723 (accessed July 17, 2019).

20. "Retirement Is on All of You." For a more detailed analysis of this topic, see Martin C. Seay and Sarah Asebedo, "Mortgage Holding and Financial Satisfaction in Retirement," *Journal of Financial Planning and Counseling*, December 2015, https://www.researchgate.net/profile/Sarah_Asebedo/publication/287240935_Mortgage_Holding_and_Financial_Satisfaction_in_Retirement/links/5674ce4808ae502c99c78903.pdf (accessed July 17, 2019).

21. See Jeff Rose, "5 Debts That Can Ruin Your Retirement," *Market Watch*, March 7, 2013, https://www.marketwatch.com/story/5-debts-that-can-ruin-your-retirement-2013-03-07 (accessed July 17, 2019).

22. National Institute on Retirement Security, "Women 80% More Likely to Be Impoverished in Retirement," March 1, 2016, https://www.nirsonline.org/2016/03/women-80-more-likely-to-be-impoverished-in-retirement (accessed June 13, 2019).

23. Frank Newport, "Update: Americans' Concerns about Retirement Persist," *Gallup*, May 9, 2018, https://news.gallup.com/poll/233861/update-americans-concerns-retirement-persist.aspx (accessed June 13, 2019).

24. Some of the articles try to estimate these costs, while others simply try to downplay these fears. See, for example, "The Fear of Running Out of Money in Retirement Is Overblown," *Financial Samurai*, https://www.financialsamurai.com/the-fear-of-running-out-of-money-in-retirement-is-overblown (accessed June 11, 2019).

25. Vernon, "Where Should You Live after Retirement?"

26. For an early news story about the possibilities of reverse mortgages, see Margaret Daly, "Reverse Mortgages: A New Cash Source for Older Folks," *Better Homes and Gardens* 67, no. 4 (April 1989): 156.

27. See, for example, Eileen Ambrose, "Selling Your Home," August/September 2015, https://www.aarp.org/money/investing/info-2015/downsize-home-for-retirement.html (accessed June 18, 2019); Suze Orman, "3 Rules on Downsizing for Retirement," *AARP: The Magazine*, August/September 2018, https://www.aarp.org/retirement/planning-for-retirement/info-2018/downsizing-suze-orman.html (accessed June 18, 2019); Jeff Yeager, "Downsizing: Ditch These Items," *AARP*, https://www.aarp.org/money/budgeting-saving/info-2015/downsizing-items-to-ditch-photo.html#slide1 (accessed June 18, 2019); Brandon Gobel, "Ideas for Clearing Out Your Home," *AARP*, August 25, 2017, https://www.aarp.org/home-family/your-home/info-2017/advice-parents-children-downsizing-fd.html (accessed June 18, 2019); and Marni Jameson, "Downsizing the Family Home—A Workbook: What to Save, What to Let Go," *AARP*, https://www.aarp.org/entertainment/books/bookstore/home-family-caregiving/info-2017/downsizing-family-home-workbook.html (accessed June 18, 2019).

28. All quotations in this paragraph are from Rubinstein, as quoted in "There's No Place Like Home," *USA Today*, December 1991, 16.

29. Vernon, "Where Should You Live after Retirement?"

30. See, for example, Barbara Beskind, "Retirement Living and Vision Loss," *Vision Aware*, https://www.visionaware.org/info/for-seniors/retirement-living/12 (accessed June 14, 2019).

31. See, for example, Vince Butler, "'Aging Friendly' Improvements for Most Every Home Remodeling Project," *AARP*, https://www.aarp.org/livable-communities/housing/info-2016/aging-friendly-renovation-improvements.html (accessed June 14, 2019); Elinor Ginzler, "Making Home Safer," *AARP*, May 2009, https://www.aarp.org/home-garden/housing/info-05-2009/ginzler_home_safe_home.html (accessed June 18, 2019); "Lighting Your Home for Safety," *AARP Assets*, https://assets.aarp.org/external_sites/caregiving/preparing/lighting_your_home.html (accessed June 18, 2019); "Make Your Home Safe for Your Aging Parent," *AARP*, https://www.aarp.org/caregiving/home-care/info-2017/home-safety-tips.html (accessed June 18, 2019); Josh Garskoff, "Make Your Home

Elder-Friendly," *Consumer Reports*, October 26, 2017, https://www.consumerreports.org/home-improvement-remodeling/elder-friendly-home (accessed June 18, 2019); and Shayne Fitz-Coy, "Steps for Converting a House into a Senior Friendly Home," *SeniorLiving.com*, https://www.seniorliving.com/article/steps-converting-house-senior-friendly-home (accessed June 18, 2019).

32. A leading personal finance adviser and journalist, Jane Bryant Quinn, has considered the question of whether retirees should rent or buy. She argues that while many people are concerned about "throwing away money on rent," instead it "frees up cash to keep you living well." Rents will continue to rise every year, and so will insurance, taxes, and upkeep costs on one's owned property. Quinn points to trade-offs in both renting and owning: "Becoming a renter has other attractions, even if you can afford to own. It's a way of checking out a new area if you're thinking of moving far away. It's a safety net, if you move to be closer to your kids—in case your kids decide to move. It also makes it easy for you to travel because no one has to take care of the house while you're away. It might be a temporary move—say, to an apartment in a culturally rich city—before making a final decision on the type of lifestyle you want. There's a landlord to handle chores and no sudden expenses, such as a new furnace or roof. For a longtime homeowner, however, the negatives are often strong. You can't modify the space to suit your style of living. The landlord might decide to sell, forcing you to move out. Pets might not be allowed. Emotionally, you might not feel as comfortable as you did in your own place." On the financial dimensions of this question, Quinn cites Harvard Business School real estate lecturer Nicolas Retsinas, who argues that renting is cheaper than buying on the two coasts (where properties are expensive), while buying is financially advantageous in the middle of the country (Jane Bryant Quinn, "You're Moving: Should You Rent or Buy?," *AARP: The Magazine*, https://www.aarp.org/work/retirement-planning/info-2014/rent-or-buy-house-in-retirement.html [accessed June 18, 2019]).

33. In helping people choose among these options for their parents, see, for example, Anne Montagnes, "When Elderly Parents Need Care," *Chatelaine* 57, no. 9 (September 1984): 49, 149–57. See also Jane Bryant Quinn, "Plan Ahead for Continuing Care," *AARP*, July/August 2014, https://www.aarp.org/money/budgeting-saving/info-2014/senior-living-cost-retirement-plan.html (accessed June 19, 2019).

34. Gary Leff, "Why You May Want to Retire to Living in Hotels (It's Cheaper)," *View from the Wing*, February 27, 2019, https://viewfromthewing.boardingarea.com/2019/02/27/why-you-may-want-to-retire-to-living-in-hotels-its-cheaper (accessed June 11, 2019).

35. Reed, "We're Semi-Retired and Living in an RV."

36. In this section, we discuss locations for living in a generic way. However, some populations, such as people with various disabilities, may have a different set of issues to consider than covered in this section. There is a considerable literature on one special population, military retirees, who may be young when they retire and want to start a second career but also need to handle issues of reassimilation into civilian life and common ailments, such as posttraumatic stress disorder. See, for example, John S. Kiernan, "Best & Worst States for Military Retirees," *Wallethub*, May 20, 2019, https://wallethub.com/edu/best-states-for

-military-retirees/3915 (accessed June 13, 2019); Extra Space Storage, "10 Best Places for Veterans & Retired Military to Retire," *Extra Space Storage*, April 25, 2108, https://www.extraspace.com/blog/moving/city-guides/best-us-cities-for-veterans-military-retirement (accessed June 13, 2019); and Sue Sveum, "Best Places for Military Retirees," *After 55.com*, January 24, 2018, https://www.after55.com/blog/best-places-for-military-retirees (accessed June 13, 2019).

37. M. T. Smith and S. Kroninger, "Retire to Florida, Not California," *Money*, July 1991, 102–5. The Extra Space Storage study identifies Florida as the best state for military retirees but also notes as other good places Alexandria, VA; Colorado Springs, CO; Minneapolis; Oklahoma City, OK; Omaha, NE; San Antonio, TX; San Diego, CA; Seattle, WA; Tampa, FL; and Virginia Beach, VA.

38. See, for example, Stacy Rapacon, "50 Best Places to Retire in the U.S.," *Kiplinger*, June 22, 2018, https://www.kiplinger.com/slideshow/retirement/T047-S001-50-best-places-to-retire-in-the-u-s-2018/index.html (accessed June 6, 2019); Melissa Phipps, "Choosing the Best Place to Live in Retirement," *The Balance*, January 7, 2019 (accessed June 6, 2019); Dan Caplinger, "The 5 Best States in Which to Retire in 2019," *The Motley Fool*, January 7, 2019, https://www.fool.com/retirement/2019/01/07/the-5-best-states-in-which-to-retire-in-2019.aspx (accessed June 7, 2019); Stephanie Faris, "What Is the Cheapest State for a Retired Couple to Live In?," *Zacks*, December 6, 2018, https://finance.zacks.com/cheapest-state-retired-couple-live-in-8519.html (accessed June 7, 2019); Joel Anderson, "Best Places to Retire on a Budget of $1500 a Month," *Go Banking Rates*, April 12, 2019, https://www.gobankingrates.com/retirement/planning/best-cities-retire-budget-month (accessed June 10, 2019); Peter Giffen, "20 Places Where You Can Buy a Retirement Home for Less Than $100,000," *MSN Money*, January 2, 2019, https://www.msn.com/en-us/money/realestate/20-places-in-america-where-you-can-buy-a-retirement-home-for-less-than-dollar100000/ss-BBNC5uE (accessed June 11, 2019); Taylor Tepper, "These Are the Best and Worst States for Retirement," *Bankrate*, July 12, 2018, https://www.bankrate.com/retirement/best-and-worst-states-for-retirement (accessed June 11, 2019); and "10 Best Places to Live after Retirement in the US," *Economy Zoom*, https://www.economyzoom.com/retirement/10-best-places-to-live-after-retirement-in-the-us (accessed June 11, 2019).

39. America's Worst States for Your Retirement, *Moneywise*, https://moneywise.com/a/ch-b/americas-worst-states-to-retire-in/p-24 (accessed June 6, 2019).

40. "Best Places to Retire in the South," *Southern Living*, https://www.southernliving.com/travel/best-places-to-retire (accessed June 7, 2019).

41. For example, one study focuses on where U.S. retirees who have $150,000 or less in retirement savings would be able to live a comfortable life (Esther Trattner, "The Top Countries Where You Can Retire on $150,000," *MoneyWise*, https://moneywise.com/a/the-top-countries-retire-on-150000 [accessed June 10, 2019]). Another study indicates that one can live "quite comfortably" in Costa Rica on $1,300 per month (J. William Carpenter, "What Does It Cost to Retire in Costa Rica?," *Investopedia*, April 2, 2019, https://www.investopedia.com/articles/personal-finance/100615/what-does-it-cost-retire-costa-rica.asp [accessed June 11, 2019]).

42. "The World's Best Places to Retire in 2019," *Live and Invest Overseas*, https://www.liveandinvestoverseas.com/best-places-to-retire (accessed June 10, 2019).

43. As quoted in "Retiring Abroad," *Wikivoyage*, https://en.wikivoyage.org/wiki/Retiring_abroad (accessed June 14, 2019).

44. This issue of "boomerang expatriates" is one that many people do not take into consideration sufficiently. What might be a good location to live in ones sixties and seventies may not be appropriate in one's eighties and nineties for health or family reasons. See, for example, a discussion of this issue in Suzanne McGee, "We Followed Our Dreams and Retired to Mexico. This Is What No One Tells You about Starting a New Life Abroad," *Money*, October 4, 2018, http://money.com/money/5414164/we-followed-our-dreams-and-retired-to-mexico-this-is-what-no-one-tells-you-about-starting-a-new-life-abroad (accessed June 13, 2019).

45. There are also articles that profile a single country without claiming that they did an international search and found that this particular country was the best choice. See, for example, J. William Carpenter, "What Does It Cost to Retire in Costa Rica?" *Investopedia*, April 2, 2019, https://www.investopedia.com/articles/personal-finance/100615/what-does-it-cost-retire-costa-rica.asp (accessed June 11, 2019); "A Guide on How to Retire in Portugal as an Expat," *Expatica*, January 29, 2019, https://www.expatica.com/pt/finance/retirement/a-guide-on-how-to-retire-in-portugal-as-an-expat-908573 (accessed June 11, 2019); The Editorial Staff, "10 Tips to Making Retirement to Spain an Absolute Success, *Expatra*, January 10, 2019, https://expatra.com/10-tips-retiring-spain-successfully (accessed June 13, 2019); and JoJo BoBo, "Real Reasons to Retire in Uruguay (or Not)," *Corporate Monkey*, December 7, 2017, https://www.corporatemonkeycpa.com/2017/12/07/real-reasons-to-retire-in-uruguay-or-not/?cn-reloaded=1&cn-reloaded=1 (accessed June 13, 2019). There is also a bevy of (self-published) books on moving to Thailand. See, for example, Scott Curtis, *How I Moved to Thailand, Retired Early, Found Love, Built a Mansion, and Live Like a King on a Dime* (Independently published, 2018); The Blether, *Why You Shouldn't Retire to Thailand* (Kindle, 2014); Godfree Roberts, *How to Retire in Thailand (and Double Your Income)* (CreateSpace independent publishing platform, 2013); and Alan Reeder-Camponi, *Nine Reasons Why an Old American Man Should Move to Thailand* (CreateSpace independent publishing platform, 2015).

46. "The World's Best Places to Retire in 2019," *International Living*, https://internationalliving-magazine.com/best-places-in-the-world-to-retire/?utm_source=google&utm_medium=ppc&utm_campaign=one-step-best-places&utm_term=search&utm_content=PILVV5GA&gclid=EAIaIQobChMIs5SU9bjN4gIVRbnACh1LDw5gEAAYASAAEgKu_PD_BwE (accessed June 10, 2019). Their survey takes into consideration the following categories: buying and investing, renting, benefits and discounts, visas and residence, cost of living, fitting in, entertainment and amenities, health care, healthy lifestyle, infrastructure (electricity, internet, pollution, transportation, and so on), climate, governance, and work and business opportunity.

47. "Retiring Abroad."

48. "Retiring Abroad."

49. William Aspray, "One Hundred Years of Car Buying," in *Everyday Information: The Evolution of Information Seeking in America*, by William Aspray and Barbara M. Hayes, 9–70 (Cambridge, MA: MIT Press, 2011).

50. Measured in inflation-adjusted international dollars for 2011 ("Economic Growth," *Our World in Data*, https://ourworldindata.org/economic-growth [accessed July 17, 2019]).

51. "Life Expectancy," *Our World in Data*, https://ourworldindata.org/life-expectancy (accessed July 17, 2019). These data are taken from the UN Population Division. The statistics about living longer are clear. The healthiness is more questionable: self-perception of health after age 64 is higher than it was two decades earlier; however, most of those gains are attributable to people who are white, have high incomes, or have high educational backgrounds. See Susan Perry, "More Older Americans Report Being in Good Health, but Most of the Gains Go to Economic Elites," *MinnPost*, September 19, 2017, https://www.minnpost.com/second-opinion/2017/09/more-older-americans-report-being-good-health-most-gains-go-economic-elites (accessed July 18, 2019).

52. Mobility is a complex issue. One might wish to separate ability to visit places from relocating one's home. According to the U.S. Census Bureau's *Current Population Survey Annual Social and Economic Supplement*, 11.2 percent of the U.S. population over age 1 moved between 2015 and 2016. This is the lowest percentage rate for any year since the Census Bureau started tracking these data, and the data show a slow but relentless drop-off over time. In 1948, for example, the annual mover rate was 20.2 percent. Richard Florida notes in *Who's Your City?* (New York: Basic Books, 2008) that empty nesters are slightly less likely to move than middle-aged or young people but that, if they do move, they are more willing to move farther away; 37.3 percent of people age 65 or greater move more than 500 miles compared to 25.6 percent of those age 45 to 54. For some of the complexity of the mobility issue, see, for example, Ryan McMaken, "Americans Are More Mobile Than Many Other Societies—and That's Not Always Good," Mises Institute, May 1, 2017, https://mises.org/wire/americans-are-more-mobile-many-other-societies—and-thats-not-always-good; Richard Florida, "The Geography of America's Mobile and 'Stuck,' Mapped," *Citylab*, March 5, 2019, https://www.citylab.com/life/2019/03/mobile-stuck-us-geography-map-where-americans-moving/584083; Adam Chandler, "Why Do Americans Move So Much More Than Europeans?," *The Atlantic*, October 21, 2016, https://www.theatlantic.com/business/archive/2016/10/us-geographic-mobility/504968; Reid Wilson, "More Americans Are Moving, Mostly to Sunbelt Suburbs," *The Hill*, April 18, 2019, https://thehill.com/homenews/state-watch/439561-more-americans-are-moving-mostly-to-sun-belt-suburbs; Claude S. Fischer, "The Great Settling Down," *Aeon*, November 17, 2016, https://aeon.co/essays/the-increasingly-mobile-us-is-a-myth-that-needs-to-move-on; U.S. Census Bureau, "Americans Moving at Historically Low Rates, Census Bureau Reports," *Newsroom*, November 16, 2016, release no. CB16-189, https://www.census.gov/newsroom/press-releases/2016/cb16-189.html; D'Vera Cohn and Rich Morin, "Who Moves? Who Stays Put? Where's Home?," Pew Research Center, *Social and Demographic Trends*, December 17, 2008, https://www.pewsocialtrends.org/2008/12/17/who-moves-who-stays-put-wheres-home, or, for their full study report with the same title, see Paul Taylor et al., December 29, 2008, https://www.pewresearch.org/wp-content/uploads/sites/3/2010/10/Movers-and-Stayers.pdf; and Jed Kolkpo, "Ameri-

cans Are Moving Way Less Than They Used To," *Citylab*, September 27, 2013, https://www.citylab.com/equity/2013/09/americans-are-moving-way-less-they-used/7046. All these articles were accessed on July 22, 2019.

53. The data were collected by the U.S. Census Bureau and reported by the College Board in "Educational Attainment over Time, 1940–2009," *Trends in Higher Education*, https://trends.collegeboard.org/education-pays/figures-tables/educational-attainment-over-time-1940-2009 (accessed July 17, 2019).

54. See "History of the Interstate Highway System," *Highway History*, U.S. Department of Transportation, Federal Highway Administration, https://www.fhwa.dot.gov/interstate/history.cfm (accessed July 22, 2019). The system was created by the Federal-Aid Highway Act of 1956.

55. In 1969, for example, there were 5.04 fatalities per 1 million miles driven, whereas by 2016, there were only 1.18 fatalities per 1 million miles driven. Cars in the 1950s and 1960s were not generally durable enough to last 100,000 miles, whereas today's cars can often last 200,000 miles. See, for example, David Henderson, "Are Cars Much Better Than 50 Years Ago?," *The Library of Economics and Liberty*, October 22, 2018, https://www.econlib.org/are-cars-much-better-than-50-years-ago, and Dexter Ford, "As Cars Are Kept Longer, 200,000 Is New 100,000," *New York Times*, March 16, 2012 (both stories accessed July 22, 2019).

56. The critical event in making air travel less expensive and more common for Americans was the Airline Deregulation Act of 1978. See, for example, Nicholas Calio, "The Democratization of Air Travel," *Airlines for America*, October 24, 2018, http://airlines.org/blog/nick-calio-the-democratization-of-air-travel (accessed July 22, 2019).

57. See, for example, Smith and Kroninger, "Retire to Florida, Not California."

58. Also, some of the financial issues are not about taxes in the place where someone is thinking of relocating. Rent stabilization and property tax relief in their current community may be disincentives to move (Henry Grabar, "Road to Nowhere," *Slate*, June 19, 2018, https://slate.com/business/2018/06/americans-are-moving-less-often-than-ever.html [accessed July 23, 2019]).

59. On the increasing ubiquity of information and communication technologies over time in the United States, see "Internet/Broadband Fact Sheet," Pew Research Center, *Internet and Technology*, June 12, 2019, https://www.pewinternet.org/fact-sheet/internet-broadband (accessed July 22, 2019).

60. Grabar, "Road to Nowhere." Other exogenous factors responsible for fewer houses being built, keeping the housing costs high, include "fewer vacant lots, land use restrictions, building material costs, and a skilled worker shortage." This analysis is drawn by Grabar from the Joint Center for Housing Studies of Harvard University, *The State of the Nation's Housing, 2018*, http://www.jchs.harvard.edu/sites/default/files/Harvard_JCHS_State_of_the_Nations_Housing_2018.pdf (accessed July 23, 2019).

61. See, for example, Vivian Marino, "Mortgages for Seniors? Available, but Exacting," *New York Times*, June 2, 2017, https://www.nytimes.com/2017/06/02/business/retirement/mortgages-for-older-people-retirement.html (accessed July 23, 2019). Forty-two percent of households headed by someone age 65 to 74 hold a home mortgage, compared to 18.5 percent in 1992, according to the Federal Reserve's 2013 Survey of Consumer Finances. See Jesse Bricker et al., "Changes in

U.S. Family Finances from 2010 to 2013," *Federal Reserve Bulletin* 100, no. 4 (September 2013), https://www.federalreserve.gov/pubs/bulletin/2014/pdf/scf14.pdf (accessed July 23, 2019).

62. Florida, *Who's Your City?*

63. See the literature reviews of information seeking in Donald O. Case and Lisa M. Given, *Looking for Information*, 4th ed. (Bingley: Emerald, 2016), 91–93.

64. Rather than cite original papers on this subject, the reader here and in the next several paragraphs is pointed to the literature reviews in Case and Given, *Looking for Information*, in this case, 190–94.

65. See Case and Given, *Looking for Information*, 193–94.

66. See Case and Given, *Looking for Information*,194–99.

67. See Case and Given, *Looking for Information*, 100–104.

68. See Case and Given, *Looking for Information*, 102.

69. See Case and Given, *Looking for Information*, 104–8.

70. See Case and Given, *Looking for Information*, 110–14.

71. Carol Kuhlthau and Reijo Savolainen have been pioneers in the consideration of affective factors in information behavior. See, for example, the following three works by C. C. Kuhlthau: "Developing a Model of the Library Search Process: Cognitive and Affective Aspects," *Reference Quarterly* 28 (1988): 32–242; "Everyday Life Information Seeking: Approaching Information Seeking in the 'Way of Life,'" *Library and Information Science Research* 17 (1995): 259–94; and *Everyday Information Practices: A Social Phenomenological Perspective* (Lanham, MD: Scarecrow Press, 2008). Also important to this topic is D. Nahl and D. Bilal, *Information and Emotion: The Emergent Affective Paradigm in Information Behavior Research and Theory* (Medford, NJ: Information Today, 2007).

Closing Statement

A house is the largest purchase an individual makes in his or her life, and the real estate sector is arguably the largest sector of the American economy. But where one lives is not only an economic consideration; it is deeply tied to the cultural meaning of an individual's existence. Given the economic and cultural significance of where to live, this topic is one that deserves continued attention from information studies and other scholars, and we were pleased to be able to open up a new line of inquiry for information studies, although we recognize that these chapters merely scratch the surface of this large and rich topic.

We have drawn on four areas of information studies in these chapters: the impact of information and communications technologies on work, industry, and privacy; community studies; information-seeking behavior; and documentary studies. Websites and social media sites, as well as internet-enabled devices, have rapidly been introduced into homes and the selling of homes; and these technologies have not only driven changes in the way that realtors work and the strategies and structures in the real estate industry but also opened up new privacy concerns for what happens in the home, the place where privacy is most expected and most highly protected.

Community is a critically important consideration in where to live, and we have seen in several studies that communities are complex places, with many different stakeholders wanting different, sometimes conflicting things from their community. The fragility of communities has led people to carry out experiments to try to better meet the needs of at least some members of the society, and we have seen that information tools and strategies are important tools in trying to better community life.

While there is some similarity among the information-seeking behaviors of adults seeking a place to live, every family is different and, to some degree, prizes certain kinds of information over others. There are some categories of seekers, such as retirees or African Americans, who have sufficiently different needs from the mainstream home seeker that the questions they ask and the sources they consult are notably different from the mainstream. This may also be true of some other identifiable groups we have not had the chance to study in this volume, such as other racial and religious minority groups, military veterans, and perhaps even millennials. We have only slightly touched on, in several chapters, the affective as well as the cognitive aspects of deciding where to live, such as for the buyer in a superheated housing market or in a retiree looking back on the emotions associated with the physical place in which they have lived.

Information studies scholars are interested in documents: who produces various types of information; how they are produced; how they are consumed; how external factors shape the creation, nature, and impact of these sources; and how consumers shape and are shaped by these sources. We have discussed several kinds of documents related to where to live in this book: home and garden magazines, television programming, how-to real estate books, and websites, among others. These studies have shown how these types of "documents" have come about and how various stakeholders have interacted with them in an active way. There is much more to be said about this topic. Why is it, for example, that the programs on the HGTV network are so popular even for people not looking to buy a new home, flip a house, or make major repairs or renovations? Similarly, why do people spend hours looking at Zillow listings when they are not actively participating in the real estate market?

This book is not only of interest to information studies scholars. It is also of interest to people seeking to buy a house, real estate professionals, regulators, and perhaps many others. Entrepreneurial start-ups, such as Zillow and Redfin, have touted the transformative nature of the information and communication technologies that they have introduced. In particular, they point to the resultant disintermediation in the real estate market and the rapid elimination of the need for real estate agents, much like the introduction of technology has severely reduced the need for telephone operators, bank tellers, and travel agents. However, our chapters show quite clearly that there is and will continue to be a need for real estate agents. The amount of information that is available to prospective house buyers has greatly increased over the past two decades—much but not all of it available over the internet. The function of the real estate agent has changed somewhat, no longer the principal supplier of that information but more as the person who understands the complex process and has a wide range of contacts across supporting professions who can guide the prospective buyer to the right information and the right professional at the right time. It has also become clear from these chapters that the information needs vary from one buyer to the next. The young family, for example, may place a much greater importance on the quality of local schools. Issues that we have not fully explored in these chapters are the growing acceptability of long-term renting over house buying as well as the patterns of change in desirable places to live, such as the trend toward amenity-rich downtown areas.

Our chapters also have lessons for real estate professionals. The market lock of the MLS has been broken, and real estate agents cannot simply rely on the ability to parcel out proprietary MLS information about houses in order to succeed in business. Information and communication technologies have become increasingly essential to the success of a real estate agent. One cannot imagine doing this job successfully today without actively using a smartphone both to gather information and to keep in touch with the various involved stakeholders. In addition to the real estate–specific information and transactions that the real estate agent deals with daily, most agents are essentially self-employed small businesspersons, and these information and communication technologies are as essential to them as they are to any other small businessperson, especially one who runs a mobile operation—much like a mobile repair or service organization or small construction company. The ready availability of multiple new kinds of real estate–related information, as well as the communicative and interactive power of the internet and social media, has implications for the real estate entrepreneur. We are witnessing innovation in the real estate industry, especially from the entrepreneurial internet-based start-up firms. One example is iBuyers, which makes instant offers on homes. This particular innovation presents a possible conflict of interest for companies such as Zillow, which has a challenging time being a fair broker in both presenting information about homes on the market and purchasing homes that might have been purchased directly by other prospective buyers (and also by reducing the possibility of buyers making successful low-ball offers). In the coronavirus era of early 2020, at the time of this writing, i-buying has proved too capital intensive and too uncertain, and Zillow and some other companies have stopped this practice. While some new secondary industries have arisen from the use of new technologies, such as virtual 3-D presentations of homes and increased use of drones to present aerial views, none of the new primary real estate business models have changed much yet. The coronavirus might streamline the qualification and purchase processes through increased use of virtual processes for notarizing documents and finalizing mortgages and closings, but it is too soon to tell whether they will have a lasting impact.

Regulators should take notice of changes occurring in the real estate industry. Some of the biggest changes in the real estate industry have come as a result of regulation being less protective of the established real estate companies and relaxing the hold of the MLSs. But it is still too complicated a process to buy a house. One might buy a decked-out semitruck and trailer on the telephone in less than an hour. This truck might cost a quarter of a million dollars—as much as the cost of a house in some communities. Both the truck and the home have to be registered by one or more government agencies, so there are similarities in these purchases. But because of regulation, it is a much more complex and lengthy process to buy a home. Buyers and sellers, as well as real estate professionals, are interested in streamlining this process and reducing government regulation (especially now that regulation does not protect the monopoly status of the MLS). Much of the innovation in the real estate industry is tied to innovations in information and communication technologies. There is a long history of the government being poor at regulating industries reliant on these fast-moving technologies, such as intellectual property issues in the entertainment industries. Regulators sometimes draft their regulation to cover a particular technology and its impacts, not recognizing that the limelight time of a particular technology may be fleeting, and such regulation is often counterproductive after just a few years. It also needs to be remembered that regulation of the real estate industry is a driver of society as a whole. As we have seen, housing regulation and other housing policies were the driver of the racial divide in Milwaukee. In a more positive example, lessening of land and existing use regulation by both the military and local governments have made possible new intergenerational housing experiments.

The question of where to live is an enduring one. The average American moves 11.4 times in his or her lifetime.[1] From the traffic on Zillow, it seems that some people are ever thinking about this issue of where to live. Choosing where to live, as we have seen in this book, is integrally tied up with information issues. As a group of information scholars who recognize that we have merely scratched the surface of this important issue, we invite others to join us in examining this enduring question, giving perspective on it from a multitude of vantage points.

NOTE

1. Mona Chalabi, "How Many Times Does the Average Person Move?," FiveThirtyEight, January 29, 2015, https://fivethirtyeight.com/features/how-many-times-the-average-person-moves (accessed April 30, 2020).

Index

Aalbers, Manuel, 183
AAP. *See* Arvada for All the People
actor–network theory, 212
affective and cognitive elements of home buying, 2
affective aspects of home sales, 38
affordable housing, 159, 161–62, 164; and elderly residents, 163. *See also* Olde Town Residences
African Americans: housing decision factors, 261, 267–70, 274–76; obstacles to home selection, 259
Age Wave, 281–82, 285
aging in place, 284–85
Alden, Andrew, 230–31
Alexander, Christopher, 211, 230–31
Allen, Anita, 98
American Beauty (1999), 60
American Magazine, or A Monthly View of the Political State of the British Colonies, 131
antipattern. *See* pattern language
apps for information, 2, 6; for agents, 7–8
Apthorpe, Noah, 113–14
architecture and site design, 231. *See also* Hope Meadows
artificial intelligence, 96, 102, 103, 111–12
Arvada, CO, 19, 151–70; affordable housing, 159, 161–62; history and demographics, 151–52; housing costs, 161–62; new development, 159–60; population growth, 154, 159; traffic issues, 156, 159
Arvada for All the People, 167–68
Arvada Urban Renewal Authority, 165
Ask This Old House, 126, 133
Atlanta, 118
Attainable Senior Housing Development Program, 163
AURA. *See* Arvada Urban Renewal Authority
Austin, TX, growth, 2, 14–25; as attractive destination, 14; creative resistance movement, 14–15, 16, 18–19; growth, 14–17; homelessness, 15; housing market, 14–15; rentals, 15; traffic, 15
"Austin Smart Growth Initiative," 16
"Austin Tomorrow Plan," 16

Barthes, Roland, 183
Bartlett, David, 181
Bastion Community of Resilience (New Orleans), 233
Beecher, Katherine, 98
Belkin, Nicholas, 239
Bendor, Roy, 97, 101, 110, 115
Bentham, Jeremy, 95
Better Homes and Gardens, 126, 131, 137
BHG. *See Better Homes and Gardens*
big data, 86–87
Bignell, Jonathan, 101
Big Short (2015), 60

313

"Blame Television for the Bubble" (WSJ), 135
Bleier Center for Television and Popular Culture (Syracuse University), 130
Blissville the Beautiful (1909), 60
Bogost, Ian, 115–16
Boling, Patricia, 98
boundary objects, 225–31
Bradford, Andrew, 131
Bridge Meadows (Portland), 230, 232, 233
Bridge War of 1845, 188–89
Brooks, Richard R. W., 263
Brown v. Board of Education of Topeka, 261
Builder, Decorator, and Woodworker, 131
Building Ohana (Spokane, WA), 233
Building Owners and Managers Association International, 21
Burgess, Ernest, 185–86

California Association of Realtors, 72
Candelas community, 160, 169; and Rocky Flats, 163–64
CARES Act, 21, 24
Carleton, Brian, 230
case studies: Austin, TX, housing market, 2, 14–19; coronavirus, 20–24; information-seeking behaviors, 2; information sources, 2–12
causality, 185–87
CCTV, 117–18
Celebration, Florida, 129
Center for Opportunity Urbanism, 269
Chanute Air Force Base, 211, 224
Charlotte, NC, 184
charrette, 231–32
Chatman, Elfreda, 276
Cherif, Emma, 77
Chicago Land Use Survey (1942), 186
Chicago school of social ecology, 185–86, 190
Chicago Tribune, 216
Child, Julia, 133

child welfare, 211
"The Cities Where African-Americans Are Doing Best Economically," 269
Civil Rights Act of 1964, 261
cocooning, 125–26
college towns, 287
Collins, Chiquita, 262
community, 212, 218–19; relational network, 218. *See also* Hope Meadows
community activism, 156, 158. *See also* "Keep Austin Weird"
community as intervention, 218
community informatics, 169–70
community processes, undermined by formalization, 184
computer-supported cooperative work, 169–70
connectivity and home choice, 115–16
The Consequences of Modernity (Giddens), 118
consumer as product, 112
consumer real estate and online search, 71–73
contemporary surveillance capitalism, 93
contextual integrity, 95
convenience v. accuracy, 266
coronavirus. *See* Covid-19
Corruption Perceptions Index, 293
Country Living, 132, 137
Covid-19, 2, 20–25, 84–85; and real estate, commercial, 21–22
Cowan, Ruth Schwartz, 98, 110
Craigslist, 74
Crang, Mike, 93
critical race theory and housing policies, 260
Crossney, Kristin, 181
Crow, Trammel, 165–67
CSCW. *See* computer-supported cooperative work
cult of domesticity, 98, 108

Damasio, Antonio, 239
Daniels, Norman, 215

data compilation for consumers, 82
Davidson, Jennifer, 134
debt, 283
decision factors: emotion, 237, 239–40; time pressure, 237, 240
decline, 186, 268
Delgado, Richard, 260
Democracy Index, 293
Denzin, Norm, 212, 213
Department of Housing and Urban Development, 43, 187, 264
Department of Justice, 66
digital assistants and surveillance, 110
digital divide, 276
Digital Scholarship Lab (University of Richmond), 180
discriminatory housing practices, 187, 199, 201–3
Dixon, Alan J., 187–88
DIY, 134
DIY Network, 143
DOJ. *See* Department of Justice
Downs, Anthony, 186
Downs, James, 186
Dukas, Paul, 100
Dupuis, Ann, 118

Easthampton, 233
Eheart, Brenda Krause, 213, 214–15, 216, 218, 229
elderly residents: and affordable housing, 163; at Hope Meadows, 214, 216, 218–21, 228, 231; smart homes, 104, 105, 108, 110
El Moussa, Tarek, 143
E-loan.com, 242
emotion: altering information behavior, 252–53; and home buying, 237, 239, 243–47, 254; and home selling, 284–85, 297; and information behavior, 247
encryption, failure to protect private data, 113
environmental benefits of smart homes, 108, 111
Equal Credit Opportunity Act, 187

ethics, 201
Expatistan cost-of-living index, 293

facial recognition technologies, 117
Fair Housing Act (1968), 177, 187
fair housing ordinance, 196
fair housing protests, 196–200
Fantasia (1940), 100
fear and security, 117
Federal Housing Administration (FHA), 178, 179, 184, 186, 264, 284
Federal Trade Commission (FTC), 66
feminization of American culture, 98
Fernández-Kelly, Patricia, 261–62
FHA. *See* Federal Housing Administration (FHA)
financial data, 43
Flip or Flop, 125
Florida, Richard, 295–96
Forbes, 269
foreclosure: financial impacts, 128; prevention, 178; racial disparities, 127
ForSaleByOwner.com, 77, 241–42
foster-adoptive care, 212–13
Foucault, Michel, 95, 211, 223–26, 229
Fox, Bonnie, 100
free housing ordinance. *See* fair housing ordinance
The French Chef, 133
Friedewald, Michael, 98, 105, 109
Friend, Lawrence, 198
Fruit, Garden, and Home, 131
FTC. *See* Federal Trade Commission (FTC)
Fulton, Crystal, 266
Furedi, Frank, 107

Gaines, Chip, 133
Galton, Antony, 177, 205
Gandy, Oscar, 94
gender and housework, 100
General Electric, 132
Generations of Hope Community model, 222–23, 227–28
GI bill, 264

Giddens, Anthony, 118
Gini Index, 293
Global Integrity Report, 293
Global Peace Index, 293
Goethe, Johann Wolfgang von, 100
Google. *See* Nest (smart thermostat)
Government Accountability Office's Center for Science, Technology, and Engineering, 96
Graham, Stephen, 93
Grant, Delvin, 77
Gray Panthers, 213–14
Great Migration, 261–62
Great Recession (2007–2009), 13, 14, 127
Griesemer, James, 211, 226
Groppi, James, Father, 195–99, 200, 204

Hackley, Chris, 101
Hansen, George T., 195
Hardeeville, SC, 233
Harvard, 128
health monitoring, 110
Henefer, Jean, 266
Her Own Money (1922), 60
heterotopia, 211, 223–25, 229; crisis heterotopia, 223, 224–25; heterotopia of deviation, 223, 231
HGTV, 125, 130, 133–34; DIY programming, 142; gardening, 142; green building, 142; house-flipping programs, 135, 138, 142, 143–44; and the housing crisis, 135–36; housing crisis-related programming, 142, 143
HGTV Magazine, 137
HGTV programs: *Brother vs. Brother*, 143; *Carter Can*, 144; *Flip or Flop*, 143; *Gardener's Diary*, 142; green building programs, 144; *HGTV Green Home*, 144; *HGTV Smart Home*, 138, 144; *House Hunters*, 125, 134–36, 138; *House Hunters International*, 144; *Income Property*, 143; *Power Broker*, 144; *Property Brothers*, 133, 137–38; *Pure Design*, 144; *Real Estate Intervention*, 143; *Red Hot & Green*, 144; *Renovate to Rent*, 143; *Rent or Buy*, 144; *Staged to Perfection*, 144; *That's Clever*, 142; *The Unsellables*, 144; *The Vanilla Ice Project*, 143
Hillier, Amy E., 180–81, 187
hodology, 182
HOLC, 178, 184
HOLC maps, 178–88, 203–4; "Area Description—Security Maps," 180; cause or effect, 181–82; data collectors, 180–81; embedded racial narratives, 178–81; Milwaukee, WI, 190–92; structural racism, 184–85, 190–94; and urban housing policy, 180–81
home: feminist critique of, 98; and privacy, 97–98; site of moral oversight, 98–99; symbolic value of, 1, 97–100, 125, 128–29, 284–85, 297
home data, 44, 67
Home Owners Loan Corporation. *See* HOLC
home sales: affective aspects, 38, 47, 284–85; locational aspects, 38; relational aspects, 38
HomeSnap, 5
home technology, 101–2. *See also* smart homes
Hope House, 231
Hope Meadows, 211–23; bureaucratic obstacles, 214, 216; community, 212, 217, 218, 219; and foster-adoptive families, 214; Generations of Hope Community model, 222–23, 227–28; Intergenerational Center, 216, 218, 219, 229; media coverage, 215, 216; senior–child system, 220–21; and seniors, 214, 216, 218–21, 228, 231; tutoring, 226, 228–29
House and Garden, 131
House and Home, 131
House Beautiful, 131
House Hunters, 125, 134–36

housework and gender, 100
Housing and Urban Development, 204
housing bubble, 83, 238. *See also* housing crisis (2007–2012)
housing communities supporting: adults with developmental disabilities, 212; foster-adoptive families, 212, 213–14; unmarried teen mothers, 212; wounded warriors, 212
housing crisis (2007–2012), 83, 125, 126–27, 296; Florida, 127; Phoenix, AZ, 127
housing decision factors, African Americans, 270–74; Black well-being, 270; education, 273; environmental racism, 271; food insecurity, 270; health disparities in African American children, 271, 273; police presence, 270; public transportation, 270; racially diverse neighborhoods, 271; racial segregation, 271
housing discrimination. *See* HOLC maps; redlining
housing recovery, 128–29
Hoyt, Homer, 185–86
HUD. *See* Department of Housing and Urban Development
HUD1, 43
Human Security Index, 293

i-buying, 86
imaginal space, 225–26
Independent Living, 291
information aggregation, 76–77
information and community issues, 152, 154, 167
Information and Emotion (Belkin), 239
information asymmetry, 48, 63, 296
information behavior: avoiding, 237; destroying, 237; and home buying, 240, 254; managing, 237; retirees, 293–97; seeking, 237; sharing, 237; and time pressure, 248; using, 237

information capitalism, 115
information failure. *See* information asymmetry
information poverty, 276
information seeking, 265; and African Americans, 266–69
information-seeking strategies, 25; African American realtors, 267; of African Americans, 25; community organizations, 267; first-order filtering, 267; racial differences in renters, 267; of retirees, 25; second-order filtering, 267–68
information sharing, 248
information sources, 265–66, 295; African American home searchers, 269; books, 9, 11; for buyers, 9, 11–12; newspaper advertisements, 3; open houses, 3; ranking lists, 269–70; real estate agents, 3, 5, 12–13; scholarly, 129–30; for specific demographics, 11; unregulated, 130; yard signs, 3, 5
information streams, 226–27
information use and QOL issues, 2
information use by proxy, 251–52
institutional racism, 129
intentional community, 211, 233
intentional neighboring, 229
Intergenerational Center, 216, 218, 219, 229
intergenerational housing, 2
intermediation of the housing market, 38–39. *See also* online information sources; relational aspects of home sales
internet-based business models, 77–78, 83; brokerage model, 78; diversified, 78; and online advertising, 78; virtual value-chain model, 78
internet-based real estate business models, 13
internet-based real estate firms, 73
Internet of Things, 96, 109. *See also* smart homes

"inversion of control," 218
IoT. *See* Internet of Things
"iron ring," 189

Jackson, Kenneth, 179, 181, 184, 187
Jefferson Center Urban Renewal Plan, 160
Jefferson Parkway project, 156–59
Jefferson Parkway Public Highway Authority, 158
Jenkins, Charles Francis, 132
Jim Crow era, 185, 259, 261
Joint Center for Housing Studies (Harvard), 128, 129
Journal of Behavioral Decision-Making, 239
JPPHA. *See* Jefferson Parkway Public Highway Authority
Juneau, Solomon, 188

"Keep Austin Weird," 14–15, 16, 18–19
Kilbourn, Byron, 188
Koppel, Ted, 215
Kosciuszko Park march, 196–99
Koskela, Hille, 101
Kranzberg, Melvin, 114–15
Krikelas, James, 130, 265–66
Krysan, Maria, 267, 268–69, 274
Kuhlthau, Carol, 239
Kuhn, Maggie, 213–14

Ladies Home Journal, 100
Landi family, 128
Lane, Laurence, 132
Latour, Bruno, 183
Leavitt, Bertie, 225
Lennar, 160–61
Levitt, William, 263
Levitt & Sons, 263–64
Levittown, PA, 263–64
Leyden Rock, 156
Light, Jennifer, 185
light rail, 166–67, 168
locational aspects of home sales, 38
location choice, 1
Love It or List It, 125
Lowe, Kenneth, 125, 133–34
Lyon, David, 94, 117

MacKinnon, Catherine, 98
magazines, home and garden, 134–38; *Better Homes and Gardens*, 131, 137, 140–42; *Country Living*, 137, 140–42; green living material, 141; *HGTV Magazine*, 137, 141–42; *House and Garden*, 131; *House Beautiful*, 131; and the housing crisis, 140; lifestyle magazines, history, 131–32; real estate-related content, 142; *Southern Living*, 137, 140, 142; subscription rates, 140; *Sunset*, 137, 140–42
Maier, Henry, 197–98, 201–2
Mäkinen, Liisa, 98–99, 107–8, 112
maps: as acts of power, 183; as boundary objects, 183; as storytelling, 182–83, 190–91, 200, 201–2, 203–4. *See also* HOLC maps
Marikyan, Davit, 103, 108
marketing the idea of home, 100–101
Mashal, Ibrahim, 96
mass media, home and garden: and the housing crisis, 140, 142, 143, 145; magazines, 2, 13, 126, 131–32, 136–37, 139; television shows, 1–2, 13, 125–26, 133–38; women's magazines, 100
Matterport, 23
McPhail, Clark, 212
Menomonee River Valley, 188–205
Mercer quality-of-living index, 293
Meredith, Edwin Thomas, 131
Meredith Corporation, 131
Merrill Lynch, 281–82, 285
meta-hodology, 182–83, 185, 187, 204–5
Metzger, John, 186
Michener, James, 290
Milwaukee, WI, 19, 177–78, 188–205; Catholic Church activism, 195–96; fair housing ordinance, 177, 196; fair housing protests, 196–200; history, 188–89; immigrant populations, 189–93, 200–201; Kosciuszko Park march, 196–200; Polish population, 189, 192, 196–97, 200–201; racial and

ethnic development, 189; racial covenants, 195
MLS (multiple listing service), 42, 69, 77, 238; defined, 63; information flow to agents, 63–65; public access, 72
More Work for Mother: The Ironies of Household Technology from the Open Hearth to the Microwave (Cowan), 98, 110
mortgage: attainment, changes in, 67–68; denials and race, 128–29; forbearance programs, 21, 24
Movement to Stop Jefferson Parkway, 156, 158
MSJP. *See* Movement to Stop Jefferson Parkway
multifamily housing, 162
Museum of Vertebrate Zoology (University of California), 226
Myers, William and Daisy, 264

NAACP Youth Council, 177, 189–92, 198; Commandos, 195, 196–99; Kosciuszko Park march, 196–200
Nahl, Diane, 239
NAR. *See* National Association of Realtors (NAR)
National Archives, 180
National Association of Real Estate Boards, 201
National Association of Realtors (NAR), 3, 21, 24, 63
Nelson, Robert K., 180
Nest (smart thermostat), 111, 112
networks of care, 212
New Orleans, 233
New York Times, 216
Nightline, 214, 217
9/11, and a need for safety, 126
nonfamily housing, 162
Northwest Multiple Listing Service, 238

Olde Town Residences, 165, 166, 169
"One Hundred Years of Car Buying in America," 293

online information sources, 3–5, 38, 44, 73, 75, 86, 295–96; apps, 2, 5–6; and demographics of users, 3; expatriation, 291, 293; offerings, 78–80; for retirees, 293; value, 78; websites, 3, 5, 74
ontological security, 118
Oosterhouse, Carter, 144
open housing ordinance (1968), 177
The Order of Things (Foucault), 223
O'Reilly, Charles T., 195–96
Osprey Village (Hardeeville, SC), 233
Owners.com, 77

panopticon, 95
paradox of exposure, 112
Park, Robert E., 185
pattern language, 211, 230–31
PBS, 133
Peña, Loralee, 225
Pennsylvania Association of Realtors, 23
Philadelphia, 180–81
Phillips, Vel (Milwaukee Alderwoman), 196
place stratification theory, 262
planned communities, 19–20, 263–64
planned shrinkage, 186
plutonium, 159
Popcorn, Faith, 126
The Popcorn Report, 126
popular media, home and garden, 130
population growth. *See* Arvada, CO; Austin, TX
Portland, 230, 233
Powell, Jerome H., 203
Power, Martha Bauman, 213
predatory data collection, 110–11
predatory inclusion, 264–65
predictive analytics, 112
predictive policing, 117
Press Freedom Index, 293
principle of least effort, 297
privacy, 2, 13; vs. convenience, 106; feminist critique of, 98; and home, 97–98; lack of concern, 105–6, 108; policies, 112

probability vs. control, 94
Property Brothers, 133, 143

race and home ownership, 190
racial bias: codified, 185–86; formalization in housing practices, 187, 190–93; in lending, 187–88; and school quality, 190
racial covenants, 194–95, 204, 263
racial disparities: in foreclosure rates, 127; in homeownership, 129; in mortgage denials, 129
racial "infiltration," 179, 180, 181–82
racial profiling, 118
racial segregation, 67, 261–62
racial zoning, 262–63
racism, 260; and real estate industry, 127, 129, 187, 190–95, 204, 262–63, 274. *See also* HOLC maps; redlining
racist narratives, 184
Rapoport, Michele, 97, 98, 104
Ray, Bill, 158
RCA (Radio Corporation of America), 132
real estate: commercial and Covid-19, 21–22; rental market, 24; residential, 22–24
real estate agents, 47, 59–62; adoption of internet-based tools, 71, 73; and associations, 62; and brokers, 41, 59; buyer's agent, 41, 47; changes in seller's agent role, 40–41, 44; control of the flow of information, 60, 62, 67; disruption by online information sources, 75–76; economic aspects, 60, 62; as information brokers, 3, 36, 47–48; in popular culture, 60; process consultants, 47; profiling and directing of buyers, 67; and social media, 45–46; specialized markets, 76; in the US economy, 37–38; use of online information sources, 44–46
real estate associations, 62–63
real estate brokers, 60; and real estate agents, 41

RealEstate.com.au, 86
real estate industry, 2, 7, 13; adoption of computer technologies, 68–70; business cycles, 85–86; changing nature of, 2; and Covid-19, 84–85; disruption by online information sources, 83; disruption of anticompetitive practices, 65–66; economic aspects, 57–58; and internet-based computing, 70–71; legal challenges, 65; and post-internet information flows, 63–65; pre-internet, 58–62, 66–67; regulation, 67; shift of balance of power, 72–75
real estate investment trusts. *See* REITs
real estate markets, 59
Real Estate Research Corporation, 186
real estate "risk" and racial bias, 178, 179
real estate websites, 241–42. *See also* online information sources
Realtor.com, 3, 5, 64, 74, 77. *See also* online information sources
Realtor's Code of Ethics, 263
Reconstruction, 259
Redfin, 5, 22, 74, 77, 78, 241. *See also* online information sources
redlining, 67, 178–82, 201, 202, 264; and cancer mortality, 180; and Charlotte, NC, 184; Chicago, 186; and enduring poverty, 180; and mortgage denial, 180
Regional Transportation District, 167
REITs, 21
relational aspects of home sales, 38
relational capacity, 227, 228, 229–30
Relative Residential Status (RRS) map, 201–2
rendition, 93
RERC. *See* Real Estate Research Corporation
retiree financial concerns: debt, 283; gender, 283–84; income, 282–83
retiree information-seeking behaviors, 2
retirement, 211; communities, 213–14; demographics, 281–82

Retirement Confidence Survey (2014), 282
retirement housing decision-making, 281–97; cultural activities, 287; endogenous factors, 293, 295–96; exogenous factors, 293–95; expatriation, 290–91; family needs, 282; financial, 282, 287, 295; health concerns, 282, 287; job opportunities, 287; location, 287; natural risk, 287; public transportation, 287; safety, 287; travel desire, 282; weather, 287
retirement housing options, 285. *See also* aging in place
Retirement Index, 291
reverse Great Migration, 273
reverse mortgages, 284
RFRK. *See* Rocky Flats Right to Know
risk, high stakes, 237
Rocky Flats, 159, 163–64, 169; and Candelas, 163–64
Rocky Flats Right to Know, 163–64
Rocky Flats Wildlife Refuge, 163–64
Roosevelt, Franklin Delano, 264
Rose, Carol M., 263
Rubinstein, Robert, 284, 285

Sadowski, Jathan, 97, 101, 110, 115
Sandler, Tara, 134
satisficing, 268
Savolainen, Reijo, 239
scaffolding, 218–19; architecture and site design, 219; communication, 222; professional services and material supports, 222; roles and expectations, 220; routine and special events, 219–20; volunteer engagement, 220
Schmidt, Deanna, 201–2
school districts and housing choice, 164–65, 168
SCOPUS, 104
Scott, Jonathan, 133
Seattle, WA: information acquisition, 255; real estate market 2012–2013, 238

segregation. *See* racial segregation
selective information sharing, 158, 164, 167
Senate Subcommittee on Consumer and Regulatory Affairs, 187–88
separate spheres, 98, 108
Sewell, Abigail A., 262
Shelley v. Kraemer (1948), 195
Shuhaiber, Amed, 96
Simon, Herbert Alexander, 268
16th Street Viaduct, 177, 189, 200
Small Business Administration, 21
smart cities, 110, 117
smart devices, 102–3, 113; packet streams, 113; skepticism about phrase, 96–97; trust in third parties, 116. *See also* Nest (smart thermostat); Zheng, Serena
smart homes, 95, 96, 100; and artificial intelligence, 96, 102, 103, 111–12; benefits, 105, 108, 111, 117; and children, 117; connectedness, 108; convenience and connectedness, 106; definitions, 103–4; and the elderly, 104, 105, 108, 110; and environmental benefits, 108, 111; and independent living, 104, 105, 108, 110; marketing, 107, 116; and the promise of a better life, 105–6; security, 107; technological bias in the literature, 104; and third parties, 106
smart neighborhoods. *See* smart cities
Smith, Nareissa, 270
social networks as information sources, 265–66
Social Progress Index, 293
Social Security, 282–83, 284
Society for the History of Technology, 114
"Sorcerer's Apprentice," 100
Southern Living, 132, 137, 287
Southern Pacific Railroad, 132
space of exception, 219; Hope Meadows, 224–25
specialization of place, 296
Spokane, WA, 233
Squires, Gregory, 181, 187, 201

Star, Leigh, 183, 211, 212, 223, 225–26, 232
Stefancic, Jean, 260
Stowe, Harriet Beecher, 98
structural racism, 2, 201–3; HOLC maps, 184–85; racial covenants, 194–95
subprime mortgage crisis. *See* housing crisis (2007–2012)
suburbanization, white, 178, 179
Successful Farming, 131
Sunset, 132, 137
supportive housing, 211
surveillance: advertiser, 93; "caring," 104, 105, 107; culture of, 95; defined, 95; and digital assistants, 110; government, 94; hidden threats, 101, 109; in the home, 115; home technology, 94–95, 104; marketed as desirable, 101; our complicity in our own, 95; predictive policing, 110; regulation of, 115; surveillance capitalism, 95, 109, 115; surveillance marketing, 101; US, contemporary, 94–95; wearable, 98

Taplin-Kaguru, Nora E., 267–74
Taunton family, 129
Taylor, Keeanga-Yamahtta, 264
techno-fetishism, 101, 116. *See also* Zheng, Serena
technological determinism, 69–70
technology, first law of, 115
technology, sociotechnical view of, 114–15
technology in homes, 101–2. *See also* smart homes
technophoria, 113, 114
television history, 132–33
"Ten Best Cities in America for Black Families to Live 2020," 269
terms of service, 112
Texas Flip and Move, 143
That Sister, 269
This Old House, 133
Thomas, Steve, 126
Thorns, David, 118

time pressure: altering information behavior, 253; and emotional information behavior, 249–50; and emotional information demand, 250–51; and search for a home, 239–40
Time Pressure and Stress in Human Judgment and Decision-Making, 240
TLC, 134
Tognoli, Jerome, 98
toll roads, 156
Treehouse Foundation (Easthampton), 233
Trulia, 5, 6, 77, 78. *See also* online information sources
Turnbull, David, 182
24/7 Wall St., 270

ubiquitous computing, 109–10. *See also* Internet of Things
unbundling of real estate services, 76
Underwriting Manual (FHA), 184, 186
University of Illinois at Urbana–Champaign, 213; Department of Sociology, 212; Institute for Government and Public Affairs, 218
urban decay, 184, 186–87, 193
urban triage, 186

veil of intervention, 227
The Victory Garden, 133
Villa, Bob, 133
Voting Rights Act of 1965, 261

Walker, George, 188
Wall Street crash of 1929, 178
Wall Street Journal, 135
Walt Disney, 100
Ware, Kristin, 273
Washington Highlands, 190
Wauwatosa, 190
Weaver, Robert C., 204
webs of relationship. *See* community, relational network
white flight, 204

whiteness equated to creditworthiness, 184
white privilege, 190, 205
Wikivoyage, 291
Wilbur, Curtis, 132
Wilkerson, Isabel, 261–62
Williams, David R., 262
Williams, Marc, 158, 167
Wilson, Thomas D., 239
Worldly Goods (1924), 60

Xome, 5

Zeng, Eric, 108
Zheng, Serena, 106, 116
Zillow, 13, 63, 70, 74–75, 77, 86, 241, 273; business model, 81–82; data, 82; growth and acquisitions, 81–82; history, 80; and the housing bubble, 83; Zestimate, 80, 82; Zillow Home Value Index (ZHVI), 82–83. *See also* online information sources
zonal theory, 185
Zoopla, 86
Zuboff, Shoshana, 96, 110, 112

About the Editors and Contributors

William Aspray is a senior research fellow at the Charles Babbage Institute at the University of Minnesota Twin Cities. In recent years, he has been a senior faculty member in the information schools at Indiana University, Bloomington; the University of Texas, Austin; and the University of Colorado, Boulder. Before that, he held leadership positions in professional nonprofit organizations: the Charles Babbage Institute, the IEEE History Center, and the Computing Research Association. Early in his career, he taught mathematical sciences at Williams College and history of science at Harvard University. He writes on computer history, information history, everyday information behavior, information policy, food studies, and broadening participation in computing.

Melissa G. Ocepek is an assistant professor at the University of Illinois, Urbana-Champaign, in the School of Information Sciences. Her research draws on ethnographic methods and institutional ethnography to explore how individuals use information throughout their everyday lives. Her research interests include everyday information behavior, critical theory, and culture. She received her PhD at the University of Texas, Austin, in the School of Information.

* * *

Steve Sawyer is a professor on the faculty of Syracuse University's School of Information Studies. His research focuses on the changing forms of work and organizing enabled through uses of information and communication technologies. Steve has also been active in advancing sociotechnical approaches to studying computing, collectively known as social informatics, emphasizing the sociotechnical basis of digital technologies. Sawyer's work is published in a range of venues and supported by funds from the National Science Foundation, IBM, Corning, and a number of other public and private sponsors. Prior to returning to Syracuse, he was a founding faculty member of Pennsylvania State University's College of Information Sciences and Technology. He earned his doctorate from Boston University in 1995.

James W. Cortada is a senior research fellow at the Charles Babbage Institute at the University of Minnesota Twin Cities. He spent nearly four decades in the IBM Corporation in various sales, consulting, managerial, and research positions. His research and writing have focused on the business history of information technology and on the role of information in modern societies.

Philip Doty joined the faculty of the School of Information at the University of Texas, Austin, in 1992 and received his PhD from the School of Information Studies at Syracuse University. He does research, teaches, and consults about surveillance, copyright, privacy, gender, and information behavior. He served as associate dean at the Texas iSchool from 2011 to 2019, is an associate director of the Technology and Information Policy Institute, and is a faculty associate of the Center for Women's and Gender Studies, all at the University of Texas, Austin. Doty has consulted with some thirty external clients: U.S. federal agencies; state agencies in New York, Texas, and Virginia; public and private universities; and other countries' legislative and executive branch agencies about freedom of information.

Hannah Weber is a recent graduate from the University of Colorado, Boulder, earning bachelor's degrees in information science and strategic communication. She also works for the National Center for Women and Information Technology (NCWIT), a nonprofit organization that works to recruit more women into computing.

Vaughan M. Nagy is a political science undergraduate at the University of Colorado, Boulder, where he also serves as a research assistant for the Department of Information Science. His areas of interest include international relations, political polarization, and online privacy policymaking. He has worked with professors and graduate students studying the teaching practices used to facilitate the retention of undergraduates in STEM as well as the privacy of online learning management systems.

Janghee Cho is a PhD student in the Department of Information Science at the University of Colorado, Boulder. His research addresses how to design technologies to support critical reflection and to empower individuals, with a focus on personal well-being and sustainability concerns. He incorporates insights from behavioral science and design to enhance understanding of how people make sense of their personal data and artificial intelligence technologies.

Judith Pintar is a teaching associate professor at the University of Illinois, Urbana-Champaign, in the School of Information Science. Her research centers around collective memory-making and collaborative knowledge practices. She is a game designer and director of an Illinois campuswide game studies initiative, "Games@Illinois: Playful Design for Transformative Education." Her interests include interactive digital narrative, narrative artificial intelligence, suggestibility, and media manipulation; the development of tools to foster programming and media literacy through collaborative game design; and social narrative approaches to trauma and memory studies. She received her PhD from the University of Illinois, Urbana-Champaign, in the Department of Sociology.

David Hopping is a lecturer at the University of Illinois, Urbana-Champaign, in the School of Information Science. His research interests include intergenerational community informatics, digital inclusion and digital literacy, relational sociology, and sociological theory. Hopping helped to build the not-for-profit community development organization Generations of Hope and served as the organization's executive managing director from 2006 to 2015 and as executive director in 2016. His current research involves the use of biofeedback and gaming technologies to enhance human capabilities and to mitigate vulnerabilities through the fostering of socioemotional resilience and the augmentation of carefully designed spaces of interaction in ways that promote bonding, learning, and playful engagement across generations. He received his PhD from the University of Illinois, Urbana-Champaign, in the Department of Sociology.

Carol F. Landry is a semiretired researcher and U.S. Navy veteran residing in Seattle, Washington. Her research draws on qualitative methods to investigate information behavior, information grounds, and the impact of digital inclusion in libraries and community technology centers. Of specific interest to her are the effects of emotion and time pressure on information behavior. Regarding these factors, she has published *The Home Buying Experience: The Impacts of Time Pressure and Emotions on High Stakes Deciders Information Behavior* and *Understanding the Information Behavior of Stay-at-Home Mothers through Affect*. She received her PhD from the Information School at the University of Washington, Seattle.

Jamillah R. Gabriel is a PhD student in the School of Information Sciences at the University of Illinois, Urbana-Champaign. Her research focuses on issues of information and race and interrogates how these issues, along with information policies and institutions, impact Black people and communities. Her research interests include information behavior, critical theory, information literacy, global librarianship, data science, and cultural heritage. She holds an MA in museum studies from Indiana University Purdue University Indianapolis and an MLIS from San Jose State University.

www.ingramcontent.com/pod-product-compliance
Lightning Source LLC
Chambersburg PA
CBHW022009300426
44117CB00005B/94